The Faces of Homelessness

The Faces of Homelessness

Marjorie Hope
James Young
Wilmington College of Ohio

Lexington Books
D.C. Heath and Company/Lexington, Massachusetts/Toronto

Library of Congress Cataloging-in-Publication Data

Hope, Marjorie.
    The faces of homelessness.

    Includes bibliographies and index.
    1. Homelessness—United States. 2. Homeless persons—United States. I. Young, James,
1916–   . II. Title.
HV4505.H66   1986   305.5'69'0973   86-45056
ISBN 0-669-13099-0 (alk. paper)

Portions of chapter 2 of the present work first appeared in "On the Street, On the Road," by
Marjorie Hope and James Young. Copyright 1984 Christian Century Foundation. Reprinted by
permission from the 01/18/84 issue of *The Christian Century*. Portions of chapter 8 first appeared
in *Commonweal*, vol. 511, no. 12 (June 15, 1984) and are reprinted with permission. Portions of
chapter 6 first appeared in *The Urban and Social Change Review*, vol. 17, no. 2 (summer 1984)
and are reprinted with permission.

Published simultaneously in Canada
Printed in the United States of America
Casebound International Standard Book Number: 0-669-13099-0
Paperbound International Standard Book Number: 0-669-14200-X
Library of Congress Catalog Card Number: 85-45056

The paper used in this publication meets the minimum requirements of American National
Standard for Information Sciences—Permanence of Paper for Printed Library Materials,
ANSI Z39.48-1984.

88 89 90 8 7 6 5 4 3 2

To "Franz"
and the countless others among us
who have slid into the streets,
still haunted by the American Dream

Contents

Photo by Nancy Miller Elliott

Preface

"To be rooted is perhaps the most important and least recognized need of the human soul."

—Simone Weil, *The Need for Roots*

For most of us, home has a special connotation of warmth, security, sharing with loved ones, and retreat from the pressures of the world. For most of us, then, it is hard to imagine what it would be like to have no roof over our heads, no place to return to at night, no place to close the door and withdraw into the quiet recesses of the self.

Is not our selfhood identified with the laughter and loving, the quarrels and reconciliations, the dreaming and planning that go on within the four walls that set us apart from those others out there? Do we not strive to embellish our turf with exotic plants, our own needlepoint, cherished books, figurines from Denmark or Woolworth's, grandmother's quilts, crystal wine glasses, bearskins displaying our hunting prowess—possessions that tell others what kind of person we are? Is not one of the first questions we ask on meeting new acquaintances, "Where is your home?"

We are often told that homeless people are different. They prefer to live that way. We tend to look past them as we walk down the street. They become invisible persons: the disheveled men slumped in doorways, the "shopping bag ladies" poking their heads into garbage cans, the human beings who clamber into odd receptacles as refuge from the cold. (One of them, a thirty-four-year-old Chicago man, was compacted to death when the out-of-order trash collector in which he had been sleeping for weeks was repaired without his knowing it.)

In almost every major city, and in some small towns as well, men, women, and children are sleeping in public parks, bus and train stations, caves, railyards, subways, alleyways, loading docks, and on rooftops and heating grates. Every winter dozens of Americans literally freeze to death on city streets. Some have perished within sight of the White House.

Even more invisible are the evicted families who huddle together in an armory or other shelter, or the battered wives carefully protected from vengeful husbands in concealed shelters, or the "throwaway kids," most of them abused youngsters, who stake out a home (without heat, electricity, or running water) in an abandoned building, or landlords who, after converting single-room occupancy hotels into luxury housing, permanently lock out tenants (many of whom are

elderly) by slinging heavy chains across apartment doors to drive people into win-
tery streets.

Large numbers of these people are "old poor" whose lives have been characterized by instability and the inability to find regular work. Others are the "new poor,"
people who enjoyed steady employment and a normal life until their jobs were
rendered obsolete.

They are not just an urban problem. On the roads of rural America dwell
thousands of hidden homeless—marginal farmers forced off the land, who join the
stream of migrants and wander from state to state in search of jobs. They live in
buses, cars, trucks, and under plastic, and in ditches along the way. Sometimes
they find occasional jobs on farms; sometimes they end up on the edge of urban
centers in sprawling tent cities.

At no time since the Great Depression has the number of Americans without
homes been so large or represented such a wide cross-section of our society as it
does today. Yet few middle-class people in America have ever talked with a homeless
man, woman, or child.

The homeless are not only roofless, they are hungry. To be sure, hunger is
more widespread than homelessness and has been growing at a startling rate. The
Physician Task Force on Hunger reported in 1985 that "Hunger is epidemic in
the U.S."[1] The task force found that despite the economic recovery, "hunger is
getting worse, not better."[2] As evidence it cited growing lines at soup kitchens and
food pantries, increases in infant mortality, and widespread malnutrition among
the elderly, infants, and the unemployed.[3] In Washington, D.C., the food bags
distributed by Bread for the City fed 10,518 people in 1982, 16,897 in 1983, and
28,510 in 1984. Hunger and homelessness are twin phenomena. The family one
sees standing in a soupline may have had to choose between eating at home or
paying the rent. They are one step away from the street.

The number of public and private shelters is growing. Yet the number of
homeless persons also continues to rise. Although joblessness has declined since
1983, the problem of homelessness is not going away. Nor will it disappear until
better ways are found to deal with technological unemployment, the dearth of services for the mentally ill, the inefficiencies and inequities of our social welfare system,
and the lack of affordable housing for low-and moderate-income persons.

As the reader will see, we not only describe America's homeless, their problems, and the services to assist them but also analyze the precipitating and underlying
causes of a situation that many have described as *the* social issue of the 1980s.

The prologue tells the story of an elderly man we found sleeping on a park
bench near the United Nations in 1977. The account of our frustrating search for
help for this gentleman may help the reader understand how we became involved
in the problem of homelessness. Although services for New York's homeless have
proliferated and improved since that time, experiences like that of Franz still occur
every day in New York and other U.S. cities. (The names of the people in the prologue are fictitious; the events are not.)

Chapter 1 explores the controversy surrounding the complex, ultimately impossible task of counting the homeless and categorizing them, describes the wide

variety of persons without homes, and shows how public attitudes toward these marginal people are changing. It also poses the question: Why is it that homelessness became such a widespread phenomenon in the 1980s?

Chapter 2 offers a cross-country glimpse of the people on the street and on the road in our land, the different kinds of facilities to assist them, the wide gaps in services, and the controversy as to whether the public or the private sector bears the greater responsibility for meeting the needs of undomiciled Americans.

In chapter 3 we turn to one American city, Washington, D.C., for a deeper look at the situation and at the successes and failures of citizen groups and professionals to deal with the problem. The national capital has an unusually large number of committed advocates and shelter providers.

For contrast, we focus on Cincinnati, Ohio, in chapter 4. Like most other middle American cities, Cincinnati has been slow to recognize and deal with the problem.

Chapter 5 examines one precipitant of homelessness—displacement—and takes a look at the widespread shortage of low-income housing.

Chapter 6 focuses on another cause of homelessness—the lack of diversified community support systems for the mentally ill—many of whom are patients discharged from large institutions.

Chapter 7 considers unemployment and the inadequacy of social benefits, which we see as symptoms of the unwillingness of society to face the consequences of the fact that our postindustrial economic climate has rendered millions of people redundant and dependent.

The final section looks to the future. Chapter 8 surveys some of the trends in work with the homeless, particularly the thrust to provide a wider range of services and to push for changes in the political arena. Chapter 9 looks at the wide range of responses to homelessness in the United States and around the world, and explores some of the ways that they reflect conflicting ideologies. In chapter 10 we present short-term and long-term proposals for a public policy that could alleviate and prevent homelessness.

Although we have tried, as sociologists, to use a balanced and factual approach, we are not detached observers. Rather, we consider ourselves participant observers who have become advocates for the homeless.

Over the years many questions have concerned us. Why is it that homelessness became so widespread in the early 1980s? How do the causes interact with one another? Do all Americans have a *right* to shelter? To decent housing? To other subsistence needs? Which sector, public or private, bears the greater responsibility for meeting the needs of people with no place to live? Is homelessness the inevitable consequence of postindustrial capitalism? How can homelessness be prevented? These are some of the issues we explore in this book.

In the past few years, growing numbers of Americans have demonstrated compassion and concern over the plight of the outcasts roaming the streets. What is needed now, we believe, is something that goes beyond compassion: a willingness to deal with the causes of homelessness and to recognize it as a symptom of problems that affect us all.

Acknowledgements

We wish to express our deep gratitude to the following persons for helpful suggestions, background information, or criticisms of the manuscript: Mary Asbury, Margaret H. Bacon, Larry Barker, Ellen Bassuk, Ellen Baxter, Winifred Bell, John Bickerman, Charlotte Birdsall, Tom Blackburn, Les Brown, Archie Bruun, James Byrne, Sara Colm, Mary Curran, Martha Dilts, Diane Doherty, Cushing Dolbeare, Carol Fennelly, Michael Ferrell, Peter Friedland, John Gaines, Lenna Mae Gara, Helen Ginsburg, Merrill Goozner, Buddy Gray, Dick Groner, Fr. Chris Hall, Chester Hartman, Bob Hayes, Lee Holmes, Mary Ellen Hombs, Kim Hopper, Frank Howard, Elisabeth Huguenin, Hayes Jacobs, Jane Jansak, Bill Jerman, Tom Joe, Becky Johnson, C.H. Johnson, Bill Kashersky, Richard Killion, Irene Schiffren Levine, Ed Loring, Floy Ann Marsh, Gerald Mc Murray, Deborah Mashibini, Fr. Terry Meehan, Mark Miller, Dick Moran, Harold Moss, Jim Mullen, Dennis Murphy, Susan Murray, Marie Nahikian, Tom Nees, Neal Newman, Leif Öjesjö, Barbara Poppe, Ann Presley, Becky Pryne, Andy Raubeson, Harrell Rodgers, Don Rohner, Dan Salerno, Cathy St. Clair, Fr. Bill Schiesl, Alvin Schorr, Barry Schwartz, Harvey Saver, Angelo Sgro, Tim Siegel, Avisa Silberman, Bob Simon, Joe Smith, Leona Smith, Chris Sprowal, Sr. Beverly Stark, Louisa Stark, Erna and John Steinbruck, Tom Styron, Don Thalheimer, Naomi Thiers, Cassandra Trimble, Sr. Mary Trzasko, Rena Van Nuys, Rob Waters, Todd Waters, Woody Widrow, Sidney Willhelm, Steve Whitney-Wise, and Leon Zecha.

We express our special thanks to our editors at Lexington Books, Margaret Zusky and Karen Maloney.

THEY SHALL BEAT THEIR SWORDS INTO PLOWSHARES. AND THEIR SPEARS INTO PRUNING HOOKS. NATION SHALL NOT LIFT UP SWORD AGAINST NATION. NEITHER SHALL THEY LEARN WAR ANY MORE

ISAIAH

Vest-pocket park opposite the United Nations, New York City.

Prologue
A Clean, Well-Lighted Bench

New Yorkers hurrying up First Avenue on a late winter evening may notice a tiny parklike recess opposite the United Nations. Walled on two sides, it is a shelter against the westerly winds, and a receptacle for the chill gusts that blow up from the East River. Under the cool lamplight and thin naked trees stand a few benches: the resting place of homeless old men.

It was on one of these benches that my husband and I saw him one November night. Clad in a worn jacket, his gray head pillowed on a canvas satchel of belongings, he looked almost like a stuffed sleeping bag. Our steps slowed, and we looked at each other. Then, by silent consensus, we moved on. After all, what could individuals do in the great jungle of New York?

But the vision of that human bundle haunted me throughout the meeting we were attending that evening in November 1977 at the Church Center of the United Nations. As delegates debated strategies for raising public awareness of the perils of nuclear holocaust, I was caught between concern for the future of life on this planet and the plight of one man, one piece of flotsam in the sea of humankind.

That evening I did speak to a secretary employed in a Church Center office about the figure we had seen on the bench. "Don't get involved!" she warned. "He could be *dangerous*. Besides, these bums *prefer* to live that way. You see," she added, with a mixture of pity and envy, "you don't know New York. It's different."

I could have told her that, although I was now teaching sociology and social work at a small college in a quiet midwestern town, I had spent fifteen years in New York, but this seemed irrelevant.

It rained that night, and I woke several times; the cold spatter on the windowpanes of the hotel room seemed to send a chill through my body.

The next morning, en route to the conference, we passed the same human bundle on the same bench. The other two benches were unoccupied. It was still raining. We walked very fast.

The following morning we passed the bench once more. It was empty. I felt uneasy yet released from a bond. Then a hundred feet ahead we saw that figure, lurching forward with the help of a cane. This time I could not stop to think.

"Sir, you slept out here last night?"

"Eh?" He gazed back at me through blurred blue eyes. There were puffs under them, and his cheeks were puffy and sallow. His mouth fell open a little; I could see half-toothed gums and smell the breath emanating from them. His softly creased face was unshaven. On his head sat a ludicrously jaunty beret, tied down with a plaid scarf. Despite his portliness and the awkwardness of his movements, his body conveyed a certain powerful quality.

"Where are you going now?"

"I am going for a so-da," he said, and I became aware of a heavy European accent.

"Would you like a real meal . . . and a place to sleep?"

He stared at me through his watery eyes, then shook his head. "What are you talking about?"

"You'll see." I took one arm, Jim the other, and together we guided our unresisting charge to the chapel in the Church Center. He sank into a pew, and my husband sat with him as I panhandled the employees for coffee and doughnuts. Dunking his doughnut to avoid the pain of chewing, our new friend munched slowly, without stopping. Then haltingly, as if speech, too, were painful, he answered our questions.

His name was Franz Ritzenthaler. No, he did not have a family or friends in the city. Yes, he had had a home in New York, an apartment in Yorkville.

How long had he been wandering about? A long time, a long time. Why had he left? Because—and for the first time, Franz's voice rose above a monotone—because the landlord was going to throw him out.

Had he gone to Welfare for help? He looked at us for a moment. Then his head sank. "No, I could not. They would say, I am a bum."

Had he been working? "Yes, before. Before the trouble with my leg." He paused. "I was a cook. At Le Faisan d'Or."

Was he French, then? "*American.* I have the citizenship. I came here with the American Army, after the war. From a village in Alsace."

Alsace! My husband and I exchanged glances. We had spent part of our honeymoon in the Alsatian wine village of Ribeauvillé, and we remembered the communal life the villagers led.

Perhaps he needed treatment at a hospital, we suggested to Franz. "*Non!*" He trembled. "Please, please do not send me to a hospital."

Upstairs, in the office of a woman moved by Franz's story, we began making phone calls. But we had forgotten that it was a holiday. The Community Service Society, the Catholic Charities, and the Department of Welfare were closed. In desperation, we began calling services that surely had to be open. The churches— were they not havens for "the least of these"? One minister expressed pity for Franz, explained that the church had no proper facilities, and recommended the Men's Shelter. Since we had heard chilling stories of the place, we did not pursue his kind suggestion. Another minister also spoke with feeling of the plight of "derelicts," apologized for his lack of facilities, and gave us the phone number of the Salvation Army. It turned out to be a service for the pick-up of old clothing. The next call was answered by a priest who commiserated with me, deplored the absence of facilities, and recommended the Holy Name Center. Responding with warmth to my call, an official of the center said that it would be happy to offer Franz noonday soup and the chance to play cards with other older men, but the center did not provide shelter; most of its clients lived in single-room occupancy hotels. Another priest suggested that we call McMahon Services. A woman there listened to my description of Franz's predicament and sighed heavily into the phone. It was a terrible shame, but their agency served only children. I called another Salvation Army service. This one, it turned out, was designed only for rehabilitation of alcoholics. Since I was reasonably sure that alcohol was not Franz's problem, I did not follow this up. Two other missions we called also were restricted to alcoholics.

The same Church Center employee who had warned me against getting involved suddenly became involved herself. With tears in her eyes, she suggested a small Catholic shelter, the Dwelling Place. But the Dwelling Place, I was to learn, took only women.

There was always Bellevue Hospital. But it served only those with acute physical or mental illness, I had been told. Perhaps some expert *could* classify Franz as senile. Perhaps only after food, shelter, and care could one assign him a label. Besides, he had pleaded not to be sent to a hospital.

Franz was not a child, or a woman, or an alcoholic, or a patient with an identifiable malady. He fitted no category. He was only a homeless old man.

My husband joined me and suggested calling the Catholic Worker, a group of mostly young people who follow Dorothy Day's precept to interpret the gospel literally and share the lives of the poor.

A weary-sounding young woman told me that she was new, and the person in charge was out for a few minutes. They could offer our friend some soup, but their beds were filled. We were reduced to the last resort: Emergency Assistance, the Welfare Department's effort to provide services even when regular offices were closed.

"Does he have *documents?*" demanded the voice at the other end of the line. "Everything's got to be *documented.*"

Since Jim had discovered a five-inch bundle of rain-soaked papers in Franz's satchel, I assured the voice that he could pass inspection, although I wanted to ask it what happened to those *misérables* who are robbed of the paper-and-plastic proof that one is indeed a real person. "Well, okay," sighed the voice. "Send him down."

By this time several conference delegates had learned about the weather-beaten stranger in the chapel and had offered to take up a collection. We accepted just enough to help pay for the cab and set off for Emergency Assistance.

In the taxi, Jim told me that he had gone through about half of Franz's documents. Our companion seemed sufficiently real; he had, *inter alia*, a social security card, a record of disability payments, an old unemployment compensation book, a membership card for the American Association of Retired Persons, three letters—all over four years old—postmarked from Switzerland, rent receipts, and a bank book showing a savings account of $9,000. Then Jim placed in Franz's lap one of his discoveries: a small photo, carefully preserved in a plastic window, of a middle-aged woman with softly waved dark hair, plump cheeks, melancholy eyes, and a sensual mouth. Was this a friend we might contact? Slowly, Franz shook his head.

The gray iron portals of Emergency Assistance at 241 Church Street were covered with graffiti, messages from those who had passed through: "No money food. Rent due. Denied help. John W. Smith." "Food stamps emergency. 109 West 17th. Denied. Why? Murderers!"

A clerk looked up from the *Daily News*. "The social worker's out to lunch," he said sourly. "Sit down."

We sat down. The seats were battered, the walls smeared, the floor littered, but it was warm.

Perhaps a dozen people were waiting: a black woman with three children, a Hispanic man with two sleeping youngsters, a middle-aged black man staring vacantly at the opposite wall, two white women draped over their seats, and a tall, thin, red-bearded man in scarlet-and-yellow plaid trousers. A policeman tapped his baton on the floor. Silence hung over the room.

Since Franz had eaten nothing but coffee and doughnuts and we ourselves were hungry, Jim bought soup, sandwiches, and cookies from a neighboring luncheonette. Franz sipped his soup slowly. It was a long time before I could follow suit. All those hungry eyes would be watching, I was sure. Yet none turned toward us; they seemed sunken in sleep or resignation, the last vestige of pride in the poor.

Suddenly a voice rang out: "I have enjoyed *every delicious morsel*!" My stomach contracted; the hand holding my sandwich stopped in midair. "Isn't there a more private place where one can partake of food?"

I turned slowly and faced my accuser. There he stood, the tall thin man, like the Grand Inquisitor: his beard neatly clipped, a halo of red hair crowning his balding pate, his head cocked with an almost theatrical dignity. His eyes met mine in a proud challenge. Then they dropped, and he sank into his seat.

I moved to his side. "We have some cookies here. Would you like to share them?"

He looked at me, then at the cookies, then back at me. "Oh, *my dear*, thank you!" And raising his eyes to heaven, he crossed himself. He clutched the cookies, then shoved them to one side. "Madame, do you know why I'm here?" Tears filled his eyes. "I was living at the Grand Hotel on Broadway. I was living at that establishment on my SSI check, I'm disabled, you see. One morning I went down the hall to the bathroom, *locking* my door. And when I returned to my abode a few minutes later, the door was open, and everything—everything—was gone." The tears washed his cheeks. "And so Madame, I am here hoping—*hoping* that the authorities will grant me some modicum of emergency assistance." He reached out and touched my hand tentatively. "God bless you, Madame."

We had missed most of the important conference meetings that day, it was already 2:30 P.M., and we had a long-standing appointment in half an hour. It seemed useless to wait any longer for the social worker to arrive. I wrote him a note, outlining what we knew about Franz and asking that he be sent to a welfare hotel, not the Men's Shelter. Franz nodded mutely and continued to stare into his lap as we explained our departure. Then he looked up through his clouded blue eyes. "*Merci.*"

Two hours later I phoned Emergency Assistance and learned that he was still waiting. At 7:30 P.M. that night I called again. A Mr. Jones told me that he was about to see Franz and would take good care of him. "Why're you so interested in this old guy?" he asked. "You're a social worker? . . . You know what happens to old people in this city? Some, they get so feeble they can't handle money. Some go down to the Bowery and drink away what they got. Others, people take their money, they get bloodied up . . . bad. And the lucky ones, we shovel them into nursing homes, and they just die away. It's not like the old days when they stayed at home. You looked up to them and you listened, and they sat at the head of the table."

For a moment I had a fleeting image of Franz at the head of a table in Alsace, ladling out *choucroute garnie* to the family he might have had.

After the caseworker promised to send Franz to a welfare hotel and to set up an appointment for long-range planning at a regular welfare office, I hung up the phone with a sense of relief.

At 10:30 P.M. I called Emergency Assistance once again. Jones had left, but his successor told me that two hours earlier Franz had been sent by cab to the Men's Shelter. Shaking with rage, I phoned the shelter. An official informed me that no such person had arrived that evening.

As I listened to the wind rattle our windows that night, shadows from the street moved across the ceiling. I saw Franz lying on the sidewalk in his own blood. Perhaps he had arrived at his destination. Perhaps he had seen the watchhouse that the city had built to shelter its good citizens from the homeless. Perhaps he had told the cabbie to drive on. To his clean well-lighted bench near the United Nations?

The bright sunshine pouring into our room the next morning kindled a new spark of hope. But Franz's bench was empty.

Seized by some fantasy that he had arrived at the shelter, after all, we decided to pay it a visit.

The New York City Municipal Men's Shelter is the nucleus of a sprawl of burned-out structures and burned-out humanity. Along the side streets stand craters of once-solid buildings, gutted by arsonists. The Bowery itself is a great wide way of hamburger joints, artists' lofts, restaurant supply houses, bars, missions, and the ubiquitous "hotels," flophouses that go by absurd names such as Sunshine, Prince, White House, and Palace. Slumped in doorways or stretched flat on pavements, men and women sleep surrounded by broken glass, tin cans, orange skins, waste paper, and excrement.

Near the shelter, a dingy building on Third Street, figures slouched against a brick wall, passing back and forth a brown paper bag from which each took a long sip. They did not speak to each other. On the sidewalk others crouched in silent circles, their eyes turned on the faces of the dice. Across the street a man was vomiting into the gutter.

In the shelter lobby, bottle pieces littered the floor, and the grime on the walls was unrelieved by an incongruous pastoral mural. There were no chairs. Ragged inmates sauntered or lurched back and forth, hobbling from nowhere to nowhere. Some were beating the air with wild flailing punches. A few were gesticulating at each other between peals of mirthless laughter. Others queued up at barred windows for meal tickets. The air smelled of sweat, urine, wine, and vomit.

From their glass-windowed cage, two guards surveyed us languidly, then finally nodded permission. "Okay, you can speak to the clerk in the office."

A maternal-looking woman with a heavy Spanish accent and dark braids wound round her head listened to our story sympathetically and made a thorough search of the files. "He's never been here." Then she shook her head. "But if he's an old man, get him out of here, and out of this neighborhood! You know what the younger ones do to the old."

Yes, we knew. I remembered tales of the Big Room here at the shelter, where hundreds of men spent the night on plastic chairs or the cold concrete floor. No one could really sleep through the night. The air was punctured with rock radio, snores, and screams of "Help!" called out from nightmares. Calls for help from the sleepless were likewise unheeded: under the eyes of the two guards, men were robbed of their wallets, their coats, their shoes; others were kicked out of their chairs and beaten at the whim of bullies.

A shelter official who had been listening approached us and nodded. "When I came here fifteen years ago, the Bowery population was made up of older, white guys—winos. A fairly stable population. Now they're mostly younger and black—drug addicts, mental patients. The median age before was fifty-six; now it's forty-one, and thirty-six for new clients. It means many of the guys you're dealing with have never worked. It's a reflection of the unemployment problem. And the drug problem. And political problems."

"How do you mean that?"

"They don't keep many mental patients in hospitals any more. Well, that philosophy is fine, if they've got enough aftercare facilities. But they don't. So the hospitals dump psychotics in the name of community medicine. And they end up here."

"It was different thirty years ago." He smiled wistfully. "There was great Yiddish Theatre then, and Sammy's Bowery Follies. Sure, the Men's Shelter was here, but it was *invisible*. Even ten years ago there were more chances for jobs for these guys. Trucks would come by and the men would line up on the street corners for a day's work—slave markets, they called it."

"How many cases do you get these days?"

"About 15,000 a year get some kind of service. Maybe 4,500 are active at any given time. We serve up to 5,000 meals a day, and send about 1,100 men to Bowery hotels. When we run out of hotel tickets, guys sometimes stay in the Big Room—on cold nights maybe 400 or more sleep there on the chairs or the floor."

On the upper floors the shelter offered some medical and dental services, the official assured us. Although I did not tell him so, I had heard about the lines of men waiting for two or three hours for cursory checkups from the only doctor. I had heard of the other lines, clients waiting for their initial interviews in a large bare room with no chairs or benches. When at last a client's turn came up, he was interviewed standing up through a hole of a window. The interviews, which averaged three minutes, were said to resemble a cross-examination in which the worker tried to force the client into some kind of admission or catch him in a contradiction.

It was the interviewer's duty, explained the official, to determine whether the client should seek other sources of assistance, get medical care, be offered tickets to a Bowery hotel, or be assigned to the second floor infirmary, which was reserved for men most in need of care. "If your friend was ill or too confused to handle money, the worker at Emergency Assistance may have made arrangements for him to go to the infirmary."

Although he was reluctant to show us the rest of the building, the official consented to take us to the dormitory. It was clean and warm enough, the antiquated iron beds were not crowded together, and two guards provided some security. But the hunched inmates ambling about the room seemed scarcely aware of our presence. In one corner a TV was blaring; the two men camped before it had closed their eyes.

Downstairs, the official hurried us past the Big Room; we could just glimpse the rows of plastic chairs. As if reading our thoughts, the official commented, "Sure, it can be hell in there. In the flophouses, the violence can be even worse. There men slit each other's pockets. They fight. One old guy last week had lye thrown in his face. To say nothing of the filthy dormitories. The mattresses are grimy, and they crawl with vermin and roaches. Sometimes there are no sheets or blankets, just a sheet of cardboard on the bed. So what do you want? In winter a man or woman is found every week frozen to death on the streets. Old men have been found in parks sleeping in the snow completely naked, their clothes stolen right off their bodies."

His lips twitched in a smile. "What do you want? You know what it costs the city to feed and shelter one of these guys? All of five bucks a day. Some people even talk of closing the place. Because it offends the sensibilities of artists and writers and other middle-class people who've moved to the Bowery. So what'll happen to these men?"

His voice had begun to rise; he had lost his bureaucratic cool. "When you get into work like this, you can't care too much. I did. I was going to change everything. Now I wouldn't even know where to start. Who's responsible? These guys—this thing called homelessness—it reaches into *everything*!"

An hour later, heading for the Lincoln Tunnel en route to our college in Ohio, we detoured to pass Franz's bench across from the United Nations. It was empty.

Another light cold rain had begun to fall, and through the drizzle I could make out the inscription on one wall of the recess where Franz used to seek refuge: "They shall beat their swords into ploughshares. . . . Neither shall they learn war any more."

If we had stayed with Franz instead of returning to normal life, if we had approached him earlier, if agencies, if the city, if . . . But we were all too late.

> Missing Persons Squad
> One Police Plaza
> New York, N.Y. 10038
> December 9, 1977

Dear Madam,

In response to your letter of recent date, please be advised that Mr. Franz Ritzenthaler has not come to the attention of the Police Department. A check of cooperating agencies was made with negative results. We will keep a record of your interest in Mr. Ritzenthaler and in the event that he does come to our attention we will notify you.

> John R---
> Detective

Presumably, that check included the morgue. Perhaps Franz was alive at least. As rain gave way to snow, he continued to pursue me: every night, as my electric blanket clicked on instant warmth, an image of Franz's shivering body snapped somewhere in my mind.

We returned to New York the following spring for another academic conference and another long search for Franz.

It seemed logical to start with his old home, a six-story senescent apartment building in New York's German section, opposite an empty area that had been bulldozed to make way for a twenty-story high rise. In the gray light of the first floor hallway, the building super, a thin-faced man with a Spanish accent, stared back at me. "You from the City?" Despite my denial, he retreated back down the hall. "I don't know nothing. Goodbye, Ma'am."

Perhaps Franz, despite his $9,000 in the bank, had sought some kind of assistance at the Welfare Department's East End Income Maintenance Center. I made my way there, passed the long lines of patient petitioners, and asked to see a supervisor. A weary-looking black woman heard me out, then shook her head.

"Try the Thirty-fourth Street office, downtown. We don't cover the gentleman's street." When I replied that he had lived close by, she looked irritated. "That's the point. The centers are *never* located in the neighborhoods where people live. Why?" She shrugged. "How should I know? Some people spend two carfares to get here."

Perhaps, I fantasized, Franz had eventually found his way to the Men's Shelter. So I returned. The same woman who had listened sympathetically five months before made a painstaking search through the files. "He's never been here. Maybe you could try the Salvation Army's Booth House—it's about the most decent place around here. But they don't take people on an emergency basis, and he'd have to be on Supplementary Security Income to get in."

Booth House II, one of the old Stations of the Cross along the Bowery, boasts clean corridors, a clean cafeteria, and services ranging from chapel to a Sobriety Club, a part-time psychiatrist, and a soul clinic. A watchman at the door informed me that since it was Sunday the only person who could answer my questions would not be there till the next day. I slipped past him and sat down in the large public room. Franz was not there. Scarcely a head turned to take in the sight of a woman alone in a gathering of men. They seemed to be gazing into some furtive beyond: the next meal, the next night of fitful sleep, perhaps the last sleep of all.

I turned to a black man in torn trousers and mismatched shoes in the next chair. Before I could finish two sentences, a tall shadow loomed over me. It was the law: a heavy-jawed guard. "Okay, lady. Out! You can't talk to nobody."

"But why not?"

"Ain't allowed. Come back Monday and ask for the supervisor."

"Can't the residents decide if they want to talk with me?"

"Just get *out*, lady!"

Fortunately, my husband, who had been attending the conference, was waiting at the Bowery bar where we had agreed to meet. On the bar stool beside us, a woman with discolored red, stringy hair and bloated cheeks began to sob. "Yah-yah-yah." Her body heaved back and forth on the stool. No one spoke to her; no one seemed to be listening. "Goddam bastards, all of them." She lifted her blouse to her face, exposing two sagging breasts. "I'm sick of living, and I'm sick of dying."

We left. As we passed the Prince Hotel, I decided to see whether my husband's presence would enable me to cross the threshold of a flophouse. Inside, an iron-cagelike door, as tall as the ceiling, barred the stairway leading to the sleeping rooms. A balding, puffy-faced man surveyed us from behind the cashier's cage. "No, you can't look around. I got orders." We looked through a glass door at the rows of men (all white) enclosed in the television room and retreated.

On the street two men were attacking cars stopped for the traffic light. Ferociously, they cleaned the windows in sweeping motions for thirty seconds, thrust their hands inside for the ransom, and retreated, pivoting on their toes and swinging their arms up to the sky.

"They're the new breed," sighed an assistant at the Bowery Mission as we sat down in his office a few minutes later. "The old-time Bowery bums are moving out, and psychotics or drug addicts are moving in."

He was a tall, reddish-blond, somewhat scholarly looking young man, without the evangelical zeal we had come to associate with the missions. Perhaps, he, too, represented a new breed on the Bowery, a response to the resentment of programs that dosed out religion as a condition of acceptance.

Men here were no longer required to take a Christian pledge, he explained, although services were held six times a week. They did have to refrain from drinking during their stay at the mission.

The rooms we saw were clean and well ordered. Yet many men left, unable to face the challenge of abstinence, our guide told us. It was easier to hide in the oblivion of flophouses: dormitories or four-by-six cubicles, separated from each other by partitions seven feet high. "The flophouses exploit the guys. When building inspectors come round, they're paid off. Stores exploit the men, paying a few cents for clothes given away at the missions. Bartenders keep the guys' Supplemental Security Income checks and give credit against them, ending up with most of the money. But if bartenders weren't 'guardians,' the men would be rolled right away. As it is, come payday the men line up on one side of the street, the jackrollers on the other. Still another racket is for labor contractors to bring in a truck and get guys drunk. They wake up next morning on a Long Island potato farm. I could go on. It's hard to see any solution, the oppression is so comprehensive."

We still had not found Franz.

The next day I returned to his apartment building. This time I found two pensioners, who introduced themselves as Tom and Charlie, sitting on the stoop in the spring sunshine. "Franz? Sure, I remember him," said Charlie, a Galway-born gentleman with a strong Brooklyn brogue. "Funny how he just disappeared. That got us worried, and we called the Bureau of Missing Persons. Yeah, Franz. Sometimes he had us in for little dinners. I'll never forget the stew with red wine he used to make. Once he showed me pictures of him in a real chef's hat!"

"He kind of kept to himself," put in Tom. "Still, he liked to sit on the stoop and talk to people going in and out."

"Every morning he went down to the supermarket on Eighty-sixth Street," said Charlie. "Then he'd come back and feed the cat and fix up his room. If it was good weather he'd sit outside the rest of the day, talking or reading the newspaper. He even read books."

"He liked the girls," added Tom. "I mean, he'd look at them and say, 'Pretty nice, huh!'"

"But he *loved* the cat," said Charlie. "He used to sleep with her."

"Then what happened?"

"Well, he had a cleaning woman," volunteered Charlie. "We asked him if she wasn't a friend, and he'd say, 'Oh no, just the cleaning woman.' And she had a key. Well, she hadn't come for awhile before he disappeared. Now that I think about it, he'd begun talking about death."

"Yeah." Tom nodded. "He'd been real friendly with a Switzy man down the street. When the guy died, that kind of shook Franz up."

"He was always worried about money," added Charlie. "He got on social security disability after some accident; it wasn't much. Then he got the idea the landlord was going to raise his rent. That does happen here. Franz, he'd been in this place over twenty years. The building's rent-controlled, and he'd been here so long, he was paying less than some of us. If the landlord gets a guy out, he can raise the rent. And it's hard to find a cheap place these days. The landlord can get about what he wants."

"Right," echoed Tom. "What's happening in the SROs—you know, single-room occupancy hotels—is worse. That's where a lot of poor people, mostly old and disabled ones on social security, have to live. There's a lot of money from converting those hotels into luxury apartments. In fact . . . " Tom paused. "That Switzy friend of Franz, he was living in an SRO. One night he came home and couldn't get in. The stairway to his room was smashed in, and a goon stood there saying he'd better not try to go farther. Well, the Switzy guy was mad, and he tried. They set dogs on him. He was messed up good, and he never really got over it. He found a room down the street, but he couldn't afford it, so he didn't eat much. And he was still shook up, it was hard for him to talk. It wasn't long till he died. That really got Franz."

"And then Franz got a funny bill from the landlord," said Charlie. "Say, I think I remember him saying he went over to the Burden Center for the Aging to get some help with that."

I was at the Burden Center half an hour later. Perhaps twenty-five elderly clients—most of them ladies in hats, stockings, and unsensible shoes—waited stoically to tell their stories of hunger, illness, eviction, rent increases, rats, lack of heat, assaults, fraud, and confusion about the myriad forms required to establish eligibility to survive.

A lanky, bearded young man in jeans listened to my story, asked a few abrupt questions, and nodded. "Think I remember him. Yeah, think he came in with a bill showing his rent had been doubled. We investigated, and the landlord claimed it was a computer error. But the old guy didn't believe it. He kept thinking the landlord was harassing him." He crushed out his cigarette. "I'll look through the files and make a few calls. Phone me tomorrow."

When I phoned, his message was cryptic. "Try Bellevue. Just a hunch."

The new wing of Bellevue Hospital bore little resemblance to the fusty institution I had once known; the endless corridors were spacious and overheated, and administration offices were decorated with coldly abstract mural paintings.

In the eighteenth-floor social-services office a Cuban caseworker greeted me warmly. "Yes, administration called. I think we have the man you're looking for. He came to us late in November—a cop picked him up in the park. They diagnosed him Organic Mental Syndrome. Me, I didn't believe it. I watch him—he's confused but not that ill. Well, now the doctors agree. We won't have to send him away to stay in Manhattan Psychiatric Center. He's staying here for awhile till we find him a nursing home.

"But he don't talk to nobody." The caseworker shook his head despairingly. "He knows English all right, but the only person he'll talk to is an aide from Haiti, she speaks French. And the lady friend who comes to visit him—she's come here five times.

"Sometimes he walks in his sleep," the caseworker added. "Funny, he always finds his way back to bed. Ask him . . . ask him why he walks in his sleep."

I opened the door of the ward and looked at the mound on a bed near the window. It was Franz.

He was clean and shaved and "respectable" now, but his gums were still toothless and an odor of sickness still clung to his breath. The tray of food at his side was untouched. I put my hand on his arm. "*Vous vous souvenez de moi?*"

He stared at me vacantly. "*Non.*"

Slowly, in French, I described the experience we had shared in mid-November. His eyes flickered, and he grunted, "Eh, perhaps."

"Tell me, what happened afterwards? Where did you go?"

"I do not remember."

"You seemed to think the landlord was trying to evict you."

"It was true. I know."

"I've met friends of yours, in the building where you lived. They were worried about you."

"They attach no importance to me."

"I know you have one friend, at least," I said desperately. "She came to visit you."

"Yes." His voice trembled a little. "Just four times."

"The social worker says she will come again soon."

"No.!"

"Why do you say that?"

"It is too late."

"Tell me, do you realize you walk in your sleep?"

"That's what they tell me. It is true, perhaps."

"Do you remember anything afterwards?"

"Sometimes. Just a little."

"When you walk where are you going?"

He stared back at me, then turned away. "Home."

I sat silently with him for a long while. At last I said clumsily, "The social worker here is trying to find you a nursing home. You can make new friends."

His watery blue eyes closed. "It is too late."

I touched his hand. "Would you like me to come back?"

"It's not worth the trouble."

"But if I want to come back?"

A faint smile warmed his lips. "Eh, if you like."

Franz's friend was a Mexican woman named Maria Maldonado, I learned at Bellevue. She had not visited recently because she, too, was ill. I finally succeeded in talking with her by phone.

"They found him on East Ninth Street, on November 28," she began hesitantly. "His legs were all swelled up, and he had a bad cold. I guess he was walking all night, all the time."

How did she know he was in Bellevue? "I called. No one lets you know anything. I kept calling all the hospitals in New York. I guess it was December 4 when I found he was in Bellevue.

"After he disappeared, I called the Bureau of Missing Persons. Then I walked around Manhattan trying to find him. I'd go up and down the streets near his apartment and all the parks. I couldn't do it all at one time. I got trouble with my legs, too.

"He wasn't like this before. There was something on his mind. He said they were going to throw him out of his apartment.

"I knew him—it was over thirty years. Something happened . . ."

Her voice broke. "But Franz and I were still friends. I always took him to the hospital, till I got sick. And now . . . " She began to sob softly. "Señora, Ma'am, I can't talk any more."

We could not leave New York without confronting the Bureau of Missing Persons. An abashed officer located a file on Franz, which included an entry stating that Maria had called the Bureau on November 6, but no entry indicating that the Bureau had called her. Tensely, he explained that we had never been notified that Franz had been found because our letter was in the "out-of-town" file. When we expressed some difficulty in understanding this explanation, since the client himself was not "out of town" and most bureaucracies keep a central file, the officer's face flushed. "Look, we've got just forty men on our staff, and each one's got to handle an average of 155 cases a week. Furthermore, you can't hold the police responsible if it's a *voluntary* disappearance. Anyway, people who are dead are of primary importance. He's alive, isn't he? We're looking for *Dead on Arrivals.*"

We returned twice to see Franz before we left New York for Ohio. We talked to Franz of our own visit to Alsace, of our liking for Alsatian wines. We asked about his favorite French dishes, his life in New York. We offered to write letters to his family and friends. Occasionally, he responded with a few words, but all the while he seemed to be looking beyond us, gazing from some shore of his own to another we were unable to see.

The tariff for the well-balanced food that Franz rarely touched, the battery of medical tests, the activity therapies he consistently refused, had been $300 a day for the past four months, we discovered. And Franz was more removed from our world than on the day we had found him on his bench.

We tried to shake hands in an awkward farewell. "Next time we'll see you in a new home."

For a lingering moment his hand clung to mine. Then his went slack. "No. It is impossible."

"What is impossible?"

"Everything. Everything is too late."

Photo by Nancy Miller Elliott

Part I
The Problem

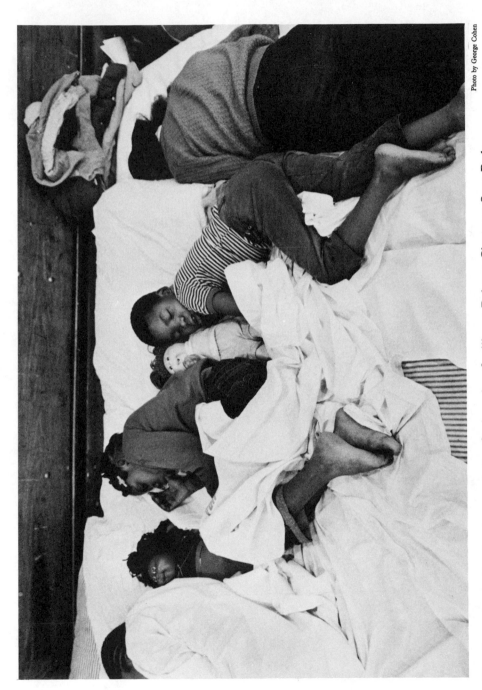

Photo by George Cohen

Sleeping arrangements in city-run shelter for homeless families at Roberto Clemente State Park, New York City.

1
The Homeless: Types and Stereotypes

I t is ironic that, although the popular media began to discover the homeless in the early 1980s, halfway through the decade public officials concerned with the problem were still focusing so much of their energy and resources in debating the number of undomiciled Americans.

In November 1983, the U.S. Department of Health and Human Services (HHS), basing its count on reports of advocacy groups, estimated that as many as 2 million people in the country may be without homes.[1] (In 1986 the National Coalition for the Homeless estimated that the number, at any given time, may be as high as 3 million.)[2] Six months after the HHS report, the U.S. Department of Housing and Urban Development (HUD) issued a report on the homeless and emergency shelters,[a] in which it declared that the most reliable range for the total number on a given night during the winter of 1983–84 lay between 250,000 and 350,000.[3]

The HUD report has encountered many criticisms. Only a few will be cited here. Close scrutiny of the document reveals that the outer range was considerably wider—from 192,000 to 586,000. Moreover, both ranges referred to a nightly count. It was conceded that one could derive a cumulative annual count ranging between two and three times the daily total, that is, up to 1.758 million, a figure not far from advocates' estimates. The latter number may be a more useful gauge of the problem since one can hardly assume that all those who leave emergency shelters do so because they have found permanent housing. Moreover, HUD excluded doubled-up or tripled-up families (and those in similarly makeshift quarters).

The researchers presented a "reliable" low estimate of 12,000 for New York City on an average night in January 1984. (Later in Congressional testimony, HUD claimed that it gave "zero weighting" to this figure.[4] One wonders why HUD published the estimate if it were to be discounted.) Yet available statistics show that on such a night over 16,000 people were domiciled in the city's emergency

---

[a]HUD used six major sources of information: (1) telephone interviews with knowledgeable observers in sixty areas; (2) a national telephone survey of shelter managers; (3) reviews of local studies; (4) site visits to ten metropolitan areas; (5) discussions with national organizations; and (6) telephone interviews with government officials in all fifty states.

public shelters, hotels, and armories, as well as church basements, private shelters, and drop-in centers. These figures do not include people in jails and hospitals who were homeless upon their arrival. In fact, they do not even take into account the great number of people on the street.[5]

HUD also found that on an average night in January 1984, 69,000 people nationwide were living in shelters. Yet it failed to include all persons vouchered into hotels, all homeless youth, and probably many of those in small shelters and all homeless people living temporarily in jails and hospitals.[6]

At a House hearing chaired by Rep. Henry B. Gonzalez, several experts strongly criticized HUD's methods; Gonzalez concluded that the report was intentionally deceptive, and Rep. Mary Rose Oakar charged that the statistics were being used to defeat legislation to help the homeless.[7]

Head-counting has been going on for a long time. In 1980 the Community Service Society of New York calculated that there were thirty-six thousand homeless adults in the city.[8] Exasperated city authorities attacked the figures and asked for an exhaustive recount, a project that would have cost $100,000, enough to lodge and feed 5,000 homeless people for five nights at many private shelters. The city ultimately decided that the study was infeasible. Yet authorities continued to make public attacks on the figures. By 1983, however, the numbers were no longer disputed.

The National Coalition for the Homeless takes the position that all this can become a numbers game. In any case, the exercise has limited value. The crux of the matter, says the coalition, is that the number of homeless persons is growing, and there are not enough beds and services for them. Every time a decent shelter is opened, beds are booked up immediately and people are still left waiting outside.

Such an exercise does have some value. Directing so much time and funding to head counts serves a function. It can divert the attention of policymakers and the public from considering the root causes of the problem. It can also present the impression of official concern.

Local counts, too, can serve a latent function. In spring 1982 New York City authorities made strange use of the fact that the winter census in the shelters did not decline with the advent of warmer weather. Instead of conceding that the reason might be that, because shelter conditions had improved, the streets were no longer preferred, the city contended that the constancy in demand was the result of artificially inflated need: people who were living with family or friends before coming to the shelter were not truly homeless. Why they left was of no concern. The implicit assumption was that many people were abandoning comfortable residences to take refuge in public shelters.[9]

Taking this line of reasoning even further, Thomas Main has argued that many New Yorkers "have discovered that the shelters are a good housing deal [hence] as capacity and quality improve, we will succeed only in enticing more people into shelters."[10] (Anyone who has visited the barrackslike public shelters or even the relatively clean and safe private ones in New York City would find it difficult to understand why any human being would prefer such accommodations to a home. Not only conditions of shelter living, but the stigma attached to it are tantamount to a means test that discourages all but those truly in need.)

On the positive side, censuses can be very useful when they serve as guidelines for action. Many shelter providers and city officials not only have surveyed the total homeless population in their vicinity but have tabulated the changes in the number of single women, families, elderly men and women, disabled people, and the like to plan for more diversified and appropriate facilities.

Still, the problems in counting the homeless are legion. In the words of Ellen Baxter and Kim Hopper, estimates are "subject to wild discrepancies depending upon the methods of estimation used, the source of figures, the time of year, and, we strongly suspect, the purpose for which the numbers are put forth. The kinds of living arrangements defined as 'homeless' may also vary considerably."[11]

Should one count as homeless only those dwelling on the streets and in designated shelters? What about those who, like Franz, end up in hospitals? Those who bed down in flophouses? Men and women who rotate via the revolving door between prison and street? People who sleep, sometimes four or six to a room, on the floor of friends' apartments? Squatters who sequester themselves in abandoned buildings? Undocumented aliens who live in such constant dread of authorities that they even fear applying for refuge at a shelter? Uprooted farmers who live in abandoned mobile homes, or who make do with tar paper shacks?

Many of those living rough are adept at avoiding researchers and reporters. There may be method in their paranoia. For example, after the *New York Times* ran a feature on men living in the tunnels of Grand Central Station, newspaper reporters and television news teams made their way into these lower depths. A few months later the two safe entrances that had allowed the men access without detection were welded shut, spigots were removed from faucets tapping hot water lines, and signs were posted warning that the area was now patrolled by Conrail police and attack dogs.[12]

Nevertheless, a working definition of homeless is essential. We prefer the comprehensive definition developed by the Office of Program Evaluation and Research of the Ohio Department of Mental Health:

A person is homeless if he or she sleeps or lives in:

1. Limited or no shelter for any length of time. (Examples include: under bridges, inside door steps, in cars, in abandoned buildings, in a bus station or all-night cafe, or in any public facility.)
2. Shelters or missions run by religious organizations or public agencies for any length of time. (Examples include: Salvation Army, Volunteers of America.)
3. Cheap hotels or motels when actual length of stay, or intent to stay, is forty-five days or less.
4. Other unique situations that do not fall into categories 1–3, and the actual length of stay or intent to stay is forty-five days or less. (Examples include: staying with families or friends, tent cities, and having spent the night in jail.)[13]

Clearly this definition is much broader and more realistic than that employed by HUD.

One point on which all authorities agree is that the number of homeless has been rising year by year in the 1980s. In New York City alone, the estimate jumped from 36,000 homeless men and women in 1979, to 60,000 men, women, and children at any one time in early 1986, according to the National Coalition for the Homeless.[14] A 1986 report by the U.S. Conference of Mayors shows that the demand for emergency shelter increased in nine out of ten of the twenty-five survey cities during 1985, and that the average was 25 percent.[15]

Who Are the Homeless?

In the mid-1980s controversy was still simmering over the composition of the homeless population. There seemed to be a growing movement to isolate and pathologize the problem. Dr. Charles Krauthammer articulated the new thrust when he argued that nearly 90 percent of the Americans without homes could be classified as mentally ill.[16] His conclusion was based on a Boston study by Dr. Ellen Bassuk and Alison Lauriat that found that about 40 percent of those studied had psychoses, 29 percent were chronic alcoholics, and 21 percent had personality disorders.[17]

There are several problems with Krauthammer's conclusions. First, the Boston study specifically focused on homeless people in *shelters*, thus excluding those living in cars, bus stations, homes of relatives, and other makeshift arrangements. The principal author, psychiatrist Ellen Bassuk, has objected strongly to the use Krauthammer made of the study's findings. She is quick to point out that her team examined only one shelter (although its population seemed to mirror the demographic description drawn from a one-day census of the homeless in twenty-seven Boston area public and private facilities). Although well-trained interviewers were used, the study was intended to be only a moderately in-depth one. She stresses that it seems indisputably clear that a significant number of the homeless, probably a majority, are mentally ill, and that her overall findings are supported by other studies. However, the definitional problems of what constitutes mental illness are immense. For example, shall alcoholism and narcotic abuse be included? How does one define social disability? Some people tend to use the term too loosely; they see it as a type of personality disorder, for example. If the latter perception were correct, says Bassuk, then obviously anyone who has lived for a sustained time on the streets could be said to be suffering from personality disorder.[18]

Ellen Baxter, whose research and personal experience with the homeless has stimulated much of the current interest in the subject, says that classifying nearly 90 percent of the homeless as mentally ill simply doesn't make sense. At the 1983 National Coalition for the Homeless Conference, those who work with these vulnerable people estimated that between 30 percent and 60 percent were mentally ill, a figure including alcoholics and narcotic abusers. Dr. Richard Roper's 1984 study of the homeless in feeding lines at the Union Rescue Mission and the Catholic Worker soup kitchen in Los Angeles reports that over 50 percent were homeless as the result of economic factors, not mental illness.[19]

In any event, greater consensus on definitions of mental illness is needed. For example, the survey by the Ohio Department of Mental Health finds that 30.8 percent of the sample had psychiatric problems (a term that excludes behavioral disturbances, which can be the result of the difficult situations faced by homeless people) and 64.2 percent said they had been drinking "some or a lot" in the past month.[20] This last description does not necessarily add up to chronic alcoholism, however, and it includes many respondents with psychiatric problems.

It is also dangerous to make generalizations about the United States on the basis of one local survey. The National Institute of Mental Health (NIMH) has estimated that up to 50 percent of the homeless may have mental disorders.[21] The American Psychiatric Association (APA) calculates that between 20 and 50 percent of the nation's homeless have serious mental disorders, an estimate excluding the homeless suffering from alcoholism and drug abuse.[22] The 1984 HUD survey concludes that about half the people in shelters are afflicted with mental illness and/or alcoholism and drug abuse.[23]

There is a larger problem, however. Defining the vast majority of the homeless as mentally ill can serve a purpose. If it can be shown that the description is valid, then the solution could be comparatively simple: institutionalize them. That is just what Krauthammer proposes: "Asylum. A place where the homeless mentally ill are taken and given food, shelter, hygiene, and a sense of order in their lives."[24]

In other words, since revolving-door shelters cannot provide psychiatric care to the homeless, community mental health centers have failed to meet their needs, and some actually refuse to come in from the cold, then the humane answer must be to put these broken souls away, even, as Krauthammer asserts, against their will. The issue becomes clear-cut: either shelter *or* an institution. He does not suggest that making good on the resolve to create a truly adequate community support system might be a large part of the answer. It is this oversimplified solution of reinstitutionalization that constitutes Bassuk's major difference with Krauthammer.

Defining the vast majority of homeless persons as mentally ill also can be useful to those who wish to mold public opinion. *They*, the homeless, are set apart as very different from *us*. They can be seen as a mere aberration from the normal processes of mainstream American society, not as a symptom of its failures. With that mind-set, we are more likely to accept certain implications for social policy. The homeless can become the responsibility of someone else—of the state department of mental health, for example. Indeed, other aspects of social policy need not be subjected to the painful process of change. This is the implication in Krauthammer's assertion: "Were our cities not overwhelmed by the mentally ill, the traditional safety nets of social welfare and voluntary charity would be adequate to handle the relatively small number of 'new poor' cases."[25]

Although citing no figures, former Secretary of Health and Human Services Margaret Heckler has expressed a similar vision: "The problem of homelessness is not a new problem. It is correlated to the problem of alcohol or drug dependency. And there have been a number of alcoholics who become homeless throughout the years, maybe centuries. They are still there. . . . I see the mentally handicapped as the latest group of the homeless."[26]

Who, Then, Are the Homeless?

It is probable that a large proportion of the homeless are mentally ill. On the other hand, alcoholics still form a high proportion of the Americans without homes. Many of them abuse other drugs as well. Many of the mentally ill, too, drink heavily or abuse narcotics.

If one includes homeless persons in hotels, doubled-up families, homeless youth, and other groups not counted by HUD and some other researchers, it is clearly hazardous to estimate the incidence of mental illness. On the other hand, if one focuses on "mental health problems" and includes moderate or severe psychiatric symptoms, behavioral disturbances, alcohol or narcotic addiction, as well as more generalized situational distress resulting from the shock of homelessness, then it seems only logical to conclude that a majority suffer from such problems.

It is therefore simpler to distinguish types of homeless persons not ordinarily considered mentally ill: battered wives, evictees, runaway or throwaway children, new poor who have recently lost their jobs, newly discharged offenders, elderly people no longer able to live on Social Security or Supplemental Security Income (SSI) payments. In the end, we are talking here about the precipitating causes that impel people to take to the streets.

The HUD study (which, for all its weaknesses, offers a useful national perspective) distinguishes between the chronically and the episodically homeless. It also groups homeless persons into three types: those suffering from chronic disabilities (alcoholism, drug abuse, mental illness) or from personal crises (battered women, runaway youth) or from economic conditions (recently unemployed, welfare recipients).[27] The three types are not mutually exclusive. A battered wife may become alcoholic to cope with abuse long before she summons up courage to leave home. An unemployed man may take to drugs as his life begins to fall apart. A youth may be asked to leave home because the family's welfare check can no longer support everyone. Street life can be so dangerous and debilitating that it exacerbates pathological symptoms. Some would say that it can even cause mental illness.

The ultimate cause may be different from the precipitating cause, yet they can be hard to distinguish. Indeed, how far does one go to determine ultimate causes? If a homeless man lost his job because of drug abuse, is the latter the ultimate cause? Or does one search back to the poor housing, second-class education, inferior health care, inadequate nutrition, crowded conditions, and general hopelessness that may have characterized the neighborhood in which he grew up?

The HUD survey, as already noted, concludes that a clear majority of the homeless suffer from chronic disabilities. Personal crises account for 40 to 50 percent of homelessness on an *annual* basis, according to the report. It adds that since people with acute personal crises tend to be homeless for relatively brief periods of time, the number of people in this category on an annual basis will be larger than at any given point during the year.[28]

The economic-conditions category covers at least 35 to 40 percent of the total, the survey asserts. It disputes the media stereotype that many in this group are middle class or skilled workers who have become homeless recently. Rather, most of the people rendered homeless for economic reasons were already at the margin: elderly persons living on small pensions, single-parent welfare households unable to afford rents, or jobless males in their early twenties.[29] (Shelter providers, too, point out that since the economic recovery of 1983 there have been fewer new poor but many more of the hard-core unemployed, people bypassed by the recovery. However, it seems clear that if before the recovery there were many new poor, who may be today's old poor, the stereotype must be at least partially correct.)

One wonders why HUD, which by definition is concerned with housing, gives short shift in this study to lack of affordable housing as a causal factor. Almost buried in a discussion of length of homelessness is the illuminating statistic that 38 percent of the homeless surveyed were recently evicted.[30] The document does make a passing reference to single-parent welfare households unable to afford rents but does not suggest that shortage of low-income units might be a factor. It also mentions briefly the decline in the number of residential hotels and rooming houses. Why, then, does it fail to refer to the decline of federally subsidized low-income housing?

The demographic profile in the HUD study supports some commonly held images of the homeless and contradicts others. (It will be recalled, however, that HUD excludes several categories of people without homes.)

Most of those in shelters are single, but there is a significant number of families. The figures break down to 66 percent single men, 13 percent single women, and 21 percent family members.

In all local studies included in the survey, the median age of homeless people (excluding children) is in the late twenties to mid-thirties, the average age being thirty-four. This represents a significant change from earlier decades when the median age for the skid-row population was some twenty years older.

Most of those without homes are white. However, minorities (primarily black, Hispanic, and Native Americans) are overrepresented. Minority members comprise 44 percent of the shelter population, according to the national telephone shelter survey, compared to 20 percent in the national population.

Contrary to the claims of many politicians who see their communities as a mecca for so-called derelicts, the national telephone survey of shelter managers found that 52 percent had lived in the area over a year; (this was also the finding of most local surveys used in the project).[31]

Moreover, HUD reported that the largest proportion were doubled up with family or friends before they became homeless. (As noted, HUD does not count people forced to live with friends or relatives as homeless.)[32] A large minority seem to be episodically homeless, moving from shelters to the streets and back again, and also spending periods of time in cheap hotels or with family, until they are evicted. The size of this group was difficult to estimate, for not all the local surveys examined the question.[33] Contrary to the commonly held view that homelessness is most concentrated in the Northeast, 31 percent of the roofless Americans in metropolitan areas are in the West, says HUD, even though only 19 percent of the country's population lives there; the other three regions have roughly similar shares of homeless people.[34] The homeless population in the North Central region has the highest proportion of long-term unemployed persons, regular users of shelters, alcoholics, and local people, and the lowest proportion of persons who were recently evicted. The West has the lowest proportion of long-term unemployed persons and alcoholics, and the highest of the first-time users and persons who were recently evicted.[35]

One of the most serious problems with this profile is that it draws a flat, static picture. It does not provide insight into the *dynamics* of homelessness. By contrast, surveys by the U.S. Conference of Mayors point up the significant rise in the numbers of women and families with children (often with a single parent).[36] In spring 1984 the conference reported that "in the past two years the number of families sheltered by New York City almost tripled."[37]

Nor does the HUD report convey any sense of the human toll in this situation. If the number of homeless families is growing, this means that thousands of American children are spending months and sometimes up to a year in shelters or single rooms in welfare hotels, without adequate health care and education, and with little sense of what it means to be part of a family. Their parents are too distraught and traumatized and too infantilized by quasi-institutional living to offer either the emotional support or the guidance that all children need in order to become mature and independent adults. Large numbers of the shelter children interviewed by Bassuk suffer from profound emotional distress and severe lags in developmental milestones.[38]

Adults suffer from the stigma of homelessness. Children suffer even more. At school, if they get there, they become known as "those shelter kids." They cannot understand how their parents became different.

Are we allowing shelter and hotel living to become routinized as a way of life? Are we allowing the scar of homelessness to pass from one generation to another?

Probing for the Roots of the Problem

We have looked at a profile of the roofless Americans of today and at some of the precipitating causes that thrust them into the streets. Somehow the profile and causes fail to make clear why this population is so much larger today than at any other time since the Great Depression. What explains the explosive increase of homelessness in the 1980s?

In the past few years scholarly studies and the popular media have cited several underlying causes: (1) unemployment, particularly among young people and minorities; (2) the grim shortage of affordable housing; (3) deinstitutionalization of patients from mental hospitals; and (4) intensive reviews of disability benefit recipients, together with tighter eligibility for recipients.[39] A fifth factor is the declining real value of public assistance benefits and a rise in the number of recipients whose benefits were cut down or cut out.[40]

By 1984, 33.7 million people, or 14.4 percent of the population, were living below the poverty level. Hunger had become what the Physician Task Force on Hunger in America has termed an *epidemic*. Many of the people who still had a roof over their heads were sinking ever deeper toward the bottom, the limbo of homelessness.

Yet as Kim Hopper and Jill Hamberg point out, in 1959, 39.5 million people, or 22.4 percent of the population, were regarded as poor and far fewer Americans received welfare benefits.[41] Moreover, hunger and malnutrition were much more widespread in the 1950s and even in the late 1960s, before federal food programs nearly eliminated such maladies by the late 1970s. Although unemployment rose in late 1982 to 10.8 percent, a record since 1940, it had been 9 percent during the 1974–75 recession. Although it was not until the late 1970s that it became commonplace to see mentally ill persons flailing their arms or babbling incoherencies on the streets, deinstitutionalization of psychiatric patients began in the late 1950s, and most of it occurred in the late 1960s and 1970s. Although tent cities in Texas, Arizona, and other parts of the Golden West have become a familiar phenomenon only in the 1980s, massive migration to that region has been occurring for decades.[42]

Simply examining each cause by itself, then, does not answer the question: Why does the poverty of the homeless in the 1980s take the distinctive form of having nowhere to live? It is more worthwhile to discern how these factors have come together and intermeshed with one another.

"Somewhere a threshold was crossed," suggest Hopper and Hamberg. They contend that "closer scrutiny of the trajectories of the economy, demography, and relevant public policy, will show how these developments have converged to create one peculiar form of marginalization—widespread homelessness—in this decade."[43]

They argue that although many of the conditions that spawn homelessness existed in the 1960s, "it was [in] the period from the early to the late 1970s that the relevant factors fell into place and their combined force gathered momentum. In the early 1980s, as the economy worsened and the housing market tightened even more, the limits of tolerance were reached and widespread homelessness resulted."[44] The rest of their argument might be summarized as follows: The first to be affected were the poor whose lives were already characterized by instability;

even in the mid-1970s large numbers of discharged psychiatric patients and young unemployed minority men were living on the streets. As the 1980s progressed and the above-cited causal factors intensified, the ranks of homeless people grew and their composition came to include increased numbers of new-poor unemployed, women, elderly persons, and families.

Homelessness can be seen as one manifestation of the housing crisis at large. The process of becoming undomiciled can be divided into two phases: displacement and the inability to locate replacement housing. Displacement can occur as a result of eviction, landlord abandonment, conversión of dwellings to higher-income housing, and other factors that reflect changes in the economy and in government policy. Dislocation can also occur as a consequence of domestic violence, abuse, or the break up of extended family households. If the displaced person can readily find replacement housing, sustained homelessness does not result. If, however, the displacee's unemployment benefit, disability benefit, or welfare stipend is too low (or does not even exist), and if low-income housing is scarce, then homelessness can become a way of life. Back in the 1960s and early 1970s even the deinstitutionalized mentally ill generally could find housing, even though it might be only miserable quarters in the SROs that today have become casualties of redevelopment.

In other words, say Hopper and Hamberg, the driving dynamic behind homelessness today is the widening gap for many people between the cost of their basic needs and the resources available. Some of the elements of this situation include the continuous rise of shelter costs, the growing incidence of abandonment and gentrification, the decline of government subsidies, and the existence of generous tax breaks encouraging speculation, conversion, and abandonment. At the same time, the economy has been damaged by significant changes. Many middle-income jobs have been eliminated and the much-touted growth of new jobs has occurred largely in the low-wage service sector. Hence the skills of many blue-collar Americans have become obsolete. During the late 1970s and the first half of the 1980s, too, income supports for people on public assistance have failed to keep pace with inflation. In addition, nearly half of the disabled poor were dropped from federal disability rolls during the first Reagan administration.[45]

Thus the common denominators for the three types of homeless people described in the HUD study are the lack of economic resources and the lack of affordable housing, denominators that have converged in the 1980s to produce massive homelessness.

In other chapters we explore each of the underlying causes and, in doing so, seek to understand how they interact with one another.

Stereotypes and Blurred Images

In the 1940s and the two following decades, the classic profile of the homeless man was that of a skid row alcoholic who inhabits New York's Bowery, Chicago's

West Madison Street, and San Francisco's Tenderloin. By the mid-1960s, the drug culture had begun to infect all strata of American society, and many narcotics abusers who were poor joined chronic inebriates on skid row, lending further credence to the popular view of the homeless man as a deviant. The image was reinforced by the arrival in the 1970s of large numbers of deinstitutionalized mental patients and other mentally ill persons without adequate community supports.

Although the mass media have presented many sympathetic portrayals of the new poor in the 1980s, some of the popular stereotypes persist from the past. Analyzing media portrayals of the homeless in his 1973 study, Bahr points to the use of words usually applied to animals or insects, rather than to human beings. "Noisy bums" are said to gether in "packs"; vagrants "swarm" to the city.[46] Even in 1980, the *New York Times,* which recently has carried generally sympathetic and accurate reports on the homeless, ran one story describing those who ride the subway all night as "the worst of life—drunks, vagrants, prostitutes, wild-eyed men with matted hair and beards who well may be insane."[47] Note the implicit identification of being insane with violence. Yet many psychiatrists find that the majority of the mentally ill are characterized by passivity rather than overt aggression.

A more sympathetic but somewhat romantic view is that of street people as independent eccentric descendants of nomadic hoboes of the past. For example, newspapers have featured stories of shopping bag ladies with thousands of dollars cached in the bank. An account of the murder of one such heiress focused on her offbeat way of life and did not even mention that the place she had been staying, a subway entrance near Grand Central Station, is occupied by many roofless people every night after they are forced to leave the station.[48]

"Morally wayward" might describe another perception of the homeless. Even today, mission directors incline toward a charitable view based on a right–wrong dichotomy. Most of those we have talked with would agree with the director who said, "These men have a lack of belief in themselves. They can't believe that God forgives."

One widespread image is that of "lazy bums." The image is a confused one, for the homeless may be seen as passive and apathetic, yet somehow aggressive enough to manipulate honest people. A story in the *New York Daily News,* for example, described how one resourceful panhandler kept her sores from healing.[49]

When Phil Donahue presented a group of homeless persons to television viewers in 1983, members of the studio audience jeered at the down-and-outs on the podium. One well-dressed woman rose and angrily informed them that her forebears had arrived in America with nothing, yet had made it in this land of opportunity. Certainly, she declared as the audience chorused approval, the homeless today could do the same if they *worked*!

The homeless seemed to make us uncomfortable. Many cities have risen to the challenge of providing facilities (after considerable prodding from concerned citizens). Yet there are other communities—Phoenix, Chicago, and Eugene, Oregon are only three of them—where authorities have tried to close shelters in response to business interests or neighborhood pressure. In Fort Lauderdale, seventy-two persons were arrested in late 1984 in a "clean sweep," and faced charges that included sleeping under bridges, urinating in public, and public indecency. Atlanta, Miami, Missoula (Montana), and other cities have carried out similar actions, including placing No Trespassing signs in city parks, and arm rests on bus station benches to discourage their use by weary people with no beds of their own. In some communities, men have been arrested on charges of vagrancy because they had no money; to be penniless becomes tantamount to a crime. New Orleans has arrested so-called vagrants sleeping in public places during the Mardi Gras, ensconced them in jail for up to thirty days, since it usually takes weeks to bring them to trial and meanwhile used them as laborers. (It has even arrested people standing in line at welfare offices.) Although one Fort Lauderdale councilman's proposal to spray trash cans with rat poison was never ratified, an ordinance was passed in 1984 making it illegal to rummage through trash cans. In Dallas (and other cities) people who camp at the city outskirts are submitted to abuse by youths who beat them sadistically.

The homeless elicit ambivalent attitudes and ambivalent policies. In one moment New York's Mayor Ed Koch brags that shelters would be opened in neighborhoods throughout the city only "over my dead body."[50] Later he boasts that New York has done more than any other city for these unfortunates.

The homeless evoke our pity and a tangle of other disquieting emotions: anger, frustration, fear, and a lingering malaise. Has something perhaps gone awry with the American dream, that persistent belief that we can all make it if we just work hard enough?

The homeless invade our downtown areas, so carefully upgraded to attract tourists, business conventions, and desirable residents. They violate our standards of decency. Should we not sweep them off the streets, wash them out of our consciousness? There are laws on the books that tell us that this is the right and proper thing to do.

Still, they need to be taken care of. We want to help, but how? They should be referred somewhere. There are so many services for the poor in this country. America has a safety net—does it not?

Todd Waters (*center*), Minneapolis ad executive, with hoboes "fixin' beans" under a bridge in Portland.

2
On the Street,
On the Road

Since 1977 we have made many journeys to search out the homeless and to talk with the people who work with them and act as their advocates. In the East we have visited New York City, Stamford (Connecticut), Springfield (Massachusetts), Washington, D.C., and Philadelphia; in Ohio, Cincinnati and Cleveland. One summer we packed our belongings into a ten-year-old unairconditioned car and set out westward to Chicago, St. Louis, Kansas City (Missouri), Denver, Laramie (Wyoming), Salt Lake City, Reno, San Francisco, Seattle, and smaller towns in between. We listened to the homeless on the streets, under bridges, beside boxcars, and in shelters, parks, Traveler's Aid offices, their own dilapidated autos, and ours. With service providers and advocates we discussed the problems of meeting the immediate needs of people with no place to live and of rousing public awareness to the need for long-term policies to avert homelessness. Over the years we have also kept in touch with many service providers and advocates by telephone and correspondence.

In our explorations we have been searching out answers to questions that have preoccupied us for a long time. Who are the people behind the statistics? What is life like for the itinerant homeless? Are many of them still haunted by dreams of success in the West? What kinds of facilities exist for them? What are their greatest unfulfilled needs? What happens to families when they lose their homes? What tensions exist between the public and private sectors over responsibility for the homeless?

The homeless men, women, and children we met defied stereotypes, even categories. For example, the "new poor." Like the mass media, we could define them as members of the middle class who have suddenly lost their jobs and their ability to keep up mortgage payments, or we could include people who had always led a marginal existence but had recently plunged into outright destitution. At what point do people who have been without jobs so long become "old poor"?

Certainly relatively few of the people we met could be called "hoboes" who refuse to work. Most of the wandering jobless to whom we offered a ride were new poor, accustomed to marginal jobs as waiters, gardeners, maintenance men, nonunionized factory hands, assistant mechanics, assistant carpenters, assistant electricians, and other assistants. "I can do anything," we heard over and over. But unlike tinkers of yore, they had little status or function. They were slipping into the underside of a technocratic society.

Marginalized though they were, our car companions held many so-called middle-class values. They were clean, neat, and polite; they even refused offers of food. With bravado, they spoke of the next job. Only gradually would we learn that for most of them, the search for work had become desperate. Texas and other Sun Belt states were not the frontiers of opportunity they were portrayed to be. "No Help Wanted" was the welcome almost everywhere. Hence many of these new migrants had turned northward, picking fruit or taking any other odd jobs.

Most of the new poor disliked sleeping in missions or shelters, which they identified with people they called "bums." Instead, they slept under the stars, in caves, in abandoned houses, in bus stations, at truck stops, or, when they had a few dollars, in run-down hotels. From time to time, they used missions for showers, for hot meals, or as a last ditch. Always they made a careful distinction between themselves and "hoboes." ("Call me a wanderer—I ain't no hobo.") They would rather risk the dangers of being robbed by a motorist or being jailed for hitchhiking than the perils of being jammed together with the rough riders of the rails.

The head of the Salvation Army in Laramie told us that he saw three types of chronic itinerants: hoboes, who ride the rails, have a loosely communal organization, and elect a king as well as other officers; tramps, who tend to be loners and are more versatile than hoboes in that they either hitchhike or ride the rails; and "home guards," hoboes or tramps who retreat into living and working in missions and thus become known as "mission stiffs."

Hoboes represent only a small fraction of the homeless, although their numbers seem to be growing. Those we met projected the same romantic image of themselves that the public at large seems to hold. "We're anti-Establishment," the Grand Duke of the Hoboes told us in Denver. "We need to be free, and we like excitement. Passengers never see or feel what *we* do on top of a boxcar, speeding through beautiful mountains and deserts."

Yet the reality of their lives is far from romantic. Most hoboes not only panhandle but also work, if sporadically; they pick fruit, wash dishes, take maintenance jobs. Like the new poor wandering in search of work, they seek day-labor jobs at agencies sardonically labeled "Rent-a-Bum." Usually such work is in short supply. Then they may sell their blood. Every large city has several plasma centers where the down-and-out line up to market one of the last things they can call their own.

Some hoboes admit that their lives are not really carefree and that, if they could do it all over again, they would choose a regular job and a home. Indeed, one year the rallying cry for the annual hobo parade was a demand that the government furnish jobs. In the following year the theme was Register the Homeless to Vote.

Todd Waters, a Minnesota advertising executive whose passion for years has been riding the rails, says that he has witnessed many changes among boxcar trekkers.

"A decade ago, I saw mostly forty-five to fifty-five-year old males traveling. Since 1980 I've witnessed an average age of twenty-five to thirty-five, with a lot of Vietnam vets and mentally ill. The latter group is victimized all the time, mostly as scapegoats for desperation. In general I've seen a thousandfold increase out there.

"In particular, I've observed a dramatic increase in women traveling, and I can't tell you how dangerous it is. One woman told me how she dealt with trouble on the road: 'You just lay down and spread your legs. It's better than getting your head split open.' I see girls—thirteen to fifteen years old maybe—traveling with older men (twenty-five to forty years old). They are usually dressed like boys and very quiet, intimidated.

"I do encounter young runaways. What I've noticed is that more tend to be pushed out of homes, with no option to return made apparent to them by their parents. (Usually they've broken with a stepfather.) I try to talk them into making a call home, even if they don't want to tell their whereabouts, or let me call their parents for them. This is a difficult situation for me because many runaways are girls. I'm afraid to approach them for fear of arrest for rape charges or contributing to the delinquency of a minor. I do it anyway, but I'm going to get my ass in a sling some day.

"As for families, the missions have been telling me they've been receiving calls from parents who want the mission to take the kids for awhile. Most transient facilities are male-oriented , so it's difficult to deal with. Many families are traveling the country by auto, heading for rumored jobs in Texas or Wyoming, when their car breaks down or they're stranded. They will often live for weeks, even months in their cars, but they know it isn't healthy for young children, so they try to give the kids up. Can you imagine the desperation?"[1]

Some families do split up, at least temporarily, rather than submit young children to the rigors of the road. In South Dakota we picked up a skinny, sandy-haired young man who sank into the corner of the front seat and stared out the window. As if surprised that motorists could take an interest in his life, he responded uneasily at first to our questions. Well, he was from St. Louis, and he'd been "traveling around" since the shoe plant where he'd been a machine operative had closed down. Like many other redundant blue-collar workers today, Bill had seen his wife obtain work—at $1.60 an hour plus tips as a waitress in a cafe—while he waited in vain at the employment office. Finally, he'd said goodbye to his wife and two-year-old son, and set off. Here and there Bill had found odd jobs, but he kept hoping to land a *real* job. Some day, he was sure, he'd have good luck. Then he'd send for his wife and son. "Yah, I miss 'em. Ain't seen my kid for eight months. My wife says she can't stand it no longer, being all alone. She wants to join me. But this ain't no life for them. I *got* to find me a real job."

Other families, we found, continue to stick together against all odds. In a Salt Lake City park where every tree shadow was occupied by a homeless person on that hundred-degree day, we found a mother, her two sons, and two daughters, together with an emaciated-looking dog, resting beside a small pick-up truck fitted with a cap over the back. All five in the family slept huddled together in the truck. While the daughter played with the dog, the mother and her sons, aged twenty-one and eighteen, sputtered out their bitterness. After she had lost her office job in Sacramento and their apartment building had been torn down to make way for new condominiums, they had turned eastward to seek better fortune. On their arrival in Salt Lake, the pickup's transmission had broken down; to have it repaired would cost $300. The older son did find a job as a busboy, but two days later fell and suffered multiple fractures in one arm. Rent-a-Bum had nothing to offer a "cripple." The mother had searched for office work in vain. The younger son went daily to Rent-a-Bum, but to date had found work only three times. There was a new family shelter sponsored by Traveler's Aid, but it held only ten families and was already full. There was also the Rescue Mission, but it was known as a rough place and took only men. "We want to stick together," they told us firmly.

Shelter providers confirm that a great many families prefer bedding down in parks, abandoned buildings, or even the streets to the separation they face when no facility can take the whole family group. What about the families that do separate? According to Stephen Crystal, there are significant differences between occupants of men's shelters and women's shelters, differences that contradict the stereotyped notion that the homeless lack involvement in intimate personal relationships. It is true, he says, that children do not appear to be a salient factor in the lives of most of the homeless men in shelters.

> But this is not the case for women. Both the number of children and their presence in the lives of shelter clients are substantial. . . . The etiology of homelessness among these women seems to have involved more troubled backgrounds than is the case among the men. Many more appeared to have become homeless as a result of chronic mental illness and "slipping between the cracks" of the mental health system. . . . They are, currently at least, unable to care for their children themselves, but this remains a goal for many of them. . . . Services for homeless women also need to focus on their needs and concerns with respect to their children. For many of the homeless women studied, children represent a still-vital link of kinship which belies the "disaffiliation" image.[2]

Surprisingly, many of the men, women, and youths we met on the street and on the road were not openly bitter. Doggedly, as if trying to reassure themselves, some of the migrant poor asserted that this was still the land of opportunity. Look at how many Americans had become rich! That they themselves had not yet made it was due to bad luck or some lack of smarts.

Some placed all their trust in God. Like the hitchhiker we picked up in the Nevada desert who settled his luggage, wiped the perspiration from his face, and opened his Bible. In proud tones he declared from its pages: "Watch therefore, for ye know neither day nor hour wherein the Son of Man cometh. For the Kingdom of Heaven is as a man traveling into a far country." He smiled, "Jesus is coming again. And I feel that the Lord is with me. You gave me a ride."

Almost invariably, the people we met on the street and on the road bade us goodbye with: "Thanks for talking with us."

A Spectrum of Problems

Some homeless persons need only a little assistance: a job, help with the rent, money to finance a trip to see relatives or an employer who has promised a job. Sometimes furnishing bus tokens so that an unemployed person can go to interviews makes all the difference in whether he or she finds work. Although assistance with such situations might appear to be simple and cost effective, only rarely does a public welfare office provide it. Emergency shelters are usually too poorly funded to offer such aid directly, but some of them have referral services that direct guests to sources of help—often churches or church-funded agencies.

Other homeless persons—especially families with a history of chronic unemployment—have a multitude of problems: poor health, poor education, emotional disturbances, even lack of know-how in applying for a job. These people require intensive support services over a fairly long period of time.

For many men and women on the streets, patient outreach work is needed because they do not know what services are available and may be fearful of those with whom they have had contact. In Denver one evening we approached a woman burdened down by two neatly bound plastic leather bags and clothes too heavy for the hot humid night. She told us shyly that she was just going for a walk, and a cup of coffee at a diner. When we told her that we were sociologists interested in people who had to live on the streets, she put down her bags. As she moved into the lamplight, we saw the face of a woman in her early fifties, with vivid blue eyes and high cheekbones. She smiled broadly. "My brother is a sociologist. At a university in California. I'm a ballet dancer. I mean, I was. Until my family put me into a hospital for changing my religion. I was born Jewish. But then I had an enlightment." We walked along the street, and eventually sat down with her in a coffee shop. Talking almost nonstop, Alice told us that she had once married, had no children, and had lived in an apartment in Ogden till her landlord raised her rent two months ago and then evicted her. With her last savings she had taken the bus to Denver a month ago. Yes, she was frightened sometimes on the streets. Men bothered her. Still, if she spent her nights in diners, her days sleeping in the park, most of the time she'd feel safe.

Alice had heard of shelters for women in Denver, but thought they must be jails, like the hospital where her family had put her. She tried to stay out of the way of the police, for they might put her in the hospital. No, the police had never hassled her, but sometimes she'd seen them get rough with men sleeping in the parks. In Utah she'd received Supplemental Security, and some of the people at the souplines told her to apply here, too, but she wasn't sure how to go about it. In Utah she'd occasionally seen a caseworker who talked to her about the importance of taking her medication. Alice could not remember anything else that the worker had ever done for her.

Somehow this fragile woman was managing to survive on the streets. "I don't mind it, being alone," she repeated several times. As we separated, she smiled wistfully. "I wish there were more people who wanted to talk with me."

Still others among the homeless present special problems. We remember, for example, a seventeen-year-old we met in San Francisco, outside the Larkin Street Youth Center, where he had been a client "till they made the rules stricter." He was short and thin, with a lined forehead and sallow skin. He lit one cigarette from another, and his gray eyes seemed constantly in movement; only occasionally would they meet ours. Yet he seemed eager to talk.

He would talk with us on condition that we not use his real name. That could get him in trouble with the police. The reason for *that* was, "I'm gay. And a prostitute." For a brief moment his eyes met ours as if in challenge.

"Call me Tony, if you like. Yeah, I work the streets. Last night I got three hours sleep. Today I'm broke. I got to go out and work, get me six dollars, so I can get a bathhouse and sleep. A bathhouse is better than a flophouse—cleaner, safer. The shelters? They can't help me."

Tony had come to San Francisco eight months earlier, he told us. At that time he didn't hustle because the Larkin Street Center gave free food vouchers; it no longer did so. He had to be eighteen to get General Assistance (GA).[a] He refused to stand for hours in a soupline. So he began hustling.

Why did he leave home? "I was kicked out for being gay. But my stepfather *never* liked me. I don't know who my real father was. I used to try to get my mother and my stepfather to love me. But if you don't get love . . ." His voice dropped. "If you don't, you release them."

"Yeah, I had a lonely childhood. I tried to find ways of getting attention, but my mother and stepfather wouldn't respond. My stepfather beat up on me. Sometimes I dished it out to the teachers at school. I put them through hell. But I hated myself. I thought there was something wrong with me. I wasn't like the others. And I hated myself. No, it wasn't because I was gay. I was always gay, ever since I can remember. At the age of five, I was messing with my male cousin. I've never felt an attraction for women.

"No, it wasn't *that*." A note of belligerence crept into his voice. "I just don't know why I hated myself. But I felt there was something wrong, and that made for a lonely life. I never had friends."

When Tony dropped out of eleventh grade, his stepfather became even more hostile. There was an explosion. "I thought, I've got to get away—maybe in

---

[a]Throughout this book we will refer to this type of relief assistance as General Assistance (GA) even though it is called by various names, such as General Relief and Home Relief, in different localities.

California I can be free. I told them I was leaving. My stepfather said, 'Fine, I'll help you pack your bags.' My mother just stood there, saying nothing.

"I wandered around Arizona and Nevada a few months. That was pretty rough. And then I came here."

"How do you feel about working the streets?"

"I like it." His fingers, yellowed with nicotine, fumbled for another cigarette. "Why? I have good friends, I'd do anything for them. All the money I get, I spend it on others. Two days ago I had $160. I blew it on them."

"Then you could ask them for help when you're down and out."

"No." He shook his head doggedly. "I'd be ashamed of myself. I can't *ask* from friends."

After a long pause, he said slowly, "Actually, I don't like the streets. I mean, I do but I don't. I don't like going without sleep. Or money. I don't like violence. I got beat up a couple of times. I saw a guy get stabbed after he'd come back from a trick. I remember seeing another guy with his arm cut off. And a girl's body all diced up, because she tried to get away from a pimp. The police don't try to do much about these things.

"I never know when I'll sleep or eat. That's why I have these wrinkles. One reason I don't sleep much is that you can be killed. And the truth is, I don't know how to handle all this."

"Have you talked with a counselor?"

"Yeah, a couple of times. But it didn't help much. They've got so many rules— like showing up when *they* think you should. Always doing things *their* way. I say, I have to deal with myself first. I have to start liking myself. So I talk to myself."

"But it can help to talk things out with others."

"They can't help me," he said, his lips set in a grim line. "All I want is a comfortable apartment, and the power to reach in my pocket and take out money."

"Nothing else?"

Tony looked hard at us, then dropped his eyes. "And . . . inner peace." He pressed his fingers to his forehead. "I've aged a lot. I know I'm going to get old. I'm going to get old and get more wrinkles. When I look at the future, I just see— nothing."

A counselor at Huckleberry House, which offers forty-eight-hour crisis services to youths who have been brought in for status offenses or have run away from home, confirmed that the present set-up was not very effective in solving the problems of the 1,000 to 2,000 young people under eighteen who live on the San Francisco streets.

Recently, a new system had been designed to offer an integrated, multitiered approach. At the first level was Huckleberry House, the receiving facility. Sometimes the staff were able to persuade runaways to return home but only when work on the basic problem with the parents was begun early enough. Otherwise, given the forty-eight-hour limitation, the staff could do little more than refer clients to Hospitality House and the Larkin Street Center. Both offered psychological counseling; referred youths to other agencies for housing, employment, and legal aid; and did outreach work with teen-agers involved or likely to be involved in prostitution. Diamond Street Youth Shelter could sleep up to twelve youths for a stay of three to five days. Although Hospitality House could not put them up on its premises, its Youth Department had a special arrangement allowing it to send six to ten clients to the nearby YMCA for a period of up to twenty-nine days. But the total number of bed nights, counting emergency and transitional shelters, was only forty-one. "That's simply not enough to help a young person figure out a new life. I do not believe the theory that unless you reach the youth in the first month, he or she is lost. I've seen kids change. Many of those here *are* looking, deep down, for an alternative to working the streets. But there's money and excitement on the streets, as well as a certain security from the group. To find satisfying alternatives takes a lot of time—usually six months or more."

Tony's case is only one of many exemplifying the need for a far wider range of services for the homeless. As shelter providers point out, such services should fulfill housing, financial, psychological, employment, and training needs, and their duration and depth should correspond to the needs of the individual. Most providers are keenly aware of the yawning gaps in the "system"; it is the general public who are indifferent.

Needed: A Spectrum of Services

The enormous growth in the number of shelters and other services for those without homes since 1980, we discovered, is due largely to the patient and persistent efforts of advocates to raise public consciousness. Some advocates are members of organizations already working for low-income housing, mental health legislation, improvements in the welfare system, and the like. Some have joined city- or statewide coalitions of groups serving the homeless in order to speak out more forcefully for the poorest of the poor. (In 1982 many advocacy groups united in the National Coalition for the Homeless, a move we describe in a later chapter.) The basic goals of coalitions for the homeless are to research public policy recommendations; foster development of services, and act as a referral center for services, donations, volunteers, and ideas. Some coalitions have a few paid staff members, but the great bulk of the work is done by committed volunteers who may be social service professionals, members of church groups, legal aid societies, civic groups, or simply individuals who become profoundly concerned with the homeless.

Yet there are still far from enough facilities. According to a study published by the U.S. Conference of Mayors, in 60 percent of the twenty-five cities surveyed, emergency shelters cannot accommodate all the people seeking assistance.[3] In every part of the country shelter-seekers are being turned away, even in summer.

The quality of services frequently is very poor. Sometimes this is due to a lack of training or of concern on the part of the staff. Some of the shelter workers we talked with did not even know what welfare services existed in the community and made no effort to refer their guests for such assistance. Far more often, however, the reason for poor shelter facilities or inadequate support services was simply lack of funding.

Emergency shelters tend to be too large; some house two hundred or even three hundred persons. One shelter in New York City, an enormous drill hall in an armory, accommodates up to one thousand every night. Obviously there can be little or no attention to clients' individual needs. Like poorhouses two centuries ago, many of these stations of the lost herd together the young and the old, chronic alcoholics and evicted families, the mentally ill and battered wives. Emergency shelters often provide no housing, employment, or psychological counseling. They also tend to limit stays, usually because there is never enough space and other roofless people must be given a chance. Some emergency shelters offer only three nights a month. Most of them are open only at night; clients often have to struggle out into soaking rain or bitter cold at six-thirty or seven every morning.

Although there are still not enough facilities for women and for families, women tend to get services of better quality. Shelters for women usually are smaller, have a less militaristic atmosphere, permit clients to remain all day, and are more flexible about the length of stay. They also provide more support services. We sometimes observed differences in treatment within one organization. At Chicago's Pacific Garden Mission, for example, the men rise at 5:15 A.M. and are forced to leave the dormitories at 7:00 A.M., except in bad weather, whereas clients in the smaller, more homelike women's facilities can remain and are encouraged to sew, wash and iron their clothes, care for their children, and gather in group sessions.

Everywhere, we found, there is a growing need for family shelters. The St. Louis Relocation Clearinghouse reports a typical situation: only two shelters in the metropolitan area accept teen-aged boys, hence many of the households turned away from shelters are intact families who could not be served as a unit and did not want to be separated. Some missions restrict their services to couples that can produce a marriage license.

Instead of a complex of services, some towns offer virtually none—and even try to close down services that exist. In Utah we picked up a young man with weary eyes who had migrated to Tucson because Arizona was supposed to be full of jobs. "But they just about chased me out of the place," he said. "There were a couple of soup kitchens and a church shelter, but the politicians tried to close them down. The police used to come around where we slept with real mean German shepherds. I heard the mayor got elected on the promise that he'd get the transients the hell out of town."

The day after that conversation in Utah, we were in Reno, the "fun city," where the chief pastime for thousands of middle-aged blue-collar people bused in from neighboring states is to pore hopefully over slot-machines. For the more affluent, the pastime is to tour the complex of casinos and girlie shows every night. The homeless pass their time moving back and forth between the Salvation Army and the Reno–Sparks Gospel Mission, where they are welcomed as sinners. The city, despite tax revenues derived from the casinos, provides no shelter. Indeed, Nevada does not have GA. What does a destitute person do? The desk clerk at the Salvation Army shrugged. "The state gives 'em directions to California."

No part of the country, then, yet offers a spectrum of services wide enough to respond to the varied needs of the homeless, although New York and Massachusetts have made real progress toward that goal.

The Shelter Providers

A rough classification of shelter sponsors comprises missions, voluntary groups (churches and nonprofit agencies), and municipal governments. How do they compare in quality of services?

The Missions

Many of the missions were set up fifty or even a hundred years ago, when most of their clients were alcoholics and the intent was to "raise them from the gutter." With some justification the directors can say that others are johnny-come-latelies. In many towns missions are still the only service available.

Other shelter providers find that in general the missions do not enter well into coalitions. Tensions also result from a difference in attitude toward rules; those in the missions tend to be very rigid. Some city officials refuse to help support missions that require even the stubbornly impious to "take a dive." The officials' refusal has had little effect on the missions, which tend to go it alone and to disdain government interference. Many mission directors told us that their *primary* purpose is preaching the gospel and that regeneration is more important than rehabilitation.

Except for some large Salvation Army shelters that have hired social workers in recent years, missions are rarely staffed by professionals. The personnel are usually converts who have felt saved from a life of sin (often as an alcoholic); "mission stiffs" who do some work in the house, pledge abstinence, attend religious services in exchange for lodging, and may or may not be sincere in their desire to reform; and a minister, who himself may be a salvaged "lost soul" and tends to run the mission like a church.

The missions themselves vary from city to city. At the two-hundred-bed Pacific Garden Mission in Chicago, every client is confronted with a spiritual counselor whose mission is to save him from perdition. The director holds the men in line by yelling at them and carries a huge ring of keys, locking himself into his office when talking with visitors and locking every door as he takes them on a room-to-room tour. At the City Union Mission in Kansas City, Missouri, a counselor explained that he tells the men about his own redemption from alcoholism and street life, but no one is forced to attend a sermon before supper. In Laramie, Wyoming, the young director of the fifteen-bed Salvation Army shelter told us that he imposes no such conditions. Instead, he cooks dinner for his guests, then sits down at the brightly painted kitchen table to listen to them. Although a few Salvation Army missions still require sermon attendance, most directors have come to the conclusion that you cannot force religion on others. Most missions, whatever their religious perspective, are apolitical; they are more concerned with individual souls than with the social causes of homelessness.

The Voluntary Sector

Unlike the missions, shelters run by church-affiliated and nonprofit community services are likely to be serviced by professionals, workers with quasi-professional in-service training, and volunteers (especially people with a religious commitment). The director is often a priest or minister who has some training in social work.

Our impressions from visits to facilities around the country confirm the conviction of most observers: shelters run by voluntary groups (which in practice, are usually church-affiliated) tend to be smaller and more familial than public shelters. Staff members and volunteers in such groups seem to be motivated by a religious or moral commitment even to difficult, unclean, or lice-ridden clients and, because they are less bureaucratic, can run the operation more cheaply.

The number of church-affiliated shelters has grown faster than others. Many church leaders also have demonstrated initiative, imagination, and courage. Most congregations are reluctant to open the church proper to street dwellers. Yet when Charles "Woody" Woodrich, pastor of Denver's Holy Ghost Catholic Church, became acutely aware that men and women were freezing in the February cold, he proposed, "Let's keep the church open tonight for people who need a place to sleep!" Woody guessed that about thirty or forty people needed shelter. Nearly two hundred showed up for the first night. Within a short time, five hundred men and women nightly were sleeping in the church on hard pews that even lacked cushions. Then the search began for a permanent facility. A closed high school was found. Under the joint sponsorship of Holy Ghost Church and the Basilica of the Immaculate Conception, it became the Samaritan Shelter. In 1985 plans were being made to construct a $6.42 million Samaritan Shelter. A model facility, it will include medical services, personal counseling, and employment counseling to an unusually broad spectrum of guests: families, runaway youths, single adults (both men and women), transients, and the handicapped, including those in wheel chairs.

In other cities—Atlanta, Chicago, Washington, D.C., and New York, for example—congregations have also made church structures available. In Atlanta, pastor Ed Loring and a group of concerned citizens have been particularly successful in convincing twenty-nine churches to open their basements, fellowship halls, Sunday school rooms, or even sanctuaries to people with no roof over their heads. Unfortunately, says Loring, fifteen of these refuges close after April 1 every year.

The St. Anthony Foundation in the Tenderloin district of San Francisco is another example of a service that has grown with the times. It was on the feast day of Saint Francis in 1950 that Franciscan Father Alfred Boeddeker opened Saint Anthony Dining Room and served the first meal to the poor in the community. Today over two thousand people line up on the streets every day, patiently waiting for the well-balanced noonday meal. On the days that we visited the dining room, seminarians, nuns clad in the sari-like garb of Mother Teresa's Missionaries of Charity, and former street people were serving the homeless; the atmosphere was one of caring and mutual support. The work of the dining room is funded entirely from individual contributions and other private sources. Over the years the foundation has expanded to include a self-supporting farm that provides work for unemployed men; a clinic with free basic medical services; the Madonna Residence for women over fifty-five with limited incomes; and an employment agency. One of the foundation's most important operations today is its Drop-In Center, where roofless men and women can sit, play cards, talk, or watch TV during the day and bed down on sleeping mats at night.

Affiliation with churches (or other voluntary groups such as Traveler's Aid, the YWCA, or the YMCA) does not automatically mean that the shelters are of good quality. A few are insensitive to the needs of their clients. In other cases, a sponsoring church body may delegate ongoing responsiblity to an insensitive or insufficiently trained paid staff. Shelters run by church groups are also constantly harassed by worries over lack of financial support. They cannot legislate funds but must depend on the generosity of congregations and individuals, all of whom feel the pull of many commitments. As a result, such shelters rarely enjoy the security of continuity. Because of lack of funds, most of them suspend operations during the summer, even though the homeless do not suspend their needs during that time. Other shelters have closed down entirely, even as the needs of people without homes have grown.

Municipal Shelters

New York, Los Angeles, Philadelphia, Boston, Washington, D.C., and Chicago are among the few cities that have set up public shelters. However, except for New York, even these cities prefer, in most cases, to contract with private groups for the actual staffing and administration of facilities. The reason these subsidized operations are still known as city shelters is that the city initiates the idea (after some prodding), usually decides to house the shelter in public buildings such as an old school or hospital, and then searches for a private group to administer it.

There are certain advantages to public shelters. The city can create and enforce standards (although this does not mean that city administrations necessarily follow them, as experience in New York and Washington attests). Moreover, shelters cannot discriminate against anyone who refuses to attend religious services. Most important, city shelters symbolize public responsibility for less fortunate citizens.

In practice, city shelters present many drawbacks. They tend to be larger, more susceptible to violence, and more bureaucratic than the private ones. In New York, the per diem cost per client has been averaging $26 (including meals).[4]

The cost in private shelters ranges from $2 to $15, depending on staffing and services offered. The chief reason for the difference in cost is that private facilities rely far more on volunteers, donated food, and workers who are willing to serve for low salaries.

Public shelters come into being only grudgingly, after a protracted struggle between concerned citizens and public officials. New York expanded the number of its shelters for single men and women from two to eighteen within four years (in 1986 there were twenty such facilities), but only after advocates had launched demonstrations and lawsuits, the media had focused a great deal of publicity on the topic, and a strong citywide Coalition for the Homeless had been formed. The coalition continues to wage battle with the city for overcrowding its facilities and for failure to provide quality care. In Chicago, the Chicago Coalition for the Homeless pushed hard for two years before the city finally agreed to open a small shelter for battered women and to contract with Catholic Charities for the administration of a one-hundred-bed general shelter. In 1985 the coalition estimated that there were nearly twenty-five thousand homeless people in Chicago and only a little more than fifteen hundred beds in all shelters.[5]

However, to blame the meagerness of support for city-operated or city-subsidized facilities on welfare officials is to misunderstand the politics of the situation and the complexity of pressures they experience from below and above—for example, neighborhood opposition to shelters. In Chicago and Hoboken, New Jersey, some private shelters have been taken to court for violating zoning codes. In smaller towns opposition may be more covert. In Laramie, Wyoming, the Council of Churches, rather than the town, helps support the Salvation Army shelter and officially, at least, limits the transient's stay to one night. On the following morning he or she becomes eligible for a one-way ticket to the nearest town, as guest of the Good Samaritan Fund.

On another level, there is dissension among city agencies and city officials. For example, the welfare department may plan to open a shelter, only to find that fire and health inspectors refuse to relax some of their criteria in the case of emergency housing.

On the mayor–city council level, there may be conflicts over allotment of funds. For example, shall some Community Development Block Grants (CDBGs) be used to support shelters or instead be directed to slum clearance, landscaping downtown areas, and other projects that actually help create homelessness?

On the city–state level, there may be heated debate between mayor and governor over who has failed to take enough responsibility for the homeless. City officials also blame state administrations for dumping mental patients into their streets and point accusing fingers at local federal officials who have refused to open empty buildings to the homeless, despite a ruling that they may be used for that purpose.

Often invisible, but always present in policy debates, are the town fathers, the prominent businessmen who claim to have the city's best interests at heart. Virtually every big city we have visited seemed to be vying to become the convention center for the nation. The homeless have no place in such a vision. Moreover, it is the business community that is likely to raise the specter of the "mecca" (sometimes referred to as "magnet") theory—that is, the proposition that building a comfortable shelter will attract "hordes of vagrants" from less generous communities to the boulevards of "our beautiful city." The theory has been contradicted in several studies, which show that the majority of the homeless in the cities surveyed have lived there for seven months or longer, and that the majority of the migrants who do move in are seeking not shelter but jobs.[6]

To pressure the city either to open a shelter or to fund a private one, then, is a formidable task.

The Frustrations of Service Providers

What is life like for the men and women who work with the homeless day after day? Although nearly all whom we met found deep satisfaction in their work, many also felt caught in the tussles of local politics or experienced conflicts over where they should be directing their energies or felt drained from the constant—and sometimes conflicting—demands on their time.

"Unless you see yourself as a saver of souls, there's nothing romantic about this work," said one shelter operator. "Most of these people are cooperative, but some are just plain difficult. I'm not thinking about their being dirty, or untidy—though many are—but rather, being hard to reach. I don't think I need gratitude. But I do appreciate some responsiveness, and people who've been traumatized from being pushed into the streets don't always have that left. As for gratitude—well, when I look deeper into myself, the less grateful people are the ones I respect more. Why *should* they be grateful for stale bread, soup made of leftovers, and second-hand clothing?"

For most service providers a more vexing problem is the constant struggle to get support from government and the public at large. Steve Whitney-Wise, who heads a coalition of service organizations and churches that work with the homeless in Sacramento, California, put it well: "As a person who has provided direct services to the homeless and hungry and also worked with and for local governments, I've often reflected on the games people play on all sides. I see—and it angers and frustrates me—nonprofit agencies in deadly competition for the meager government monies to provide Band Aid services to the poor. I also see people who genuinely want to help in some way but don't know how. Or they may just want to drop something off without getting involved. I remember a Christmas time in San Francisco some years ago. A young man wearing an army jacket and sunglasses came by St. Anthony's drop-in center, which I headed at that time, and handed a staff person an envelope containing $5,000. The envelope was sealed with a Band Aid. At least three other drop-in centers received the same kind of gift, with the same kind of Band Aid, that day.

"You see, charity is a word that makes me nervous. It's a word that lets us all off the hook. Charity can actually be a means of perpetuating injustice, hunger, and homelessness by throwing money at the poor without changing the systems that promote poverty."

The service providers we met felt that they could not leave the front line because the urgent survival needs of desperate people had to be met. At the same time, however, many asked themselves whether they would not in the end serve the homeless better by focusing their energies on working for policies that could prevent homelessness.

The Ongoing Debate

Throughout the 1980s a controversy has been simmering: which sector, public or private, bears primary responsibility for the homeless?

When President Reagan took office, he promised the American people that he would turn over far more responsibility for "our unfortunate citizens" to the voluntary sector in order to get "big government off our backs." The superiority of voluntaryism, he declared, was a matter of principle: "This can be an era of losing freedom or one of reclaiming it."

That message set the tone. It was a message heard not only by ordinary Americans confused about the source of their tax burdens but by state, county, and city officials as well. Today, when service providers seek government support, officials usually talk of their limited funds and emphasize the predominant role of private groups in a free enterprise society.

One might have expected voluntary groups to bask in such recognition of their importance. Curiously, only a minority of the shelter providers—most of the missions and a very few church groups—would subscribe to this philosophy.

In part this is due to the common inertia or unwillingness of almost all groups or institutions to recognize troubling issues and realign their priorities accordingly. The response of churches and synagogues illustrates the point. On the one hand, both Judaic and Christian precepts enjoin the haves of the established society to offer hospitality to the wandering poor in their midst. During the Middle Ages, Christians set up networks of hospices as places of refuge for travelers and as homes for the sick and the poor. The churches themselves were often used as refuges for men and women fleeing from persecution and for other undomiciled people. Even in earlier decades of the twentieth century the Catholic Worker and some Franciscan groups began to open small houses of hospitality to shelter alcoholics, battered spouses, the disabled, and other people living on the fringes of society.

Despite these traditions, it cannot be said that the religious community as a whole immediately sprang to the challenge˙ of homelessness in the 1980s. A characteristic response of leaders of congregations as well as their flocks has been "Let some other parish handle them. We must take care of our own." Only slowly have a few priests, ministers, or rabbis opened the doors of their houses of worship to the unwashed. Typically, the rationale is that "neither the community nor my own parish would put up with this."

Nevertheless, as we have already seen, some religious leaders and parishioners have succeeded in breaking through this resistance and have opened their own houses of worship to street people. Others have volunteered in shelters or assisted in various supportive efforts. There can be no doubt that churches and other voluntary groups have assumed leadership in direct work with the homeless, as a look at the time, energy, skills, and funds they have invested clearly attests.

Do they have the resources to meet the ever-growing need? For almost all the voluntary groups with whom we have been in contact the answer is no. Only government, they believe, is in a position to finance programs on the scale necessary. Here they part company with the Reagan philosophy.

The great majority of sevice providers with whom we have talked believe that, in general, religious and other voluntary groups can do a better job in the actual operation of shelters. They would agree with Archie Bruun, Director of the Office of Social Action and World Peace of the Archdiocese of Cincinnati: "City governments often do their best to demonstrate that there's no homeless problem. So if they do create shelters, they're likely to make the places as unpleasant as possible. I've seen large city shelters where they harass guests by treating them roughly, keeping the lights on, making noise, and pushing people out very early in the morning. Church groups not only treat their guests as human beings but also have less red tape. Still, if the churches try to undertake large projects, they too will fail. As long as our programs retain a human-hearted quality, they will succeed. For bureaucrats, providing shelter is just a job to be done. For a church person it is a commitment. Naturally, government should provide funding."

Many municipal governments have come to agree, at least tacitly, with Bruun's philosophy. In recent years, a growing practice has been for the city to contract with private groups for services. As we have seen, sometimes the city initiates the idea and offers the use of municipal buildings, in which case the facility usually comes to be known as a city shelter. More often the city offers to help support an already existing private operation. In still other cases, the city or county vouchers homeless people (usually families) into welfare hotels or boarding houses. For their part, churches can furnish food, clothing, volunteers, and sometimes basements. Voluntary agencies such as Traveler's Aid or the YWCA can provide food, social services, referrals, and, in some cases, a building.

Is the answer a partnership between the public and private sectors? In concept, partnership sounds like an ideal solution. In practice, it presents many difficulties. Service providers have told us in frustrated tones how precious time can be lost in applying for government grants through complicated bureaucratic procedures. Government often comes in with its own agenda, which may reflect little understanding of the homeless or the ideas of service providers. Sometimes city administrations fail to follow federal guidelines in awarding federal grants and instead favor those who have offered favors. Cities and counties, the levels of government that traditionally have borne most direct responsibility for the indigent, are also most subject to local politicking and subtle control by business interests.

Federal funding has been grossly inadequate, say most of those who work with the homeless. The major source has been the Federal Emergency Management Administration (FEMA) grants. After prolonged pressure on the part of advocates, Congress appropriated $100 million for emergency services as part of the so-called Jobs Bill in fiscal 1983, another $40 million in fiscal 1984, $90 million in fiscal 1985, and $70 million in fiscal 1986. If there are 2 million homeless people in the United States, this averages $38 per person a year. Moreover, the emergency funding is not intended for the homeless alone. A large portion has gone to soup kitchens and other programs to meet emergency needs, which may or may not include the homeless.

Although federal officials are subject to far less local politicking, the actual administration of federal funding presents many problems. In the case of the above grants, FEMA has been charged with distributing the funds to voluntary umbrella organizations such as the United Way and the National Conference of Catholic Charities, which allocate monies to local service providers. Despite some frustrating restrictions imposed in the early years of the program, by 1985 the overwhelming majority of the FEMA-funded service providers interviewed in an Urban Institute survey felt that the program did respond to a great need. At the same time, most service providers agreed that the ongoing need for food and shelter was a structural poverty problem that the program could never solve.[7]

Teamwork That Works

Despite all the problems involved in partnership, some collaborative efforts do succeed. In Seattle the city government has been unusually supportive. It has no shelter of its own but provides financial assistance to private groups serving those without homes. For example, it has cooperated with the Emergency Housing Coalition and other groups to convert a vacant school building into a temporary shelter for homeless women and children. The city elected to use portions of its federal CDBG as well as interest from a foundation (the H.H. Dearborn Trust). Seattle also has allocated some of its federal revenue-sharing funds for the homeless. The money goes to the Survival Services Coalition, a group of nineteen agencies.

In addition to providing private groups with technical assistance, the city has established the position of emergency food and shelter coordinator, who serves as liaison between private organizations and various city departments and monitors city contracts concerned with emergency assistance.

In the course of our visit to Seattle's Downtown Emergency Center, where 230 men and women were sleeping in a dilapidated turn-of-the-century ballroom, we learned that the facility was funded by CDBG money, the county (which supports two mental health case manager positions), churches, businesses, and individual donors.

The lack of transitional facilities is filled to some degree by the Seattle Emergency Housing Service. Supported by CDBG and United Way funds, the service offers apartment housing to some fifty families for up to five weeks. Without this extra time, says director Martha Dilts, many families would have gone to temporary shelters. The security of living in their own apartment, even for a few weeks, has been a key factor in helping them to stabilize their lives. Yet the service can assist only a fraction of the families who need it.

In St. Louis, where 20,000 people were estimated to be homeless in early 1986, the city funds the operating costs of the St. Louis Relocation Clearinghouse and the local shelter. On our visit, Susan Murray, executive director of the Clearinghouse, described how the agency had played a central role in bringing hope to the homeless. "In 1980 the mayor decided that the overhead of the relocation department was too high, so he looked for a voluntary group that could take over moving families displaced by fire and code enforcement agencies. We said we'd put the program together only if it also involved social and health services that could solve the problems these people face. We also stipulated that funds be provided for research, which would help in getting legislation passed."

Today a chief function of the Clearinghouse is a referral service (said to be a model of its kind) that provides homeless persons or their advocates with immediate information on where bed space is available in the emergency shelters in the St. Louis metropolitan area; an attempt is made to match people with an appropriate facility. Since many shelters are unable to provide casework, housing referrals, and training, the services are often provided by the Clearinghouse. The agency also has helped found the St. Louis County Emergency Housing Council, which set up a program, administered by the Clearinghouse, to place county residents in hotels for brief stays.

Because decent housing is hard to find, the Clearinghouse helps people locate marginally substandard units and inspects replacement units. Staff members teach new tenants how to make improvements and run classes on their rights and responsibilities. Because of clients' short attention spans, the sessions last only one hour. Yet the program has proved remarkably successful; problems involving tenants' rights and responsibilities have been cut by two-thirds.

In 1981 the city's budget for relocating families was $500,000. By 1983 the budget was down to $300,000, yet the Clearinghouse program was relocating 50 percent more people than when it was directly managed by the city. Moreover, the program now includes research, referral, educating the homeless, educating the community, and moving people from emergency into more permanent accommodations.

Yet the program could not possibly exist without financial support from city, state, and federal governments. In addition to operating funds from the city, FEMA money and an interest-free loan from the Missouri Housing Development Commission have been crucial. This loan supports Project Re-Do, an innovative and far-sighted response to the needs of the homeless. Under the plan, the Clearinghouse purchases vacant buildings and gut-rehabs them into apartments for families, who live in them while receiving vocational training. Once trained and employed, the families move to permanent housing located by the Clearinghouse. "The real need," says Murray, "is for adequate *permanent* housing for low-income families."

In Massachusetts, the state has taken the initiative in creating an alliance between the public and private sectors. When Michael Dukakis became governor in 1983, he promised to make the homeless a top priority. Under his leadership, Massachusetts has instituted legislation that resulted in funding some eighteen shelters on a 75 percent–25 percent basis with the groups that operate them. Some are transitional facilties; the state funds all the operating costs of three such shelters in Boston.

As Neal Newman of the Massachusetts Coalition for the Homeless points out, it was in response to prodding from the coalition that the state also instituted measures that can help to prevent homelessness. Today it offers AFDC families (or families with children under twenty-one who are financially but not categorically eligible for AFDC) assistance that can include four months rental or mortgage payments, utility or fuel payments, and in some cases, one month's advance rent or security deposit as well as thirty days furniture storage or $150 moving expenses.

Massachusetts also has changed welfare rules so that people without permanent addresses can receive GA, expanded medical coverage for the homeless under GA, opened twenty-four hour hotlines for referrals, and committed its Department of Mental Health to do case management services in shelters.

In addition, the state set up the mechanism for the Fund for the Homeless. Started with $25,000 seed money from a foundation, the fund provides a way for private donations from individuals, groups, and corporations to be funneled into shelters.

In Boston, the city has set up the Emergency Shelter Commission. Among other things, the commission coordinates city efforts with those of the state, federal, and private groups; locates facilities and resources for shelters and transitional housing; helps private groups in the recruitment of volunteers; and makes lists of foreclosed properties available to shelter providers for potential conversion to SROs. It also works with unions, business leaders, and local foundations that have contributed time, money, and materials.

In New York City, churches and the municipal government have embarked on an unusual cooperative venture. The Partnership for the Homeless unites more than three hundred churches and synagogues in the joint management of some one hundred private shelters, many of which are located in houses of worship. The city has furnished cots, blankets, and other kinds of technical assistance, while FEMA provides funds to purchase food. Other monies come from foundations. However, the lion's share of responsibility is borne by religious communities, which contribute the site of the shelter, referrals of homeless guests, and volunteers. In 1985 over twelve thousand people were donating their services.

According to founder Peter Smith, the first reaction of most ministers and rabbis to the proposal was that they would not be able to arouse their parishioners. "Those leaders were astonished at the number of people who volunteered," he told us. "They often underestimate the concern in their congregations." One secret of the partnership's success is that its shelters are not warehouses but small communal-type places. The maximum number of clients is nineteen, and the average is eleven. Another secret is that no shelters are opened without involving community residents in planning.

In addition to providing emergency shelter, the partnership offers furniture, towels, blankets, and kitchenware to homeless people who move into city-owned apartments. Its volunteers help people find child-care programs, health services, and social activities in their neighborhoods.

Since the partnership's network is the largest in any U.S. city, the group has established a National Technical Assistance Project that visits communities across the nation and provides them with help to mobilize the religious sector in similar ventures.

The partnership also has been working with the city to place families and individuals in permanent housing: city-owned *in rem* (transferred to the city for failure to pay taxes) buildings that have been rehabilitated through funds from the city, private foundations, corporations, church groups, and individuals.

A look around the country reveals that municipal governments perform a wide variety of functions in cooperation with the work of the private sector. Sometimes the mayor's office organizes a task force on the homeless with representatives from government, religious groups, voluntary agencies, and the business community. Some cities set up or support hot lines to tell homeless people or referring agencies where shelter services are available. A few municipalities have organized outreach teams that roam the streets at night, inviting those who are "sleeping rough" to accept food and a bed. The city may expand its own social services to the homeless or provide more financial support to voluntary groups that offer such help. It also may contribute comestibles and space to a food pantry.

Growing numbers of cities rehabilitate unused municipal buildings and lease or donate them to private shelter operators. Some also contribute funds to rehabilitate existing shelters. More frequent is the custom of providing families, and sometimes singles or couples, with vouchers for cheap hotels. In a few parts of the country, the city pays landlords several months rent for homeless families. New York City has initiated, with state approval, a program that pays landlords four months rent at the emergency rate on a two-year lease for an apartment. Since a number of families sheltered in New York City find permanent housing on their own, the city also may pay for rent deposits, moving expenses, and if appropriate, a broker's fee. A few communities, concerned with preventing homelessness, help households in danger of eviction to meet rental payments.

Although the 1984 HUD survey revealed that local Public Housing Authorities (PHAs) have not played a significant role in sheltering the homeless, they have the power to do so. They can, for example, set up emergency priorities. Usually the definition of *emergency* covers only those persons displaced because of fire, government programs, natural disasters, or, in some cases, evictions. People living on the street typically are not included.[8] PHA officials frequently declare, with some justice, that they cannot meet the needs of the homeless because their waiting lists are already too long. Yet housing authorities in Seattle and Dayton, Ohio, have leased units to nonprofit groups to house people without homes, and in Alabama, the Birmingham Housing Authority works with the city and a church group to operate one shelter.

Although states generally have not played an active role in working with the private sector, at least two of them provide examples of what could be achieved. New York has created a program providing for construction or rehabilitation of housing for the homeless and awarded grants to municipalities and nonprofit groups for these purposes. California, through its Department of Housing and Community Development, furnishes funds to local governments and nonprofit organizations for temporary shelter.

Theoretically, at least, the federal role in partnerships offers a wide variety of possibilities. On occasion the Department of Defense has transferred non-marketable food from its commissaries to food banks. Even more rarely, it has offered surplus facilities for emergency shelters to be operated by voluntary groups. In at least one instance—a demonstration program in Memphis—HUD has provided the units for transitional housing. The program has been called a success that could serve as a model in other communities.

The major sources of federal funds that could serve the homeless are FEMA, CDBG, Social Services Block Grants (SSBG), and Community Services Block Grants (CSBG). FEMA has provided vitally needed assistance, although its usefulness is limited because funds are insufficient and are provided only on a year-to-year basis. Municipal governments also can opt to use portions of their CDBG funds for housing the homeless. However, since only neighborhood-based nonprofit organizations, local development corporations, or small businesses can build new housing with CDBG funds, and then as part of a neighborhood revitalization or community development project, emergency shelter operators have been able to use such funds only to rehabilitate a shelter. In principle the SSBG offers good opportunities for creative collaboration with voluntary gorups. However, during the first Reagan administration, its funds were cut 23.5 percent, despite the augmented need for services for the poor. CSBG funds were cut even more: 37.1 percent.[9]

Although cities can use general revenues, many are financially pressed, partly because of cuts in block grants. If the 1984 HUD report on the homeless is correct, only about 20 percent of the local governments have been using locally generated funds to help the outcasts wandering the streets.

Reflections

Over the years we have come to the conclusion that several conditions must be met to ensure that partnership between the public and private sectors be successful:

Government sources should furnish what they are in a position to give: money (in the form of revolving, not one-time grants), buildings, technical aid such as assistance with renovations, and liaison personnel.

Corporations and foundations should offer funding. Many shelter-providers feel that thus far there has been only a feeble response from the corporate world. Contributions from both corporations and foundations are growing, however. The Ittleson Foundation, the J. M. Kaplan Fund, the New York Community Trust, the New York Foundation, the Robert Wood Johnson Fund, Morgan Guaranty, the Astor Foundation, the Pew Memorial Trust, and the Chicago Community Trust, are only a few of such groups that help support research, direct services, or advocacy work for the homeless.

The attitude of various government levels must be both positive and realistic. They need to recognize that funding should be based on an ongoing commitment and act accordingly. By the same token, government personnel who work with private service providers should have experience in human services, preferably in work with the poor. Unfortunately, government people in such liaison positions are almost always bureaucrats with little understanding of the work of service providers. Bureaucrats also are more likely to be motivated by political interests. In states such as Arizona it is expedient to proclaim a hard line on the homeless. In a few others, such as Massachusetts, it is advantageous to be on the side of the underdog. Even in such states, the dominant concern may not be the well-being of the homeless themselves.

The various levels of government should be willing to work on long-term problems such as housing.

If city or state decides that shelters should be licensed, this should be seen as a positive opportunity to raise the number and quality of facilities, not as an excuse for shutting them down.

Government should participate in rallying public support, by contributing to media campaigns, for example.

For a partnership to work, ideally there should be a President and/or a governor and/or a mayor who clearly care about the welfare of the homeless, or at least have been pressured to care. Officials need top-down sanctions in order to bring out the best in them. Today the reality is that ambivalence permeates the whole hierarchy of government. Officials realize that the more government is involved, the more clear is the admission that homelessness is an affliction that will not go away until government at every level assumes more responsibility for dealing with the underlying problems.

Genuine desire to do something about the situation is, of course, crucial. Any survey of work with the homeless verifies the old adage, "Where there's a will, there's a way." Where there is active concern, somehow, miraculously, funds are discovered.

Photo by Nancy Miller Elliott

Part II
A Look at Two Cities

ANYONE leaving
the building After
1:00 AM will not be
welcome back
inside.

Please —
No men
on the steps!

WOMEN'S
SHELTER
ENTRANCE

ANYONE leaving the
building after 1:00 A.M.
will not be welcome
back inside.

CCNV Second Street shelter before renovation.

3
Homeless in Washington

On long winter nights in the nation's capital, the bodies of men and women lie stretched over heat grates within sight of the White House. Other street people sleep fitfully in boxes, bus stations, abandoned cars, or emergency shelters.

Estimates of the number of homeless in Washington, D.C. range from seven thousand to eighteen thousand. Most are black. Many have been living on the streets for years and have coped with fate by outward resignation and turning their anger inward.

To others, however, life on the sidewalks is new. They can remember regular jobs, three meals a day, living under a roof, and their rage simmers close to the surface as they look at the White House.

Washington is a city of contrasts. It is symbolized by the White House, but its population is nearly 70 percent black. With its stately embassies, fashionable town houses, carefully planned broad avenues, and lush green lawns surrounding marble monuments, it is the most elegant of all U.S. cities, yet it also has some of the country's worst slums. Only a mile or two from the White House, block after block of craterlike areas contain charred skeletons of abandoned buildings, some of them memoirs of the 1968 riots. The city has taken no responsibility for making them habitable. Today children play in open spaces littered with trash and garbage. Opposite them stand rehabilitated condominiums with brick facades and sculptured shrubbery. Down the street dilapidated-looking buildings display the invitation: "Buy Now—Suitable for Conversion."

In the Pentagon, the Secretary of Defense entertains experts in technological warfare in four plush executive dining rooms. According to the Children's Defense Fund, just the $1 million annual subsidy for the dining rooms would buy 800,000 school lunches.[1]

In the past thirty years Washington has grown from a sleepy southern town to a prime center for conventions. Today development is a key slogan. By 1980 the city had become the national leader in revitalization. Washington has an abundance of singles and young couples—people with high-status white-collar jobs— who form the core of the urban pioneers seeking homes in the city. A majority of the new arrivals are white. Almost all the people they are displacing are black, many of them impoverished migrants from the South.

Some of the economic and political problems of the city are related to its peculiar step-child status. Formerly governed by a commission under Congress, residents of the District of Columbia waited until 1961 for the privilege of voting in Presidential elections. Only in 1974 did they gain the right to elect their own mayor and city council. The District has won the authority to levy its own taxes, but Congress has retained power to veto actions and review the city's annual budget. The District's geographical area is rigidly confined to sixty-seven square miles; it cannot expand into the suburbs.

The Precipitants of Homelessness

As in other parts of the United States, homelessness in Washington stems from four principal causes: unemployment, inadequacy of social benefits, lack of shelter and treatment for the mentally disabled, and lack of affordable housing.

Unemployment

The population of the District of Columbia is over 70 percent black. According to Dick Groner of Washington's Office of Employment Services, in 1984 (the latest year for which statistics are available) overall unemployment was 9 percent, but the figure for whites was 2.3 percent and for blacks, 12.1 percent.[2] Authorities blame the situation on the lack of skills among blacks to meet today's needs, and on the federal government's slashing of programs to provide jobs and training.

Many of the black unemployed have been displaced from southern farms as mechanization has grown. All too often their hopes of finding security in the city are illusions. They line up in long queues for work, live in crowded dwellings, send their children to crowded inferior schools, and hope that their welfare checks (if they happen to be eligible for assistance) will last into the second half of the month.

Inadequate Social Benefits

Unless a poor family is fortunate enough to live in subsidized housing, the chances of making it till the end of the month are extremely slim. In the District of Columbia, in 1985, a mother with one child received a maximum grant of $257 from AFDC (known in D.C. as Aid to Dependent Children). There is no rent supplement. The amount of food stamps is based on family size and disposable income after rent. Mike Hildebrand, of Lutheran Social Services, describes a situation that illustrates how far a grant of $257 can go. A twenty-four-year-old AFDC mother (pseudonym Janet) with a three-year-old child was living in a tiny apartment for a rent of $256—a rent considered very cheap in D.C., especially since it included heat. The landlord would not accept the welfare check in payment of rent, so she had to purchase a money order, which cost a dollar. Janet borrowed twenty-two cents to mail the money order. How did she manage to pay for other necessities with less than zero income? She did receive Medicaid and food stamps. When the latter ran out toward the end of the month, Janet stood in line at soup kitchens and food pantries. That did not pay her $12-a-month electric bill, however. It was for assistance with that bill that she approached Lutheran Social Services. How did she pay for carfare, phone calls, clothing, hand soap, cleaning supplies, non-prescription medications, furniture, ad other items not covered by food stamps? "Who knows?" says Mr. Hildebrand. "But I do know what happens to many other young women in such circumstances."

The stipend for a single person on SSI with no other income is $336 a month (1986 figures). A person on GA (known in Washington as General Public Assistance) can expect the lowest stipend of all: in 1986, a maximum of $206 a month. However, in D.C., only temporarily disabled persons qualify for the program. Unemployed single persons and couples who are considered able-bodied and have used up their unemployment compensation (if indeed they ever received it) get no benefits whatsoever.

Many people, especially the elderly, fall through the cracks of the system. One December day, outside a soup kitchen, we talked with a thin, weary-looking black woman huddling in her threadbare coat as she waited for the doors to open. She was only sixty-two; her drawn face and bent figure made her look older. A widow, nearly crippled with arthritis, she could no longer do domestic work. Her disability was not considered severe enough for her to receive Social Security Disability (SSD) or SSI for the disabled. She did qualify for a widow's pension of $229 under Social Security. Because her Social Security income was deemed too high to entitle her to GA, she was not eligible for medical assistance—she would have to wait until her sixty-fifth birthday to qualify for either Medicaid (under SSI) or Medicare. Her rent was $200. Hence she had $29 left for all the so-called discretionary expenses described above as well as medical and dental care, and all medication. "Sometimes I wait and I wait for that Social Security check to come. Lots of times it's several days late," she told us. After we had chatted for a while, she confided: "I get $75 worth of food stamps. And I . . . well, the welfare department would call me a 'cheat,' but you've been nice talking to me, so I'll tell you. I sell some of those stamps. Don't get much—about half what they're worth. That doesn't leave me much to eat. But what else could I do?"

Inadequate Services for the Mentally Disabled

The general estimate among those who work with the homeless in Washington is that 50 to 70 percent of those who walk the streets are mentally ill.

Saint Elizabeths Hospital, a federal psychiatric facility, has stringent deinstitutionalization policies, and 80 percent of the mentally ill on the streets are said to be discharged from there. Approximately sixty persons are released each month.

In the 1950s the hospital's inpatient population peaked near 8,000;[3] in 1985, it averaged 1,500.[4] Mentally ill persons admitted to Saint Elizabeths are no longer allowed to stay for more than seventy-two hours if a psychiatrist does not deem them a danger to themselves or others. Women have been known to go to a shelter and violently attack someone in a desperate attempt to be returned to the hospital.

In 1974 a court decision, the Dixon Mandate, established the right of mentally disabled patients of St. Elizabeths Hospital who do not need institutionalization to receive suitable services in the community. In 1980 the federal and local governments agreed to follow a detailed plan for creating such services. Yet in March 1982, the Mental Health Law Project filed a court motion detailing the extensive deficiencies in compliance found by the Dixon Implementation Monitoring Committee and asked the court to help enforce the consent order.[5] St. Elizabeths, responding to growing pressure, expressed willingness to institute improvements. Partly because of federal budget cuts, however, progress was stalled. In 1985 the situation took a new turn: a plan was inaugurated for the gradual transfer of administrative and financial responsibility for the hospital from the federal government to the District. By 1991, the district is to assume all responsibility and to have an integrated, coordinated mental health system, including community-based programs and a continuum of inpatient and outpatient mental health care and support systems.

Yet according to several experienced workers at private shelters for women, some guests are still arriving from St. Elizabeths with nothing more than the clothes they are wearing and the address of the shelter. Cathy St. Clair and Diane Doherty point out that often shelter providers find it extremely difficult to track down the client's social worker and doctor at St. E's. In cases where they do succeed, shelter providers often discover that hospital staff have developed no plan for a secure source of income and no treatment plan other than returning to the hospital once a month for group therapy and medication. After accomplishing the difficult task of getting a woman to one of the district's community mental health centers, shelter providers often encounter a general lack of knowledge by center staff about appropriate facilities. There are excellent private programs under contract to the city that can meet the special needs of mentally ill homeless women, yet many slots have gone unfilled.

Another problem is the lack of continuity among center personnel. Within a short period women will see two or three different doctors or counselors. As a result, patients do not develop relationships with the people treating them. Moreover, center personnel sometimes do not respond to the gravity of crisis situations. When a woman is brought to a center in the middle of the night because she was engaged in violence toward herself or others, it is a serious problem. Frequently shelter providers and their violent clients have been turned away and told that there is no need for immediate care.[6]

The article by St. Clair and Doherty was published in 1982. Three years later, despite community pressure for adherence to the Dixon Mandate, all these problems still existed, according to Elisabeth Huguenin, a psychiatric social worker who has worked at Sarah House and the House of Ruth. "St. Elizabeths prefers to take only the more stabilized patients, so many of those who need hospitalization—including some who *want* to get in—are not admitted. At the mental health centers, workers are overloaded, so their work is superficial; the stress is on quantity, not quality. The emergency service at the centers is for the birds. Often workers there will say, 'This person is not crazy enough.' At the shelters the big problem is that they seldom keep the women long enough. Transitional shelters often provide a three-months stay—longer than at emergency shelters— but even three months isn't enough time for most women to get their lives together. The shelters don't have enough money, so they rely too much on volunteers or staff members who have had little training. Many of them don't realize that we shouldn't be acting like parents but instead should gradually give people more control over their lives. But the women who don't get themselves into a hospital or mental health center or shelter are the worst off. They're afraid of contacts with people, so they're afraid of shelters. But life on the streets still forces them into contacts with people and brings other stresses. They're treated very badly, and that accentuates their paranoia."

For any Washington resident, low-cost housing is nearly impossible to find. For the fragile mentally ill, the search is even more difficult. Only a few are fortunate enough to find asylum in a foster home, a halfway house, or group home. Yet such housing is not expensive; it runs $2,800 to $3,200 a year in comparison to the $95,000 (based on average per diem cost of $244.47 in 1985)[7] required to keep a patient at St. E's.

The Shortage of Low-Income Housing

According to the Metropolitan Washington Planning and Housing Association (MWPHA), between 1970 and 1980 there was only a 4-percent increase in rental units in the metropolitan area, and in the district, as a result of conversion, abandonment, and demolition, there was actually a net decrease—a loss of 25,522 rental units.[8] During that period, according to estimates by housing advocates, rents increased almost 50 percent.

The loss of rental units, says MWPHA, can be attributed to co-op and condominium conversion, abandonment, and demolition. In 1970 there were less than 1,000 condominium units in the metropolitan area; by July 1981 there were almost 95,000 units.[9] By February 1986 there were 11,728 families in D.C. alone waiting for public housing and assisted housing; the list was seven years long.[10]

Many of the applicants have been paying 60 to 80 percent of their income for shelter alone. The problem is compounded by the acute shortage of rooming houses and boarding houses that could meet the needs of many single persons and couples. SROs have been disappearing. All these could bridge the gap between emergency night shelters and independent apartment living for homeless people.

In contrast to most other U.S. cities, Washington does extend housing protection to the poor in the form of rent controls, eviction laws, relocation assistance, restrictions on conversion, limited home purchase assistance, and a prohibitive tax on rapid sales for quick profits.

Despite rent controls, landlords enjoy considerable protection. Rents go up automatically every year; the increases, regulated by City Council, parallel the consumer Price Index. Automatic raises of 10 percent are allowed for each new vacancy. Hence long-term tenants are frequently pressed to leave. Hardship increases of 30 to 40 percent are available in many cases. The landlord also knows that it takes six to twelve months for tenants to get a hearing in the courts. Even if the owner is convicted, he or she is likely to get a minor fine.

Although evictions of public housing tenants have virtually ceased, dislodgment of private tenants has been increasing, as poor renters find it increasingly difficult to meet their payments. Moreover, landlords, citing the high cost of heating, close their buildings as winter approaches. Speculating owners may evict tenants in order to keep a building empty until the most advantageous moment for a quick hassle-free sale.

On the other side, small landlords of low-income housing find it increasingly difficult to get a fair return on their investment. When tenants have to be evicted for nonpayment of rent, the landlord may also suffer. Since evictions must be carried out by marshals, and there are not enough marshals to do the job, tenants often remain in apartments for six months or longer. Today some advocates for the homeless and many small landlords are pushing for an aggressive technical and financial program, funded by the District, to help such owners maintain rental units. They particularly favor incentives for owners who house low-income people.

In 1978 citizen pressure resulted in the nation's first tax on real estate speculation, a levy on profits of the sale of residential property that is held less than three years and does not comply with the housing code. If the residence is owner-occupied and if the owner provides a two-year warranty for repairs, the property is exempt from the tax. In practice, owners falling outside the generous exemptions have ignored the law. There are many loopholes, and city officials complain about the nightmare of enforcing it.

Recent progress includes a law stipulating that evictions shall not take place when the temperature falls below 32°F. Moreover, Rental Housing Acts substantiate the principle that if the tenant has been paying rent the landlord is no longer able to evict the person for no reason at all; the conditions under which he can do so are defined. Unfortunately, most poor tenants do not know their rights. The D.C. Law Students in Court Program has observed that in the 1980s the number of contested cases has been falling; more tenants seem to be simply giving up, signing consent judgments to pay back rent, or moving without a fight. The biggest problem, according to the program's executive director, Rick Carter, is the growing scarcity of assistance from advocates such as housing counselors, lawyers, and law students; rights on paper are meaningless without the ability to exercise them.[11]

Since 1981 District of Columbia law has provided that no rental property can be converted to a cooperative or condominium unless, in a special election, at least 51 percent of the tenants qualified to vote opt for conversion. Those aged sixty-two and over with annual household incomes under $40,000 are entitled to remain as renters in the converted property. Tenants are granted the first right to purchase their unit or a co-op share; those who do not wish to purchase must be given at least 120 days written notice to move. The city government also stipulates relocation benefits: the owner must make a payment of $100 to $150 per room for moving expenses for any relocating tenant household as well as a lump-sum payment equaling the difference between the rent in the old housing and that in any comparable housing to which the renter is moving. In addition, the city government must provide housing assistance payments for three years to low-income tenants who do not purchase. The amount of assistance varies with family income and monthly housing expense.

Although these protections represent notable progress, most of them do not address the heart of the problem. The right to first purchase, for example, is meaningless to a family that cannot afford to buy a converted unit. Assistance with moving expenses and a lump-sum payment cannot compensate for the higher rent that most people pay. Nor do these protections create more housing.

As in the rest of the United States, a more fundamental cause for the housing crisis in the District of Columbia is the general indifference of the federal government to the housing needs of low-income Americans.

Despite the discouraging situation, several organizations are continuing to fight for decent affordable housing. MWPHA, for example, provides tenant support and assistance, offers policy analysis and direct planning assistance for community development, monitors fair housing and metropolitan issues, and testifies on local legislation.

One form of tenant assistance is support of efforts to increase the housing supply. MWPHA has developed a program that encourages the development of accessory apartments—small living units such as granny flats and quarters shared by low-income singles—within single family houses. It promotes policies to lower the construction costs of new housing, for example, by reducing zoning restrictions to permit prefabricated and mobile homes. It also promotes construction of housing on small vacant lots, especially those owned by the city.

To accomplish its goal of geographic, economic, and racial diversity, the MWPHA advocates a program to assure equitable distribution of housing for low- and moderate-income families in all eight wards of the city, a requirement that at least 15 percent of newly constructed housing units be affordable for low- and moderate-income persons, and the creation of a community development corporation to undertake housing rehabilitation, acquire real estate for the benefit of the community, and provide technical assistance.

In recent years MWPHA has fostered home ownership opportunities through housing counseling and a program to support tenant purchases and conversion of multifamily units to home ownership. It also has established a homesteading program and a funding pool for rehabilitation of tenant-purchase multifamily housing.

Perhaps its greatest success, however, lies in its efforts to get landlords and tenants together. As Bob Simon of MWPHA put it, "Today we have to recognize that *both* groups have problems. We try to get tenants to work things out with landlords, rather than rely on battles and rent strikes—except as a last resort. Because tenants are staying longer, with little prospect of moving elsewhere, they're locked into a relationship with the landlord. So they're more willing to put in their own time doing things like sweeping the halls and making minor repairs."

Some of the tenant associations formed under MWPHA's guidance acquire tenant control: they manage the building without buying it. It is they who make major decisions as to where the money is going. Energy conservation workshops run by MWPHA teach landlords and tenants how to caulk, use water properly, control thermostats, and the like. Thus landlords save on utility bills and management. The association also works with tenant groups in negotiating voluntary rental increases, that is, tenants agree to pay rent above the standard increase in return for certain improvements such as more security, maintenance, or appliances.

MWPHA, a small organization, forms eight to ten groups each year. This is a very modest step forward, considering the vast need. Yet such efforts do represent a trend in the movement among low- and moderate-income people to gain some control over their housing and their communities.

The Struggle to House the Homeless

Washington can boast more services for undomiciled people than most other cities in the nation. It was not always that way. Before 1975 the city took no responsibility for single homeless people. It did operate two small apartment buildings as family shelters, but each could accommodate only twenty families at a time when some 10,000 were being evicted annually. The Central Union Mission had fifty beds for men (offering four free nights a month) and twelve beds for women. The Gospel Mission took in 150 men with one free night each month. In addition, the Salvation Army had space for ten women. There was a total of twenty-two beds for women and 200 for men. No shelter worker could recall a time when all women's beds were not in use.[12]

Today there are some thirty shelters; the number varies from year to year, even month to month. Over two-thirds of the bed space is allocated to men; about 15 percent goes to women, and 12 to 15 percent to families. Missions or church-affiliated groups run most of the men's facilities, but two are sponsored by the city, which contracts with the D.C. Council of Churches to do the actual administration. Of the women's shelters, only one is funded by the city. The battered-spouse shelters are run by independent groups. One of the family shelters is sponsored by the city, the others by churches.

Although the number of refuges sounds impressive, only about half of the men's and women's shelters take in more than twenty-five persons. According to C.H. Johnson, director of the Anacostia Men's Life Center (a project of the D.C. Coalition for the Homeless), the number of people actually housed on a typical night in early 1986 averaged less than 3,000, including families (of a population ranging from 7,000 to 18,000). Moreover, most of the shelters (except those for families) are open only from six or seven at night until early morning. During the day the homeless must walk the streets or find food and warmth at a soup kitchen or drop-in center. Most of the drop-in centers and day programs offer food, clothing, asylum from the elements, and sometimes laundry service, showers, medical assistance, and counseling. In addition, a dozen small legal service groups provide counseling and some limited advocacy to poor people entangled in housing problems. Since these organizations are staffed by volunteers—lawyers, law students, and other counselors—services always fall short of demand.

Volunteers, most of them from church organizations, also staff the soup kitchens and the storefront community centers that provide packaged food and used clothing to the homeless.

Over the years many volunteers have been sent out by the Coalition for the Homeless. It has also been active in analyzing local issues such as rent controls and rent subsidies, and in publishing action alerts designed to influence legislation affecting the homeless. Today the coalition's chief function is running one center for homeless men and two for women.

These services are far from sufficient. The greatest unmet need is for more family shelters; when they are not available, families split up. Moreover, most services for the homeless are concentrated in the downtown area—in fact, the majority are in one quadrant, Northwest. The suburbs of Washington refer outcasts roaming the streets to this so-called Homeless Belt. Shelter providers feel strongly that other neighborhoods should be taking more responsibility for the unfortunate in their midst.

Nevertheless, the existing framework marks a tremendous step forward. Its success is due to a sensitized core of citizens who have created a network of private services and have prodded a reluctant government to open public shelters. Many groups have been responsible for this progress. One of the most active—and certainly the best known—is the Community for Creative Non-Violence (CCNV).

One Group's Approach: Nonviolent Confrontation

In contrast to the quiet, task-centered approach taken by the church groups, CCNV tends to use confrontational tactics and to focus on changing public policy. It has become a gadfly, irritating the powers that be, goading them into action.

CCNV has made headlines around the nation for dramatic and imaginative actions that include erecting a tent city dubbed Reaganville across the street from the White House, occupying the Capitol Rotunda to demand that federal buildings be made available as shelters during the winter, engaging in a successful series of protests over the sacrilege of naming a U.S. submarine *Corpus Christi*, organizing demonstrations against the widespread waste of food, and fasting to dramatize the plight of the homeless. CCNV members Mitch Snyder and Mary Ellen Hombs wrote *Homelessness in America*, one of the first books to document the scope and complexity of the problem. In 1983 CCNV helped to organize the first congressional hearings on homelessness in fifty years. Members worked closely with congressional leadership in shaping the emergency food and shelter assistance component of the 1983 Jobs Bill. Over the years, CCNV also has continued the less dramatic task of opening and staffing emergency shelters, drop-in centers, and an infirmary for homeless persons recuperating from injury or illness.

The history of CCNV reflects the history of the struggle to establish services for D.C.'s homeless. Hombs, who has been with the community longer than any other member, traces its origins back to late 1970, when Ed Guinan, a chaplain at George Washington University Catholic Center, was granted permission to found a community. Mary Ellen was pursuing a bachelor's degree at the university, and by 1971 found herself increasingly attracted to joining the group, which focused on the Vietnam War and larger questions of war and peace, violence and nonviolence. An Episcopalian, she could find no answer in "coffee house" religion. "But going into community where people were permanently committed—I liked that," she says.

Mary Ellen does not fit the stereotype of a radical living in a hippie commune. Tall and slender, with rosy cheeks, long dark hair, a clear complexion, and large blue eyes, she speaks slowly and gently. "While we continued to talk of peace and justice, we also prepared to make peace and justice with our immediate neighbors," Mary Ellen recalls. "So in 1972 we opened Zaccheus Community Kitchen, and in no time at all we were feeding four hundred people a day, seven days a week. The kitchen is still going on.

"While living here at the community I got an M.A. in urban planning. But what can you do with that? Real estate or government work. I wanted neither. And after our involvement with the soup kitchen, I began to do my own analysis of what should be done."

By spring 1973, Mitch Snyder, a huskily built young man who had learned about nonviolent resistance and community organizing from conscientious objectors of the War Resisters League while he was incarcerated at Danbury Federal Prison, arrived to open a CCNV pre-trial house for homeless persons who would otherwise stay in jail while awaiting trial because they had no verifiable address.

Meanwhile CCNV expanded rapidly, launched a free medical clinic, and began hospitality work in three houses on N Street belonging to Luther Place Memorial Church. After a dispute with the church, CCNV moved to a house on Euclid Street.

On a raw Christmas Eve in 1976, CCNV members kept the soup kitchen open through the night to offer warmth and shelter to those on the street. As CCNV members watched their guests settle down on the makeshift mats, and as they talked with each other, a simple realization emerged: everyone has the right, on any night of the year, to get inside. On Christmas morning, as those who had passed the night at the kitchen began drifting out, CCNV members wondered where these people would spend the next night, and the next.[13]

Reluctantly, but with a sense of inevitability, they decided to open the living room of their home on Euclid Street to the destitute. And they began driving through the streets looking for men and women huddled around open fires, lying in gutters, or stretched over heat grates. Baked potatoes and hot tea were offered to those who preferred to stay behind.[14]

CCNV, Luther Place Memorial Church, and Sojourners, a group of activist evangelicals, launched a joint appeal to all 1,100 churches, synagogues, and mosques in the area, asking that they too make sleeping space available. A few responded with money and clothing, but only Luther Place offered to shelter the homeless.

For the rest of the winter, 160 or more people were lodged at the church each night, in addition to the thirty-five to forty-five at the CCNV house and at Deborah's Place (a newly opened shelter for women). The action of Luther Place kindled a growing awareness that clergy and laypersons bore responsiblity for participating in this work.

Hence in 1977 a separate shelter for men opened at St. Stephen and the Incarnation Episcopal Church, and Luther Place took in women. Growing numbers of volunteers staffed the shelters and joined CCNV in making the rounds of the streets to offer warm food and an invitation to take refuge.

No real demands were made on city officials until the winter of 1977–78, when the freezing deaths of three men on the same night made newspaper headlines. D.C. Department of Human Resources Director Albert Russo attributed the three deaths to extreme temperatures, alcohol, and bad luck but not to a lack of shelter.[15]

Russo and CCNV members met and discussed the situation. Two days later, a vacant city-owned building on C Street became the District's newest asylum for the homeless. Within a short time more than seventy-five men were sleeping there every night.[16] Still, homeless people continue to die of exposure. CCNV gave the city a choice: either officials would provide additional space by February 8, or four members would move to the street in front of city hall and live there until a new shelter opened. Less than twenty-four hours before the activists were to move, the Department of Human Resources, reacting both to CCNV and the quieter efforts of a persevering Catholic priest, Father Eugene Brake, announced that it was replacing the shelter on C Street with a larger, 200-bed refuge at Blair School.

Thus from December 1976 to February 1978, the number of beds in the city rose from twenty-two to fifty-two for women and from two hundred to four hundred fifty for men. A very different kind of accommodation, the city-run shelter, was developing. Municipal funds were used to pay for utilities, building expenses, and salaries. Dinner was prepared by a government contractor, although a usable kitchen existed in the old school building.[17]

To Mitch and Mary Ellen, the biggest difference was in the atmosphere created by using city workers at C Street and Blair School. The workers seemed to communicate a feeling that the homeless were people not so much to be served as to be regulated. By using admission logs, filing incident reports, checking identification, rejecting those receiving benefit checks, storing possessions, serving each person just one portion of food, and keeping an armed uniformed guard at all times, the staff created barriers between themselves and their guests.[18]

In late 1978 Luther Place again opened its doors to women for the winter, but no other church offered space to the homeless.

In November 1978, CCNV occupied the National Visitor Center, and invited street people to sleep there. The episode drew considerable public attention, and resulted in a major breakthrough. The city succumbed to pressure by finally coming through on a promise. Previously it had agreed to use the vacant Pierce School as a backup shelter, but no homeless people had been able to use it because the doors remained locked. The city opened up the school, and also made rules easier for the clients. The school filled up quickly.

At the Pierce School CCNV used volunteers and guests in the place of paid staff. To Mary Ellen and Mitch it was clear that a difference in atmosphere was attracting more people. Guests served meals to each other and helped to maintain the building and staff the shelter. Control over their environment gave them some of the dignity and self-respect they had been denied.[19]

The city reneged on a promise to open a much-needed shelter in the northwest quadrant, and no additional buildings were opened after Pierce reached capacity. As a result, guests and staff decided to take over the Lenox School building themselves. It soon filled. Overcrowding was temporarily relieved by this move. Many problems remained. Still, CCNV members felt that they had made their point. Such facilities were vitally needed because men who had not seen shelter as available to them were now staying at these schools.[20]

In the following years CCNV turned to other actions to focus attention on homelessness and force a response from both the religious community and local government. For example:

Community members and advocates from other cities planted more than five hundred crosses, each bearing the name or date of death of a homeless person. After remaining there all winter, each cross was delivered to a member of Congress.

Public funeral services have been conducted for people who died from exposure. In January 1980, for instance, a cortege led by a horse-drawn carriage carrying the body of "John Doe" marched through downtown Washington to city hall.

Community members poured blood on the altar of St. Matthew's Cathedral after cathedral officials refused to keep the building open during a snowstorm and two people died of exposure within the next three days. The group also confronted Holy Trinity Catholic Church over its plan to spend $400,000 on renovation rather than to help the poor. Five CCNV members fasted forty-two days, but the church refused to alter its position. Then Mitch Snyder fasted alone for eleven days. According to Mary Ellen, the church leadership said he could die, but it would not change.

CCNV has also remained committed to the nitty-gritty work of caring for the homeless. For several years it operated two adjoining drop-in centers (one for younger people, the other for older men and women, who often feared the young ones). The community turned over some of the management to the people it served. "That's a slow agonizing process, full of pitfalls and false expectations," admits Carol Fennelly, a member since 1975. "But it's as important as anything we've ever tried to do." It has also opened a seventeen-bed infirmary for homeless persons recovering from severe illnesses such as leg and foot ulcers, pneumonia, severe hypothermia, malnutrition, and injuries resulting from beatings and rape.

Serving food at drop-in centers made CCNV members increasingly aware of the enormous amount of waste in this country. "Every year approximately 20 percent of the nation's total food production is thrown away—enough to feed almost 50 million Americans," says Mary Ellen. "To dramatize waste, we approached the Giant Food supermarket chain and asked it to make available the food discarded in dumpsters. Giant officials flatly refused. So we mounted a demonstration. Twenty-eight CCNV people and other supporters were arrested, and the story made headlines: Giant locks up trash bins to keep hungry out. Just one week later, Giant did a complete turn around! It agreed to give the Capital Area Food Bank unsold food headed for trash. Then we decided to discuss this waste situation with members of Congress. Out of that came a bipartisan House resolution urging government agencies and other organizations to make available to the needy food that otherwise would be wasted. To prove to Congress that much of the food is still good and is pulled from market shelves only because cans are dented, sale expiration dates are reached, or fruits and vegetables are blemished, we asked Representatives Tony Hall and Pete Stark, who were key sponsors of the resolution, to join us in what some people called a scavenging trip of supermarkets."

The community invited thirty members of Congress to the Rayburn Building's Gold Room for a luncheon of crudites with dip, cold cuts, crab quiche, fresh green beans with mushrooms and bacon, potatoes au gratin, salads of crunchy raw vegetables and fresh fruits with pink yogurt dressing, and a shortcake made with large sweet boysenberries. The meal, pronounced very good by the guests, seemed to help pass the resolution.

CCNV's long struggle with the National Park Service over the right to sleep in tents in Lafayette Park marks another point in the community's involvement with politics at the federal level. On Thanksgiving Day 1981, it served its traditional turkey dinner to seven hundred hungry people in the park. Then members erected a tent community, naming it Reaganville in honor of the President whose home stood opposite the park. The tents lasted only one night: at daybreak six protesters were arrested by park police. After prolonged wrangling and two court appearances, the group was granted the right to keep the tents up provided no one slept in them. CCNV members planted forty-one crosses in front of the tents to memorialize victims of previous winters and continued to press the case. On 22 December 1981, federal judge Charles Richey reversed his earlier decision. Enlightened by two hearings and the testimony of Mitch Snyder, who talked of his experience living on the streets, Richey ruled that the homeless had been discriminated against and could sleep in the tents since in the past others—farmers, veterans, and blacks—had been allowed to do so.

In June 1982, the Interior Department officially changed its regulations, and banned sleeping in the parks in order to prohibit any repetition of Reaganville. Hence in December 1982 a U.S. District Court judge ruled that CCNV might erect tents, but the homeless had no constitutional right to sleep in them. CCNV brought the case back to the U.S. Circuit Court of Appeals, arguing that by sleeping in the sixty tents street people would give symbolic expression, protected by the constitutional guarantee of free speech, to their poverty and homelessness. Again CCNV won a victory: in March 1983 the appeals court ruled that sleeping is part of a political message and is protected by the First Amendment. But again the victory was shortlived, for after Secretary of the Interior James Watt declared that he would join the U.S. Attorney's office in an emergency appeal to the Supreme Court, Chief Justice Warren Burger blocked the circuit court's order. Eventually the Supreme Court rejected CCNV's appeal, and threw out the case as frivolous.

Over the years the CCNV has sharpened its confrontations with the U.S. government. In December 1982 Mitch and Mary Ellen testified at the House hearings on Homelessness in America. The hearings resulted in an appropriation of $100 million to FEMA for the alleviation of hunger and homelessness. Mitch also testified at the 1983 Senate hearings on Street People, and at the January 1984 House hearings on Homelessness.

During the winter of 1982–83, it proclaimed a "People's State of the Union" message by gathering a group of unemployed persons and elderly poor, together with their supporters, to occupy the Capitol Rotunda. There they demanded that the government provide food, shelter, and jobs, and that federal buildings be made available for use as shelters throughout the winter. Secretary of Defense Weinberger responded by issuing an order to make military buildings available. However, they were often unusable, located in virtually inaccessible places.

Continuing to dramatize the hunger issue, in the summer of 1983 over thirty-five CCNV members and supporters set up an open-ended fast in Kansas City, near the limestone caves housing some of the 727 million pounds of dairy products stored by the U.S. Department of Agriculture. Mitch posed the question for the group: Why store billions of dollars of food at a cost (if grain storage is included) of more than $1 million a day, when record numbers of Americans were going hungry? There was so much food that increasing quantities were rotting or being sold as animal food or discarded. Carol Fennelly voiced CCNV's answer: "When the Administration is singing 'Happy Days are Here Again,' it doesn't want pictures of long distribution lines." After thirty days of fasting, during which several of the fasters who were taking only water nearly collapsed in the July heat, the federal government agreed to release more food.

When an order was issued to make federal buildings available as shelters, CCNV decided to focus its efforts on securing a clearly accessible federally owned building located in D.C. that had been used as a community college. The campaign could demonstrate that the federal government has vast resources to deal with the problem.

After long months of hard work CCNV triumphed. On 15 January 1984 the building opened as the 1,000-bed "Second Street shelter," the largest in the country. The festive inauguration, attended by Health and Human Services Secretary Margaret Heckler and many high-ranking officials, marked a breakthrough in federal resistance to admitting responsibility for the homeless.

In the fall of 1984 CCNV made national headlines for two actions. In order to persuade President Reagan to bring the dilapidated Second Street shelter up to habitable condition and to make it a model facility, Mitch undertook a widely publicized fast. (CCNV had already raised $50,000 for the minimum repairs necessary to open the shelter.) On the fifty-first day—just two days before the election and a few hours before Mitch was to appear on television—President Reagan yielded to both demands.

During the same months CCNV engaged in a vigorous campaign to get a right-to-shelter initiative on the D.C. ballot and then to convince voters to support it. After the Board of Elections approved placing the initiative on the ballot, the District government went to court to challenge the Board. The lower court ruled that the ballot should stand, and Initiative 17 was supported by an overwhelming 72 percent of the electorate. In October 1985 the D.C. government took the issue to the Court of Appeals. In April 1986 a decision was still pending. The city, then, was continuing to fight the initiative—but at the same time it admitted that it had underestimated the number of homeless in D.C. (It raised its count from 5,000 to 7,000; CCNV sees the number as between 15,000 and 18,000.)

Community Members at Home

A visit to the CCNV house on Euclid Street offers insight into the structure of a community that has proved remarkably cohesive and durable over the years. Unlike many other intentional communities that emerged during the Vietnam War, it has not only survived, but has continued to practice nonviolent action. Although CCNV sees its role as a prophetic one, its approach is essentially secular: its emphasis is on work in this world.

Today the community is a group of some fifty activists—adults and children, whites and blacks—many of whom live (together with a dozen homeless cats) in a nine-room rambling house in a racially mixed low-income area of D.C. The house on Euclid Street is furnished with donations of battered tables, paint-worn chairs, and sagging sofas. Yet flowering plants fill the bay windows, colorful cushions brighten the sofas, and the presence of an upright piano suggests that on many evenings community members come together to sing.

A meeting on lobbying Congress may take place in the living room while orientation of new volunteers goes on in the dining room, a third group congregates in the kitchen to make soup for the Drop-In Center, a fourth group meets upstairs to plan a new storefront clinic, and neighborhood children wander in searching for their friends. Visitors are likely to feel that the place is a three-ring circus. Yet everyone seems to know where he or she is going. Laughter and cheerful comaraderie pervade the house.

CCNV's work is sustained by small donations and some large gifts. It does not accept contributions that are encumbered in ways that could impair its ability to respond to the dictates of conscience.

In a reversal of the stereotype that it is America's manifest destiny to minister to the less fortunate peoples of the earth, CCNV has even attracted foreign volunteers, particularly Indians, Japanese, and Germans. Bernie Neidlein, a young German sent by the Church of the Brethren Volunteer Service to various practice projects in Washington, found that when he came to CCNV, he automatically wanted to stay. "This was something I'd always been looking for, living in community. I like the simple life style. You can really devote your whole life to something meaningful. In Germany, too, we withdraw from each other. We become involved in material things, our own family, our house. It's very dangerous. But the way CCNV people try to live here can be an example for other people. It could change the whole society."

Bernie also enjoyed the variety in his day. On a typical morning he might unload donations of food from farmers, then work at the Calvary United Methodist church free food store. A typical afternoon might include sorting discarded food in CCNV's basement, cooking the vegetables and meat into a hearty soup, sweeping floors, then carrying the soup, bread, and fruit salad dessert to the Drop-In Center, where the homeless queued up for supper every evening at five-thirty. Evenings were filled with "good talk, good fun, and planning more actions."

Taking to the Streets

Although there are committed groups all over the country working with the homeless, only a few individuals have taken the ultimate step of voluntarily going to the street to share the lives of urban exiles. CCNV members Harold Moss and Mitch Snyder have done so. This is their story. Because we had more opportunity to talk with Harold and because, as a black man, he can identify with the blacks who make up the majority of Washington's homeless, we have focused on his experience. Having read about his life on the streets in *Homelessness in*

America, we asked him to recount it and also tell us about his earlier life and his feelings about himself.

Moss is a tall, slender man with a neat clipped beard and a quick smile. Despite his soft voice and easy friendliness, his restless eyes, lined forehead, and gesturing hands convey intensity.

"I was born in Memphis in 1941, and grew up with twelve brothers and sisters. I guess you'd say my family was middle class. My father worked for the post office, and my mother was an incredibly intelligent woman who was first in her class in French at a Chicago high school. She got me to college. We were raised Catholic. People like Saint Francis had a big influence on me.

"After getting a B.A. and M.A. at Howard University, I began to work as a chemist with the National Cancer Institute. I was making good money, I was married, I had a future. But I felt intensely lonely. I was having problems with my marriage, and other things were bothering me. I began to paint, nearly eight hours a day. But art and research both were isolating me from people. I didn't know it, but I needed community. The Vietnam War was bothering me, but I wasn't in the demonstrations. Then one day I heard on TV: 'If you're not part of the solution, you're part of the problem.' I knew I was out of touch with the world.

"I was working with white people who were extremely intelligent. But their lives were screwed up. They couldn't function as family men. Their kids were on drugs. They came to *me* for advice!

"I did talk with them, and I talked with their kids. But I began to wonder: how can I best use my male image and whatever sensitivity to others I've developed? Then I began to see people on the streets. Lonely—lost."

Harold heard about the Zaccheus Soup Kitchen from his priest, began volunteering there, and joined CCNV. "One night I was about to paint murals on the kitchen walls, when I heard a noise. I went out to locate it and discovered a man sleeping in a huge box. That got me. I became involved in trying to do something fundamental about housing. CCNV was planning a land trust. I became president of the group. We accomplished some good things. Eventually, though, we passed the land trust on to others because we were grappling with the problem of how to maximize our time. I began to concentrate more on nonviolent actions."

On 5 December 1980, Harold and Mitch finished their dinner at the community's Drop-In Center and walked off into the night. For the rest of the winter, till 21 March 1981, they lived on the streets, sleeping on heat grates, lining up for meals in a soupline, hiding from guards—struggling for sheer survival.

Two years before, Mitch and Ann Splaine, a crippled woman who helped found Hannah House shelter, had spent two weeks on the streets. Like Mitch, Harold had fasted and engaged in other actions. Once he had spent two days and nights on a grate with a sick black man who was refusing official offers of help. That experience lingered in his mind. "I began to have problems with living in when others were outside," he recalled. "I came to see going 'out' as a kind of pilgrimage. An effort to educate myself. And I always wanted to walk the streets as Christ walked the streets. I wanted to be a friend. Maybe offer a little advice, eventually. But first of all, listen. A lot of those people are lonely. What I've found is that *they* have given to me, too. They have nothing, so whatever they give is powerful."

When Harold and Mitch set off that December evening, it took them two hours to discover two small grates that were not already taken. The air coming out of them reeked of sewage; this seemed to be the reason they were still vacant. After a few hours of fitful tossing, they finally fell asleep in the blankets they carried in plastic bags.

Awaking at dawn, they made their way to the public bathroom in Lafayette Park, across the street from the White House. After waiting in line for over an hour for the bathroom to open, they relieved themselves. Then they went across the street to a church, where they found comfort in warmth and prayer.

"By the time the soup kitchen began serving breakfast at 9:30 A.M. nearly two hundred people stood in line," Harold recalled. "Many of the men who are turned out of the city shelters at six or seven every morning go straight to the kitchen because there's so little to do at that early hour. In some shelters the staff have been known to pour ammonia in the middle of the dormitory floor. The men are awakened by the fumes, gasp, and then rush out. All this, so the men won't take too long getting back on the streets.

"We soon found that the big question facing every homeless person is what to do with the day, which seems to stretch out infinitely before you. Mitch and I did carry a Bible and a couple of other books. Most street people, though, are too depressed to read. So what do they do? Pass the time between bowls of soup at nine in the morning and five in the evening, walking, sitting, *trying* to sleep.

"Libraries, churches, hospital emergency rooms, and bus and train stations, are places they go for. But sleeping in libraries is forbidden. To remain awake hour after hour when your body and mind are aching for rest—that is just torture.

"The churches? There are only a few that remain open; most are shut tight except in times of worship. Many keep their bathrooms locked to discourage their use by harmless men and women. Many street people are more willing to suffer abuse from bus station personnel than contempt from servants of God. *That* really hurts.

"Besides, there are no public bathrooms that stay open around the clock, except for the bus stations, and we were pretty far from them. Our activities became centered around bathrooms. We came to understand what happens to the dignity of street people when they have to defecate in an alley, like animals, or behind a bush, while praying not to be seen.

"Where else did we spend time? In hospital emergency rooms sometimes. Usually the personnel are sympathetic, though if too many people begin to gather, they'll be asked to leave. We went to bus stations, too. But station guards are always looking for vagrants, and they insist pretty vigorously that you get out if you don't have a ticket. Museums? Security guards can evict you pretty fast there, too. And there's no real place to sit and rest.

"After the morning meal we generally spent a couple of hours at either a church or the public library. Usually our day ended up where it began, in Lafayette Park, visiting people who live there.

"I'll never forget them. Women like Jean, who spent her days on street corners yelling at passersby, and her nights curled up on the White House sidewalk. And Mary, who slept sitting up beside the guard tower at the White House. And Ross, who slept on a heat grate and woke up one night with a strange wailing, full of pain and grief and anger with a world that allowed him to live this way. These were people trembling in the cold—surrounded by heated, lighted, guarded, and empty government buildings! This is the world we live in.

"We wanted to be accessible to people sleeping raw. Actually, it wasn't easy to reach them. I never drank before, but pretty soon I saw I'd better have a bottle of cheap wine as introduction to other guys—something we could share. The funny thing is that after a month, I looked forward to drinking. When there's no food in your stomach, that's when you need it. You begin to drink early in the morning and get really bombed out. You drink to get rid of anxiety. It smooths out the rough edges. And when it's cold and they offer you a drink—you just can't sit outside in the cold unless you're half drunk.

"The trouble is, alcohol can make your temperature drop to a dangerous level. You can get pneumonia, hypothermia, gangrene. I've seen the bodies of men who have frozen to death.

"I'd tell the guys that. But they knew it already. They still drink because a stiff drink makes it possible to take a little more cold and harassment.

"You can't get a job. Even if they're available, you have to look decent for an interview. But you can't get a shower or a change of clothes. So what's the use?

"Passersby harass you. Mitch was nearly killed when some young guys threw beer bottles at us on a grate—one smashed into fragments just inches from his face. The police harass you. You can't be seen too often in one place. If something happens in the area, you're seen as a prime suspect. If *you* are robbed on the streets, the police won't deal with you. And if you *want* to get into jail, to get out of the cold? You have to break a law. Throw a rock, but make sure the police see you.

"So what happens is, you try to stay invisible. You get paranoid. And you become a weird category.

"People know you're a street person, a 'bum.' I remember people driving by, looking through or beyond us when we caught them glancing in our direction. And the incredible thing that happened was that our *own* sense of our worth dribbled away. We kept regular contact with members of our community. But in less than one week on the streets, we couldn't make or maintain eye contact, even with them.

"Street people come to see themselves as bums. It terrifies the young ones to see the old ones—to feel that they're just one step away. Maybe that's one reason some of the young guys beat up the old guys when they get their SSI checks.

"You're surprised at what violence you're capable of. You've got to act macho to keep people from abusing you. You turn your anger against those who are vulnerable. You're too frightened to take it out on the middle-class person, so you take it out on the powerless. And you become racist as a defensive tactic.

"Still, most street people aren't outwardly violent. They turn their violence against themselves and become passive. At some point it's become clear that they can't do very much.

"No wonder that most of them are emotionally and mentally incapable of dealing with life., That comes not just from the fact that maybe 60 percent are mentally ill. It's also because—as we found—a few weeks or months of rejection and homelessness can make you 'crazy' even if you weren't before."

Yet Harold has retained a certain optimism. "I've seen incredible things happen. Demonstrations do confront consciences. Like the action to retrieve wasted food. You try to find one person in Congress with a heart, someone who'll go out to the dumpsters. We found him: Representative Pete Stark. Then you plan the dinner, and other members of Congress come. Pretty soon this whole thing begins to explode. When Giant changed its policy on food dumping, other stores began to do the same. We got three hundred pounds of turkey in three weeks! Some farmers contributed food. People donated old cars for transport. It's beautiful. You've got to have faith that if you're doing something right, others will begin to see it that way, too.

"For me personally, the answer has been to belong to community. As an individual you can't do much. CCNV's success comes from working and *being* together. It's devastating to be alone. But here, my talents have been maximized by being in community."

CCNV is not a perfect fellowship. As in most communities, there have been internal divisions, resulting in the departure of some individuals and in the formation of new groups.

On the outside, critics have charged the community with creating a "cult syndrome," using "ego-serving" tactics, and pursuing "an exotic life style." Others have blamed the group for its "lack of accountability," its "disdain for record-keeping." The most frequent criticism concerns the confrontational style of some CCNV members, notably Mitch Synder. "To fast unto death before Holy Trinity Church because the congregation is spending money for renovations instead of the homeless is not nonviolent, but coercive," says one church minister. "Renovations, however expensive, may be necessary to preserve a roof. Actually, Holy Trinity has done a great deal for the poor and is forever expanding its ways to help them."

Basic to the criticism are fundamental differences in outlook. What CCNV perceives as a restrictive atmosphere in some shelters, especially public ones, seems quite necessary to some shelter providers. "You have to have some rules in order to keep order, to prevent violence," says one minister. "In some shelters a police officer may be necessary. The public shelters in the schools do have regimentation. The men have to give up their things and be quiet at night. There was so much confusion in the Pierce School when CCNV ran it that the city canceled its agreement and eventually handed the shelter's administration over to the Council of Churches."

According to another observer, "CCNV does have a point. Some chronic street people are so afraid of rules that they won't come into most shelters. CCNV would let them keep their weapons and liquor, or sleep in the halls—in other words, do their own thing. That is fine for some people. But it's a mistake to extend that philosophy to everyone. And I'm afraid the group has a reputation for tolerating chaotic, unsanitary conditions.

"Because it's committed to confrontation, CCNV doesn't work well in coalition," he adds. "What's irritating is that what they do—like Mitch sleeping in a cardboard box before the mayor's office—are things that the media eat up. There are quieter groups doing a fine job, and they need publicity, too."

CCNV's penchant for publicity is epitomized in Mitch Snyder's successful fast to pressure President Reagan to fund the Second Street shelter and the subsequent year-long fight to get him to live up to his promise to make it a model physical shelter. (In 1986 a film inspired by these events was being made of Mitch's struggle for the homeless.)

After the election, architect Conrad Levenson developed plans to create five shelter areas, one for women and four for men, all accessible to handicapped people. The plans also included a laundry room, infirmary, legal clinic, social services, and separate drop-in centers for men and women. HHS declared that the renovation would cost $10 million—$10,000 per bed—a figure that was cited at the last moment and never documented. CCNV, on the other hand, presented a contractor's bid for just under $6 million, which included insurance guaranteeing the price of the bid. HHS, however, declared it would close the shelter rather than do the renovation envisioned by the Levenson plans.

When CCNV took the issue to court, a Federal District judge ruled that the shelter could be closed only after the federal government had made alternative arrangements. HHS finally accepted a proposal from the D.C. Coalition for the Homeless to create three shelters, two small ones for women and a 500-bed facility for men in an old Navy building to be renovated. For this the coalition received $3.7 million in federal funds.

The action infuriated many residents of Anacostia, the neighborhood where the renovated shelter for men was to be situated, as well as local activists, CCNV, Mayor Barry (who insisted that Reagan had made a "social contract") and many residents of the Second Street shelter, who protested that they were frightened by the prospect of being uprooted from the place that had been their home for months. Just as Federal Protection agents were about to assault the shelter and forcibly eject the residents, President Reagan intervened; the shelter was allowed to remain open, at least until spring. The D.C. government offered CCNV $250,000 for repairs.

The long dispute left some unresolved issues. Will the facilities run by the coalition satisfy the growing need? C.H. Johnson, director of the new Anacostia shelter, admits that they cannot. Indeed, by March 1986 that facility was harboring over 500 men a night. In the three months since it was supposed to close, CCNV's Second Street shelter was taking in more people than ever before; the nightly count often ran above capacity, to 1,050.

What is a "just price" for a shelter? CCNV and Levenson have pointed out that the guaranteed estimate of less than $6 million (about $6,000 per bed) covered the cost of constructing service facilities as well as semiprivate sleeping cubicles. They add that even the undocumented estimate of $10 million cited by HHS would be low by national standards; across the country construction costs for shelters average between $15,000 and $25,000 per bed. (It is worth noting that the federal government spends an average of $34,480 per bed in prisons; state prisons average $49,851 per bed.)[21]

Is it important that the government keep its word?

Who won? If existing facilities still cannot offer enough beds to the growing numbers of homeless people, then the argument behind CCNV's Initiative 17—the proposition that the city has the responsibility to provide shelter to all who need it—still holds. Moreover, despite President Reagan's efforts to ignore the homeless issue and even deny funds to Congress-approved programs, he did back down twice—first in response to Snyder's fast and then when the imminent closing of the Second Street shelter threatened him with a poor public image. Hence the federal government today finds itself "in the shelter business." Ironically, although CCNV lost the skirmish over remodeling the Second Street shelter, it was victorious in the bigger battle. It has succeeded in pressuring the Reagan administration to acknowledge—and assume—responsibility for the homeless.

Even critics admire CCNV members for their dedication and their willingness to share the lives of the people they serve. (One Second Street shelter resident declared that CCNV staff treated her like "visiting royalty.") Many critics also praise the group for its sensitivity to the political roots of the problem, its willingness to go out on a limb, and its talent for finding dramatic ways of exposing the situation to the public. "CCNV is necessary to the movement," they say. "It has national impact. If it didn't exist, it would have to be invented."

Another Approach: Down in the Trenches

Equally necessary to the movement are those quieter groups that, in the words of one observer, "are staffed by tough, persistent, overworked, underpaid people whom you seldom hear about because they don't seek publicity. But they *get things done!*"

Contributions of the Catholics

The Catholics have done outstanding work with Washington's homeless. Mt. Carmel House for Women was set up under the auspices of Archbishop James Hickey. A clean, well-run, brightly decorated place, it is staffed by four nuns and a lay social worker paid by the archdiocese. The archidocese was also responsible for establishing the Calvert Emergency Shelter for men; it is now run by the Capuchin Friars and Associated Catholic Charities. In a major pioneering move, the archdiocese renovated a three-story apartment house for use as a transitional shelter. Named McKenna House after a Jesuit priest who beame particularly concerned about the homeless, it provides a warm environment to twenty-five men while intense efforts are made to find them employment and a permanent home. Another shelter, housed in St. Aloysius Church, demonstrates what a parish can do at the grassroots level. The basement has become a small overnight refuge for seven elderly men, while another section of the basement has been turned into a daytime drop-in center for men seeking asylum from the elements. The St. Francis Catholic Worker House offers a cheering welcome and long-term shelter to four men and four women, while the Dorothy Day Catholic Worker Community provides temporary shelter on a twenty-four-hour basis to five or six families.

In the suburbs, where there are far fewer facilities for the homeless than in D.C., Catholic Charities operate five shelters. As individuals, too, Catholics have made important contributions to work with the homeless. Hannah House, an interfaith ministry to women, is staffed by a Sister of Mercy and a laywoman who left her religious order after forty years. As noted earlier, Father Eugene Brake's quiet, persistent dialogues with the city helped persuade city authorities to open Blair School as a shelter. Parishioners from Holy Trinity Church often volunteer at the Luther Place Memorial Church emergency shelter for women.

The Community of Hope

Each year the number of homeless families rises in both D.C., and the suburbs. The District sponsors one family shelter at the Pitts Motel, at an average cost of $70 per day per family.

"We decided there was a better way," says Tom Nees, minister of the Community of Hope mission church of the Nazarene. "Our program takes families from motels, families that have the ability to survive on their own, and lodges them here in this apartment building. In the same building we have a large room on the first floor that is used as a church on Sunday and as a place of refuge during the week. In the back, and on other floors, you'll see a community health clinic, a law office, a jobs program, and a program for children and youth—all offering services to help people through the crisis period."

What impresses visitors the most is that the apartment building in which the church, apartments, and services are housed was rehabilitated by the community members' own labor.

The clinic, which serves the neighborhood as well as homeless families, is small, simply furnished, and spotlessly clean; the ambience is so cheerful that the place hardly seems like a clinic. Bulletin boards announce a variety of activities in the neighborhood, and easy-to-read booklets lying on the tables explain better ways for clients to care for themselves and their families. At the desk, a receptionist chats with clients, and a young woman physician fondles a baby in her arms as she talks with the mother. The health service staff is committed to holism, and sees more than six thousand patients a year.

Rev. Nees, a lean, fortyish man with slightly graying hair and intense blue eyes framed by horn-rimmed glasses, is cordial yet low-keyed in manner. As he moves across the room to answer two phones that seem to be ringing continually, he emits tightly controlled nervous energy.

"We began our project in 1973 with another abandoned building, rehabbed it with unskilled volunteers, and in the process learned a lot of skills together. That first building is now a cooperative for low-income people. They run it alone and do a fine job. It's quiet, secure, clean. And the occupants are able to rent at one half the market value.

"Homeless families are of special concern to us. Crowding a family into one motel room is not only expensive but artificial. Even their meals are taken care of. This fosters dependency and isn't appropriate even for chronically homeless families, where parents haven't the inner *or* outer resources to provide for their children. What *can* be done for such families is hard to say.

"We choose families that have the potential to get it together in about ninety days. The city pays us for the apartment rent—about $300 a month, a far cry from the $2,000 it would pay monthly to voucher an average family into a motel. We hold that money in escrow, and give it to the family at the end of their stay here, to help meet the costs of moving and setting up an apartment."

Rev. Nees believes that unlike individual homelessness, family homelessness is rarely the result of addiction or psychological problems. "Rather, it's the result of the failure of our economic system to provide the opportunity for every family to have decent affordable housing," he says. "Families come here because they haven't met the rent, then have gone to relatives or friends, who eventually evict them."

In our conversations and in his testimony at Senate hearings on Street People, Rev. Nees emphasized that most families are dismembered before they reach a shelter. Children are separated from parents, then placed in foster care, or in the homes of relatives or neighbors. It may take years to reunite them. Many of the families at the community have been fairly independent until recent years. If they had the funds for rent, they could maintain a household. Nees believes that one micro solution is creating nonprofit corporations like the Community of Hope, which can enter the housing market and because of their tax-exempt status purchase apartment buildings at below-market value. On the macro level, says Nees, it is up to Congress to provide housing subsidies for the millions of Americans who need a home.

The Houses on N Street

An outstanding example of the work of the quiet groups is a complex of services known as N Street Village, a row of old buildings across the street from Luther Place Memorial Church. They belong to the church, which for years rented them out as a source of income. In the mid-seventies, as the situation of the homeless became more visible, the congregation decided to use them for ministry. Gradually other churches joined the effort. Today the village represents a highly successful interreligious endeavor serving the homeless and other poor persons.

First in the row is Bread for the City, a bustling storefront center providing free clothing, free food for home preparation, food stamp advocacy, nutrition classes, counseling on jobs and housing, referrals to social services, and an outreach program to home-bound citizens. Many of the staff belong to the Lutheran Volunteer Corps and live communally in Dietrich Bonhoeffer House on N Street. Volunteers from the Emmaus Churches and from the Jesuit Volunteer Corps have also helped staff the center. Elderly and disabled persons, as well as poor families with dependent children, are eligible for a two-day supply of rations, which come from the Capital Area Food Bank. Other items are purchased by Bread from local grocery salvage companies or are donated by local supermarkets or the Department of Agriculture.

The Zaccheus Clinic, which opened in 1974 under the aegis of CCNV but is now independent, focuses particularly on preventive measures such as screening for tuberculosis, diabetes, veneral disease, hypertension, and pregnancy—areas where the needs of the poor are least likely to be met. Physical examinations and follow-up care are also offered.

In 1983 Luther Place Memorial church opened the Raoul Wallenberg House as a temporary refuge for poor families undergoing crises such as eviction or unemployment. They are allowed to remain up to ninety days while getting their lives together.

The only church in Washington that has had an ongoing program of opening its own doors to the homeless, Luther Place continues to offer emergency overnight shelter to women. The arrangement is simple: mattresses are stacked against the wall of the chapel during the day; volunteers from various churches, colleges, or civic groups arrive before the shelter opens at eight in the evening; the women file in from the church steps (where many have been waiting for hours); and the volunteers help the women settle their belongings and set up their mattresses. After breakfast coffee and a roll, the women are back on the street.

Most of them wander across the steet to Bethany Women's Day Center, which offers warmth, lunch, sewing facilities, recreation, and counseling during the day. (Bethany was located in the basement of a church several blocks away until it was evicted by the church. Said its leader: "Why should we cast our pearls before swine?")

At the time of our visit the small rooms, sparsely furnished but clean, were crowded with clients. Most of the women huddled on the worn sofas and chairs sat wrapped in their own silence, barely communicating with each other but smiling blandly at visitors. "Perhaps 90 percent of the women who come here are mentally disabled," explained Erna Steinbruck, director of the center and wife of John Steinbruck, pastor at Luther Place Memorial Church. "Most of them were discharged from St. Elizabeths without adequate planning for after care. Before long they stop taking their medicines, begin to deteriorate, and end up in shelters—if they can get in."

Another haven on N Street is Deborah's Place, a transitional shelter for eight women, homeless or not, who have been traumatized by abuse, illness, or some setback but have the capacity to come back and cope. Women can stay up to four months and receive counseling as they search for housing and jobs.

Neighboring Sarah House is a transitional shelter for women whose mental health is much more fragile than that of women at Deborah's Place. Here fourteen women who would otherwise spend the night on the street can receive an evening meal, bed, and breakfast. It opens at 3:00 P.M. and closes at 9:30 A.M., when most of the clients go to Bethany Women's Center. Unlike emergency shelters, Sarah House goes beyond fulfilling the women's immediate physical needs. In the words of Elisabeth Huguenin, "Our goal is to move clients to independent living or a group home. Since over 75 percent suffer from severe emotional and mental health problems, we provide social and medical services, group counseling, and some individual counseling. Unfortunately, the small budget limits our ability to offer sufficient counseling. The aim is to help women accomplish the immediate and long-term goals they've worked out in their Individual Development Plans. To achieve group living, we require that the women assume specific household and personal responsibilities, including cleanliness, sobriety, chores, participation in counseling, and cooperation with staff in achieving their development plans. If they have not met their goals in three months but are progressing, they may stay on, up to six months in all."

Women must go outside the Village for another level of care, semi-independent living in a group home. Such facilities had been virtually nonexistent till recently, when Sarah House, together with Mt. Carmel House and other women's shelters, helped set up a group home known as Abbey Place House. The five residents pay $135 per month toward rent and utilities. A live-in house manager helps build an atmosphere of community and handles the daily routine of running the house. Now that Abbey Place has proved a sound model, Women's Shelter Providers (a coalition of seven facilities) is working to create several types of housing, including group homes for more stable women. "The facilities belonging to Women's Shelter Providers have become more effective each year, as we work more closely together," says Erna Steinbruck. "I've seen women move from being terribly chronically ill to managing on their own. We have to needle them often, keep them to their plans. We *are* patient, because we know they need supports all along. But the progress of some women—they're miracle stories."

In late 1983 the N Street Village produced a daughter shelter at St. Peter Evangelical Lutheran Church, in a middle-class section of the northeast quadrant. Rev. Steinbruck had asked St. Peter's Rev. John Ellison if he knew of any churches that could open a winter refuge for fifteen women to relieve crowding at the emergency shelter in Luther Place. Ellison brought the question to his parish council that night, and members immedjtely offered their own building.

Church or State?

In Washington, as elsewhere, government and churches continue to argue the question of primary responsibility for the homeless. The controversy reflects the larger ongoing debate sparked by the Reagan administration's attempts to solve social problems by asking the voluntary (private) organizations and individual volunteers to take more responsibility for the poor.

In the early 1970s the only religious groups sheltering D.C.'s homeless were two missions. In the mid-seventies, the appeal sent out by CCNV, Sojourners, and Luther Place touched off a slowly growing realization that the churches have great power. A few rose to the challenge.

Most shelter providers in Washington believe that the churches can do a better job than the city because they are less bureaucratic. "The church brings a compassionate, caring dimension that you don't see in the big city-run shelters," says Erna Steinbruck. "Here we treat them like brothers and sisters. And small budgets are stretched better."

As noted before, the "city-run" shelters in D.C. are actually administered by private groups in a contractual arrangement. The House of Ruth, a nonprofit facility for women, is administered by its own staff but funded by the city. The Council of Churches runs the men's shelters, which are lodged in two vacant schools.

In 1980, after the city granted permission to use the Pierce School as a shelter, it was run by CCNV, but the following year, because of CCNV's alleged mismanagement, the city took control. In 1982 it handed responsibility for administration of the facility over to the council.

It is an old building, dingy and battered on the outside, and dingy and decaying on the inside. The aging walls of the interior have turned gray, and the fluorescent lighting accents the harsh monotony of the scene. The place is fairly clean, and it is warm.

On the day we visited, the temperature was in the teens, and a raw wind blew through the streets. Although the shelter closed at 6:00 A.M. through most of the year, and at 7:00 A.M. during the winter months, because of the cold the men were allowed the special privilege of staying inside that day. We looked around, and did not see them.

A neatly dressed, polite employee showed us the dormitories. The beds were clean. He also showed us the offices on the first floor, where men could get counseling on whatever job or housing opportunities existed. Although the offices were closed because it was after four o'clock, we could see that they were clean and well ordered.

In his dark, unpretentious office, a courteous and poised young black man introduced himself as Michael Ferrell, executive director. He was not a member of the council but had been hired by the group presumably because of his degree in business administration and some experience with city agencies. He liked the contractual arrangement, he said, because it was more cost effective than if the city ran it directly. "You don't have to worry about union wages, cost-of-living increases, or incremental increases."

The staff came from diverse backgrounds, he explained. Most had a high school education. Eight or nine were former street people.

The official capacity of Pierce School was 150 per night, but it was their policy not to turn anyone away. The number of clients was increasing, for the upsurge in employment applied only to people with skills.

At last we were allowed to see the men permitted to stay in that day. They were all lodged in the basement. "We keep them there," explained our guide, "until we begin processing them in at seven."

As he opened the basement door, we saw that the men were all slumped against the streaked walls or sitting on the grimy floor. There were no chairs. The long basement hall was their only refuge; there were no rooms for reading, playing cards, watching TV, or gathering to talk. Very few men were talking. The hall seemed almost silent. The slouching figures in their scruffy clothes looked up at us, then dropped their eyes. They were, indeed, "processed" men.

We were led to a damp, smelly shower and toilet room, and then to the tiny dining room in the basement. Four long tables and benches served 150 to 250 men, who were expected to eat in rapid shifts. The huge vats of ravioli stood on a serving table without a burner. In two hours the food would be tepid. This was the only home of these men. Yet as we walked, like visiting inspectors, through their midst, there was no visible resentment in their eyes or their movements. They seemed to have lost their capacity to feel hurt pride.

All but one of the fifty-odd men we saw that afternoon were blacks. Shoved out of sight in that underground, they were the redundant human beings of our time.

Reflections

Affiliation with a church body is no magic formula for a humane approach to the homeless. Across the United States, some of the large shelters run by the Christian missions are comparable to the Pierce School.

When shelters are small, and when churches and parishioners take direct responsibility, the atmosphere is almost always one of warmth and caring. However, when citizens delegate responsibility to a city government, which in turn delegates it to a bureaucratic church body, which in turn delegates it to an administration mandated to be primarily concerned with order and cost effectiveness, then *caritas*—true human heartedness—is lost.

On the other hand, thus far religious and other voluntary groups have been able to offer beds to only a fraction of the homeless in Washington.

John Steinbruck openly criticizes both church and state. "There is a great need for established religion to be born again. I'm afraid that today it is in complicity with principalities and powers. One Protestant church spent $3 million for cosmetic changes and nothing for the homeless.

"Do the churches open their own doors? Rarely. It's easier to get into Fort Knox than into most churches. I say, the church should be a hospice, as it was in the past. To be hospitable means converting the *hostis* into a *hospes*, the enemy into a guest. Hospitality is not to change people but to offer them space where change can take place. Luther Place tries to be an oasis in our capital's asphalt desert.

"To welcome the stranger is to insure your own survival, as mandated to biblical Israel. The churches have the option of becoming Abrahamic tents to shelter the urban nomads of the city.

"Still, they can't do it alone. Government bears a tremendous responsibility to participate in funding shelters and to create a real safety net. The Reagan administration has reached a new zenith in cruelty to the less fortunate members of our society.

"But that mentality had been growing for years. It's the life-boat ethic. Urban blacks and other poor people can die, just be written off. So that we don't have to deal with the problem. We don't call the solution gas chambers, but what else is it?"

Pastor Steinbruck relishes the question of what he would do if he were President. "I'd pick *hospitality* as the theme. I'd make the country as hospitable an environment as possible. With all the passion our recent Presidents have expressed for weaponry, I'd seek to shelter the 'dense pack' of humanity on our streets.

"It's a measure of our civilization today that we throw these sick, vulnerable people onto the street. The men in power obviously have hate and contempt for the poor. They think that the poor are the embodiment of sloth, and think of themselves as the embodiment of frugality. Frugality—yet they spend billions on weapons of destruction. While our every appeal to the White House for left-over food from state banquets is ignored! The officials we've approached say, 'The idea is disgusting.'

"What would I do if I were President? I'd open Blair House, the President's guest house, to the homeless. Why not?

"I'd employ hundreds of thousands of workers to create housing for the poor. Not enough Americans realize that public programs like the Trident submarine actually employ *fewer* workers than do programs like public housing. The urban housing for the poor could be similar to what exists in military bases. It's effective, complete, decent, and economical.

"That would result in employment. It would be merciful, pragmatic, and just, and it would result in the redistribution of wealth.

"Funds? I'd take them from the military. Friends of mine, admirals and generals, tell me that we don't need all this weaponry. It only brings us closer to annihilation."

Photo by Bill Kashersky

Buddy Gray (*left*), octogenarian Joe Bean (*center*), and Kim Headen (*right*) of the Drop-Inn Center.

4
Down and Out in Cincinnati

One hundred years ago Cincinnati was a peaceful town, nestled on fertile hills rising from the Ohio River. Paddle boats plied the water route to the Mississippi, and vineyards climbed the slopes ringing the town. To the German immigrants who formed the major part of the population, this was the Rhineland of America.

Today Cincinnati, the Queen City, is a hustling metropolis of nearly 400,000 inhabitants. The vineyards are gone; skyscrapers and smog obscure the hills that once bore grapes for wine. Over-the-Rhine, a small neighborhood near the city's center, has almost no German residents; they have been replaced by blacks, Appalachians, and other low-income people. In the last decade it has become a battleground between developers and ambitious civic leaders intent on gentrifying the area and a coalition of groups determined to prevent displacement and homelessness. A central actor in this jousting is the Drop-Inn Center, till 1984 the city's only open shelter, which refuses to move from its prime location near elegant Music Hall. During the 1980s, it has been the driving force in increasingly successful efforts to secure services for the homeless, and to prevent displacement of low-income tenants.

Although Cincinnati, like Washington, is a border town, residents will tell you that the Queen City is "really a Southern city—more like Louisville or St. Louis than Cleveland or Columbus." They are referring to Greater Cincinnati, which includes the Kentucky towns of Covington and Newport, impoverished industrial communities that many middle-class Cincinnatians tend to forget.

The Queen City has a Southern cast in many respects. Its racial minorities are not well-integrated. Black families are concentrated in a few areas, and efforts by the Cincinnati Metropolitan Housing Authority to disperse housing opportunities into the suburbs and outlying neighborhoods have met with fierce opposition. For nine years the school system took a number of steps to avoid court-ordered busing. In the end it reached an out-of-court settlement that involves the magnet school concept and voluntary busing. Although Cincinnati prides itself on having been a crucial stop on the Underground Railroad, it was also the point where slave hunters captured slaves and brought them to the city magistrate to have them returned. Cincinnatians could hardly be described as hospitable to Southern migrants these days. In 1980, 16,577 out of 21,216 (78 percent) of the city's poverty households were black.[1] Although Cincinnati's blacks never rioted on the massive scale of Washington's blacks, block after block of the Queen City went up in flames during the 1960s, especially after Martin Luther King's assassination.

In Cincinnati, the electorate tends to be more conservative than political constituencies in other major Ohio cities. A bias against unions is also evident among many of the top entrepreneurs. There are only a few strong labor unions. The city is known as a family company town. Although no elites hold absolute sway, companies such as Cincinnati Milacron and Procter and Gamble (which are nonunion) have great power with the school board, zoning regulations, entree into the Commercial Club, and plans for the city's future. Indeed, in one section of the city, St. Bernard, Procter and Gamble has established a community unto itself. Since this is an enclave within the city limits, P&G can pay taxes to St. Bernard rather than Cincinnati. Tax rates are lower than for the city, hence the arrangement represents a tax shelter.

Middle- and upper-class Queen City residents seem to take special pride in being Cincinnatians. Although most live in the suburbs, they speak glowingly of the fine stores, chic restaurants, and sky-top cocktail lounges downtown, as well as the museums and concert halls that represent Cincinnati's long cultural traditions.

Fountain Square is the heart of downtown. In the summer, when secretaries, students, clerks, families, and unemployed workers gather round the fountains to munch sandwiches and listen to fledgling musicians strum guitars, the place looks like a people's square. It belongs, however, to the businessmen, who see Fountain Square as the center of new boutiques, restaurants, department stores, and hotel/ convention centers. Most of these entrepreneurs are members of the Cincinnati Business Committee, which has been described as a "top-heavy group of business powers," who "convene to advise on city schools, city government, and downtown development."[2]

Like many other Northern cities, during the 1970s Cincinnati experienced economic decline. From 1970 to 1980, the population dropped 14.6 percent to 387,467. At the same time, the county (Hamilton) lost over 50,000 people.[3] Cincinnati's business elite has been making dramatic efforts to make up for the decline. As some industries have left for the Sun Belt and the manufacturing base has diminished, the service sector has greatly expanded. In the Fountain Square area alone, between 1982 and 1984 a new convention center emerged, the Omni Netherland-Plaza Hotel was completely remodeled, the Westin and Hyatt-Regency hotels opened their doors, Saks-Fifth Avenue opened a Cincinnati branch, and several smaller enterprises acquired new facades. Between 1980 and 1984 office space doubled in the downtown area.

The visitor is struck by the number of parking lots in the downtown section and in nearby Over-the-Rhine. Once the site of family life and neighborhood commerce, these bulldozed areas have turned into fields of concrete, gravel, and tar. Although they seem to represent a waste of valuable space, any Cincinnatian will tell you that the lots are awaiting future development.

Revitalization has not reached a massive scale in Cincinnati. The process, however, is well underway. When "60 Minutes" ran a documentary on gentrification, it chose to focus on the Queen City, to the outrage of the city fathers and the local media.

The city's dreams extend far into the future. The business community and city officials have prepared a detailed blueprint of the metropolis for the coming decades. The real estate in Over-the-Rhine plays an essential part in the plan. Poor residents who are homeless, or perched on the brink of homelessness, do not.

No one knows the number of homeless in Cincinnati, for no one has ever attempted to count them. Until recently, most Cincinnatians, like citizens of many other middle-sized cities, seemed only peripherally aware that in their own metropolitan community such people exist. Rarely are they seen lying on heating grates or curled up in doorways in downtown business areas; the police are quick to shuffle them elsewhere.

Yet almost everyone who works with the homeless estimates the number in the thousands. The Greater Cincinnati Coalition for the Homeless believes that the annual count exceeds ten thousand. Although they appear less numerous here than in many other cities, as soon as a new shelter is opened, it fills up quickly.

Most of the homeless are invisible people. True, they are more visible in Over-the-Rhine than elsewhere because most of the shelters and other sources of help are clustered in that area. (As a result, Over-the-Rhine has a reputation for being a dangerous section.) Some of these urban exiles can be seen lying on benches in Over-the-Rhine's Washington Park until 10:00 P.M., when police officers herd them away. Where do they sleep? Some live in abandoned buildings. Some camp on the riverbank. Some make the rounds of the missions. A few, those who are said to prefer the streets, huddle around fires in vacant lots. The makeshift home beside them may be no more than an old wooden trailer where four men ("whoever gets there first") squeeze in at night.

Others wander from one arrangement to another, from homes of relatives to those of friends. Families attempt to share apartments; community workers say it is not unusual for two or three families to live in the same unit. When the situation explodes, the guests may find asylum in a shelter. Often, however, hosts and guests simply tolerate the intolerable, and continue their lives of not-so-quiet desperation in the same quarters.

It is the women whose homelessness is most likely to be hidden, says Becky Johnson, formerly of the Contact Center, a neighborhood advocacy group in Over-the-Rhine. "In our society homelessness is still more acceptable for men than women. And there are always far more programs for men. In Cincinnati, the city has no women's shelter, and almost all the private programs offer only temporary refuge. As a result, women—and children, too—are forced into nasty situations. Some become prostitutes. Others are forced to seek shelter with any man. The men abuse them. But these women—especially those who are alcoholic—have such low images of themselves that often they can't break away. And where *can* they go?"

Let us take a look at the interaction of the four main contributing causes of homelessness: unemployment, inadequacy of social benefits, inadequate services for the mentally disabled, and lack of affordable housing.

The Precipitants of Homelessness

Unemployment and Inadequate Social Benefits

The latest official figures with a racial breakdown on unemployment in Cincinnati come from the 1980 census. They show overall joblessness running at 8.7 percent; the rate for whites was 6.0 percent, and the rate for blacks, 15.2 percent. In September 1985 the overall unemployment rate was 9.3 percent. City planner Dick Moran observes that in those five years the gap between whites and blacks has probably been widening.[4]

In any case, the plight of the poor has worsened in Hamilton County since 1980. One clear sign of this is the jump in the number of cases on GA (known in Ohio as General Relief), the welfare program designed for the poorest of the poor, who cannot fit into any other category of eligibility. In February 1980 the number of cases on GA rolls was 3,587. By February 1985, despite the much-vaunted economic recovery, the number had expanded to 13,901; since then it has declined very slightly. The caseload was also significantly younger and included more women and more middle-class people.[5] Rental evictions have been climbing: in 1981 there were 2,527 such actions in Hamilton County; in 1984, 3,718.[6] Mortgage foreclosures have also continued to climb. In 1982 there were 573; in 1984, 696.[7]

What resources does the Hamilton County Department of Human Services provide to deal with these needs? It has not sponsored any emergency facilities for families. The only family shelters available are private efforts (although most of them now get some assistance from various government sources). Nor has it followed the example of some welfare offices in other parts of the country by offering financial assistance to retain occupancy of housing. Unlike some other welfare departments, too, it does not provide vouchers covering hotel accommodations till the homeless person can manage on his or her own.

The department does have an emergency program that can provide aid once in twelve months, for one thirty-day period, to persons whose utilities have been cut off, or who have been rendered homeless by eviction (but only if court-ordered), or need for security deposit after eviction, disasters, or condemnation of housing. It is not designed to meet the needs of people who cannot make do on their meager allotments. (Advocates for the homeless and the potentially homeless point out that many families on welfare receive so little that they have one or two genuine emergencies a month.) Nor does Emergency Assistance help people whose applications for GA, food stamps, or AFDC (known in Ohio as ADC) have been delayed or whose checks arrive late, because of some error on the part of the Post Office or Department of Human Services.

Moreover, such assistance is not granted until one has found a landlord who will accept payment through a voucher system. If it can meet the emergency needs of people for such items as rent, utilities, security deposit, and furniture, a voucher will be issued. Applicants can apply for food stamps, but emergency assistance is not intended to cover transportation, phone calls, soap, or other necessities. The maximum for one individual is $184, and for a family of four, $343 (1986 figures). Sometimes people rendered homeless by these circumstances are given vouchers for cheap hotels; in such cases, this is the single form of assistance they receive.

Emergency assistance is a federal–state program and, as such, sets up the restriction limiting aid to one thirty-day period once in twelve months. Any county can elect to supplement that assistance on its own. Hamilton County has not done so.

The other features of the so-called safety net in Cincinnati are somewhat typical of medium-sized American cities. The average payment per person in the AFDC program runs under the national median. (In 1983 the national median was $106.38 per person; the Ohio median was $85.75.)[8] In 1986 a family of three with zero income and minimal assets could receive $302 from AFDC. For many years this has been a flat grant; housing is expected to come out of that sum. In addition, the family is eligible for Medicaid and food stamps.

GA is still referred to in the Ohio Revised Code as Poor Relief—a term inherited from the Poor Laws of Elizabethan England. In Cincinnati, as in most parts of Ohio, the maximum stipend for a single person with zero income is $134 a month, plus $15 for expenses if the recipient is on work relief. Of this sum, welfare workers budget $67 for housing if the client is living in two or more rental rooms. If he or she is living with another person, the housing allowance is cut according to the number of rooms and the number of people.

Welfare workers admit that they cannot imagine how their clients manage to live on such sums. Yet Kentucky, just over the Ohio River, has no GA programs at all. Some poor Kentuckians living in Cincinnati fear returning to their home state to seek work or join relatives because they know that if they cannot find jobs, there will be no safety net at all.

The county does run one homeless facility, the Mount Airy Shelter, fifteen miles from downtown. Only single men are eligible, and the county welfare department screens all applicants.

Beyond referring them to Mount Airy, the city–county responsibility for the homeless largely consists of telling clients about services run by private organizations. In the words of one welfare supervisor, "We can't take on all the problems of the poor. Private groups can do the job." No transportation is provided from welfare offices to the private shelters.

Gaps in Services for the Mentally Disabled

No one knows how many deinstitutionalized mental patients there are in the county. The Hamilton County Mental Health Board estimates that they number between 4,000 and 5,000. Statistics on deinstitutionalization policies of Lewis Center, the long-term state mental hospital in the area, suggest that their numbers might be higher. In 1963 it had a population of 3,013.[9] In early 1986, the average daily count of patients was around 401; admissions and discharges were roughly equal— about 295 people a year.[10]

In 1963 the annual budget of the center (at that time known as Longview State Hospital) was $5,001,466.[11] By fiscal 1986 it had climbed to $20 million—or about $50,000 per patient.[12] Funding for community-based programs in Hamilton County, on the other hand, ran about $20 million in 1984. Since between 5,000 and 6,000 chronically mentally ill persons (including some who were never hospitalized) are in community-based treatment at some point during the year, this averages out to around $3,600 per patient.[13]

These statistics do not tell the whole story. Good hospital care is expensive. As Don Rohner, associate executive director of the Hamilton County Mental Health Board points out, "The rise in Lewis Center's budget was a good sign in many respects. In the 1960s state institutions resembled warehouses. They did little more than keep the lid on. The decision in the mid-1970s to get out those who could make it also meant higher quality care for those who remained.

"It wasn't until 1975 that the Community Mental Health Centers Act required some transitional halfway housing. Considering that fact, Cincinnati has made very good progress. In 1975 there were no halfway houses for the mentally ill; today there are four halfway houses and other residential services serving four hundred fifty persons each year.

"In most other states, large hospital populations were deinstitutionalized too fast. Ohio went more slowly but also more carefully. My observation is that there has been more coordination with community agencies here than in the country as a whole. As a result, fewer people have fallen through the cracks. Ohio is at about the middle in the development of community-based facilities."

One reason for the increase after 1980 in efforts to establish such facilities and to coordinate them with discharge policies is the growth of public concern over deinstitutionalization. Today the official policy at Lewis Center is that no patients shall be discharged without an aftercare plan, including housing, income, and treatment through either a mental health center or a private therapist.

As a result of studies underlining the need for housing for the chronic mentally ill, between 1980 and 1984, the number of residential placements tripled, to a new peak of four hundred fifty; that number included group homes, supervised apartments, halfway houses, and foster homes. In addition, two new programs—a crisis stabilization center and a discharge planning unit at Rollman Psychiatric Institute (an acute-care facility)—were launched. Yet mental health officials admit that the need for adequate housing, particularly for adult foster care and group homes, is still far from fulfilled.

In practice, making arrangements for income supports and housing is fraught with problems. Although applying for GA or SSI can be started in the hospital, it takes several weeks to process the application. Moreover, patients cannot actually receive benefits until after leaving the hospital. In order to receive the portion of GA allotted for housing as well as the portion for living expenses, the patient must have an address in the community. Yet in order to get an address, that is, to rent lodging, he must have money to pay the landlord. After paying transportation and other necessities, few GA recipients have much left from their living expense stipend to pay rent. In some cases, the Mental Health Board will pay for a room temporarily. The Department of Human Services ("Welfare") takes no responsibility for finding housing.

It is often impossible to withhold discharge on the grounds that a patient has no place to go. Today he or she can request discharge in writing, and unless the case can be probated within seventy-two hours (that is, it can be proved that the person is a danger to self or others), the request must be honored. It is extremely difficult to find cheap lodging or supervised residential care within seventy-two hours. The only solution may be the Drop-Inn Center. Sometimes deinstitutionalized persons have been sent to the Drop-Inn, with only a note bearing the address; it may take hours for them to find the place. Most patients are released to their families, who are unlikely to have the resources, the patience, or the training to care for them.

Since Lewis Center has no outpatient clinic of its own, patients are referred to nonprofit mental health clinics supported by the Mental Health Board, a state–county body concerned with funding and planning. Unlike the system in some other cities, such clinics are not run directly by the city or county. Instead, the board contracts with a number of nonprofit agencies for clinic treatment, rehabilitation, and supportive residential programs.

One of the most successful mental health and rehabilitation agencies is Cincinnati Restoration, Inc. Focusing on adults who have a significant history of emotional problems, usually with multiple psychiatric hospitalizations, it offers ongoing therapy, supportive residential programs, prevocational training, and socialization services, as well as case management and crisis intervention.

A continuum of residential arrangements is available: (1) a residential assessment center provides assessment and planning for community placement; (2) halfway houses offer treatment and assistance in handling day-to-day responsibilities; (3) group homes, which have less intensive supervision, help the mentally disabled live in the community; (4) supervised apartments offer residents a chance to share three- or four-person units and household responsibilities, with support services offered through the adjacent halfway house program; (5) satellite apartments represent a further step toward independence, with no supervision at the apartments but support services and meals available at the center; (6) coordinated apartment living provides even more freedom, with clients living without day-to-day supervision and responsible for purchasing food, cooking, and paying bills (the Restoration staff is used as a resource); (7) family-care placements offer supportive housing in a family setting, through partnership with the Mental Health Board; (8) supported independent living furnishes outreach services to former residential clients through telephone counseling, individual contacts, social activities, and case management. The overall goal is to avoid rehospitalization. In addition, Cincinnati Restoration sponsors a psychosocial center with drop-in facilities for hard-to-reach clients and those needing sustaining care in order to succeed in semi-independent living arrangements.

The cost of each level of living differs, but the average is about $20 per patient per day, in distinct contrast to nearly $97 at Lewis Center.

Cincinnati Restoration's Kemper Center is open to all clients. Designed to enhance socialization, vocational abilities, and life skills, Kemper's program provides a variety of activity groups, ranging from food-buying and preparation to social development, maintenance, housekeeping, or business.

A glimpse of one meeting of the social development group offers insight into the work of the center. Three blacks and nine whites are discussing plans for a shopping trip to Shillito/Rike's, a local department store. The social worker, acting as leader, makes a strong effort to involve everyone. A blond, curly-haired woman, whose tongue moves in and out continually while her body jerks back and forth, blurts out that the stockings she bought last time are too tight for her. A stocky young man with short-cropped hair, slumped shoulders, and a fixed stare murmurs, slurring his words, that he wants to buy something for his mother. Will the leader help him? She assures him she will, and then turns to a young black man who has been staring fixedly at his finger nails. Does he know what he wants to get? The youth shakes his head, still not looking at her. Meanwhile, a red-haired woman on the sofa is loudly announcing that she wants to buy a big rhinestone bracelet for herself. The leader listens patiently, tells her that they can discuss this later on, turns to a woman who has been staring out the window and asks where she got the pretty dress she is wearing. The woman smiles shyly and says that it came from a thrift shop.

During all this, there have been several interruptions: two young men who have wandered in to give brief wipes to the windows, an elderly woman who keeps telling the leader that she is running out of medicine, and an Oriental youth who walks through the room, arm raised, shouting "Charge!" No one seems to be upset by these interruptions, and the meeting moves on, as the clients plan the details of their expedition downtown.

Were it not for such programs, many more people would be homeless or would have returned to a hospital. By the end of 1986 the agency expects to have 144 beds, and to reach more than 350 clients. Other residential services in the area have some 350 beds. About 800 persons have been discharged into independent living or to homes of families. In the course of a year between 5,000 and 6,000 people are served at mental health clinics. Unfortunately, this may mean no more than irregular and infrequent visits. They may get medication, but there is no assurance that they will take it. Even regular clinic visits do not fulfill the needs of the mentally ill for rehabilitation, socialization, and protective housing.

Mary Asbury of Legal Aid in Cincinnati points out that despite strong efforts on the part of the Mental Health Board to establish group homes, some neighborhoods resist them. "Then, too, some of the mentally ill don't *want* or even need group homes. They need a boarding-house type of lodging. It's this no-frills type of housing that has been lost in Cincinnati. Legal Aid is working with the City Planning Commission on the problem.

"Legal Aid is also involved in representing prospective tenants when there is neighborhood opposition to establishing group homes. The need for more community-based facilities is serious."

What happens to those who just drop out of programs? Who go off medications? Who fail to show up at clinics? What about those who never entered a mental hospital (a group conservatively estimated at four thousand)?

No one really knows what happens, for no system has been set up to track these people. Some of them do show up at the Drop-Inn or other shelters, although such facilities are not equipped to handle them. Some end up in the streets. Many attend out-patient clinics but on an irregular basis.

Moreover, it has become increasingly difficult for the deinstitutionalized to return to a hospital. As one advocate put it, "They have to blow up. When we drive them to a hospital, sometimes we deliberately try *not* to calm them down. Or we drop them inside and rush away before admissions can say no. Recently the procedure has changed for probated patients. The probate orders aren't cancelled on departure but merely suspended; they can be reactivated when a psychiatrist at the University of Cincinnati Psychiatric Unit, which now does the screening, considers it necessary."

Despite the obstacles in returning to Lewis Center, over a third of the patients go back. Social workers there speak in frustrated tones of how difficult it is to engage young chronics in the system. If this is true, one might ask if the system is not at fault.

What happens to those who fall through the cracks? Buddy Gray and Pat Johnson of the Drop-Inn Center tell the following story of a woman whom they were able to help only in a marginal way because the Drop-Inn is not equipped to handle such cases.

Susan (pseudonym), now fifty-one, was discharged seven years ago from Lewis Center, where she had spent ten years. During that time she received weekly group therapy, occupational therapy, art therapy, and several drugs. Susan was sent to a community mental health center, where her medication prescriptions were renewed and a caseworker talked to her, emphasizing the importance of taking her medicine. Sometimes Susan returned for her monthly appointment; sometimes she forgot.

Even normal women in their fifties were having a hard time finding jobs. With her lack of working experience, and her disheveled hair, vacant stare, fixed smile, and habit of scratching herself in intimate places, Susan did not impress prospective employers.

At the Social Security office, she did get accepted for SSI. From her stipend (currently $336 a month) she pays $230 in rent for an SRO room. Her food stamp allowance amounts to $76 a month. Susan finds it difficult to stretch these allotments to the end of the month. Several times she has approached the mental health center in great distress to talk of the difficulty; each time the case manager has gone over her budget and called her a poor manager, while the psychiatrist in charge has changed or increased her medication. During the following days Susan often feels so listless or depressed that she simply decides on her own to cease taking any medication for awhile.

There is some truth in the label poor manager. Occasionally, when Susan feels particularly lonely, she gives dollar bills away to homeless people she meets on park benches or in the Drop-Inn.

Susan has often been hungry. One day she acquired a "new" hat and coat, together with a fake fur scarf, at a church clothing center. That night she approached a restaurant where she had often stood longingly, staring at the roast beef, garnished salmon loaf, cheese cake, and other delicacies standing in the window. This time she swept through the door, sat down at a table, and ordered a full meal. When the waiter approached with the check, Susan asked if she might wash the dishes. Instead, he and the manager returned with the police.

After listening to her story, the officers took her to the Drop-Inn. There an eighty-one-year-old gentleman who lived in a run-down SRO in the neighborhood and came in every day to volunteer his time "because these folks are lonely like me" dug into his pockets and found enough to pay for Susan's dinner.

A few weeks later Susan again felt so hungry that she entered another restaurant and ate another full meal. This time the police took her directly to the police station, and she was jailed.

Today Susan wanders in and out of facilities for the homeless. Several times when her SSI check has run out, she has been evicted. Sometimes she seeks refuge at the Drop-Inn, sometimes with men. Invariably they abuse her sexually and physically. Eventually she flees from these relationships, hurt and confused, but not quite able to articulate her anger. "I'm no damned good," she says

The Drop-Inn staff have developed an affectionate concern for Susan. They have no authority over her, however. No one on the staff is empowered to dispense medications, for example. Covertly, they do manage to do this by keeping them in a medicine chest, bringing them out at the prescribed time, and urging her to take them. When she disappears for days or weeks at a time, there is nothing they can do. They can only hope that their caring will cause her to come back. Nor is it easy to maintain their concern for Susan. Although she never engages in physical violence, her language can be violent. She often curses the coffee, the doughnuts, the men from the street, and the staff. Sometimes she calls Pat, who is black, "a Jew—just another goddam dirty Jew!" Yet a few minutes later she may smile a thank you to Pat.

Caring is important, staff members agree, but it is not enough.

At this point in time, the most successful actions in reaching those who have fallen through the cracks seem to be the efforts of individual advocates working in the interstices of the system. Some advocates are paid workers; others are volunteers. Jane Jansak, who has a master's degree in social work and seven years of experience on the staff of the Welfare Department, now donates her time to working with society's cast-asides, particularly the mentally ill, at the Prince of Peace Lutheran Church in Over-the-Rhine. "The kind of work I do is very labor intensive," she says. "No computer could be programmed to do it, and that might not be considered cost effective. For instance, I've been acting as payee for twenty-two mentally ill people. They can't manage money, and are easily victimized by the tougher men in the neighborhood. Everybody knows who these ill people are, and when they're robbed, they end up homeless.

"When SSI checks arrive late, which sometimes happens, they are frightened. Some may be evicted. If they're people I know, I become their advocate.

"Others, some of them sick people who never were hospitalized, are just unable to negotiate the whole system. They have to provide documentation, and if they can't read or write, or have only a second grade education, or are emotionally incapacitated, they simply can't do that.

"Unfortunately, there is no provision for payees in the GA system. Nor is it always easy to get on GA. Sometimes people who manage to do that, fail to show up once for the work relief days they're required to put in every month, so they get put off the rolls for ninety days. What happens then? They become invisible people. The easiest thing to do is to get into the criminal system.

"The real problem is the lack of resources. When Lewis Center has only seventy-two hours to discharge a patient, they sometimes ask me to find housing. That's all the time available to make a discharge plan! How can I find a place? Who's going to pay for it? You can't get SSI in three days. The patient might be eligible for GA, but that takes about thirty days. He could get emergency assistance till GA arrives but would need a permanent address. Sometimes I have to ask landlords to accept someone on the promise, or hope, that they'll get the rent eventually!"

Jansak is also concerned about the lack of resources for long-term accommodations. "Some of the people I work with have grown up in Lewis Center. They're chronic patients, often with dual diagnoses. Yet they are discharged to community living. There aren't enough transitional accommodations, and living in their own apartments is too unstructured for them to handle. Hamilton County now has more residential beds than almost any other county in Ohio, but the number could be doubled and still not meet the need.

"Actually, even if there were enough halfway houses, such facilities wouldn't suffice. Halfway implies halfway to something—to a fairly normal life in the community. Many of these people probably will never get there. They need an *endway* house, where recreation, meals, medication, and all other activities are supervised. Not necessarily by professionals but by people with heart and a certain minimum training. There should be a lot of freedom in such places but plenty of activies, too. Nothing is worse on the human spirit than having nothing to do. Every person needs a structure. Some of my people come in to see me every day just because they need human contact and some pattern in their lives. The endway houses should be small. Most mentally ill people are *prickly*. If you get too many prickly edges together, they become a herd of porcupines! I think the churches could be doing far more of this kind of work than they are doing now, using their own funds and their own *people*."

The Lack of Affordable Housing

As Goozner makes clear in his perceptive *Housing Cincinnati's Poor,* a seeming paradox exists in the Queen City: there is a surplus of housing units, yet at the same time a tremendous unmet housing need. The poor cannot afford to rent the housing that is available.[14] This is especially true of poor families headed by women, a category growing in Cincinnati as in the rest of the nation.

With rising costs, landlords have been unable to get enough rent to keep up their properties, hence they are likely to rent at the lower rates but let the building deteriorate. Eventually they abandon the building. In 1986 disinvestment was still the chief cause of displacement of low-income people in Cincinnati, according to Ken Robinson of the Department of Neighborhoods.

At the same time, government programs have declined. There have been three types of federal assistance: public housing directed by the Cincinnati Metropolitan Housing Authority (CMHA); privately owned housing that receives either below-market interest rate subsidy or rent supplements for tenants or both; and existing private market rental housing where the landlord receives a rent subsidy on behalf of a tenant (Section 8 certificate, and the experimental voucher program).[15]

On the other hand, such assistance has improved a situation that was far more deplorable before public housing was born in the late 1930s. Until then, Cincinnati had some of the worst housing in the United States. The dwellings that have emerged through federal programs have provided simple but substantial and affordable housing.

The large influx of blacks and Appalachians in the 1950s added to the demand. In the 1960s Cincinnati became one of the fifteen Project Rehab cities in the nation. Developers, both profit-oriented and nonprofit groups, bought and rehabbed 6,500 inner-city rental units, using below-market interest rate loans guaranteed by the federal government. Housing was rented to low-income people who paid either 25 percent of their incomes or 30 percent of the base rent, whichever was higher; the balance, a rent supplement, was paid by the government.[16]

Many problems arose with the private sector ownership portion of the program. Some tenants of existing housing did not want to be moved. Poor workmanship and the use of poor materials characterized many projects. Large numbers of investors were in the game only for tax benefits. Waste and fraud were common. As for the private, nonprofit sector, many social activists were too inexperienced to make their programs viable.

Despite such problems and failures, Project Rehab did create 6,500 subsidized housing units out of the city's existing housing stock—more subsidized housing than had been built in over thirty years of public housing construction.[17]

The energy crisis of 1973–74 had a devastating impact on existing subsidized units and on private landlords of low-income housing. Owners of units whose subsidies were controlled by the federal government could not raise rents at a pace that kept up with rising costs of utility bills. Eventually several thousand subsidized units were foreclosed and repossessed for resale by HUD.

The private sector rents for low-income housing remained fairly stable, but landlords' utility bills skyrocketed. The result was that owners at first failed to keep up the buildings then abandoned them entirely.

The introduction in the 1970s of the Section 8 program, providing for new construction, substantial or moderate rehabilitation for existing housing, and Section 8 certificates, seemed promising. However, says Goozner, the requirements that low-income housing be decentralized into communities that had no subsidy programs aroused bitter resistance; the newly targeted neighborhoods wanted to keep families with children and poor black people out. Many landlords stated openly that they would not put a welfare person next door to a middle-income family. Hence by the early 1980s, about 40 percent of the holders of Section 8 certificates were using these vouchers in the dwellings where they already were living.[18] As critics of the voucher idea have pointed out, such programs may merely subsidize landlords without assuring expansion of housing choices.

As a result of discrimination, most of the city's subsidized housing is concentrated in a few neighborhoods, which remain or become segregated. According to the Over-the-Rhine Comprehensive Plan, 26 percent of the housing in that area was subsidized in 1982, and in 1980 (the latest year for which census figures are available) 63 percent of the population was black, and 68 percent of the householders were living at or under the poverty level.[19]

Most of the subsidized building has been undertaken by profit-oriented builders. Private developers make their real profit not from ownership and management of low income real estate but from syndicating the ownership to wealthy investors, who buy the depreciation of the building for tax purposes. If the building's total value depreciates an average of 10 percent each year, an investor in the highest tax bracket can recoup all of his or her original investment within a short period of time. The depreciation continues until the investor may have more than doubled his or her money. Furthermore, the investor still owns his or her share of the building and its residual value.[20]

Two developers who have profited from the ownership and management of subsidized low-income housing are Tom and Norb Denhart, the biggest landlords in Over-the Rhine. Beginning in the Project Rehab era, within a few years the two brothers accumulated twelve hundred units, and created their own building supply, management, and insurance companies.[21] According to their tenants and community advocates, the Denharts have made the fewest repairs possible, used the cheapest materials, and charged tenants for repairs that are either not made or unsatisfactory.[22] To thousands of Over-the-Rhine residents they have become the symbol of landlord abuse, greed, and corruption.

Public housing (where, according to CMHA executive director John Nelson approximately 89 percent of all tenants were black, and the average income for all *households* was about $6,000 a year in 1986) has been roundly criticized for poor maintenance, excessively strict rules, a tendency to perpetuate segregation, and, especially since recent cuts of CMHA subsidies, escalation of rents.

In theory, homeless persons have priority in gaining access to public housing. However, only those displaced by government action or code enforcement are eligible. The great majority forced out of their homes are not accepted.

Another source of low-income housing—cheap hotels and other SRO dwellings—dwindled rapidly. According to a 1984 Planning Commission Report, which used 1980 census figures, between 1970 and 1980 the city had experienced a dramatic decrease of 1,685 SRO units, from 6,519 to 4,834, mostly in the Central Business District.[23]

By the mid-1980s, the costs to private landlords of operating unsubsidized housing were still marching ahead of their ability to squeeze a few more dollars out of their impoverished tenants. The number of people who could afford even HUD's fair market rent has been declining. The rent gap was causing Cincinnati's housing stock to deteriorate. The result has been increased abandonment.

Abandonment not only causes low-income people to move from one run-down place to another, often paying higher and higher proportions of their income for shelter, it also creates a pool of cheap land and buildings that, if located in potentially desirable areas, can eventually be used for gentrified housing. This is the fear of residents in Over-the-Rhine, where a quarter of the housing units stand empty. In some parts of the area, the process is well underway; in others, the abandoned properties are still only a threat.

Services for the Homeless

Because large numbers of urban nomads are not visible on the streets and homelessness has never reached the proportions it has in many other cities, Cincinnati was relatively unprepared to meet the problem. It was not till 1982, in response to the growing need for emergency facilities for families, that the Greater Cincinnati Emergency Services Coalition was formed. Until 1984 Cincinnati had no citywide coalition of groups concerned with undomiciled people. In March of that year the Ohio Coalition for the Homeless was formed. Then Buddy Gray of the Drop-Inn Center and Barbara Poppe of Bethany House got together to crystallize long-standing plans for a Greater Cincinnati Coalition for the Homeless. It was founded in May 1984, and less than a month later the new group was testifying at the Ohio Senate Hunger Task Force hearings in Cincinnati. Today the coalition brings together some thirty shelters, residential programs, soup kitchens, churches, community centers, and other services for low-income people in the Greater Cincinnati area (including Covington, Kentucky). Members of the coalition have presented City Council with plans to respond to the need for low-income housing, addressed city hearings on the CDBG program in order to underline the need to serve homeless people, held a candlelight vigil at city hall to protest lack of government action on the issue, met with a wide range of city officials, and engaged in broader political action, such as a drive to "Evict Reagan" during the 1984 Presidential campaign.

Although municipal officials, in response to pressure from service providers and concerned citizens, have gradually allocated more public funds to assist facilities for the homeless, their basic assumption has been that these monies supplement the efforts of the voluntary sector, which bears primary responsibility. Private agencies, missions, and church groups have tried to meet the challenge, but their resources have been strained. For example, the Housing Authority did offer to make several apartments available to agencies at the unusually low rent of $50 a month (including utilities) for use as temporary shelters for homeless families. Private agencies were too strapped for funds to take up the offer. As for the shelters, all of them have had to stretch their resources to meet the increased need in the 1980s.

The response of private groups also occurred later than in many other cities. It was only in 1982 that the City Gospel Mission, which had served men only, launched a separate shelter for families, and only in 1983 that the Catholic Worker and Bethany House opened their doors to women and families. (The Catholic Worker now serves men only.) Yet it soon became apparent that the number of homeless families was growing so fast that even these new shelters could not fill the gap. In 1984 God's Shelter House, intended primarily for families, was founded. That year the Inner City Mission opened a hot meal program and at the same time unofficially made beds available to families and anyone else in need of a place to stay; the mission is not recognized as a shelter.

What are the principal services for the homeless?

Women Helping Women has no shelter of its own, but it assists abused women and children with counseling and referrals to shelters and attempts to educate women and the community about rape and family violence.

Women Helping Women works closely with Alice Paul House, a refuge for battered women and children established in 1981 by the YWCA. Because it is important to hide battered women from abusers who may be pursuing them, the location of the house is not disclosed, and the procedure for admission is extremely complicated. The applicant is interviewed intensively over the phone, then given directions to a social service office, where a worker from the house meets her, questions her again at length, and finally takes her to the shelter. It is a spacious, comfortable, brightly furnished house with single rooms offering women the privacy to lie on their beds and cry. Staff members are on board twenty-four hours a day and provide extensive counseling. The atmosphere is warm and caring; most women who have stayed there say that it has helped them discover their potential for new lives.

The Salvation Army maintains an emergency home for women and women with children, who may or may not be abused. In principle the stay is limited to three days, although in some cases it is extended. The sleeping arrangements offer double rooms rather than dormitories, the food is good, and the place is quiet and clean. The atmosphere is regimented, however, and the women complain that there are just too many rules. Although women may bring their children, boys over ten years of age are not admitted.

What happens in such cases? The boy may be separated from his mother, and sent to Allen House, a county home for children who for some reason cannot be with their parents, or to the Lighthouse Runaway Shelter. Although the City Gospel Mission has a family shelter, the father must be present, and the stay is usually limited. The mission also has a women's shelter, but it is open only to lone women, not those with children; if a single mother with children applied, the youngsters would have to go elsewhere. Jack Meisenhelder of Catholic Social Services has dealt with families in which the mother and younger child were staying at the Salvation Army, the teen-age son was living with runaways at the Lighthouse, and the father was domiciled at the Drop-Inn Center where the majority of residents are alcoholic. The opening of God's Shelter House and the Temporary Housing Program at the St. John's Social Service Center marked a real change for such families. Both facilities accept children of any age, have a more relaxed approach than the traditional missions, attempt to provide a familylike atmosphere, and set flexible limits on length of stay. St. John's is a unique service in Cincinnati in that it offers apartments and its primary focus is the two-parent family, the most underserved homeless in the area. (It also takes single-parent families and single persons.)

The City Gospel Mission is strict in its definition of couples and families. No trial marriages or common-law couples are accepted, and applicants must present a marriage certificate. If they do not have one, a staff member will phone the appropriate county registrar to ascertain that the ceremony was performed.

Like many other missions in America, this one makes a sharp distinction between transients and those on the program. If male clients are transient, they are allowed just three nights lodging, breakfast, and dinner. During the day transient males must leave the premises, regardless of weather. Men and women on the four-month program—those who have made a commitment—agree to attend Bible classes five days a week, both morning and afternoon. For the first two weeks they are on restriction (they must remain on the premises) but after that they may go in and out at will, providing that they sign out and also attend all required services. These rules apply to all categories of clients, whether they be alcoholic, drug-addicted, battered, burned out of housing, or otherwise rendered homeless. As one assistant explained, "The program is to *change* them."

Reflecting the old stereotype that identifies homelessness with excessive drinking, most of the shelters for men in Cincinnati have been built for the purpose of rehabilitating alcoholics. The City Gospel Mission attempts to do this by persuading them to follow its fundamentalist tenets. Volunteers of America places some emphasis on attending Alcoholics Anonymous meetings (and similar programs for drug abusers), but its major stress is on work as rehabilitation. Almost all the work is manual labor, ranging from baling paper to repairing furniture. Prayer is encouraged; each man must attend services on two successive Tuesdays, but after that attendance is optional. Men can remain indefinitely, as long as they maintain sobriety. The Salvation Army, which describes its services to men as "not a shelter, but a rehabilitation program for alcoholics and men discharged from prison," has a similar approach. Prayer and work are seen as the primary avenues to rehabilitation, and work consists of tasks such as building maintenance and repairing clothing. This approach seems to work well with some men, but others resent the emphasis on religion and also feel that they are being used as a source of cheap labor.

In contrast, Prospect House, a state-funded rehabilitation program for alcoholic men, does not focus on work and prayer. Varied treatment approaches are used, and church service is not compulsory.

The Mount Airy Shelter, run by the Hamilton County Welfare Board, takes not only alcoholics but also drug abusers, ex-offenders, and a few who are just down and out. "Mental cases" are not accepted. The shelter provides three meals a day, real beds, and referrals to rehabilitation programs. To many men, there are drawbacks to staying at Mount Airy. Because it is situated fifteen miles from downtown, they find it difficult to look for jobs or meet old friends. Indeed, it is difficult both to get into the shelter and to get out. Mount Airy is not listed under that name in the phone directory; one would have to be knowledgeable enough to think of looking it up under Hamilton County Human Services Department. To be admitted, a man must be screened by the department, and once in, he cannot leave the premises without a pass.

Since services for the homeless are generally inadequate, responsibility often tumbles into the lap of the church. This has been particularly true for families. Although voluntary agencies have sometimes received FEMA funds for the purpose, it is usually individual parishes with a strong commitment to aid the poor that voucher individuals into hotels for temporary stays.

Hotels are not the answer for people who need on-site supportive services. Some do well in transitional residences. Others, particularly those who are chronically mentally ill, need what Jane Jansak calls an endway house. Jane herself runs a boarding house called New Morning for mentally disabled men on SSI. The simple facility has been adequate for relatively independent residents, but the arrival of more disturbed men has heightened the need for supervision. Jane hopes to work out an agreement with Tender Mercies, a residence opened by Catholic priest Chris Hall in 1985, to manage her place as well.

Situated in an old graystone on Washington Park, Tender Mercies offers a certain autonomy yet a communal atmosphere to a dozen mentally ill women. Each room has a stove, refrigerator, desk, bathroom, and divider separating the bed from the cooking facilities. With considerable pride, the women show visitors their rooms and respond to Father Chris' gentle queries. After getting permission from the resident, he may tell visitors how they met—usually in a mental hospital, jail, or the Drop-Inn Center—and a bit about how she has been doing since. In the sunny office a motherly looking nun has frequent friendly talks with each of the women. The residence derives much of its support from the guests' SSI checks; the rest comes from various church and government sources. Around the corner from Tender Mercies, Father Chris has been developing a similar residence for men.

Since Bethany House—a joint effort of Catholics, Episcopalians, and the United Church of Christ—opened in the fall of 1983, it has become a sought-after transitional residence for women and women with children. The house is a light, airy, tastefully furnished place on a hill overlooking the central part of the city. A Sister of Charity, a Sister of Mercy, a Franciscan Sister, and two laywomen staff the home; their gentle concern lends it an ambience of serenity. Bethany House is more flexible than the missions in deciding length of stay, the atmosphere is more relaxed and familial, and guests receive more personal attention. As a result they are able to work out plans for the future.

One guest is a fifty-three-year old white woman whom we shall call Constance. She is not alcoholic, addicted to drugs, abused, nor mentally disabled.

Bethany receives many women who, like Constance, seem to fit no category. She tells you that she was once a model for Macy's department store in New York and that she sang western and country and gospel music in professional orchestras. And it is clear that she was once a good-looking woman. She has small delicate features, her skin is fresh, and her gray hair is brushed into neat waves. But she speaks haltingly, and her large blue eyes are sad.

For ten years she was married to a Southern Baptist preacher. "He was a good man. And I've always been a Christian. We didn't have no children. But we got along real well. Then he died." Later she married a mechanic, but he fell onto hard times, exacerbated by the expenses incurred from a cancer operation on her colon. Yet they somehow managed to stay off welfare. Then he died. A few months later her cataracts worsened, and she went blind. A year later she had a stroke, which paralyzed part of her body and affected her voice. After a cataract operation she did regain the sight of one eye. The Welfare Department sent her to a foster home, but she felt lonely there because the other clients were "all old people, senile. I couldn't really talk with them." Constance tried living alone, but found that difficult because of her handicaps. Then the landlord announced that he was converting the apartment building into upper-income units. Frightened, Constance accepted the offer of a friend to share an apartment. "But she *wasn't* a friend. She knew I was on SSI; she took my money. And she was talking in a real threatening way. So one night I went to that drop-in place. The staff there were nice, but I wasn't used to sleeping on the floor, and besides I was the only woman who wasn't inebriated. So the drop-in people brought me here. I like it real well. They've helped me find a special apartment for the disabled. I'm lucky. And I believe in the Lord Jesus Christ, my personal savior. But you know . . ." Her voice turned wistful. "I don't really want to live alone. I'm going to miss these nice people here." Staff member Sister Dee says they follow up on the women who have lived at Bethany and invite them to potluck suppers. "We want them to feel part of a family." However, neither temporary shelters nor privatized apartments are the real answer for homeless people like Constance, she believes. "There ought to be something more."

One private shelter for men that neither is intended primarily for alcoholics nor seeks to reform its guests is the Saint Francis Catholic Worker House. Like the eighty-odd Catholic Worker houses across the country, the Saint Francis in Cincinnati offers hospitality in a family atmosphere to the down-and-out from all walks of life.

Indeed, the Catholic Worker philosophy is that we are all children of God, all members of one communal family, hence we are responsible for one another. Robert Ellsberg, who worked for many years at Saint Joseph House in New York, once summed up the Catholic Worker approach: "The kind of service we're trying to share is different from that sold by the state and the missions. If everyone practiced works of mercy, at a personal level, at a personal sacrifice—not through taxes via the welfare system—and if we allowed our surplus to supply the needs of neighbors, there would not be this misery in our cities. But you have to live it; you try to act as you would have everyone act. And the Catholic Worker tries to provide this example. The point is not that we ourselves should house everyone on the Bowery, but that we should follow Christ's commandment and pray that others will do the same."

The Cincinnati house of hospitality is one three-story building in Over-the-Rhine, which can domicile up to fifteen men at a time. It is clean, light, and simply but brightly appointed with donated furniture. The flowered wall paper, television, carpet, orange plastic-covered chairs, and two fish aquariums, together with posters proclaiming peace to all humankind, offer a refreshing welcome to men coming in from drab, littered streets.

Saint Francis was opened in 1983 by Jim Mullen, a tense, wiry man in his thirties who had been operating two bars in the city when he began to "feel the emptiness of it all." He sold the bars, and in the search to bring more meaning to his life, began donating his time at the soupline run by Saint Francis Church. There he discovered many men and women who had no home. Jim managed to find and rehabilitate a dilapidated house, where he offered hospitality to women and women with children, since they seemed to represent the greatest unmet need. Fire broke out, damaging an already run-down building.

Eventually Jim found a better house for $16,500, wrote a letter to the *Catholic Telegraph* explaining his plan, and in two weeks raised $8,000. Partly because Bethany House was just opening its doors to women, he decided to use the newly purchased building for men. "Since then, the place is almost always full, even in summer. Sometimes I jam an extra ten men or so into the attic. Agencies, churches, everybody calls here. It makes you wonder what they did before."

The Catholic Worker takes many men who fall through the cracks. During our visit there was a call from Human Services (Welfare). Could they take a man in a wheelchair, one who insisted he could go up stairs with a banister? Hesitantly, Jim agreed. A few minutes later the van arrived, and two workers deposited the new guest in the middle of the living room. Squat, square-jawed, with a once-powerful body, Pete (pseudonym) surveyed us tensely, his bright blue eyes radiating subdued anger. Yes, he was glad to be here. Maybe things were going to be better now. He had just come from three days at the Drop-Inn. "Maybe it's an okay place for alcoholics, but not for me. I ain't no alcoholic. The commotion was terrible. Some of those guys practically puked on me, and they stepped all over me, while I was sitting in this chair. I had to fight to get food. Sure, the staff was decent to me, but I didn't see much of them, for all the commotion. That's because I had to sleep in the front room, the one where the TV is. They wouldn't let me sleep in the dorm because you have to go up a few steps. I told them I could pull myself up the banister, but they wouldn't believe me.

"Yeah, you're probably right, they were worried about responsibility. But still I had to sleep on a hard bench, out in that room. They never gave me a chance.

The deeper source of Pete's anger, we learned, was his experience before coming to the Drop-Inn. He was a battered husband. In January, while living in Kentucky, he had met a woman who said she loved him. In March she became his third wife, and everything went just fine for two months. But nowhere could she find a job in her field, office work, and by May she was back into drink. Then she took up with a boy friend. Last week the two had beaten him up in his own apartment, emptied his wallet, and thrown it out on the street. The shrieking became so loud that neighbors called the police, who came to his rescue.

"I'd like to work," Pete told us. "I was a truck driver for GE. What happened to my back? I got a tumor on the spine. They *could* operate, but there's an eighty percent chance the operation would kill me. I'm not a gambler. Sure, I went to Rehab in Kentucky. But they didn't give me no training. Just tested me, and sent me from place to place looking for work. Nobody'd take me. I can drive. I'm still a good driver. A state trooper approved me. Him and me drove all over the county. But employers won't take me. They say the insurance costs too much. They never give me a chance.

"Now what's going to happen to me? Maybe they'll give me an apartment for the handicapped like they did in Kentucky. But what'm I going to *do* all day?"

We thought of Mary Asbury and her idea that many mentally disabled people need a boarding-house kind of home. Would not people like Pete and Constance also do best in such an arrangement, one combining considerable independence with care and community?

The Drop-Inn Center

Situated on Twelfth Street near Washington Park, the Drop-Inn Center is lodged in two contiguous buildings, one of gray sandstone and the other an old garage of brick painted over in bright red and yellow.

Visitors entering around five in the afternoon will see several dozen figures in the waiting-room, seated on folding chairs and quietly watching television. The brick walls of the interior are painted in faded yellow and brown and are adorned with friendly reminders, such as a poster depicting a long slope with many precipices and plateaus, bearing the inscription: "Where are *you* on the mountain of sobriety?"

At six-thirty they begin to line up for dinner in the next room. A staff member or special volunteer asks each person in line his or her name. Tonight the one in charge is a volunteer in a plaid shirt, worker's cap, and name-tag saying Bill. It turns out that he is Father Bill Schiesl, a Catholic prison chaplain who lives in the neighborhood and volunteers at least once a week.

No ID, no proof of need, is required. Some of the clients eye the floor and mumble their names. Others look at Father Bill askance but blurt out their names with bravado. Father Bill knows many of them. Gently he steers those already drunk to a nearby table, where volunteers will bring them dinner. "We don't want these guys slopping food over others and starting trouble," he explains.

The food is ladled out to the hungry at a long stainless steel serving counter. The menu is basically the same every night: soup of the day (the ingredients depending on whatever was donated that morning), stale rolls and bread, Kool-Aid, tomato or fruit, perhaps an outdated doughnut for dessert. Volunteers from schools, colleges, the neighborhood, or church groups serve the food. Some smile and chat with the men and women who have become the recipients of society's bounty. Other volunteers simply hand out the filled plates.

The cold fluorescent lighting, the dark concrete floors, the dilapidated wooden tables, and the iron ceiling beams give the converted garage a barnlike quality. Yet some guests talk with each other, and occasionally laughter breaks the subdued atmosphere. When a visitor tries to strike up a conversation, almost invariably the clients respond eagerly. A man with bleary blue eyes and tattooed biceps tells you that he was a kid in the Depression and things weren't as bad as they are today. A youthful black man in a hooded sweat jacket says he's been looking for work for two years. A gentleman with one eye, long curling white hair, and elegant beard begins to shout incoherently to the whole room and the world at large. A maternal-looking woman named Sherry approaches him, smiling, and quietly guides him to the office. A few minutes later, he emerges, looking calmer. Sherry leads him to the door where a volunteer car is waiting to take him to the detoxification center.

At the door he turns and yells, "Give me a call and I'll be there!" as he strums an imaginary guitar and dances up and down. "Detox will help. George has been building up to this for a long time," says Sherry.

The dimly lit office, furnished with a battered desk and two chairs, is cluttered with papers, sleeping mats, today's donations, and individual bags of the guests' belongings. On the wall is pasted a homemade poster: The FACTS—City Jail: $69 per day. University of Cincinnati Hospital: $550. Drop-Inn Center: $2.00.

The big hall, part of the sandstone building, is the dormitory. Around seven every night the hall begins to fill. Men line up for plastic mats, quietly spread them on the floor, and lie down in their clothes. A few spread coats over themselves; no blankets, sheets, or pillows are provided. Since there is seldom enough room for everyone to sleep on the floor, some men sit on chairs in the big hall through the entire night; others gather noisily in the waiting room.

In contrast to most city-run shelters in other parts of the country, no policeman is on hand. Joe Bean, a portly, smiling man in his eighties and one of the live-ins who work at the center, walks up and down the aisles of sprawled bodies. "Just checking up to see they're all right," he explains. "Of course we get troubles sometimes, but nothing we can't handle. These guys are okay."

Indeed, the hall of over one hundred fifty men is remarkably quiet. Some turn fitfully, moaning in their sleep; some break into coughs; others mutter an incoherent dialogue with themselves. But most of the men, even those sitting sleepless in their chairs, seem wrapped in silence.

In an inside room, space has been set aside for a dozen women. They also have a small television alcove of their own, which assures them of a little privacy. Myrtle, an untidy but affable woman in her late sixties, beckons to you with a smile. She is "a bit senile," and also "loves the bottle a little too much," according to the staff. Perhaps her problem is that she is too generous, they say, for she is always getting evicted by landlords for inviting all her friends to sleep in her apartment, which becomes a little Drop-Inn of her own. After being displaced, Myrtle always ends up here. "But I like it," she tells you. "It's not like my own place. But they treat me nice."

As you leave the big hall and its cargo of sweaty bodies, some of the men on chairs smile at you, as if seeking recognition. Many on the floor have curled themselves into sleep. Others lie inert, eyes wide open, staring up at the ceiling.

Anyone who is out of pocket, out of luck, can pass through the Drop-Inn Center's portals with few questions asked; although all are encouraged to seek more permanent lodging, no one is turned back to the streets when some deadline has passed. The Drop-Inn is a kaleidoscope of fissured American dreams. Here you see the men and women who once made it, or expected to make it, and have slid into a struggle just to survive. In the eyes of the average Cincinnatian, they are failures. To many developers, City Councilors, and establishment families, they are also a hindrance to the orderly gentrification of the area. Since its founding in 1973, the shelter has had to put up a fierce fight to exist. Unlike many shelterhouses in other cities, the Drop-Inn is not opposed by the neighborhood. On the contrary, Over-the-Rhine residents have supported its struggle, and workers at the Drop-Inn have joined other campaigns in the community.

On the average, 170 people sleep at the center every night, and 215 (but up to 260) eat there every evening. The number of clients grew 70 percent between 1981 and 1986 and continues to rise, despite the fact that other shelters have opened during that time.

The center derives its principal support from the South West Ohio Regional Council on Alcoholism (SWORCA) with a grant averaging about $2 per person per night. In 1985, however, alcohol programs in Ohio were cut back 18 percent. In 1984 it received $34,000 and in 1985, $20,000 from FEMA, mostly for feeding programs. It has occasionally received small CDBG grants, funneled through the city, for specific projects such as improving the bathroom, but it was not till 1985 that it was awarded the comparatively generous sum of $18,000 from CDBG funds, as the result of a political hassle to be described later. Hence the center continues to rely heavily on donations from individuals and religious groups.

The structure of the Drop-Inn reflects its grassroots democratic philosophy. The governing board is composed of one-third staff, one-third residents, and one-third volunteers. The twelve-member staff is half white and half black, half male and half female. All staff members are paid the same, $10,000 a year—a salary that almost no professional would consider. Staff members are not professionals, but they receive on-the-job training. About half are recovering alcoholics who have come to know, through tough experience, the personality makeup of substance abusers as well as the steps toward recovery. Some of the other workers have proved their skills in working with a difficult population through volunteering.

Who are the Drop-Inn guests? "The tough ones," say the staff, "Those who won't fit in elsewhere. The police always seem to think of *us*." Roughly 85 percent are men, but the proportion of women grows every year. Occasionally, whole families have been domiciled. Some 80 percent are alcoholics; the rest are from the ranks of the new unemployed, the mentally disabled, and those displaced from their homes. Growing numbers are mixed abusers who both drink and take drugs. About half the guests are black, the other half white; occasionally Hispanics and Native Americans wander into the center. Eighty percent come from the notoriously poor Appalachian region. Despite a widespread myth that they flock here from distant places, Drop-Inn workers estimate that 75 percent were born in Ohio or Kentucky. The real transiency, they say, is the movement within the Cincinnati area—in and out of apartment, jail, hospital, abandoned building, riverbank, and shelters.

"Most of these people have a history of work, often in dangerous, debilitating industries such as mines, railroads, or foundries," says Bill Kashersky, a long-time staff member. "Most still work when they can. On any given day, three-quarters will try day labor. Sometimes only half a dozen guys—the younger, stronger ones—get such jobs. The ones that are overlooked get frustrated. Some sell their blood at the local plasma center. Maybe they drown their frustration at a bar afterwards.

In day labor, the men tend to get the dirtiest or most dangerous jobs, like cleaning acid out of barrels. And they work here at the center—painting, cleaning, running errands. Our people also go to agencies to get housing, welfare, or social security. The common thread running through their lives is unemployment.

"Often Welfare gives them the run-around. They can't get on full GA and food stamps unless they have an address. They can ask landlords for a place because Welfare's going to pay, but many won't take you on a promise. So they stay here till they find a landlord who'll take them.

"Other people who come here can't make it on GA. Some drink their check away. But even those who don't drink, or drink only a little—how can they make it on $134 a month? By the last half of the month, our soupline has grown longer and longer. And some have been evicted."

Although the Drop-Inn has not kept statistics on the reasons for seeking shelter there, according to Bill the staff knows clients well enough to say that almost all have been displaced—whether through fires, condo conversions, eviction by their own families, or inability to pay rent.

The center opens its TV room at four o'clock, its dining room at six-thirty. Its goal for the future is to be open twenty-four hours a day.

As part of its educational program, the center shows films on alcoholism and tries to involve clients in counseling. A dozen chronic drinkers who can demonstrate progress toward sobriety participate in the live-in program. Although it is not as rigid as the Salvation Army or Volunteers of America programs, there are some rules. One must attend Alcoholics Anonymous or a similar program, help out with work at the center, consent to stay on the premises for the first thirty days, and set progress goals. "The difference between us and the Army or volunteers is that there they make the guys fit into work *they* want performed, and conform to *their* ideas of rehabilitation," says Bill. "Here we do a lot of counseling and work out a different program for each person.

"But it's frustrating for us not to be able to feel part of a strong coordinated network of services for alcoholics and narcotics abusers. In spite of the increased *need,* since 1980 in Cincinnati the number of beds in detox centers has been reduced from fifty to fifteen, and the number of halfway houses from five to just three. It's even more frustrating not to be able to do much about the causes that lie in society. What the public still doesn't understand well enough is that there's a close relationship between job insecurity on the one hand, and domestic violence and alcoholism on the other."

In contrast to the highly structured approach of some professionals, Drop-Inn staff make themselves available for on-the-spot counseling. For example, a man in the soupline says he used to have a drinking problem, but now just drinks a few beers a day. "That could be a few too many," says Bill. "I used to tell myself things like that, too." The two chat awhile, and agree to talk again the next day.

The Drop-Inn opened its first shelter in 1973: one small room on Vine Street. For over two years, however, Buddy Gray, one of the center's founders, had been housing urban nomads in his own Over-the-Rhine apartment. Buddy is still the guiding spirit of the center. Some would use different language. He has been called, among other things, a poverty pimp and a Black Panther. (Buddy is white.) His presentation of self makes him vulnerable to such attacks. With his wire-rimmed glasses, beard, hair drawn back into a ponytail at least a foot long, and blue farmer's overalls, a uniform he wears even to court, Buddy looks like a throwback to the sixties. Yet he is always neat and polite, and his boyish smile can disarm even some of his critics. Buddy has no training as a social worker or community organizer. He has never even been to college. How did he become involved in the struggle to help drop-outs drop in at the center?

Our first meeting with Buddy took place on the stoop of an old building that Drop-Inn residents were rehabbing. As he talked, people on the street waved and called out, "Hey, Buddy!" We remarked that he seemed to know everyone.

"This is my neighborhood. It's a real good place to be if you're with the people here," he said, his eyes moving quickly up and down the street. "Two of those guys you see there have graduated from the Drop-Inn. I'm not sure they're really sober, but they've made progress. Lots of the other people are neighbors.

"But you were asking how I got involved. My grandfather, to whom I was very close, died a street alcoholic after losing his farm. Then even in high school back in the mid-1960s, I was concerned about the Vietnam War and the rioting of blacks in Cincinnati. This woke me up to the injustices of the inner city.

"My family was working class. I probably could have worked my way through college, but I was more interested in doing something active. After saving money from a summer gas station job, I moved from a rural area east of Cincinnati to Over-the-Rhine. My free time I spent volunteering at a church, where I saw hungry, homeless, lonely people in need of material and emotional support. So I volunteered for the tutoring program at the church.

"Of course, I got into other activities, like finding clothing for these folks, even sleeping them in the church basement without permission. That made the elders uptight. They didn't want smelly, raggedy, unshaven, poor people sleeping in a *church*. That was sacrilege! So they let me go. I went over to another church, but the same story happened all over again.

"So I began putting people up in my own place. Homeless people who were victims of street violence or were freezing in empty buildings. They'd call up from the street: 'Hey, Buddy!' and I'd go down. Some guys were so drunk, or just exhausted, that I'd carry them up the four flights on my back. Sometimes eight, ten, twelve men would be spread out on the floor of one room."

He paused, and waved to a little black girl who was looking at us hesitantly. "You can come up, Yolanda." Gently, he put her on his knees. Without saying a word, she put an arm around his waist, and settled into his lap. For the next hour she sat there in contented silence, occasionally tugging at Buddy's ponytail.

"I also became increasingly aware of housing issues," he went on. "I got to know the people involved in rent strikes. I began to see how slum landlords like the Denharts were exploiting both the tenants and the taxpayers. Over the years I've seen the Denharts involved in racket after racket. Even when they were taken to trial, what happened? They were found guilty of defrauding the government of $875,000—and got a $25,000 fine! When two children died in a fire because the Denharts had heavy steel screens bolted over windows, which prevented the children from getting out, they got a *suspended* sentence! Plus they had to give $5,000 to the community. These men are white-collar criminals.

"Over five thousand people were uprooted during Project Rehab. I helped some of those folks move. In the early years, the city gave them hardly any relocation funds. I realized what displacement can do to people's lives."

By 1973 Buddy began to see that running a little pad for homeless people could not get very far. He had discussions with Rev. Joel Hempel, who wanted to set up a permanent shelter. Joel organized a meeting with concerned people, including Bates Ford, a black community activist who had been involved in similar efforts in Boston and later became the first paid staff person. The group obtained a grant from SWORCA and, later, one from the Franciscans of the Over-the-Rhine Mission.

In 1974 the center moved from its one-room quarters on Vine Street to a five-room building on Main Street and gradually became the center of controversy. The owner of the building, "Slumlord Leslie Fox," tried to evict the group because publicity had begun to spread about the bad building conditions. The Health Department also threatened eviction, claiming that the building was unfit for serving food and sheltering people, despite the fact that it had already granted the center a food-operating license. "What was happening," says Buddy, "is that the center was being fingered by the Health Department head, Arnold Leff, to be taken over by the city. The center refused and was then attacked."

To compound all these problems, a split developed between the community people and volunteers on the one hand and the professional staff on the other. "These professionals wanted a nine-to-five therapeutic program, five days a week—in total opposition to what the community saw as a priority," says Buddy. "We wanted a seven-night-a-week program that could keep our people *alive*. About forty Over-the-Rhine residents and volunteers from other social agencies organized a committee of volunteers to run the center on weekends. When they took a list of all their needs to the board, the director and the professional staff protested and eventually resigned. They said shelter and rehabilitation couldn't work together, and community involvement threatened their control of the center. Eventually, Over-the-Rhine folks took control, and we got what we wanted—a community-based program that runs all week and has a staff that suits our needs—one that's racially balanced, has half men and half women, and uses recovering alcoholics.

"As for the Health Department, we *inherited* the problems of that Main Street building! We put hundreds of hours into upgrading that leaky, rat-infested place. But the department attacked *us* rather than Fox! We saw we could *never* pass inspection. Why? Because those officials had a hang-up that people from the community, without degrees behind their names, couldn't run such a program.

"We weren't magicians who could mysteriously get money and materials to meet all health and building code standards. The Health Department was ordering us to buy a new freezer, get a new building with fifty square feet per person, give complete medical exams to all residents, and get workers with college degrees. There were five hundred food operating places downtown and only three inspectors. Yet the Drop-Inn got eight inspections in two months. We failed all of them, even though we complied with every original order. Each time they found new violations. And they insulted us. Like the administrator with the air-conditioned office who accused one of us hard-working people, somebody working in the kitchen in 110-degree heat, of having body odor."

The conflict with the city was beginning to awaken many citizens to the situation, however. Television, radio, and newspapers gave the center good coverage. Community residents, doctors, workers, students, even small children and senior citizens stopped by with clothes, small money donations, or offers to volunteer their time. Paul Sullivan, who was director of Pine Street Inn, a shelter in Boston, flew in to speak at city hall about the importance of the Drop-Inn. Seven of the nine City Council members visited the center and expressed concern. The wind seemed to be shifting a little.

The Drop-Inn staff finally discovered a new location, the former Teamsters Union Hall, and the Building Department helped develop an estimate of $80,000 to bring the building up to code standards. In the five years of the center's existence, it had received no funds from the city. Since the new shelter was larger, the center staff asked the city to match the 1977 state health grant of $80,000 with $80,000 for the operating fund, and also approve $80,000 from CDGB funds for needed building improvements. On January 5, 1978 the City Council voted 5–4 to award $25,000 to the center. The staff knew, however, that they had enemies at city hall and in the business community who opposed the project.

"Eight days later, on the night of Friday the 13th, we moved to our new home without telling the city," recalls Buddy. "It was the night of the city's worst blizzard. We got volunteers from all over the city to help us. It was a people's move! We moved secretly because city officials and social elites had declared their opposition to our relocating there. They wanted us to move to another site far from Over-the-Rhine.

"The move infuriated the city. We could see that the struggle was not over—instead, a new phase had begun. Exactly one week after our move, the city fire and building departments tried to set our residents out on the street—in zero weather, fourteen inches of snow! They called the place an extreme safety hazard. If they were so concerned with the residents' safety, how could they put people out on the street? When they arrived at four in the afternoon, we called the media. Of course they came, ready to take pictures of those guys sticking our folks outside. A special emergency hearing was held at ten that night, and Judge Outcault ruled that despite fire and health code violations, the city was in the wrong. 'I just don't think you can put these men out in the cold,' he said. Five days later City Council reneged on its promise of $25,000—money we'd counted on for rent, gas, and electricity. On February 10 the building department changed the center's classification to hospital. They were really bent on making requirements impossible. They also ordered immediate repairs, but denied a building permit for the repairs until the hosptial classification was re-evaluated."

During all this time there were numerous inspections, emergency service provided by the police was stopped, and the City Council denied further funds—this time a CDBG grant already approved by the Community Development Advisory Council. On three separate occasions the fire department insisted on a drill in the middle of the night. Drop-Inn resident George Dunson says: "I can remember one of the coldest nights of the winter. I was in the shower about 3:00 A.M., when the fire inspector showed up. I and everyone else was told not too kindly to get out and go across the street. I managed to grab something to wrap up in. It wasn't too warm in subzero weather, but it helped some. We got out under our allotted time, handicapped, alcoholic people, and all."

"We were going to stay, no matter what," says Buddy. "The media were very supportive, television especially. They followed every move. We also mustered a good crowd at a music rally in March. And the unions helped pull us through. Many of them donated material and hundreds of hours. In May Cincinnati's major unions came to a mass meeting and publicly backed the Drop-Inn. A month earlier religious and professional leaders, who'd been paying rent and utility money when the city cut off its funds, confronted City Manager Donaldson, asking him to stop attacking the Drop-Inn. He listened.

"The more the city attacked us, the more public support grew. All this finally forced a change in the city's stance. In May 1978 we won an appeal for classification as a transient home. The council approved a Community Development grant of $15,000."

However, as the staff had begun to suspect, this change did not signal a real reversal in policy. The hidden agenda of the city had become apparent, especially after community people had smuggled out of city hall a secret document known as the Washington Park Master Plan revealing designs for gentrification of the area. The new shelterhouse was in the middle of a redevelopment project. According to Buddy, "Luxury high-rise apartments were planned despite historic strong Over-the-Rhine opposition. Instead of revealing their real intentions, the city was attempting to force the program out of existence on the pretext that the building was not suitable for the shelterhouse residents."

During the next few months the center submitted plans to meet the building department's requirements. It refused to approve the plans and issue a permit for repairs but at the same time threatened criminal charges for the failure to make urgently needed repairs. When the permit was finally granted in September 1978, it was accompanied by a deadline (1 February 1979) that center workers termed "*highly unusual* because it was obviously impossible to complete the work demanded in that time span." The city also threatened to arrest center leaders for violation of public safety if the deadline was not met.

Drop-Inn residents, staff, and volunteers dug in to meet the February 1 deadline. Six new exits and three major fire-wall partitions were built, a fire-alarm system was installed, and more improvements were made in the kitchen. Public support for the center also was growing. The building department extended its permit for sixty days.

The victory had broad implications. To Mike Maloney, director of the Urban Appalachian Council, "The struggle exposed the way politicians and bureaucrats get together to talk over problems developed by neighborhood groups."

In December 1979, a new city manager, Sy Murray, a black, visited the Drop-Inn. On March 5, 1980, he made a public statement: "I want to set the tone that the city government is not anti-Drop-Inn. . . . If not for you, the problem would fall on the city."

"Still, our enemies hadn't given up," says Buddy. "It's interesting to ask who the people who opposed us were. There was Mrs. Bobbie Sterne on the City Council, who would not support the funding for the Drop-Inn being situated on 12th Street. There was Arnold Leff, chief of the Health Department, who just happened to be Bobbie Sterne's son-in-law. He tried to make a deal with social service agencies that they take over the work of the center, in exchange for a doubled budget for operating funds and a new building. That backfired, because David Whitaker, the director of SWORCA, went on TV to expose the deal and to support the Drop-Inn. That gave us a boost! Who else was in the opposition? There was Nell Surber, head of Urban Development, or what *we* call Black Removal, which just happened to be the federal agency that gave tax credits to big businessmen for things like air-conditioned skywalks downtown. She opposed funding because 'derelicts'—her word for homeless alcoholics—would ruin the Music Hall area. And James Luken of City Council, who claimed that Cincinnati already had too many black and poor people, too many services. According to him, if the Drop-Inn were supported, it would attract homeless people from all over the country to come to Cincinnati. And then there was Irma Lazarus, the rich socialite and great patroness of the arts, who just happens to be the wife of Fred Lazarus, Chairman of the Board of Federated Department Stores and was dead-set against having the Drop-Inn near Music Hall.

"Fred Lazarus just happened to be president of Queen City Housing Corporation, which was begun by the Cincinnati Business Committee," says Buddy. "Queen City set up Heritage Preservation, which was involved in low-income housing. Of course, Fred Lazarus was on its board. So was James Winberg, president of Eagle Savings, which funded Neighborhood Housing Services. It was also funded by Community Development. Winberg, coincidentally, was president of the Neighborhood Housing Services Board. Carl Westmoreland was director. And who was Carl? President of Mount Auburn Good Housing Foundation, which managed Neighborhood Housing Services and also Heritage Preservation. Fred Lazarus paid Carl's salary to be director of Heritage Preservation. Carl also managed other apartments for Community Development-funded housing corporations. During our struggle in the early 1980s the CDBG board was chaired by Joan Hammond, a prominent socialite, and a promoter of Queen City/Heritage Preservation/Neighborhood Housing Services. And Lazarus was on that, too."

Linking the Homelessness and Housing Issues

It did not take long to see that opposition to the shelter from all these forces was part of a larger threat to low-income housing in the entire Over-the-Rhine area, says Bill. "We've always been close to community groups here," he points out. "Their support for the Drop-Inn showed it was a community that was taking care of its own sick and troubled people. Now we're working with community organizations more than ever. Like Over-the-Rhine Community Council, which brings together tenant associations, area clubs, churches, and interested individuals from the neighborhood. The city promised to involve the council in deciding how CDGB funds should be spent for housing in Over-the-Rhine. Our community's request for $500,000 to develop housing was denied because they said our proposal was not specific enough. But the housing department's plans get approved without any specific work done on them at all—at least, not to show the community when we question them. We've demanded that CDBG funds be used for *low-income* housing, excluding middle and upper.

"In August 1981 the city's promise to involve us in decisions was flagrantly violated when it awarded funds to Heritage Preservation. Westmoreland said his primary focus was on low-income housing, but admitted that 'eventually' he'd do middle- and upper-income units here. We knew his real interest was gentrification—his ties with the powers that be proved that. Well, it's interesting that in 1983 Westmoreland was dumped by Heritage Preservation because he had too many problems with our community and too many financial deals under public investigation."

Tom Blackburn, long a fellow staff-member at the Drop-Inn, points out that in the last few years the demolition of cheap housing and hotels around the south part of Over-the-Rhine has left more and more people homeless. "Like the YMCA deciding to close the top floors of its residential facility, and make the bottom floors into recreational space for downtown businessmen. It got to be known as the Young Men's Racketball Association. Approximately three hundred men, most of them elderly, were forced out. Some had lived there on Social Security or disability for ten or twenty years. A number found alternate housing at higher rents. Some wandered off alone—where? Some came to us. A few went to pieces, from the shock of it all, and died soon after the move."

Many Over-the-Rhine residents were angry over the Y's closing. Denise Crew, vice-chair of Washington Park Block Club, wrote to *Voices,* the community newspaper: "I will say to all the Y board members, to all the Lazaruses, to all the Westmorelands: . . . I personally commit myself to help put your ravaging of this neighborhood to an end. . . ."[24]

Buddy speaks bitterly of Andy Wolf, a symphony orchestra musician who bought property on the edge of Washington Park, next door to Music Hall, in order to transform the building into a fine restaurant he called Bacchus. Says Buddy: "The Gospel Mission, which takes in homeless people and is situated just a few doors away, had also put in a proposal for the building, because it wanted to open a shelter for families. Guess who got it. And *how* did he get it? There was supposed to be no rehabilitation or demolition without public review. City officials didn't seem to know how Wolf's permit transpired."

At the same time Over-the-Rhine residents witnessed the arrival of an office project that would completely replace low-income housing. The project was sponsored by Kathy Laker and Phil Adelman, who had become two of the most-hated developers in Over-the-Rhine for transforming nearby Liberty Hill from what *Voices* called a "low-income white and black rental area" to "an upper-income-professional-urban-pioneer-fancy-renovated homes area." Laker and Adelman are leading characters in *We Will Not Be Moved,* a vivid slide–tape documentary on displacement, which has been shown in many cities around the country.

Despite these setbacks, Over-the-Rhine residents were scoring significant victories. In June 1980 an organization known as People Against Displacement (PAD), together with Legal Aid, succeeded in pushing through an Anti-Displacement Ordinance. The new law attempted to minimize displacement by making it unlawful to discriminate against people with rent subsidies, gave the right of first purchase and first return to tenants, and allocated relocation benefits up to $2,500 to persons directly displaced by city-assisted development.

A month later, a new measure was passed, providing that indirect displacement in four areas of the city (including two in Over-the-Rhine) would bring the same relocation benefits as displacement that is the result of city assistance.

These victories were due in large part to the militant efforts of the Over-the-Rhine Community Council. Says Buddy, for many years a guiding force on the council: "Among other things, we're fighting displacement and bulldozing, demanding that all development receive approval of the Community Council, and trying to force the city to make a commitment to provide new and rehabilitated apartments to meet the needs of people. We'll fight actions to generate an income mix of population in rehabilitated housing until there's assurance that 5,520 units— the present number of all occupied units—be reserved for low-income folks."

"In time, the Community Council forged a coalition with two delegates on the Planning Task Force who were social professionals, as well as some key business delegates," recalls Buddy. "We finally won a new Neighborhood Housing Retention Ordinance, which puts permanent controls on housing demolition. It requires a public hearing on all such requests. If the landlord wants to tear it down, he must first delay one year, and in good faith seek government aid to remodel the building for low-income people.

"As for the Drop-Inn, now we own the place. They can't force us out—except by asserting right of eminent domain. And that *could* happen."

Indeed, by 1982 Over-the-Rhine residents' struggle to stay put had already reached a new phase. In the late 1970s the Cincinnati Business Committee conceived the idea that the area be declared a historic district. Developers gave enthusiastic support to the idea, for it meant they could deduct 25 percent of their rehabilitation costs from taxes and could also depreciate the bulk of their redevelopment expenses from taxes for the next fifteen years.

One of the most articulate supporters of the historic preservation proposal was Jim Tarbell, owner of two popular restaurants and spokesperson for the Over-the-Rhine Property Owners Association. Although he and Buddy Gray have cast epithets upon each other for years, they have certain qualities in common: a genial but earthy manner, a beatnik-of-the-sixties appearance (Tarbell's beard was longer and bushier till he shaved his head completely), and almost overpowering self-assurance. Their philosophies are different. Tarbell, who owns several properties in Over-the-Rhine, is against "too much" government intervention, yet welcomes subsidies such as those for historic preservation. He is a proponent of mixing various income groups in an area, claiming that a low-income ghetto will never survive. To Buddy, this apparently democratic philosophy is a sham. "If he's so interested in helping low-income people, why does he buy up just the good-looking apartments, the ones with Victorian trim? As for mixing, we know what's happened in other cities when rich people come to live in revitalized areas. Rents and taxes go up, and the poor get displaced."

People Against Displacement and the Over-the-Rhine Community Council organized a racially integrated coalition of nearly one hundred neighborhood residents, religious leaders, local business persons, and social service professionals. On 3 December 1982 they journeyed to Columbus for the hearing of the Ohio Historic Site Preservation Advisory Board. Armed with more than one hundred twenty notarized statements from Over-the-Rhine land owners, a petition signed by some fifteen hundred community residents, a statement signed by more than forty Catholic clergy, and statements of support from union representatives, five of the nine City Council members, and three state legislators, the coalition argued its case passionately. Only developers, not present homeowners, would be able to receive the tax credits, it pointed out; the prestigious historic label fanned speculation, and the designation did nothing to control demolition or to promote low-income housing. The advisory board voted eight to seven to reject the historic nomination.

A few months later, the coalition's jubilation turned to bitterness. The State Director of Historic Preservation, who had superior power to question the board's decision (a power never attached to the post before the Reagan administration), sent the proposal on to his superiors at the Department of the Interior in Washington. This time the state board's majority vote was overturned; the superiors won.

Despite their bitterness, coalition members turned their efforts to pressing the city to amend the Anti-Displacement Ordinance with a provision that if displacement occurs because of historic designation, any benefits that apply to the revitalization district shall apply to the whole neighborhood. In a separate campaign, the Over-the-Rhine Task Force continued fighting for a commitment from the city that at least 5,520, housing units be retained for low-income occupants in the community.

Existing units, and those destroyed or rehabilitated to make way for upper-income housing, would have to be replaced on a one-for-one basis.

In 1984, in a surprise move in the ongoing battle between low-income housing advocates and the city, the latter offered to convert a health center in the West End (adjacent to the Over-the-Rhine but farther from Downtown Cincinnati) into a thirty-five bed facility for emergency shelter and longer-term housing. The project would have cost $350,000. "We were furious," says Buddy. "What they really wanted was an excuse to close down the Drop-Inn. By that time, we had our Greater Cincinnati Coalition going. We said, 'Does it make sense to spend that sum on a new shelter of thirty-five beds when the Drop-Inn sleeps 170 people a night, and we still don't even have enough bathroom facilities?' Two hundred and fifty homeless people and concerned citizens staged a peaceful demonstration at city hall, demanding that the city give that sum to upgrade shelters that already existed. Well, the city backed down, and offered to split $100,000 of CDBG money among eight shelters for capital improvements. That's a real victory."

Today the Drop-Inn Center, the Greater Cincinnati Coalition for the Homeless, the Over-the-Rhine Community Council, and other community groups are girding themselves for a prolonged struggle to preserve Over-the-Rhine as a neighborhood for low-income people. Keeping the Drop-Inn has become a symbol of resistance. "The Drop-Inn has come up before the City Council at least fifty times already," says Buddy. "We're sitting in a prime area. We have no illusions. But they have a fight on their hands."

A Grassroots Network

Whereas the Drop-Inn is a haven for those already homeless, many other groups in Over-the-Rhine are working to prevent conditions that contribute directly or indirectly to homelessness. Although there has been considerable tension among some of the groups over the years, the one issue that can unite them in times of crisis is preservation of low-income housing.

The Contact Center, a grassroots organization of Over-the-Rhine residents, has focused a great deal of effort on fighting exploitative landlords, building tenant councils, and combating displacement. It also has sponsored a low-cost clothing store, a food-buying club, a cooperative garden, and a sewing club; sent delegations to public hearings and City Council meetings; won a class action suit forcing HUD to cease selling vacant subsidized housing to profit-oriented developers and upper-income buyers; crusaded for jobs for residents of the community; and organized People Against Displacement. The best part of all this, according to its staff, is that poor people became empowered to do things for themselves.

One of these indigenous leaders is Thelma Stone, an energetic black woman in her sixties who began working at the age of nine chopping cotton in Alabama, and for decades worked as a domestic in Cincinnati. In the late 1970s she became active in tenant councils and then became a leading spokesperson for People Against

Displacement. "The Contact Center gave us direction," she says. "Here we can get help, but we have to do it ourselves.

"I feel especially good about People Against Displacement. Our slide show, *We Will Not Be Moved*, is a real tool for organizing. Some of us have traveled around the country with the Center for Community Change in Washington to give inspiration to other grassroots organizations working on housing and employment issues. We monitor the Anti-Displacement Ordinance to be sure it's enforced. The media cover our activities. And we use leaflets, posters, buttons, and word-of-mouth inside the neighborhood. We're going to go on fighting. We're *not* going to let historic preservationists preserve us out of the neighborhood!"

In 1985 the center lost most of its funding. Nevertheless, because of the determination of people like Thelma, local volunteers have managed to keep the project going a few hours every day.

Legal Aid, too, has been a forceful advocate for low-income housing. One of its principal attorneys, Mary Asbury, was a prime catalyst in the big steps that were taken in 1984 on the homelessness issue; in January of that year she sent a letter to City Manager Sy Murray stressing that this was a problem with which the city ought to be dealing. Legal Aid was co-sponsor, with People Against Displacement, of the Anti-Displacement Ordinance. In 1984 and 1985, when the Garfield Place area was being redeveloped as a new downtown residential community that would include some office space, many SROs were slated to disappear. City officials admitted that poor singles would be moved out as affluent singles moved in; the new community would be a nest for empty nesters. SRO residents were not covered by the Anti-Displacement Ordinance at that time, and before the city had formed any plan for displacees, many were already wandering the streets.

Legal Aid then sponsored a resolution to minimize displacement in Garfield Place and the rest of the Central Business District, which passed City Council. As a result, funds have been made available to renovate two hundred units in the YMCA, develop more Section 202 housing in the future, provide low-interest loans to maintain and improve existing housing, and extend the relocation benefits available to areas covered by the Anti-Displacement Ordinance to the Central Business District. Legal Aid also has been fighting for a tougher Neighborhood Retention Ordinance, which would make it harder for a developer to get a demolition permit and provide for one-for-one replacement of demolished units in most situations in Over-the-Rhine. The group has also supported the Over-the-Rhine Community Council in its successful fight for a guarantee of 5,520 low-income units as part of the Over-the-Rhine urban renewal plan.

In the Over-the-Rhine Neighborhood Strategy proposed by the city, Legal Aid is supporting the push for $2 million from the city and federal governments for developing an integrated set of housing and commercial development programs. That sum is far greater than any previously spent on the neighborhood.

The Urban Appalachian Council includes housing as one of its prime concerns. The Over-the-Rhine Community Council sponsors a housing referral office and has a Housing Task Force that works to defend and expand low-income housing. The Prince of Peace Lutheran Church runs an active social service program and co-sponsors work retreats to rehabilitate neighborhood housing.

The Office of Social Action and World Peace of the Catholic Archdiocese of Cincinnati has taken a special interest in housing as a social justice issue. Archbishop Bernardin put the archdiocese on record as supporting Anti-Displacement. In addition, three Catholic parishes provided signature guarantees for collateral for the Drop-Inn Center, and the archdiocese contributed funds for rehabbing.

Sign of the Cross is an ecumenical ministry and construction management firm that acquires, renovates, and leases or rents property to lower- income people with the goal of building community and assisting residents eventually to purchase the houses in which they live. Asbury Management (sponsored by the Wesley Chapel United Methodist Church) and St. John's Social Service Center (run by the Franciscan Sisters of the Poor) are nonprofits that operate on similar principles. O-T-R, Inc. (which actually stands for Owning the Realty) is the housing arm of the Over-the-Rhine Community Council. Like the last three groups, it uses not only donations but CDBG and city funds in its efforts to build low-income units. ReStoc, a nonprofit project of the Drop-Inn Center, buys up old buildings, and citywide volunteers, together with live-in Drop-Inn residents, rehabilitate the units. The project renovates not only buildings, but lives, for residents who make it through the program and go on the wagon are offered the opportunity to live independently in one of these low-rent apartments and work for pay in rehabilitating others. Most of the apartments in these cooperative groups rent for about $100 a month, plus utilities—$40 or $50 less than similar apartments owned by private landlords.

As Archie Bruun, director of the Social Justice and World Peace Program puts it, "Housing decisions are usually political decisions. But self-help projects are one way of saying that low-income people can have some control."

All these groups form an informal network. Is it a network that reflects a true sense of community? To Buddy Gray, Over-the-Rhine *is* a real community. "This is one place where blacks and whites work together. It's a neighborhood that cares for itself."

Don Thalheimer, who works at the Social Justice and World Peace Program of the Cincinnati archdiocese and lives in Over-the-Rhine, agrees. "Athough it's not true of other parts of Cincinnati, in Over-the-Rhine blacks and whites get along remarkably well—and certainly better than in any other neighborhood I've seen in this country. There's a sense of community that comes from the feeling of being outside the mainstream of American life where everything is more commercialized. There's bonding from feeling that we're fellow lost souls."

To Jane Jansak, it is the "eyes of the street" that make this a community. "In *The Death and Life of Great American Cities,* Jane Jacobs points out that for a neighborhood to be safe, there must be eyes belonging to those we might call the natural proprietors of the street," says Jansak. "You don't see many eyes appearing in the windows of high-rent buildings. The tenants who live there haven't the vaguest idea of who takes care of the street. Over-the-Rhine isn't like that. When you drive through, it looks like a decaying neighborhood. But when you've lived here, and worked here, you feel the eyes. You feel the people. Many planners think you can transform an area just by fixing up the buildings. That *is* a tool. But it's not enough. You have to make an investment not so much in housing as *people*. I see that happening here."

If you visit the Wednesday night community suppers of Jane's Prince of Peace Church, you understand better what she means. The church basement vibrates with lively commotion: children scamper across the floor, adults—black and white—get up to speak to their neighbors at the next table, the piano pounds, everyone seems to be talking and laughing at once. The noise level is high.

"What you see here is family," Jane shrieks above the din. "It's a place for people to bring their families. It's also church family. And for singles, young and old, it's substitute family. The kids have a great time. You can't tell whose child is whose, because everybody looks after them.

"Officially we have only sixty-five members, but hundreds attend our church suppers, which are always followed by a service and then a special program. As you can see from the way they're mixing, black and white relations are excellent. And we even have half a dozen seminarians—Catholic, Mennonite, Lutheran, both women and men—who work here, using the experience to get credit for Inner City Mission work. This place is a great human mix. All working together to make *communal* family."

Yet there are many who find divisiveness in Over-the-Rhine. Some say that this is a reflection of our modern society, a society that emphasizes separateness, rather than bonding. To Floy Ann Marsh of the Contact Center, "The politics here have been incredible. This neighborhood tends to live from crisis to crisis. That's the way poor people live."

Much of the divisiveness centers around the Over-the-Rhine Community Council, and the role of Buddy Gray there. Although he always denies it, many observers say that he—together with a couple of close friends—runs the show. During the struggle from 1978 to 1981 to keep the Drop-Inn open, Buddy became known, in the words of a *Cincinnati Magazine* writer, as a "feisty radical" for his "fiery appearances at city hall." Even people from various Over-the-Rhine groups have called him domineering and intolerant. Some say that he is frequently tactless, unreliable, hard to get hold of, and reluctant to share power.

His defenders say that he is typical of many community activists, that he follows the organizing style of Saul Alinsky. "Besides," says Floy Ann Marsh, "even though he can be rude, you *can* tell him that, and next time he'll come on more easy. Buddy has mellowed."

"The most important thing", says Jane Jansak, "is that Buddy is incorruptible. Other activists have been bought off, or co-opted by the Establishment. But Buddy's not for sale. And he has a talent for getting people involved."

You can sense that talent of Buddy's and glimpse some of the community spirit in Over-the-Rhine, if you sit in the storefront of *Voices*, the irreverent neighborhood newspaper that speaks out on local issues, minority rights, and third-world struggles. The storefront is primitive by prevalent standards: the furniture is battered, the floor is bare, and the only heat comes from a woodstove. Although the place is known as the office of *Voices*, it is a multipurpose meeting place for many neighborhood groups.

On the wall an enormous poster depicts the progress of a campaign of the Over-the-Rhine Community Council to transform the abandoned Peaslee School into a community center.

At a long table, volunteers are working on mailings for that project. Five volunteers—three black men and two white men—are from Drop-Inn. Two women from the neighborhood are packing circulars. Joe Bean, the octogenarian "live-in" who works at the Drop-Inn, comes in with a message and pauses to chat with each one at the table. Bonnie, the dark, curly-haired young woman who seems to be in charge, offers you coffee. As you chat, you learn that this is her real work. Her bread work is doing spot typing. "Of course I can get along on that." She looks surprised at the question. "I live simply." What has made her choose such a life? She shrugs, "Well, it just makes me feel good to do what I can for this neighborhood."

Buddy Gray comes in from the back room. With a quick light step he moves from one volunteer to another. "Good work!" or "Looks fine!" he says, putting his hand on their shoulders. "You guys did a great job with voter registration. You'll make this a success, too."

Buddy has perceived that housing and homelessness are interrelated; he has fused the two issues in his own life and work.

Planning for the Future

A walk through Over-the-Rhine reveals the need for housing. On Vine Street, the main thoroughfare, dreary-looking apartments are perched above stores. Most of the latter seem to be pawn shops, fast-food joints, or second-hand clothing stores, all interspersed between bars and storefront pentecostal churches promising a better life in the next world. On the side streets children play in littered alleys, unemployed youths pass the bottle in vacant lots strewn with rubbish, and older men tinker with broken-down cars. Many buildings are gutted out or otherwise abandoned. Some are so rat infested, deteriorated, and hazardous that they are past rehabilitation. A decade ago, most were salvageable. Today they are a monument to the reluctance of an individualistic, profit-oriented society to plan for the future. At this point, there is no alternative to demolition and new units. In these cases, displacement is not the real issue. The real need is for new affordable housing.

On Fifteenth Street we talked with a black woman in an apartment building that reportedly was being purchased by Kroger's, the giant supermarket chain. As

Bertha stood in the dimly lit hallway, perspiring as she tightened the sarong-type wrap around her heavy body, she seemed to emanate weary resignation. No, the tenants here had received no notice. No, she didn't know how true the rumors were. Some said the building would be demolished for a superstore, some said it would be a warehouse, and others had heard it would be a parking lot. All she could do was wait and see. The place where she was living was a dump, but the thought of moving was "hanging real heavy" on her mind. "Where can I go? You just get settled somewhere, and they tell you, 'Leave!' "

She was used to displacement. Once, while living in a Denhart apartment, she lost her job and unemployment compensation was delayed. Denhart evicted her. Once she and her husband quarreled and he beat her, then kicked her out. She took refuge in the Salvation Army shelter. "They was real nice to me there. But no, I couldn't stay. Anyway, you're not supposed to lean on people just because they want to help you." Another time, she withheld rent because the landlord cut her water; he retaliated by evicting her and her three sons. The marshal who evicted the family told her, too late, that the building was about to be abandoned anyway. First she lived with her daughter, but the latter could not keep her because the apartment was tiny and she had two young sons of her own. Then she went to her mother, who welcomed Bertha, but had to squeeze her family into one room because Bertha's brother, his wife, and a child were sleeping in the other bedroom. Bertha soon left.

"I works," she said proudly. "At a laundry. It's hot, heavy work. But I tell myself, the steam is good for my arthritis. Had that job since I was fifteen. And I'm not on welfare. I could pay up to $225 a month. But the projects is full, and they don't offer you no privacy, anyway. I ought to find a subsidized housing, but their list is too long, too, and landlords, they don't like families. What's going to happen to us?"

If Bertha is forced to leave, will she and her children join the ranks of the homeless? Families like Bertha's would have the good fortune to be covered by benefits under the Anti-Displacement Ordinance, even if the move is not city-assisted, because they happen to live in a district targeted by the city for redevelopment. However, the benefits would amount only to moving expenses, the first month's rent, and the deposit. It would not assure them of finding decent affordable housing.

As she observed, the waiting lists for subsidized and other assisted housing are long. In 1986, for example, CMHA was working on its 1983 list for public housing.

The queue for apartments through cooperative neighborhood corporations is also long. The one hundred fifty or so units currently available hardly answer the need.

Assessing Progress

By 1986 it was clear that Cincinnati had made remarkable advances in creating services for people already homeless. In 1980 the problem was barely recognized, and in just six years the number of services had nearly doubled (from eight to fifteen, if one counts the two Tender Mercies houses, which provide permanent accommodation). In addition, Clermont County, which is part of the Greater Cincinnati area and had no shelters in 1980, had created a multipurpose shelter and a refuge for battered women. At the same time, a wider spectrum of other services had developed to assist people—especially women and families—whose needs had been largely overlooked a few years before.

The Drop-Inn Center had acquired new bathrooms, a dumbwaiter, and the services of a regular volunteer doctor as well as several nurses. More important, it was operating with the assistance of more regular government grants, and, as staff member Tom Blackburn observed, a tacit, though sometimes broken, truce seemed to have evolved between the Drop-Inn and the city. Many political and business leaders had come to tolerate the presence of the shelter in its prime location. Indeed, Irma Lazarus had accepted an invitation from Buddy Gray to visit the Drop-Inn, and according to Buddy, had been favorably impressed.

In the past the Community Chest devoted a large portion of its resources to middle-class beneficiaries such as the Boy Scouts. Today it is giving much more to survival services, including the Free Store. At the Free Store, too, the Community Chest is funding two social workers who act as payees for mentally disabled persons on SSI.

The Emergency Services Coalition (a committee sponsored by the Community Chest) has also shifted its focus. Only a few years ago it emphasized the role of the voluntary sector. Now that FEMA money is available, and is funneled to the Community Chest for distribution among service providers, the coalition's major emphasis has become how to spend that sum.

The city has made significant changes in allocating its general revenues. In the past it never used such revenues for shelters (except in the case of the Alice Paul battered women's shelter). Now 1.3 percent of that fund is awarded to the city's Department of Human Services (distinct from the county department of the same name), and the department's allocation for operating expenses of shelters has been increasing each year. (In 1986 it was $150,000.) Such monies are important because CDBG grants pay only for renovation, not running the shelters. At the same time larger portions of CDBG funds coming from HUD have been steered by the city to shelters for the homeless. (In 1986, they amounted to $200,000). A great deal of this progress is due to the persistence of the Greater Cincinnati Coalition for the Homeless. Although its membership largely consists of voluntary groups, it has pressed for public funding, especially the use of CDBG monies. The coalition also has taken a leadership role in deciding how such funding should be shared. Co-chair Barbara Poppe describes the unusual way the FEMA grant was apportioned. "Usually service providers compete for fixed sums and some outside committee makes decisions. With us, the service providers in the Homeless Coalition each requested a certain amount, then sat down around a table, discussed each other's needs, and gradually pared down the requests till they all totaled the award sum. In this way the competitive spirit evaporated. We were all sensitive to the other groups' needs, and to the total situation we're trying to address. We amazed the Emergency Services Coalition. The same thing has happened with allocating CDBG funds."

Barry Schwartz, a city staff person who acts as liaison between the Human Services Department and service providers, confirms that the whole process has gone marvelously well. When decisions are made by providers themselves, through open discussion and with the aim of reaching consensus, resentments are minimal, he says.

State funds, too, had finally begun to emerge in 1986, after the Ohio legislature had passed a bill allocating $2.4 million dollars to private nonprofit agencies that provide shelter and emergency assistance to the homeless. Members of the Greater Cincinnati Coalition for the Homeless took an active role in promoting the legislation and influenced several state senators and representatives from the area to give it their crucial support.

Cincinnati, then, has made steady advances in expanding both its emergency and transitional services. It still has far to go in the more difficult task of preventing homelessness.

On the one hand, the city passed the Housing Retention Act and the Anti-Displacement Ordinance. However, these neither create nor rehabilitate units. Nor does the city always follow through to see that the laws are enforced. The resolution passed by the city (after the Garfield Place project drew bad publicity and considerable pressure from community groups) to preserve SRO housing does provide CDBG funds and low-interest loans for rehabilitation. One such undertaking is a grant of $250,000 (to be followed by another $250,000) in CDBG funds to a developer who would supplement that sum with private investment funds in order to convert the upper floors of the YMCA back to SRO units. A few of the older people displaced from SROs in the Garfield Place area had found housing in the YWCA, which had been purchased by a developer who had leased the two lower floors back to the YWCA for its own programs, and converted the upper floors into 100 units of Section 202 housing for the elderly. The five principal nonprofit housing groups in Over-the-Rhine expected to receive a total of $500,000 in CDBG funds. Another hopeful note was a CDBG start-up grant for a citywide redevelopment corporation, which would use a variety of public and private sources of funds, an idea suggested by Merrill Goozner several years ago.

On the other hand, almost all these projects depend on CDBG funds. That source can hardly solve the housing problem. For one thing, restrictions preclude the use of CDBG funds for rent subsidies. Nor can CDBG monies go into new construction, except in very unusual cases. Many units are beyond rehabilitation or need gut-rehabbing, which is generally more expensive than new construction. (For developers, it is not more expensive because they can get tax advantages from rehabbing in a historical area; for taxpayers it is more costly.)

Moreover, CDBG funds have been dwindling. In Cincinnati the program's overall budget was cut 20 percent from 1985 to 1986. In general, about half of the budget goes for a variety of programs such as economic development, recreation, public works, and administration. In the half devoted to housing, 80 percent has been going for low- and moderate-income units. Eugene Beaupré, acting director of the Department of Neighborhoods, says that, partly because of pressures from the Gramm-Rudman Act, outlays for low-income housing are bound to decline, both absolutely and proportionately, in the future. President Reagan would like to abolish CDBG entirely.

At the same time, Section 8 programs have been reduced or eliminated. To get Rental Rehabilitation assistance (another program) the landlord must match the maximum of $5,000 with $5,000 of his or her own. Most rental units need more than $10,000 worth of work. Only the Section 202 program for housing elderly and handicapped tenants (many of whom are middle-income people) has been constructing a few units.

As for public housing, federal funds steered to the CMHA for that purpose declined by 40 percent between 1981 and 1986. These monies have been used chiefly to maintain units rather than create new ones.

If one looks at the overall picture, for all types of federally assisted housing in the metropolitan Cincinnati area, only one-third of the people who are eligible manage to get it, says CMHA executive director John Nelson. Families are suffering the most.

How will the gap be met? Although the city government has used a generous portion of its CDBG funds for low-income housing, under present Ohio law the city cannot use its own general revenues; these go for operating expenses such as public works and fire and police protection. In any case, its general revenue pot shrinks in 1987 when federal revenue-sharing ceases.

The city can sell more abandoned houses to nonprofit neighborhood groups. It can use city funds for small capital grants to tenant groups that invest sweat equity in a project. It could sponsor a citywide low-income housing coalition made up of the Housing Authority, the city, program directors, developers, neighborhood nonprofit groups, concerned professionals, and most importantly, tenants. Possibly with some change in the state law the city could create an insurance fund for socially inclined capital that already has reduced rates of return (such as government-backed revenue bonds), thus building a permanent financing mechanism for low-cost capital. These proposals advanced by Goozner could at least make a dent in the problem.[25]

On the state level, a campaign might be launched to get Ohio to fund some low-income housing as a few other states have done.

Even if all these ideas were transformed into reality, they could hardly satisfy the need. The one point on which almost all Cincinnatians involved in housing seem to agree—bureaucrats and low-income advocates alike—is that there is no substitute for federal funding.

When the Cincinnati 2000 Plan was first formulated, it spoke of buildings, zones, spaces, greenery, security, parking facilities, lighting fixtures, industry, public art, cultural centers, and skywalks but almost nowhere of people. When people were mentioned, they were perceived as consumers. Nowhere was the possibility of dislocation discussed. Today, in response to demands from community groups, city ordinances have been passed that at least partly deal with displacement.

How much impact have such groups had? In almost any conversation over homelessness and low-income housing, city officials concede, almost always with a mixture of irritation and respect, that they have had to "modify" their plans because of "pressure" from organizations that have made "skillful use of the media."

Father Terry Meehan, who worked several years for the Community Land Trust in neighboring West End, observes that Over-the-Rhine groups are politically sophisticated; when they are aroused, City Council has to sit up and take notice. "Buddy, especially, has a knack for sensing when pressure is coming from the city or a developer—and then rallying people around the issue." Buddy, then, has become the symbol of the struggle; he is the watchdog for the underdog.

One reason for the successes scored by Over-the-Rhine groups is that they have slowly learned to get together. "For many years," says Father Terry, "there was a lot of turfing going on. But when there's a crisis, the community really unites. And they're all coming to see that the only way they can survive is to coordinate their planning by sharing power."

Clearly, Over-the-Rhine community groups have reached closer agreement on overall goals. They all are working for legislation to minimize displacement, for implementation on assurances of a reservoir of at least 5,520 units of low-income housing, for funds to bring these 5,520 units up to code, for zoning changes to protect Over-the-Rhine as a residential neighborhood, and for guarantees that its residents will have a strong role in all planning for their community.

Today these groups are talking less of displacement than of replacement. They are pushing for recognition of the principle that one low-income unit shall be built for each one demolished. One step toward this goal would be to follow the example of San Francisco, where low-income housing development groups sell certificates for the apartments they build to landlords who want an equal number of demolition rights. Already a Low-Income Housing Replacement Fund is being proposed, which would help accomplish this purpose.

Looking Toward the Year 2000

Little displacement resulting from gentrification has occurred in Over-the-Rhine through 1986, partly because of community actions and partly because of the high cost of building. It is bound to accelerate, however, especially if historic designation continues to offer attractive tax benefits to developers. At the same time, the Central Business District will be spilling more potentially homeless people into Over-the-Rhine; there will be greater competition for existing housing.

A city planning map of Over-the-Rhine reveals that by the year 2000 it will be a mixed neighborhood with areas for commercial establishments, light manufacturing, new shops, and what planners call housing for mixed-income levels. They claim that the major emphasis will be on low-income housing, but admit that home ownership (that is, private dwellings and condominiums) for moderate and upper-income levels will be encouraged.

Washington Park will be redeveloped and improved. Designated R-7, it will be mostly residential, but because of its many amenities, says Senior Planner Charlotte Birdsall, the park can include "certain kinds of restaurants and shops."

Over-the-Rhine people know what this means: the slow encroachment of gentry bringing a style of living that will escalate housing costs and change the character of the neighborhood. They are even more alarmed by the city's hope to zone an area that borders the park and stands between Central Parkway and Twelfth Street as 0-1 for "low-density office use." Since the Drop-Inn is located on Twelfth Street, the city could invoke the principle of eminent domain in order to oust the shelter from its crucial location. The little regiment of housing advocates is digging in for a long opposition struggle.

People in Over-the-Rhine have demonstrated a reluctant willingness to compromise by allowing moderate- and upper-income housing to be included in the Over-the-Rhine urban renewal plan, although they had originally hoped to keep their neighborhood for low-income people. However, the city's pledge to preserve 5,520 low-income units (which, in some way that developers have not clarified, are also supposed to cover the needs of the homeless) is the cause of anxiety. Residents of Over-the-Rhine fear that there will not be enough investment to implement that promise.

What will happen to the Drop-Inn Center? "I guess by now one would have to concede that it belongs to Over-the-Rhine," says Birdsall with a sigh. Still . . ." She hesitates. "If only it were not *that* near Music Hall!" Where would she like to locate it, then? "Well, it would be nice if they moved just a few blocks up, say, to Fifteenth Street. But Buddy has made it a *point of honor* to keep the Drop-Inn where it is." She sighs again.

No one denies that the heart of the vision for Over-the-Rhine is Washington Park. It is a lovely place, with tall trees, soft grass, a few gracefully converted old houses, and Victorian-style Music Hall, imposing as a *fin-de-siècle* queen surveying her subjects. The park could be lovelier still, say Cincinnati's future-designers. It could be like a large courtyard for condominiums, boutiques, and restaurants, many of them in late nineteenth-century German style. And all that is needed for this transformation to take place is that the town fathers cite their right of eminent domain.

Meanwhile, on warm evenings Music Hall patrons stroll in the park between acts. Homeless people from the Drop-Inn and other shelters sit on benches and stare at the promenaders. Most of the Music Hall people are afraid of the people they label "derelicts." But the urban exiles are more afraid of those who stroll past, their eyes averted. The two worlds never meet.

City-run shelter for homeless families at Roberto Clemente State Park, New York City.

Part III
The Causes

A U.S. Marshal and a bank mortgage company representative oversee a foreclosure eviction. *Inset:* One resident forced from his home.

5
Displacement and the Housing Crisis

On an icy January day, the lifeless bodies of Norman and Anna Peters, wrapped in ragged blankets against the cold, were found in the dilapidated twelve-year-old station wagon that had become their home. With no resources and no other shelter, they had died of carbon monoxide poisoning while running the engine to keep warm. Two months earlier they had been evicted from their badly weathered two-story Chicago home.

Mr. and Mrs. Peters are not typical of the majority of the people now living on the streets. Yet their story does typify some of the processes by which growing numbers of lower-middle-class persons lose their resources and eventually become displaced. Today many of them end up on the streets.

Like millions of other American families, the Peters's big dream had always been to own their own home. Mr. Peters, who had been employed for twenty-six years as a machine mover for trade shows, worked hard but found that jobs had become more rare in the past four years. The family's financial problems, however, began some fifteen years ago, at the time of the birth of the last of their five children. Born with serious defects, the infant underwent nine reconstructive operations, but died within his first year. The cost of the surgery led the Peters to bankruptcy; they could not even afford a gravestone. Financial difficulties persisted, and the Peters took out a second mortgage. A proud man who could not confide his troubles in his friends, Mr. Peters turned his despair inward and began to drink more heavily than ever before. When faced with the prospect of losing their home, Mrs. Peters, long opposed to liquor in the home, began drinking, too.

After the eviction, they lived with one son until the friction became too great. The couple received treatment in the alcoholic rehabilitation ward of a hospital and seemed to show considerable improvement. On checking out, they told the son with whom they had lived that they would stay with friends or in a motel. That was the last that any of the Peters children heard from their parents. A few days later a passerby noticed the couple in the station wagon. The rear of the car was loaded with bags of crumpled clothing, unemployment compensation records, and foreclosure papers from the home they had lost. Said one of the daughters, "I think everything culminated into an attitude by them that 'there is no way we can win—so why fight it?' "

n which the couple had about $20,000 equity, was sold at auction
being advertised by the Cook County Sheriff in an obscure
away free of charge. It was bought by a tax lawyer, who said that
ledge of owning the house and that it was probably purchased in
brother, a lawyer involved in real estate, "for corporate reasons."[1]

Homelessness: A Symptom of the Housing Crisis

Displacement is one of the most frequent precipitants of homelessness. Beneath
displacement, however, lies a much broader problem, the widespread scarcity of
low-income housing. Beneath that lies a social system more concerned with profits
than with the welfare of its citizens.

As noted in chapter 1, Hopper and Hamberg point out that the process of
becoming undomiciled can be divided into two phases: displacement and the inability to find replacement housing. If the displacee finds housing fairly easily,
prolonged homelessness does not result. Since the 1970s, however, displacement
has been growing as the stock of affordable replacement housing has declined.

Most often, the path from home to the streets is a two- or three-step process.
When occupants are forced to leave because of eviction, arson, conversion to condominiums, rent increases, loss of job, or other reasons, some do find housing on
their own. Like the Peters, thousands of others, however, double up with friends
or relatives in already overcrowded quarters. (Between 1978 and 1983 the number
of American families living with others as subfamilies doubled from a low of 1.3
million to 2.6 million.)[2] The arrangement almost always creates tensions. Even for
middle-class families with a house to share, there are pressures from portioning
out space, conflicts of life styles, and feelings of resentment on one side, guilt on
the other. For poor families squeezed into smaller quarters, there are constant anx-
ieties over how to find money for the bare necessities to ensure the survival of
everyone. Eventually tensions are likely to erupt into explosions. Many shelters
report that the most most frequent reason for seeking admission is eviction, and
that over half the evictions are from the home of a friend or relative.

Some displaced families are forced to split up. A mother may find some kind
of haven for herself and an infant with relatives but may be forced to place her
older children in foster homes. Having no home for her children is often considered
proof of poor parenting; hence it may be years before the Welfare Department allows
the family to be reunited. Still other displacees go directly to the streets. They find
refuge in automobiles, parks, cardboard boxes, or emergency shelters.

Uprooted families that do find their own housing may eventually become
homeless. Their new quarters are usually more dilapidated and expensive than the
old, and as other living costs rise or as welfare benefits are cut, the family finds
it impossible to cope with all the demands on its resources.

"Displacement is just a calm word for a frequent and shattering experience: people losing their homes against their will," says the Legal Services Anti-Displacement Project. "Displacement afflicts some 2,500,000 Americans each year. Beyond that statistic, some 500,000 lower-rent units are lost each year through conversion, abandonment, inflation, arson, and demolition."[3]

Drastic loss of lower-rent units can be observed across the United States. In Atlantic City, New Jersey, the casino boom has disrupted long-term households; elderly residents have been evicted from beachfront lodging-houses to make room for hotels and luxury housing, whereas in minority neighborhoods landlords have forced tenants out by stopping maintenance, then bulldozing the buildings and selling the land. In Salt Lake City, the Mormon Church tried to evict forty-two tenants, many of them elderly women who had lived there thirty years, in order to convert two buildings to office space. In San Francisco touristification of the Tenderloin has pushed costs of housing far beyond the ability of low-income persons to pay; hundreds of old-time residents have been uprooted.

Evictions have increased sharply in the 1980s. Hopper and Hamberg observe that

> In New York City, with a total of nearly 2 million rental units, there were nearly half a million such actions in 1983. Fully half of these actions were taken against public assistance recipients and 80 percent of these involved tenants paying rents above the maximum housing allowance. Welfare-rent ceilings had not been increased since 1975, while rents had nearly doubled.[4]

Displacement is not confined to urban areas or to renters. Today thousands of rural people who could not make their mortgage payments or who have become redundant as agribusiness takes over have been shoved off the land. The position of farmers continues to worsen. The Mortgage Bankers Association reports that by the first quarter of 1985, the national delinquency rate for one- to four-unit residential mortgage loans reached an historical level of 6.19 percent.[5]

Displacement will continue to grow as the costs of housing rise and the stock for low-and middle-income Americans shrinks. In the 1970s and early 1980s, the price of new homes rose so rapidly that many people had to turn to rental housing, thus increasing the demand for the latter.

Rental housing has become prohibitively expensive for low- and middle-income persons in many parts of the country. In April 1985 Jack Newfield observed in the *Village Voice* that in New York rents had increased, on average, 25 percent over the past three years, while the number of rental apartments had declined by thirty-six thousand since 1981—mostly as a result of co-op and condo conversions. For affluent buyers, one-bedroom condos in Manhattan were selling briskly for $400,000 and two bedroom units for $600,000.[6]

Housing costs have risen more rapidly than incomes since 1970. The renter has suffered more than the homeowner, however. In 1980, there were 80.4 million occupied housing units in the United States.[7] In the same year, according to the Annual Housing Survey, there were 7 million households paying more than 50 percent of their income for housing (including utilities). Almost 70 percent of those households were renters, and their median income was between $4,000 and $5,000 a year.[8] Newfield says that in 1984–85 about 30 percent of New York City renters were paying more than half of their income to landlords.[9]

In 1980 (the latest year for which census statistics are available) a family with an income of $3,000 who paid the median rent for a household of that income class, spent 72 percent of its income on shelter, compared to 34 percent in 1970. In 1980 such households (numbering nearly 2.7 million) had only $71 a month left for all other needs.[10] Low-income households paying more than half their incomes for rent cannot afford both housing and other necessities of life; if they are not yet homeless, they totter on the brink of homelessness.

The 1983 median household income for owners was $24,400, whereas that for renters was $12,400, only 51 percent of that for owners.[11] Clearly renters are worse off; they have lower incomes to begin with and pay more of their income for shelter.

According to Cushing Dolbeare, "Our housing need is on the order of 16 million units, just counting households now living in substandard housing or paying more than a third of their income for shelter."[12] Gerald McMurray, staff director of the House Subcommittee on Housing and Community Development, says that today about 4 million housing units are subsidized by HUD and about 1 million by the Farmers Home Administration (FmHA). In other words, he says, we face a shortfall of some 11 million low-income units.

Behind the Shortfall

Why is there such a widespread shortage of shelter, especially rental housing for low- and moderate-income persons?

A common assumption is that the shortage can be attributed to high interest rates, the shortage of mortgage credit, and the high cost of materials, land, and labor. Another commonly accepted reason is that the number of people, particularly single persons, looking for homes has increased because the average number of occupants per household has declined from about five in 1900 to less than three in 1980.

Although this is true, the explanation overlooks the fact that the number of low-income rental units in the private sector is not only inadequate but is actually shrinking. Many still exist as physical structures, but, because of inflation, rents are no longer low. Removal of units from the lower-rent housing stock also increases the squeeze of rent inflation and other displacing pressures on the growing low- and moderate-income population, which must compete for a smaller supply of housing.[13] Moreover, renters have borne the brunt of rising property and energy costs passed on to them by landlords. Most important, government programs, which might have provided alternatives to reliance on the private sector, have never been adequate and in the 1980s have been declining drastically.

Why is the number of rental units shrinking so rapidly? Displacement is a principal cause. It is far more widespread than many Americans assume. George and Eunice Greer cite twenty-six precipitants of displacement. Among them are abandonment, accidental fire, airport construction or expansion, arson, code enforcement, conversion of rental apartments to condominiums, demolition to make way for new housing, demolition for safety or health reasons, foreclosures, highway or transit construction or expansion, institutional expansion (universities, hospitals, and so forth), military base expansion, natural disaster, planning and zoning decisions, public housing construction, redlining, rehabilitation, renovation of public housing, rising market prices and rents, rising assessments and tax rates, and urban renewal.[14]

This still does not explain why affordable replacement housing has not materialized. The root of the problem is the so-called free market, a system that works against meeting housing needs of low-income people. In this system, real estate speculators, builders, and landlords use housing to maximize profits, not serve human beings. Moreover, the system is larger than is commonly realized, for real estate, banking, insurance companies, and government sectors tend to work together.

As the All City Housing Organization (ACHO) of Boston points out, "Housing for people with low- and moderate-incomes has not been 'profitable' on its own, without government subsidy, since the Second World War."[15]

Unlike transportation, retirement, education, and other areas of federal concern, the U.S. government has not moved to take over the costs of making the housing system work, says urban planner Chester Hartman.

> Partly that is due to the heavy pressure of the real estate industry, which enjoys the money it can make from the shortage. But partly it also reflects the fact that ownership and marketing of real estate is the oldest, most hallowed form of capital accumulation in the war chest of private enterprise. To mess with that seems like messing with the basic roots of the private profit system, and the U.S. government is too fond of that system to institute fundamental reform.[16]

In almost all European countries the government plays a far more active role in subsidizing and controlling building activity. In Denmark, for example, the great majority of apartment buildings are built and owned by nonprofit building societies, which receive substantial financial assistance from the government. In fact, all Danish building activity, not only the nonprofit portion, is financed through long-term mortgages obtained from traditional mortgage institutions that are nonprofit organizations under public control.

In the United States, the housing industry is closely linked to the banking industry. Peter Hawley says that interest rates (debt service) can consume 50 to 60 percent of the rent dollar.[17] Thus the banks wield great power. Redlining, described later in this chapter, is another example of that power.

As we shall see, government policy has done little to alleviate the displacement problem and often has exacerbated it.

The Federal Housing Program and Its Beneficiaries

Virtually all American housing is subsidized in one way or another. "Contrary to public opinion, the wealthy have greater access to housing subsidies than the poor," says Roger Sanjek. "The richer you are, the greater the federal housing subsidy you receive. . . . It is only the homeless—the poorest of the poor—for whom no categorical federal housing subsidy program exists."[18]

The largest federal housing program is the tax deduction for mortgage interest payments and property taxes. This indirect subsidy for homeowners is an entitlement; no eligibility other than home ownership is needed. First, second, and vacation homes are all equally eligible.[19]

Another important form of tax expenditure is the investor deduction. According to Barry Zigas, president of the National Low-Income Housing Coalition:

> In fiscal year 1984, housing spending by the federal government amounted to a total of $57 billion, of which the Housing Subcommittee and its appropriation committee had direct control over only $10.8 billion [that is, this amount went to low-income housing programs]. The remaining $46 billion [homeowner and investor deductions] went out in subsidies through the tax system. . . . Fully 75 percent of tax subsidies in 1981 went to the top 15 percent of the income distribution.[20]

The tax system has been a major factor in encouraging the purchase of housing as an investment. The tendency of people who are already generously housed to buy more expensive homes, or second or third homes, or rental income housing, drives prices up.

For low-income people, federal housing subsidies are much less widely distributed and are not entitlements. One must go through an onerous filtering process to establish need. Only 9 percent of those eligible for Section 8 rental subsidies have been receiving them. Most of those eligible do not benefit because Congress has failed to appropriate sufficient funds. The Section 202 units for the elderly and disabled meet only a small part of the need recognized by the 1961, 1971, and 1981 White House Conferences on Aging.[21]

Real estate owners can also deduct property taxes from income tax, although the tenant pays them as part of his rent. In addition, landlords enjoy a wide variety of tax shelters. To list only a few: depreciation deductions, developer subsidies and abatements, real estate investment trusts, syndications, lease-backs, the inflated mortgage, and the bondable net lease.

To change such a system is difficult. Real estate and banking interests are intertwinerd. They also exercise enormous political power. According to Hartman, the

National Board of Realtors Political Action Committee led all other PACs in contributions to the 1982 congressional races, contributing over $2 million—$400,000 more than the American Medical Association's PAC. The National Board of Realtors has over 600,000 members and 1,800 local boards that strongly influence state and local legislation through political contributions and lobbying. In addition, since state and local legislators do not work full time, some also act as lawyers, insurance agents, realtors, and even landlords.[22]

Federal Programs for Low- and Moderate-Income Americans. To understand how the federal government has failed to supply adequate shelter, a short overview of its involvement in housing may be in order.

In 1937 Congress first passed a housing bill for the poor, conceived as a public-works program to make jobs for the unemployed. In the late 1940s, slum clearance and urban renewal became the key issues, and Congress passed the 1949 Housing Act. The goal was a lofty, some would say radical, one: "a decent home and suitable living environment for every American family." Yet the government failed to develop a true national policy.

In 1968 Congress reaffirmed the goal of a decent home for every American family and set as its goal the construction and rehabilitation of 26 million housing units over the next ten years; 6 million of them were to be federally assisted in order to provide housing for people of meager or moderate means.

Ten years later it was clear that the private market had performed well, producing 18 million units (3.8 million of these, however, were mobile homes, which in the original 1968 plan were not viewed as satisfying projected needs). On the other hand, of the 6 million lower-income units mentioned in the law, only 2.7 million units had been constructed or rehabilitated under federal housing programs.[23] The failure can be attributed in large part to the resistance of middle- or upper-income taxpayers to public housing as a handout, although it is these very income groups that benefit most from the largest federal housing largesse of all, the income tax deductions on mortgage interest, property taxes, and other housing-related expenditures.

As we have seen in the case of Cincinnati, it is the local public housing authority that develops, owns, and operates low-income public projects, under the guidelines of the federal government. HUD furnishes technical and professional assistance in planning and managing the projects, as well as up-front loans for planning, annual contributions to pay the authority's debt service, and, in most cases, operating subsidies.

Until the mid-1960s, the financing mechanisms of public housing sufficed to permit rents that most low-income families could afford. In the late 1960s and early 1970s, however, operating costs rose dramatically. Yet the federal government became increasingly reluctant to advance the necessary subsidies. Housing authorities were forced to cut back on maintenance and essential repairs, and the net result was the deterioration of housing projects.

One must add that public housing, occupied by the poorer segments of society, naturally attracted a high proportion of hostile, alienated people. The tension that has prevailed in many housing projects was predictable.

Moreover, compared to the Scandinavians, U.S. authorities have made generally weak efforts to create a mix of ethnic and income groups. Many public housing projects are unattractive, poorly constructed, and lacking in sufficient space for children to play.

On the other hand, the common image of public housing as monster high-rise projects is an erroneous one. This misconception has led to the belief that housing programs are not worth fighting for. Actually, fewer than 10 percent of public housing units are in such projects, which are often failures.[24] The more successful efforts are not known because they look like everyone else's housing.

By the late 1960s, provision of public housing units for the poor was overshadowed by a new approach: subsidies for mortgages at below-market interest rates for building by nonprofit and profit-oriented groups.

Although this new approach stimulated the most massive subsidized housing production in U.S. history, the boom of 1969-1973, the situation changed in 1973, when President Nixon declared a moratorium on all subsidized housing programs. During the postmoratorium period of 1974–1976, the number of assisted new housing starts and newly rehabilitated units totaled far less than 200,000 a year—a 90 percent cutback, resulting from the moratorium. (It takes several years for an appropriation to run through the pipeline.)

The decade 1968–78 also was characterized by confusion and inconsistency; each Administration brought its own programs, some so poorly structured and subsidized that their failures could have been predicted. Mismanagement occurred frequently.

Between 1974 and 1983, the principal housing assistance program for low-income people was Section 8. There were four types of Section 8 assistance: for new construction, substantial rehabilitation, moderate rehabilitation, and existing housing. In the last type, a tenant pays a fixed percentage of his or her adjusted income (formerly 25 but raised to 30 percent under the Reagan administration), and the government pays the landlord the difference between that and the fair market value of the unit.

Other important federal housing programs have included Section 236 and Section 202. The former provides mortgage interest subsidies to nonprofit and limited-dividend groups that develop and manage rental units. Section 202 benefits moderate-income elderly and handicapped occupants with a maximum income considerably higher than the public housing limit, by means of direct government loans with reduced interest rates to nonprofit housing developments, together with Section 8 certificates to the tenants.

By 1980, only about one-quarter of the need for federally subsidized or federally assisted housing had been satisfied. ("Subsidized" and "assisted" are generally interchangeable terms.) Instead of increasing appropriations to respond to this crisis, the Reagan administration has made a concerted effort to withdraw from the low-income housing field. For example, in 1985 the National Low-Income Housing Coalition testified that since 1981 Congress had approved cuts that reduced the federal housing assistance budget by 60 percent. It added that the 1986 cut, unless rejected (Congress did indeed reject so drastic a cut), would mean a 98 percent reduction since President Reagan took office. Moreover, the cuts already made had hurt the truly needy, for the median family income of households receiving federal low-income housing assistance was under $6,000 a year.[25] Cuts in publicly subsidized housing accounted for approximately half of the Reagan administration's domestic budget cuts in the first two years. These housing cuts are not immediately apparent to the public because of the interval between the date an appropriation is passed and the time it materializes into housing. Funding for units constructed in 1986 may have been appropriated as long ago as 1978.

At the same time, military spending was showing an enormous increase. For each dollar authorized for national defense in 1980, nineteen cents was authorized for subsidized housing programs. In 1984, only three cents was authorized for subsidized housing for each military dollar.[26]

The Reagan approach, according to Hartman, has had four major goals: (1) to end all programs that directly add through construction and substantial rehabilitation to the stock of housing available to lower-income households; (2) to reduce subsidies by forcing recipients to devote higher proportions of their own inadequate incomes (that is, proportions have risen from 25 percent to 30 percent); (3) to reduce the existing stock of subsidized housing through demolition, conversion, sale, and planned deterioration; (4) to move toward relying almost exclusively on the existing supply to meet low-income housing needs, through introduction of the voucher, a limited direct cash housing payment designed to cover the gap between rent levels and what lower-income households can afford. This approach seems to assume the existence of large numbers of moderately priced vacancies in decent condition, and a housing market that does not discriminate against applicants because of race, income, family size, or life style.[27] As the situation in Cincinnati demonstrates, this is not the case.

During the first three years of its tenure the Reagan administration acted as if the homeless did not exist. Some HUD officials openly declared that no Americans were living without a roof over their heads.

Since 1983, however, the Reagan administration has been forced to recognize the homeless. As previously noted, in winter 1982–83 the Senate held hearings on Street People, the House heard testimony on Homelessness in America, and Congress appropriated $100 million to FEMA for food and shelter programs. Since then, FEMA has remained the funnel for such funds. As we shall see, the Reagan administration has resisted attempts to appropriate HUD funds expressly for housing the homeless.

HURRA—A Fresh Start?

In November 1983, the Reagan administration reached a compromise with housing advocates—not because it had changed philosophy but because it placed great importance on approval of International Monetary Fund monies, which congressional proponents of housing had cleverly tied into the same bill (the Housing and Urban/Rural Recovery Act of 1983, known as HURRA). The two-year act authorized new federal subsidies for 100,000 units (about a third of what Congress provided annually in the mid-1970s).

In a key concession, the Reagan administration agreed to a new program to assist construction or rehabilitation of 30,000 to 40,000 rental units, a move that would at least partially fulfill the need for more units. Except for the Section 202 program, the enabling legislation for the Section 8 New Construction and Substantial Rehabilitation programs was repealed. The Section 8 Moderate Rehabilitation and Existing Housing programs were continued, as was public housing.

An experimental voucher program was created to pay the difference between the tenant contribution (30 percent of adjusted income) and the payment standard, which is based on fair market rents for Section 8 existing units.

Other significant features of this complex and detailed legislation included: (1) extension of rural housing programs, under the Farmers Home Administration (FmHA); (2) reauthorization of the CDBG program for another three years, with tighter target requirements; (3) expanded assistance to shared housing for the elderly and handicapped, a program for which advocacy groups such as the Gray Panthers had long been fighting.

Several provisions of the bill demonstrated the impact of the Reagan administration philosophy. Private investment was encouraged: one passage in the bill declared that development projects with a greater proportion of private funds to government funds would be more likely to be approved. Rent control was discouraged: state or local governments might control rents in structures assisted by moderate rehabilitation or development grants only if controls were imposed under a law in effect on the date of enactment or if the requirements would also apply generally to nonassisted structures. Nor were the grants for the new rental housing rehabilitation and development program aimed principally to benefit very low-income people. Instead, at least 20 percent of the units in housing under the development grants were to be targeted to lower-income families.

On the other hand, the moderate rehabilitation grants were targeted so that 100 percent of the assistance was to be used to benefit lower-income families. Moreover, families paying more than 50 percent of their income for shelter were given priority for housing assistance in the low-income housing programs.

Several features of the bill demonstrated that many members of Congress had become concerned about the homeless. One provision stipulated that up to $60 million might be appropriated in 1984 so that HUD could make grants for shelters and other essential services for homeless persons. Another regulation provided that

Section 8 assistance might be used for SRO units that meet local hea... standards (rather than Section 8 Existing standards). Still another sti... that, in both rehabilitated and newly constructed apartments, there... displacement of very low-income families with higher-income tenan...

Finally, funding was authorized for up to fourteen thousand more S... units for the elderly or handicapped. Significant here is the fact that in 1982 HUD finally had agreed to include the mentally disabled under handicapped. Although the number of units envisioned in HURRA 1983 was tiny in the light of need, this move (and the support for SRO housing) meant that some progress was being made toward provision of permanent housing for the homeless and potentially homeless.

President Reagan, however, refused to go along with the appropriation of $60 million for shelters, announcing that he would veto it because "enough" had been done for the homeless. A few months later Congress responded to this move by appropriating $70 million to FEMA, a sum that came to be known as FEMA III.

It is worth noting that the process by which a budget request eventuates in actual housing is extremely complex. The fact that a certain proposal has been made may say very little about the end result. Space does not permit a full description of the many steps it takes through Congress and Administration offices. However, it is relevant to note that the Administration tried to prevent release of all the monies appropriated in HURRA 1983 by use of a surgical procedure known as recision (permanent cancellation of already approved budget authority). Such a move must be approved by both the House and Senate, and in this case it was unsuccessful. The Reagan administration has sometimes been more successful with the use of deferral (putting off the spending of one year's budget authority), which can stand unless overturned by a resolution of Congress. The Administration can then speak of a surplus, and use this as a reason for requesting even less funding the following year.

How Does Displacement Work?

Of the twenty-six causes of displacement listed by the Greers, the most important are rising market prices and rents, disinvestment and abandonment, demolition, arson for profit, conversion, housing rehabilitation, and uprooting resulting from government programs.

Rising Market Prices

Between 1970 and 1980 the median income for renters rose 66.7 percent, whereas among owner-occupants income rose 104.1 percent. Meanwhile, inflation drove up the Consumer Price Index by 112.2 percent.[28] Clearly, this was the beginning of what Hopper and Hamberg term a gathering storm.

For elderly people living on small Social Security or SSI checks, the situation can be devastating. One afternoon in Cleveland we met two aging sisters in a park.

Eyeing us suspiciously, and hugging their coats closer to their thin bodies, they moved down the bench as we made attempts to initiate a conversation. However, within five minutes, the two women were telling us that until a year ago, they shared a two-room apartment. "It was small, but we could make do. Then the rent went up from $220 to $300. Now we sometimes sleep in shelters, sometimes in bus stations, sometimes in parks."

Disinvestment and/or Abandonment

Disinvestment refers to an owner's disuse of his properties: letting buildings run down, withdrawing services, cutting down maintenance, and finally abandoning them. A landlord discards what he has invested in buildings that no longer return the profit he wants. The process, which almost always occurs in low-income neighborhoods (such as Over-the-Rhine) where tenants cannot pay rents that bring owners attractive profits, demonstrates the inability of our socioeconomic system, as it is presently structured, to serve the housing needs of the poor.

For people with money, says the Legal Services Anti-Displacement Project, the free market system can work almost as well in reverse as it does for the normal expansionist form of investment. Hence disinvestment can still bring profits. Sometimes the process is relatively innocent. A landlord gets in over his head, cuts back on maintenance and taxes in order to maintain a cash flow, and ends up with a property that he can sell only at below-market prices. The solution is abandonment. More frequently, however, there is a series of owners, each of whom neglects the property and then leaves the new owner with the accumulated neglect of the past. Although the process appears natural, it is often a conscious strategy of abandonment.[29]

Thus landlords may buy property with very little cash down (using several mortgage loans), fail to make repairs, pay no property taxes, fall behind in utility bills, and simply collect rent, using some of the money to pay off loans and keeping the rest. Eventually, code inspectors and tax officials confront the delinquent operators. Then the landlords, having milked the building, simply walk away, leaving a tangle of run-down apartments and unpaid bills with which the city and others must deal. Sometimes there is a tragic final step: arson. The landlords have the building torched and collect the insurance.[30]

Redlining is an illegal but nevertheless common *institutional* form of abandonment. Banks and insurance companies target certain declining areas as poor credit risks—they withhold mortgage money and insurance coverage from entire neighborhoods or offer funds and services at discriminatory, often unaffordable rates. Since minority groups usually cluster in such neighborhoods, the practice reflects racist or class-based ideas that it is not worth putting money into these areas. Homeowners who need to fix up their property are unable to get the loans they need. If fire insurance is not available, otherwise willing lenders will withhold funds from investment. Even well-meaning landlords cannot obtain money to do necessary renovations. The result is a self-fulfilling prophecy of further deterioration, which in turn causes more disinvestment, more displacement, more deterioration. Money that has been deposited by neighborhood residents in local banks flows out of the neighborhood and is invested elsewhere.

Demolition

Demolition removes rental units from the market at the same time that it removes renters from housing. According to Dennis Keating, a leading consultant on housing and planning, both demolition and arson can make money for speculators by *shrinking* the number of housing units for rent. Larger profits for property owners who are seeking to replace the building with higher-density or upper-income housing are almost always the motive for demolition. For the rest of the population, this reduction of units—even if they are vacant when they are knocked down or torched—means that the cost of rental housing goes up even faster as people scramble for whatever is left. Some are left on the street.[31]

Today private demolition is a far greater cause of displacement than the publicly sponsored version (urban renewal) of the 1950s and 1960s, says Keating. However, a great deal of private demolition is supported and triggered by public policies, ranging from development incentives in tax laws to the ripple effects of government investment and expenditures.[32]

Arson for Profit

The purposeful burning of rental housing has become a major source of displacement. Between 1951 and 1977 the number of arsons reported by local fire departments across the United States to the National Fire Protection Association (NFPA) increased by 3,100 percent, from 5,600 cases to 177,000 cases.[33] During each year between 1977 and 1980 about 1,000 civilians and 120 firefighters were killed in deliberately set fires; in addition 30,000 civilians and 4,000 firefighters were injured. Most of those killed are members of minorities and poor people living in the central city, many of them children and elderly persons.[34]

Arson brings big money to some people. According to the Legal Services Anti-Displacement Project, the estimated annual cost of property damage from criminal burning is $1.5 billion, most of which is recovered from insurance companies by property owners.[35]

The public labors under the delusion that deliberately set fires are the isolated acts of pyromaniacs or vandals and pose no serious threat to cities guarded by modern fire-fighting companies, says James Brady, director of the City of Boston Arson Strike Force. Actually, he says there is "a clear link between the politics of banks and insurance companies on the one hand and the arson-for-profit schemes of organized crime professional arsonists, shady landlords, and corrupt public officials."[36]

It is also a cheap way to clear a site for development, to remove buildings protected by historic preservation restrictions, or to get rid of decaying property once it has been depreciated for tax purposes, says Keating. With the insurance award (tax free) the owner can make a down payment on other property; the awards become a convenient source of funds when conventional mortgage sources dwindle. Significantly, arson rates tend to go up when the economy goes down.[37]

Typically, the burning of even a long-vacant building is only the final chapter in displacement resulting from disinvestment. Behind the process is a concerted drive to force people out and cause neighborhood change. Speculators may use arson to remove stable tenants and provoke block-busting, to empty properties in order to expedite remodeling or condo conversions, or to capitalize on rent control laws that allow unlimited increases upon change of tenancy.[38]

Speculators and landlords do not operate alone. They are connected with banks and, in some cases, with organized crime. Using maps, Brady shows that poor neighborhoods such as Roxbury, Dorchester, and East Boston have been the centers of arson. The questions to ask, he says, are Why do so-called pyromaniacs respect neighborhood boundaries? and Why do fires take place more often in buildings that are owned by absentee landlords, and less often in HUD-subsidized buildings? We have to ask where buildings are situated, and *who* owns them, he declares.

More than half of the arsons take place in abandoned buildings, says Brady, and it is usally white landlords who abandon them—particularly absentee landlords with high incomes who own a number of buildings and hold titles through holding companies and real estate trusts, which means they cannot be identified personally. Studies show that abandonment patterns follow closely the discriminatory lending policies that deny credit to certain districts of the inner city in order to invest in more profitable suburban real estate.

Directly or indirectly some bank policies may be closely linked to schemes of organized crime, according to Brady. Foreclosing on unpaid mortgages is one side effect of redlining. By the time foreclosure procedures have been completed, the property is often run down and abandoned. Organized crime racketeers offer to buy these problem buildings, often at a price far exceeding the market value, providing the bank will give them a new mortgage for near the purchase price, and sometimes more, to include the cost of renovation. The racketeers then call on "friends" to do the renovation (often a fake job). Second, third, and fourth mortgages enhance the total value far beyond its actual worth. Since reputable banks have issued the mortgages, it is not difficult to acquire fire insurance. Professional torches then go to work on the overmortgaged and overinsured buildings. Banks often profit more than the racketeers, even without consciously joining in the conspiracy and without violating the law. The potential losses from foreclosed properties are converted into substantial profit for the bank because the new mortgage paid by the insurance company far exceeds the old bad debt assumed under foreclosure.[39]

Whole neighborhoods can be decimated. In 1975 alone, thirteen thousand fires broke out in the twelve square miles of the South Bronx. More than half of the fires were recorded as cause unknown. Even today, many blocks are still in ruins.[40]

Because of arson, city governments lose tax revenues, often in the tens of millions of dollars. Yet the U.S. Fire Administration says that arrest rates run 9 percent, conviction rates 2 percent, and incarceration rates 0.7 percent.[41]

Conversion

Washington, D.C. is only one of many urban areas where *condomania* has run rampant. According to one leading authority on housing, about five hundred thousand apartment building conversions into condominiums and cooperatives occurred in the period 1977–82 alone.[42] By 1985 the rage for condos was subsiding in many areas, according to the *Wall Street Journal*, which reported that in some cities values were falling 15 percent to 35 percent.[43] Nevertheless, condos are still in great demand in a number of cities, and prices are expected to rebound eventually.

Conversion usually takes place against the background of a wider phenomenon known as gentrification, which refers to a concerted effort to revitalize a declining neighborhood by bringing back business, improving the quality of services, and attracting middle- and upper-income households. Since conversion of low-cost housing is a central factor in this process, the terms conversion and gentrification often are used interchangeably.

To neighborhood residents affected by the process, the terms simply mean that younger, more affluent people, usually white, arrive on the scene, and the elderly, poor, and minorities are forced to move to more crowded and dilapidated quarters—or to the streets. The available number of housing units in the neighborhood also declines so that remaining residents pay higher rents.

The basic reasons for conversion to condominiums or to involuntary cooperatives are simple: high profitability and strong market demands. It is true that a landlord often can make high profits from the cash flow, tax benefits, and appreciation in value of rental properties. However, because of rising operating costs and grassroots movements to strengthen rent and eviction controls (which weaken a landlord's ability to treat tenants arbitrarily), it is usually much more profitable today to sell an apartment as a condominium.

There has been a large market for condominium and cooperative conversion, especially in cities where housing is scarce. Although condos and co-ops are expensive, they usually are cheaper than single-family detached houses, have lower operating costs, and still offer the tax advantage of home ownership. As we have seen, these tax advantages are an indirect government subsidy. One of the principal reasons that production of new unsubsidized rental apartments fell drastically in the late 1970s is the immense attraction of home ownership.

Real estate attorney Julius Yacker observes that a rental project may change hands every ten or twelve years, and only one building is to be insured. "However," he says, "if you convert the building to condominiums, the units change hands more frequently. As condos, there are now perhaps hundreds of little title insurance policies to be issued, one for each unit. . . . this has been an exceptionally good thing for the title company."[44]

City planner Daniel Lauber asserts that there are three types of buyers of condos. Some people voluntarily wish to live in and own a condominium. The majority, however, are primarily motivated to buy because they fear they cannot find affordable replacement housing in the same community, or, if they do, it too will be converted. The third type of purchaser is the nonoccupant investor. "Nonoccupants," he says, "tend to hold on to their units for eighteen to twenty-four months. . . . Many investors follow a developer around the country, purchasing from one to ten units in each of his conversions." Such speculators benefit from high inflation and from paying a low tax rate on capital gains when they sell. In addition, they have the advantages of deductions for mortgage interest, property tax, and depreciation. Says one attorney for Chicago Investors: "In one building we had over five hundred individual mortgage closings in five days. There just aren't enough owner-occupants around to sell that fast."[45]

As political scientist Cicin-Sain points out, there are many potential benefits in gentrification. Obviously, the real estate and construction sectors realize profits. Residents who remain in the upgraded neighborhoods usually enjoy improved municipal services and a better physical environment. For home-owners, equity appreciates, and the availability of hazard insurance improves.[46]

Residents coming in from outlying areas can live nearer their employment, enjoy city amenities, pay less for transportation, and accumulate equity in the new home. Neighborhoods may benefit from upgrading of the housing stock and municipal services. Cities profit from an expanded tax base and from increased employment in the real estate, building, and other service sectors. The metropolitan area as a whole may benefit from a revitalized central city and from redress of the socioeconomic disparities between the central city and the suburbs. The nation may be served by the revitalization of central cities and the conservation of existing housing stock.[47]

On the other side, the costs of gentrification are great. Condo conversion decreases the total housing stock available to the poor. Since relocation expenses are rarely borne by private developers, residents who have to leave the neighborhood pay for moving charges, security deposits, and utility deposits. The psychological costs are often much greater; there is always trauma in a forced move, and for people who have lived in a neighborhood for decades, the loss of community bonds may be shattering. Uprooted elderly people are rarely able to form new ties in a new community; they become isolated and deteriorate prematurely. Poor people living on welfare assistance must go through the complex and often degrading process of applying at a new welfare office, a new hospital, a new unemployment office.[48]

Female-headed large families and ethnic or racial groups face discrimination when they seek housing, and the latter lose social ties based on ethnicity or race. The revitalized neighborhoods suffer the disruption of neighborhood networks and information institutions of self-help. Racial and social tensions often mount.[49] As in the case of Cincinnati, where dislocated Garfield Place area residents are spilling into Over-the-Rhine, the neighborhoods that receive the uprooted are also likely to suffer such tensions. In addition, they may have to endure an increased load on municipal services. As for the metropolitan area as a whole, it may simply experience a shift in the focus of problems from central cities to other parts of the metropolitan areas.

Finally, costs of local goods and services go up, property taxes rise, and developers pressure residents to move. Some end up on the streets.

Witness the changes on New York's Lower East Side, the legendary home of poor immigrants and of homeless people living rough on the Bowery. Today even the flea-bag hotels where many so-called derelicts passed the night are disappearing. Martin Gottlieb describes the neighborhood today as "a place of overnight real estate fortunes, of enormous displacement of the poor, and of settlement of a new class of educated but downwardly mobile young white people."[50] Actually, a great many of the young newcomers are not living in converted gentrified buildings, but in dark narrow walk-up tenements with bathtubs in the kitchen and icicles inside the windows in winter. So great is the shortage of housing that such quarters may cost $300 or more a month. Their value has been pushed upward by gentrification in the area. The eventual goal of speculators and builders is transformation of the neighborhood through construction of market-rate housing like that on the Upper East Side.

Gottlieb gives a vivid description of conditions and forces at work: tenants living for months with no heat or water, amid the constant scurry of rats, till the ceiling falls in; young whites being favored as tenants over blacks or Hispanics; commercial rents quintupling, forcing many small shopkeepers to close; harassment of rent-strikers, including an 82-year-old woman served with an eviction notice; and a burgeoning of deals that result in escalating real estate values.

On close analysis, says Gottlieb, a two-pronged pattern of gentrification emerges. "The 'first generation' landlord either cleans out the building or gets rid of tenants who are problems and those who occupy the low rent apartments. Within a couple of years he will sell to a second landlord, who will run the building as a long-term investment, for a significantly changed tenancy."[51] Thus rental buildings that used to sell for one or two times their annual rent rolls are being "flipped" at enormous profits.

Gottlieb cites many examples:

Consider the case of the five-story tenement at 270 East 10th Street. On April 1, 1976, with a number of tenants and a huge bill of back taxes, it sold for a mere $5,706 plus assumption of debts. Nearly four years later, on January 7, 1980, it was still occupied by tenants, according to city records, and tax bill paid, it sold for $40,000. But when Morris Leisner, an active East Side real estate man, bought it on June 12, 1981, the tenement was empty—and its price was three times higher, $130,000. Four months later, Leisner 'flipped' the building, selling it to Mag Reality Associates of Leonia, New Jersey, for $202,500. That's a $70,000 profit in four months on a building that gave shelter to no one. (Typical of the present pattern, the assessed value of this property—that is, the figure on which the city bases its taxes—has *dropped* from $26,000 to $18,000, less than a tenth of its current value.)[52]

The last sentence suggests that city governments are not likely to be neutral bystanders in this process. New York has practiced the curious custom of raising assessments of certain buildings only a fraction of their actual rise in value. Marcuse, citing evidence from a city report, says that assessed values went up 26.3 percent over nine years ending 1982–1983, although real estate values went up 200 percent to 300 percent over a shorter period of time.[53] Nor has the city ever tried to count the people displaced under such circumstances. Its rent stabilization laws are poorly enforced. Indeed, Mayor Ed Koch has argued that people who cannot afford to live in Manhattan should find a home elsewhere. In 1955 the city passed the J–51 program, allowing property tax write-offs to encourage modest improvements on older housing that could be carried out while tenants remained in place, but in the 1970s it was expanded to allow conversion of buildings into luxury apartments and displacement of the original tenants. Under the Koch administration, J–51 conferred enormous tax rewards in affluent neighborhoods where the developers would have done the renovations without concessions. This policy also led to the illegal dumping of low-income tenants, particularly those living in SROs. Although some modifications of the law have occurred as the result of growing political opposition, J–51 still is very much alive. Other cities have somewhat similar tax abatement programs.

Traditionally, SROs have represented a last-ditch source of housing for poor people living not far from the brink of homelessness. Such dwellings frequently are dilapidated structures, with peeling walls and floors sprinkled with plaster and resident roaches. Yet SROs represent an irreplaceable source of housing, especially for the elderly poor and the mentally disabled who make up the hard core of the nation's homeless. Most residents of SROs feel that such hotels at least offer some dignity and are infinitely preferable to shelters. Today many dislodged SRO tenants find that their independence has been reduced to making a free choice between shelters and streets.

The shortage is growing at an alarming rate. Between 1970 and 1982, 1,116,000 SRO units disappeared—nearly half of the nation's total stock. During the same period New York City alone lost 110,000 such units of low-rent SRO housing—representing 87 percent of the total low-cost SRO stock—as a result of conversion, rent inflation, and demolition.[54] If this trend continues, lower-priced hotels will soon be extinct.

SROs are not removed by private developers alone. Rehabilitation subsidized through HUD may be the spearhead in some communities. Publicly sponsored downtown redevelopment clearance projects may also trigger the process. In most cases the destruction of SROs occurs with the tacit cooperation of the city. The J–51 tax abatement program is one example of congenial relationships between government and "free" enterprise.

Rehabilitation

On the surface, rehabilitation sounds like an attractive and sensible process. Yet it can uproot human beings from dwellings that mean home. Almost invariably, it results in fewer units of low-income housing. Rehabilitation is often part of a wider gentrification process. Keating cites an example: in 1979 the Canterbury, a seventy-five-year-old apartment building in Los Angeles, was finally declared a health hazard after it had been torched by arsonists, littered with garbage, and invaded by rats. Having made all they could from disinvestment, the owners evicted the tenants, most of them elderly, to find whatever shelter they could from charitable groups. Less than a year later the Canterbury reopened, with a fresh facade and newly renovated rooms. The new owners refused to let former tenants return. Even if the owners had allowed it, none of the old inhabitants could have afforded to go back. The rent for a one-bedroom apartment had shot up from $185 to $495.[55]

Rehabilitation can be both private and public. The distinction is misleading, since landlords have been able to take accelerated depreciation benefits for each unit rehabilitated for low- and moderate-income use. Cities, too, may offer tax abatements to encourage rehabilitation of substandard housing, as has been done under New York City's J–51 law.

Historic preservation is another area where federal and local tax policies work in concert with real estate interests. The Tax Reform Act of 1976 gives accelerated depreciation tax shelters on rehabilitation by owners of historic properties and provides no displacement compensation whatsoever. Hence a rehabber can get a building certified as a historic structure, evict low-income tenants, convert the buildings into condominiums or luxury rental housing, and also enjoy handsome tax shelters and a resale profit.

Antidisplacement groups recognize that it is important to conserve our historical heritage and important to rescue basically good housing stock from deterioration. They are not fighting against historical preservation or rehabilitation per se; they are asking that people be considered as important as buildings and that laws be carefully structured so that displacees will be adequately protected.

Displacement Due to Government Policies

Most Americans think of the government as a source of low-income housing, not as the agent of its destruction. Yet as we have seen in the case of Cincinnati, each year thousands of people have been uprooted from housing subsidized through HUD or FmHA. Others have been victims of displacement resulting from activities of the CDBG and the Urban Development Action Grants (UDAG) programs.

How can government trigger displacement? As more affluent people move into low-income areas, they are dismayed by the sight of public housing projects. Pressure mounts to convert developments that house families to units for elderly tenants, to sell them off as cooperatives or condominiums, or even to demolish them. Hence in the midst of severe rental housing shortages, public housing in basically good condition may be razed, or sold to private owners.

Displacement is most likely to occur when a project's federal subsidies expire, or when local housing authorities decide to disinvest, or when large-scale renovation is undertaken. For example, at the end of the bond repayment period, the local housing authority can own the project and dispose of it. Cuts in operating and maintenance subsidies also contribute to the process. The Reagan administration has encouraged such practices. In some cities up to 25 percent of the units under public ownership have been sold off to private interests, often at bargain prices. According to Hartman, such practices may reflect deliberate political decisions to close out a project by attrition and replace it with something preferred by the power structure.[56]

Public housing units may also be lost when older projects receive renovation funds through HUD's Modernization Program to thin out the project, for example, or to combine small units to make room for large families.

When an owner defaults on the HUD-insured mortgage and it is assigned to HUD, the latter must dispose of the property. Since HUD is legally limited to bidding no more than the unpaid indebtedness plus certain other costs, speculators can use foreclosure sales to obtain properties for higher-rent use. Tenants are displaced; the lower-income housing supply is reduced. If HUD becomes the owner at the sale, officials may decide that it is simpler to demolish the project they may have been forced to take over.[57]

Tenants may also be displaced because of activities under CDBG. CDBG emerged in 1974, when the federal government decided to bring six programs (urban renewal, Model Cities, water and sewer facilities, open space, neighborhood facilities, and public facilities loans) under one funding source. Every U.S. city with fifty thousand or more population is entitled to receive a certain amount. Smaller cities can also obtain funding, but on a competitive rather than entitlement basis.

Since such funds can be used not only for providing decent housing but also for developing small business investment corporations, landscaping downtown areas, clearing slum areas, and a wide range of other politically expedient uses that principally benefit upper-income people, it is obvious that CDBG programs can actually contribute to displacement.

Such was the case with SRO tenants uprooted from the Garfield Place area in Cincinnati. Even rural people may be affected. The village of Beauty, Kentucky, was almost relocated in toto through CDBG actions. Although the welfare of families to be relocated out of the Beauty flood plain was cited as the reason for the plan, the vast majority of the town's residents opposed it, and subsequent evidence suggests that coal company pressure may well have been behind the whole proposal. Residents fought the plan vigorously and it was dropped.[58]

Fighting Displacement

Low-income housing activists have discovered that some federal programs do include provisions that can be used to combat displacement. Federal standards, explicitly stated and uniformly applied, have provided greater protection for low- and moderate-income people than have the provisions of local or state governments, where legislators tend to speak for the business community and special interests unfriendly to the poor. For example, the federally sponsored Uniform Relocation Act (URA) provides relocation benefits but only for displacement directly caused by government action. Hence as government assistance has shifted toward more and more support of private development, the number of situations where it applies has diminished. Moreover, the URA employs such restrictive wording that people displaced by CDBG do not enjoy its protection. Nevertheless, the act represents a partial reform and, perhaps more important, serves as a model for negotiation of relocating benefits for those displaced by private or CDBG development.[59] Cincinnati is only one of the cities where housing activists have achieved some success in securing such benefits.

This kind of action represents the tip of the iceberg. The broader strategy is founded on the same principle that forms the foundation block of a broad progressive housing policy—the principle that housing is a *right*, a public right, rather than a private commodity.

Groups fighting displacement have two overall goals. The first is defense of the right to stay put. The other is the requirement that there be one-for-one replacement of lower-rent units withdrawn from the market. Antidisplacement groups recognize that frequently they will not be able to win such demands and will have to compromise by struggling to get all they can to compensate displacees for the pain of dislocation. However, the push toward basic goals is always important.

The objectives of the movement include rent controls (now in place in more than two hundred cities); rent subsidies; resale controls (to prevent speculation); stronger eviction controls; demolition controls; relocation benefits; tougher anti-arson laws with tougher enforcement; ordinances banning or regulating condo conversions; the right of return to a unit that was rehabilitated; attachment of antidisplacement provisions to CDBG programs; and preferences for displaced persons in government housing.

The movement can cite some striking successes. In Boston, *Inquilinos Boricuas en Acción* (Puerto Rican Tenants in Action), or IBA, succeeded in resisting displacement for Parcel 19 of the South End urban renewal project. Then it went on to become a housing developer. In addition, IBA operates a wide range of community-oriented programs, including social services to families and the elderly, day care for children, and advocacy work. The architecture does not have the austere style of most public housing; the buildings are attractively designed, around a Spanish-style piazza with trees and a covered, arched shopping arcade. IBA and its subsidiaries are a $3 million-a-year operation, with nearly one hundred employees, most of whom are residents of the area.[60]

The New Jersey Tenants Organization has mobilized 80,000 dues-paying members. Using litigation, direct action (rent strikes, demonstrations, picketing, rallies) and political action (campaigning for pro-tenant candidates in local and state elections), it has won rent control in more than 100 cities, as well as the toughest tenant–landlord laws in the nation. In 1985 alone, it was a crucial force in busting the antirent control mayors of Hoboken, East Orange, and Jersey City from office.[61]

Today the antidisplacement and tenants rights movements have working groups in every major city across the United States. In rural areas, traditionally resistant to community organizing, farmers have been mobilizing to fight displacement from their land. All over the United States, sometimes clandestinely and sometimes with the support of community organizers, the homeless and the borderline homeless have been squatting in abandoned housing.

These movements will almost certainly spread further. The housing inflation has drastically decreased the possibility of home ownership. At the same time, the shortage of low- and moderate-income rental housing has brought extremely low vacancy rates in a great many cities. Tenants have come to feel that they are locked into a relationship with a landlord for a long time. Hence they are more willing to put in the necessary time and effort to organize for their rights.

The Long View

Between 1950 and 1970 the proportion of substandard housing in the United States declined from more than 40 percent to 9 percent. The need for decent housing, together with war-induced prosperity and the increased productive capacity of the economy, triggered a huge housing construction boom. The interests of the poor and other housing consumers coincided. Expanded federal mortgage insurance and tax incentives for home ownership made it possible for the suburban single-family tract house to become the vehicle for this explosive growth.[62]

Although politicians and developers often talked of the needs of the poor, middle-class Americans were the real recipients of the below-market interest rate mortgages, the government guarantees, and the state housing finance agencies. As this country became a nation of home owners, the interests of the poor and middle class no longer coincided; government housing became identified with the poor. Suburban home owners, home builders, and banks became less concerned with housing as shelter than with housing as a tax refuge and form of protection from inflation.[63]

In the 1970s housing in the public sector increasingly focused on subsidies and tax advantages to developers, rehabilitators, and landlords, especially through the Section 8 and Section 202 program. Public housing projects, which have never enjoyed political support commensurate with that for subsidies to developers, fell into further disfavor.

Thus government policies have reinforced a system in which housing is viewed not as a social good but as a commodity. Instead of focusing on the needs of low-income people, government policies have tended to create a profitable situation for the building, banking, and real estate industries. Housing policy, says Hartman, is made in Washington through the interactions of the administration, Congress, and pressure groups such as the National Association of Realtors, the National Association of Builders, the U.S. League or Savings institutions, the American Bankers Association, and the Associated General Contractors Associations, all of which have well-heeled Political Action Committees.[64]

Achtenberg and Marcuse argue that the quest for profits limits the production of housing because privately controlled resources are allocated only when it is profitable for developers, land speculators, materials producers, and mortgage lenders to do so. Moreover, there is an overreliance on private credit building and buying housing. The result is an extremely cyclical pattern of construction, which inhibits the productive capacity of the industry.[65]

It is increasingly clear that we need high production of new units if low-income people are to get decent housing. Free market economists who adhere to the trickle-down theory assumed that the poor would get decent housing, second hand, because, as the affluent leave new (or relatively new) housing for something better, the less advantaged move in. In reality, the trickle-down policy has not trickled down many units to the poor because rents can be lowered only so much and may still be too high for the poor. Moreover, although private building of housing at the high-income levels seems to cost the American people less, the indirect subsidy of income tax deductions can make it as expensive as subsidizing low- and moderate-income persons—and in the latter case they get new, decent units.

The paramount goals of a progressive housing policy, then, are to secure public recognition that housing is a basic human right, to further the concept of ownership of housing as a public trust, and to remove housing as much as possible from the drive to maximize profits.

Perhaps the purest and most effective way to accomplish the last two goals is by means of community land trusts, which are designed to alter the way land is held so that social needs supersede individual profits. The basic idea does not oppose private ownership; it makes a distinction between personal property, which human beings create through their own efforts, and resources such as land, minerals, or water which belong to nature and therefore should be held in trust for the community. As a nonprofit corporation chartered to hold land in the best interests of the present and future community, the trust can purchase land or receive it by donation.[66]

In Cincinnati, the Community Land Cooperative (which is actually a trust, but is known as a cooperative because the state has strict laws on how the term *trust* may be used) has applied the principle to inner-city housing. Instead of being at the mercy of a landlord who could put them out by selling the building or replacing them with tenants who pay more, members live in a building owned by the trust. They pay a lease fee, which is used to maintain the building and pay the debt on it. The members receive a share or life-time lease and, as long as they participate in the trust, cannot be put out. When the building debt is discharged in full, they pay only the operating costs. They have the right to leave the share to anyone, providing that the person is willing to live in the building and be a member of the trust. Members who move sell their shares to the group and receive an amount of money based on what they paid over the years. All this is made possible by loans from investors.[67]

Community land trusts represent a clear alternative to the dominant pattern of housing for profit and reliance on government. For the present, they can make only a tiny dent in the shortage of low-income housing, however. Given the enormity of the problem, there is no way to avoid seeking government funding, and only the federal government has the extensive resources needed.

Some proposals for the future envision a radical restructuring of the relationship between government and private construction: they eliminate the middleman—the lending institution. Says Hartman:

> Just think, a $60,000 mortgage to purchase an $80,000 home, repaid over thirty years at about 12–14 percent interest, requires the owner to pay back up to $256,000 during the life of the mortgage, nearly four-fifths of which is interest—profits to the bank. Suppose, instead of mortgages, housing credit were abandoned and housing built with one-time government capital grants? Monthly housing costs—for taxes, utilities, maintenance, insurance—would be more than halved.[68]

Hawley goes further. Most multiple dwellings, he argues, should be placed in the public domain. New housing would be built by direct allocation of government funds to a housing board consisting of tenants. The board would coordinate tenant committees elected by a majority of all tenants in each multiple dwelling. Tenants, Hawley believes, can learn the technicalities of financing, operations, construction, and design as well as the skills to hire personnel. Direct allocation would mean paying for construction in cash, out of government revenues that have already been raised. Hence borrowing, mortgages, and bond issues can be eliminated. Direct allocation, he says, would reduce rents 50 percent, since financing—the cost of borrowing money from banks and other lending institutions—doubles the construction costs and operating expenses of a building.[69]

Obviously, in the present context of political realities, such a scheme is at best a long-range goal. In the foreseeable future, most aspects of housing production will continue to be performed by the private sector. Yet in order to meet the goal of an adequate supply of housing, the production and rehabilitation processes must be increasingly subject to government control.

In their program for housing decommodification, Achtenberg and Marcuse outline several goals in the overall objective of limiting the role of profit in decisions affecting housing: social ownership, social production, social control of land, public financing, resident control of neighborhoods, and affirmative action and housing choice.[70]

Social ownership may have a communist ring to some, but it simply means controlling the speculative private ownership of housing and expanding the amount of housing under public, collective, community, or resident ownership. Examples of social ownership exist in many parts of the United States. The concept takes a variety of forms: collective ownership by resident-controlled corporations (such as community land trusts); direct ownership by government bodies or nonprofit entities (such as public housing projects, Section 202 housing for the elderly, and church-sponsored housing nonprofits); nonequity or limited-equity cooperatives (which prevent cooperative share values from inflating along with the market, thereby retaining the economic benefits of the arrangement for the entire cooperative); and nonspeculative resident ownership of single-family homes. Ideally, residents' rents would be based on their ability to pay.

The goal of social production would be to upgrade and expand the housing supply and increase social control over production, including housing design, development construction, and production of materials. The long-term objective would be to move toward social ownership of materials-production industries.

Social control of land would restrict or regulate the speculative private use and disposition of land. Nonprofit land banks would make it possible for municipalities to acquire and hold land for future development.

Public financing, say Achtenberg and Marcuse, is necessary because as long as housing remains dependent on private mortgage credit, it will continue to be costly to society and in short supply. In the immediate future, we should create measures to allocate more private credit to housing as well as alternative public sources of housing credit (such as state housing banks and public pension funds). As for the long term, in much the same way that government military facilities make direct payment to building contractors, production and rehabilitation should be increasingly financed through contracts between government and community developers.[71]

Similarly, Dreier suggests direct government grants and low-interest loans to encourage building of limited-equity cooperative housing and rehabilitation of existing housing. The loans would be to nonprofit, community-based developers, who would grant life-time leases to tenant cooperatives and residents of single-family houses.[72]

The more immediate goals of most advocates of housing reform are (1) protection of existing government-aided stock; (2) an expanded stock of decent housing (new, rehabbed, or existing units in good condition) permanently available to low-income people; (3) a housing allowance that is available to both renters and owners and is seen as an entitlement; (4) more government support for nonprofit groups that can build and manage housing, involving the community in every phase of the process; (5) modification of monetary and credit policies to counteract high financing costs for housing; (6) assistance for alternative delivery systems such as community-controlled credit unions and housing trust funds; (7) a firm declaration by the federal government that it will use its resources to prevent displacement by either public or private action; (8) tougher local laws to control demolition, eviction, condo conversion, and rent increases; (9) strengthening of measures enforcing fair housing laws to protect minorities from being excluded; (10) a strong commitment from federal, state, and local governments to support emergency shelter and transitional housing for the homeless; and (11) revision of the tax system as it affects housing.

Genuine tax reform lies at the heart of the problem. As the system stands now, the myriad tax shelters seem to represent an illogical jumble. Homeowner deductions consume by far the greater proportion of tax expenditures. As for investor deductions, it is important to realize that today people tend to invest not in real estate but in tax advantages. For example, in syndications—partnerships that raise money from investors to buy properties—the tax write-offs sometimes amount to $2 for every $1 invested. As Goozner points out, this concealed tax subsidy is never included as part of the cost to taxpayers; if it were, actual construction costs per unit built by the so-called private sector would be as much as 50 percent higher.[73] As a result of these advantages, it can often be profitable to overbuild real estate such as office buildings. (Of course, eventually developers can reach a point of diminishing returns.) Such a system is hardly a free market, although it is promoted as such.

Moreover, says Dolbeare, at least three-quarters of the housing-related tax expenditures (mostly home-owner deductions) have gone to people in the top 15 percent of the income distribution. Cutting their tax subsidies by only one-half would release enough to pay for entitlement housing allowances and substantial preservation, rehabilitation, and construction.[74]

A new tax reform such as that contained in the 1985 Reagan plan would abolish some of the breaks, simplify the present complex system, and provide solid tax relief to low-income families. However, certain tax advantages would remain. Among housing-related tax expenditures, the most important is the home-owner mortgage interest deduction.

Moreover, the complete elimination of tax breaks could cause chaos. The reduction or elimination of such benefits for builders could virtually halt construction of low-income rental housing and cause cutbacks in most other types of multifamily construction. Hence the supply would decline, pushing vacancy rates lower and putting pressure on rents.

Low-income nonprofits and neighborhood groups that have come to use tax advantages as the only way to secure housing funds would also suffer heavy losses. In early 1986 low-income housing advocates were waiting to see what compromises would be made. As Dolbeare put it, housing advocates would once again have to go to bat to keep low-income programs alive despite their manifest shortcomings, by trying to protect the small flow of cash still coming through the tax-shelter process. The ideal, she stressed, would be to transfer the savings from tax changes into direct low-income housing assistance.[75]

In November 1985 President Reagan reluctantly signed an omnibus piece of legislation—a fiscal 1986 appropriation bill that covered HUD and seventeen independent agencies. It funded $14.7 billion for HUD (in contrast to the $2.3 billion requested by the administration), with $9.9 billion of that sum earmarked for assisted-housing programs. CDBG was cut 10 percent, UDAG 25 percent, and General Revenue Sharing 8.6 percent over the previous year. FEMA was allotted $70 million for emergency food and shelter.

In early 1986 the outlook for even the more immediate goals of housing reform advocates appeared grim. Although the amount committed for additional low-income housing had already been cut by nearly 70 percent since 1981, it was clear that the Reagan administration wanted to eliminate CDBG, UDAG, the Rental Rehabilitation and Housing Development Grant programs, and the Section 312 rehabilitation program, and to suspend the Section 202 program for the elderly and handicapped. Only public pressure on Congress had helped many of these programs survive thus far. Application of the Gramm-Rudman-Hollings budget balancing act could accomplish their demise. Housing Subcommittee staff director McMurray says that the deficit has been deliberately contrived in order to sacrifice the programs that are least viable from a political point of view and to convince the public of the necessity to shift responsibility to the private sector.

The outlook for the homeless was no brighter. There have been many ardent congressional supporters of programs for people without homes, among them, Representatives Henry Gonzalez, Barney Frank, Augustus Hawkins, Bruce Vento, and Mary Rose Oakar, and Senators Daniel Moynihan and Slade Gordon. They have proposed a variety of programs, many of them designed to go beyond mere stop-gap measures for emergency shelter and to provide for transitional housing and a range of supportive services, especially for the mentally disabled. However, in early 1986 none of these programs had passed Congress.

In Washington, the ultimate decision makers still seem to look at the absence of a home as a problem to be dealt with on a year-to-year basis, despite widespread acceptance of the reality that homelessness will not go away next year, or the next, or the next.

Ninety-seven thousand units of assisted housing were funded in fiscal 1986. Dolbeare says that at least 750,000 units should be added to the permanent stock of affordable units each year. Ironically, during the Reagan administration the total number of subsidized units has continued to increase, a fact that can confuse people who hear about cuts. It is important to realize that this "increase" occurred only because of appropriations passed during previous administrations. In the future, the federally assisted low-income housing coming through the pipeline will slow to a trickle. Thousands of deteriorating units will not be rehabilitated, and thousands of the needed new ones will not be built. Hence competition for the diminished supply of low-income dwellings will grow. More people will be displaced, and many of them will slide into homelessness.

The crisis of homelessness has illuminated the more pervasive crisis in affordable housing. Will the interests of middle-class tenants—the millions who are seeing their dream of owning a home disappear—once more coalesce with the interests of the poor who may pay more than half of their incomes for housing? Some analysts find that this is already happening, that groups are beginning to unite in a growing renters' rights revolt around the country.

A nationwide effort to give substance to the right to housing will take not only imagination and commitment but also money. However, a country that can spend $293 billion on defense in one year can find the resources to house the people the military is designed to defend.

Are the longer-term goals to limit the role of profit making in housing unrealistic? They have become reality in many other Western societies, whose experience with certain forms of social ownership, social control of land, and public financing suggests that many of these proposals can be compatible with a private market economy.

In general two kinds of strategy have been used. One approach employs housing allowances. Prevalent in West Germany, Britain, Sweden, Austria, France, and many other countries, such allowances help low-income citizens afford decent housing. In 1984, a Swedish family with two children, an annual income of 85,000 Swedish Kronor ($10,200), and housing costs of 20,500 Kronor ($2,460) per year would receive a housing allowance of about 9,800 Kronor ($1,176) a year.[76]

The second approach is expansion of the housing base by financing, subsidizing, and/or regulating home construction. The latter strategy is exemplified by Britain's efforts to build quality public housing. People from all income groups, not only the poor, live in such flats. By the mid-seventies, one household out of every four in England was living in public housing.[77]

In Sweden there are three housing sectors: the public, which has built about 45 percent of all housing since World War II; consumer cooperatives, which have constructed about 20 percent of all units; and the private sector, which has contributed about 35 percent. In all sectors, the Swedish government provides most of the financing. The government also plans housing construction, designs satellite cities, and establishes building standards and location requirements. Builders must take the needs of all income groups into account.

France, West Germany, and Holland do not directly own a large proportion of the housing sector, but, like Sweden, they subsidize quasi-public housing authorities and private home builders. As previously noted, in Denmark traditional mortgage institutions are nonprofit organizations under public control. The same is true of building societies in Great Britain.

While Britain and France still have substandard housing, it is far better than America's worst neighborhoods. In Switzerland, West Germany, Holland, Belgium, Sweden, Norway, Denmark, Finland, and Austria, it is virtually impossible to find slums in the cities. The share of the public budget allocated for housing is from two to five times higher in Western Europe than in the United States.

In the United States about 4 million housing units are subsidized by HUD and about 1 million are assisted by FmHA. This means that less than one household in sixteen is living in directly assisted housing. That is the lowest proportion among the so-called civilized countries. It is no coincidence that in other industrialized nations homelessness is not as serious a problem as in the United States.

6

Back Wards, Back Alleys:
The Deinstitutionalized and the
Never-Institutionalized Mentally Ill

After twelve years of childlike existence in a mental hospital, 31-year-old John Jones was discharged to independent living with a bus token and directions to the welfare office and the community mental health clinic. He had no relatives in the community.[a]

After three days of wandering the streets in confusion, he found the office. There the intake worker gave him a list of shelters so he could have a temporary address in order to qualify for SSI. The first two shelters were full; the third managed to give him a mat on the floor of a dormitory. That night a fellowsleeper stole his coat. Frightened and demoralized, John returned to the streets.

For the next four days he lived on handouts from passersby and on scraps retrieved from garbage cans. The nights were getting colder, however. With no coat, little food in his stomach, and none of the medication he had been receiving in the hospital, John began to develop the shakes. He managed to find the first shelter, and this time was accepted. The next morning a shelter worker, recognizing his confusion, accompanied him to the Social Security office and verified that he had an address. After a long investigation that John seemed unable to comprehend, he was deemed eligible for SSI. For food stamps he had to find his way to the food stamp office, however. For a medical card he had to return to the welfare office. For help in finding permanent housing, he had to go to a separate department in the welfare office. Since the shelter worker was overwhelmed with other duties, John had to negotiate all this on his own.

After days of waiting in line at these offices, John triumphed. He had food stamps, a medical card, and even a foster home. A welfare worker persuaded him to apply for treatment at the community mental health center.

Victory soon gave way to defeat, however. As the weeks passed in his new foster home, John began to complain that the food was poor, that the foster parents were nasty, and that he was being ripped off because they appropriated his SSI check every month. The counselor at the mental health center did not investigate the

---

[a]The story of John Jones is based on actual incidents. The name and some details have been changed to preserve confidentiality.

situation because that was the province of the welfare office. For two hours one afternoon and one hour on another afternoon, John waited for his welfare worker until the office closed. The next day he saw her. Since twenty other clients were waiting, the harassed worker simply made a quick call to the foster parents, listened to their story, and decided that John's complaints could be attributed to his "paranoid tendencies."

One day John left the foster home. This meant leaving all his social benefits behind as well. For six weeks he roamed the streets without his medication. At night he found refuge in an abandoned building, where he cooked over a wood fire and huddled close to the coals for warmth. By this time the temperature was hovering around zero, however. John felt dizzy and weak. A man living in another part of the building failed to wake up one morning; he had frozen to death. Seeing that body rocked John out of the cocoon he had spun around himself. Dazed though he was, he made his way back to the Social Security office. There a worker looked at his unshaven face, torn shirt, and ulcerated legs, shuddered slightly, and told him that in order to be reinstated for SSI, he would have to go through the whole process again, beginning with establishing an address at a shelter.

He made it. This time the welfare worker placed him in an SRO hotel. John even visited the mental health center a few times, where he received medication and short sessions of group therapy. He seemed to be better. Six months later, the SRO was converted to condominiums. When John resisted eviction, the landlord simply put all of his belongings out on the street, locked him out of the building, and threatened to set police dogs on him if he dared to come back.

Shaken, fearful of the world that seemed to be closing in on him, and fearful of the rage that seemed to be taking possession of his body, John sat down on the sidewalk beside his possessions. Passersby kicked at him. Others commented about "that drunken bum there." John's fists clenched as he struggled with the violent emotions running through his body. Then a policeman came up and ordered him to move. That did it. The fear of authority seemed to override his anger; meekly he moved off the sidewalk.

For John now the only solution was to stay as far away as possible from the police, landlords, welfare workers, Social Security, shelters, the mental health clinic—from the system. He took to the streets once more. Much of the time he sat in a stupor, occasionally conversing with his dead mother and father. From time to time he did odd jobs such as painting houses and hauling furniture to supplement his meager income from panhandling and selling his blood. Occasionally he visited the mental health clinic and received medication.

The next winter, after the first blizzard, John struggled through still another redetermination process and again was recertified for SSI. Four months later, an SSI review board appeared on the scene to scrutinize every case, so that chiselers could be weeded out. John's case was among those dropped from the rolls; because he had worked occasionally in the last twelve months, he was not truly needy, not truly disabled.

Because he was fortunate enough to live in one of the states that offer GA, John was able to qualify for the GA stipend of $103 a month (then about one-third of the standard SSI payment). A room in the most run-down hotels in the city would cost $140 a month. The overcrowded shelters could offer only temporary accommodation.

This time John is out on the streets, living rough, for good. John is not rebelling; he has no energy left for that. Twice a day he stands in a soupline, muttering "thanks" as the volunteers dole out stew or macaroni. In the evening he finds refuge under a bridge with two dozen others. During the day he usually sits on a park bench buttoning and unbuttoning his pants, and carrying on long conversations with his parents. Passersby cannot see his companions, but to John they are the only real friends he knows.

Today most mental hospital patients are not discharged to the streets. Many meet before discharge with hospital caseworkers who make plans for treatment at community mental health centers and discuss living arrangements with welfare workers. Even in the 1960s and 1970s, before the furor over the failure of deinstitutionalization prompted hospitals to do better aftercare planning, the majority of such patients returned to their families or went to nursing homes, group homes, board-and-care facilities, or SROs. When the formerly hospitalized end up on the streets, it is usually the result of a several-step process.

On the other hand, discharges like John's are by no means uncommon. During fiscal 1979–80, 23 percent of the releases from New York State psychiatric centers were to "unknown" living arrangements.[1] A 1985 Ohio Department of Mental Health study of the homeless revealed that only 60 percent of the respondents said that community living plans (including arrangements with families) had been made for them.[2] Although considerable progress has been made in the 1980s, the lack of integrated planning designed to coordinate mental health care and living arrangements remains a serious problem.

Most of the public debate surrounding the disposition of the homeless mentally ill has focused on deinstitutionalized patients. The reality is that a large and rapidly growing proportion of the mentally disabled on the streets have never been treated in a state hospital. Some in this group have received short-term care in outpatient clinics; others have had no treatment at all. They are nonetheless casualties of the deinstitutionalization philosophy—or rather of its implementation.

Public debate on the issue has also tended to center on the lack of community-based mental health care for people discharged from state hospitals. Dr. John Talbott, past president of the American Psychiatric Association (APA) has declared that fewer than a quarter of such patients remain in any mental health program at all.[3]

Although the adequacy of treatment facilities still constitutes an urgent problem, more significant is the inadequacy of basic life supports, especially shelter. The mentally ill are the most vulnerble victims of the low-income housing crisis.

As we have seen, in the 1960s and 1970s it was much easier for the mentally disabled to find some abode of their own, however miserable it might be. Federally subsidized urban renewal projects, however, removed some of the SROs and cheap rooming houses. In the second wave of displacement, mainly the result of abandonment and gentrification as well as publicly sponsored urban renewal in some cities, much of the remaining cheap housing (including Skid Row flophouses) was demolished.[4] The increasing shortage not only destroyed homes of many deinstitutionalized singles who were maintaining a fragile independence in SROs, it also shrank the housing supply for families. Many of those who were playing host to a discharged family member were forced to move to tighter quarters or to double up with others. As tensions mounted, increasing numbers of the deinstitutionalized and the never-institutionalized were eventually evicted by their families.

Moreover, even in communities where mental health treatment facilities may be fairly adequate, the mental health system rarely assumes responsibility for implementing a comprehensive plan for the patient, including living arrangements. The latter problem is more often assigned to the welfare system. Small wonder, then, that for many poor mentally ill people, the streets have become home.

Many passersby on the avenues, repelled by the bizarre behavior of such patients and unaware of the complex process that led to the spectacle they are witnessing, conclude that these unfortunate creatures prefer living that way. They may be running through garbage, flailing their arms wildly at some invisible being, shouting incoherently in response to voices, or playing rounds of hopscotch with an imaginary companion. They may also be quiet ones, who sit on doorsteps for hours, a fixed smile on their faces, waiting passively for doors to open and offer shelter for the night—quiet ones, who only stare and then move furtively away when you speak to them. These are the ones who have given up fighting.

To the mentally disabled homeless, the world looks quite different from the way it looks to passersby. It is a frightening place. Unless they have been fully prepared for discharge, they are unable to negotiate the bureaucratic maze that is supposed to offer material and emotional support. For people who have led an almost childlike existence of enforced dependency in an institution, life suddenly becomes a tangle of complex application forms, searches for myriad documents, and appointments in different parts of the town for food stamps, housing , medical checkups, SSI certification and recertification, and the like. If they do find lodging in an SRO or in other low-cost housing, they may well be displaced.

The stresses of living on the streets exacerbate emotional disturbance. In some cases disorientation may be the result rather than the cause of homelessness. The day-to-day search for a toilet, for food, for refuge from the police, for an empty heating grate or bus station seat causes a state of perpetual exhaustion. Sleep deprivation can disorient and confuse even the healthiest human beings. When it is combined with poor nutrition, lack of shelter, constant exposure to the elements, physical and mental infirmities, and little or no medical care, the results can be total breakdown of the body and spirit.

The Growth of the Deinstitutionalization Movement

In 1955, 558,922 people were residents of state mental hospitals in the United States. By 1982 that population had shrunk by more than three-quarters to 125,200.[5] The reduction was due to a general reduction in the length of stay as well as discharge policies per se. Nevertheless, no other industrialized nation has reduced its public mental hospital census as rapidly or has left such a large proportion of its citizens homeless as the United States, says Gittelman.[6] Even in the United Kingdom under Margaret Thatcher, the number of mental hospital beds has been reduced by only one-half, and the reduction has been accompanied by an increase in hostels and rehabilitative facilities.[7]

Three factors contributed to this phenomenon: (1) the widespread use of antipsychotic drugs, which meant that more patients could be maintained outside a hospital setting; (2) the growth of a movement upholding the civil rights of mental patients, including the right to refuse institutionalization unless there was a clear danger to self or others; and (3) the development of the philosophy that most patients should be treated in the least restrictive setting possible, preferably in small, decentralized, multiservice facilities in their own communities, near their homes and families. Hospitals should be used only for *treatment* of the mentally ill; nursing homes, board-and-care homes, and similar congregate facilities could house and care for them.

That philosophy grew out of a series of exposés revealing deplorable conditions in many state hospitals. Before deinstitutionalization and the emphasis on patients' rights, some patients were physically mistreated or were submitted to experimentation. Some residents did not belong there. Husbands sometimes committed wives instead of dealing with the underlying marital problems. (Occasionally wives committed husbands, but more often it was the other way around.) Children might be committed because their parents could not deal with them. Some children spent their growing-up years in institutions. Today, in most states, involuntary commitment is far more difficult.

A less frequently stated factor in the growth of the movement was the desire of the state governments to save money by cutting down the resident population. In 1963 Aid to the Disabled became available to the mentally ill. Such federal grants-in-aid, in some states supplemented by state funds, made it possible for discharged patients to support themselves either at home or in such places as SROs and board-and-care homes. States found that it cost less to maintain these people outside the walls of the hospital.

In the same year President Kennedy, declaring that "reliance on the cold mercy of custodial isolation will be supplanted by the open warmth of community concern," signed the 1963 Mental Retardation Facilities and Community Mental Health Centers (CMHC) Construction Act. The legislation funded construction of outpatient centers around the country that included a variety of programs. To qualify for federal funding, the centers had to include at least five basic services: outpatient, inpatient (for those who were acutely psychotic but did not need long-term hospitalization), emergency, partial hospitalization, and consultation and education for the community. This bold new approach was motivated by the same concern as the federal stand on civil rights: the belief that Washington had to set certain national standards of treatment to protect citizens in less-enlightened states. It thus helped establish deinstitutionalization as national policy and provided another means by which states could economize on the cost of treatment.

After Medicaid was legislated in 1965, its reimbursement mechanisms were broadened to cover mentally ill persons who could be cared for in skilled nursing facilities (SNFs) and intermediate care facilities (ICFs) rather than state mental hospitals. Since the federal government pays a larger share of Medicaid costs than do the states and nursing homes are less costly than state hospitals, which are supported only by state funds, deinstitutionalization quickly became public policy in states across the nation.

Efforts to economize also played an important role in the Veteran's Administration's deinstitutionalization policy, which began in 1963, before most states had introduced similar procedures. Between 1963 and 1981, the VA reduced the number of psychiatric beds nationwide from 59,000 to 28,500, a cut of over 50 percent.[8]

To sociologist Andrew Scull, the decarceration movement reflects a deliberate effort on the part of capitalist society to find cheaper methods of social control. "In particular, it reflects the structural pressures to curtail sharply the costly system of segregative control once welfare payments, providing subsistence for elements of the surplus population, make available a viable alternative to management in an institution."[9]

The Casualties of Deinstitutionalization

The basic requisites for the maintenance of chronically mentally ill people are threefold: subsistence (food and shelter), mental health care, and supportive services. In state hospitals, comprehensive services were provided to meet all these needs, however inadequately. Where have the deinstitutionalized gone? How well have their needs been met in the community?

Most of the deinstitutionalized have not gone to situations envisioned by architects of the policy. The basic reasons for the failure of deinstitutionalization are rooted in overoptimistic assumptions and inadequate planning.

Few communities have greeted "those crazy people" with open warmth. On the contrary, many have set up zoning and other restrictions to limit congregate housing for them.

The policy, based on the implicit assumption that families would welcome back the mentally ill, failed to recognize that chronic mental patients often exhibit such bizarre or hostile behavior that even close-knit loving families cannot tolerate them for long, especially if they are living in extremely crowded conditions.

One might have expected the Comprehensive Mental Health Centers to provide for the three basic requisites. The centers have turned out to be anything but comprehensive. In the first place, many never got off the ground. The original plan envisioned two thousand centers nationwide by 1980; in early 1984 that goal was 1,283 short.[10] A fundamental reason for this failure lies in the structure of planning. The federal government provided only seed money; as the grants were gradually phased out, the centers were expected to become self-sustaining through a combination of fees, private insurance, Medicaid, Title 20 money, and state and local sources. The centers found it particularly difficult to get Medicaid for its indigent patients, however.

A significant flaw in the CMHC plan was omission of provision for living arrangements, such as special housing with appropriate community support. Furthermore, although rehabilitation (vocational or psychosocial) as well as precare and aftercare services were among those eligible for federal funding, an agency did not have to offer them in order to qualify for federal support. Yet rehabilitation and appropriate housing are even more vital to many chronic patients than psychotherapy. Some centers do provide special housing, help with job training, and other support services, but it is often difficult to find funding for them. It was not until 1982 that HUD included the mentally ill among handicapped people for whom Section 202 housing was available and approved $10 million for 259 housing units for the chronically mentally ill.[11]

Add to all these structural obstacles a human element: the reluctance of many clinicians to work with poor and/or seriously ill mental patients. As Irene Schiffren Levine, coordinator of the Program for the Homeless Mentally Ill of the National Institute of Mental Health, observes, staff members have preferred to work with the "worried well." In a report for the American Psychological Association, Smith and Hobbs have offered this assessment of services:

> The more advanced mental health services have tended to be a middle-class luxury; chronic mental hospital custody, a lower-class horror. The relationship between the mental health helper and the helped has been governed by an affinity of the clean for the clean, the educated for the educated, the affluent for the affluent.[12]

CMHCs, then, have been no solution for a great many low-income discharged patients with multiple needs. In 1975 Congress did enact P.L. 94–63, which amended CMHC legislation to include mandates for some community support and rehabilitation programs (such as halfway houses). In 1980 Congress passed the Mental Health Systems Act to mandate a federal-state effort to improve care of seriously mentally ill children and the elderly. A year later, however, the Reagan administration rescinded the act. Congress then passed the Federal Omnibus Budget Reconciliation Act, which lumped funding for all alcohol, drug, and mental health programs into one block grant (called ADM), and cut the package by 25 percent. All the remaining CMHC funds were funneled into this ADM grant. Title 20 funding for social services, an indirect source of CMHC support, was also cut by the Omnibus Act. Today CMHCs increasingly rely on fees and private insurance. As a result, the focus of service of many centers has been toward a middle-class clientele, to the neglect of the largely poor chronics. In 1983 the Mental Health Law Project observed that although four times as many people were served by community-based mental health programs as in 1965, most of the programs were not caring for the chronically mentally ill.[13]

Many discharged patients have gone to nursing homes. Partly because of the growth of that industry and a broadening of Medicaid and other welfare benefits, the percentage of Americans residing in state hospitals and in homes for the aged and dependent replaced each other between 1950 and 1970. Talbott, perhaps the most widely respected authority on deinstitutionalization, points out that in 1950, 39 percent of institutionalized Americans were in mental hospitals and 19 percent in nursing homes; in 1970, 20 percent were in mental hospitals and 44 percent in nursing homes.

Many others have been sent to foster or group homes. Between 1963 and 1972 some of them paid for their board and care through Social Security benefits or Aid to the Disabled. In 1972 SSI was set up to replace and federalize the inequitable programs known as Aid to the Blind, Old Age Assistance, and Aid to the Disabled. Since SSI was a federal program and generally offered somewhat more generous benefits than its predecessors, it provided the means for more patients to live outside the hospitals.[14]

Still other ex-patients have found refuge in SROs through caseworkers' efforts or their own. They have lived in cell-like rooms, used bathrooms and kitchen facilities at the end of the hall, and sometimes shared their quarters with roaches and rodents. Some SROs are fairly clean and well managed. A great many, however, fit Lorber's description of such a dwelling:

> The halls and stairways are dimly lit, unswept, littered with debris and fallen plaster. Throughout the halls, there's the stink of toilets with overflowing paper, feces, and urine. Some of the toilets haven't worked in months. Electrical wires are exposed where plaster has been knocked out of the walls. Doors to the rooms have been broken with boards. Locks have been gouged.[15]

Yet to the indigent mentally ill these quarters offered some measure of privacy and dignity.

As the overall shortage of low-income housing has shrunk and many SROs have been converted into middle-class condominiums, it has become difficult for the mentally ill to find lodging even in such quarters. Since the competition for housing has been accelerating, managers can discriminate against clients perceived as strange, lice-ridden, or noisy. When more conventional customers appear, the mentally disabled are often pushed out.

Some of those expelled from SROs have ended up on dirty, flea-ridden cots in the dormitories or the wire-ceilinged cubicles of flophouses. Many have discovered that these accommodations are more dangerous than the streets. Today even the flophouses are dwindling under the pressure of urban revitalization.

Sooner or later many discharged patients end up in local hospitals because they lack either housing or mental health care, or both. As a result of dumping mental patients, says Talbott,

> Emergency services of local municipal and voluntary hospitals began to reflect the discharged patient population rather than their previous diverse acute-onset group. Even after deinstitutionalization decreased the hospital rolls, the money theoretically saved by the need for fewer staff and less building space was not passed on to the localities. The local hospitals became "chronicized." They fought back by trying to send patients to state facilities as quickly as possible rather than treat them for adequate periods of time with appropriate methods, as they had in the past.[16]

Battles between state and local officials over implementing services continue unabated.

It is not a simple matter to send patients to state facilities today. That is not because the hospitals are no longer there. Although their populations have dwindled, very few have closed, and funding for community care has risen very little. In New York State, for example, the number of hospital residents decreased from 85,000 to 23,000 during the years 1965–81, yet the number of hospital employees declined from 32,400 to only 31,400. In the years 1977–82, the state spent $3.1 billion on the hospitals and only $340 million on community based-services.[17] In 1982, the state spent 85 percent of its mental health budget (more than $1 billion) for institutional care for the 23,000 remaining patients, while allocating only $170 million to medical and support services for the 80,000 chronically ill men and women in communities across the state.[18] Why this anomalous situation? The answer is politics. Hospital employee unions and towns near hospitals wield enough influence to prevent hospital closings. State mental hospital administrators have responded by defending themselves and their institution instead of addressing the need to adapt to new situations.

Yet it has become increasingly difficult to enter or re-enter state hospitals. One agency administrator has observed that today it is easier to get into Harvard than a state hospital. Whereas deinstitutionalization has been ebbing in most states, the policy of restricted admission has taken its place. In a sense, it is the flip side of deinstitutionalization.

As Angelo Sgro, director of the Emergency/Aftercare Service at the Hall-Mercer Community Mental Health/Mental Retardation Center of Pennsylvania Hospital in Philadelphia puts it, "The Philadelphia State Hospital used to have 7,000 patients and now there are less than 800. Generally, patients cannot be admitted to the state hospital unless they have first been treated for at least thirty days in an acute-care hospital unit in the community. These acute-care beds are costly and in great demand."

If patients do get into state hospitals, they are not likely to stay long enough to make any real progress. In California, for example, the median stay is now sixteen days.[19]

Some private hospitals reject a patient if he or she has no insurance. Even state hospitals sometimes dispute the diagnosis of a patient who has been involuntarily committed and refuse admission even though the psychiatrists who originally committed the patient remain convinced that he or she is a danger to self or others.

In some communities there is great pressure to institutionalize mentally disordered people needing twenty-four hour care anywhere there is a room, including jail. As a result, many receive incarceration instead of treatment. Some studies describe what has been called a criminalization of mentally disordered behavior.[20]

Disabling Service Systems

The locus of living arrangements and mental health care is less important than their quality. Theoretically, the mentally ill could receive good care in nursing homes and board-and-care homes. Many of these facilities are excellent.

However, since board-and-care homes are products of the private sector and have an incentive to maximize their profit margin, it is hardly surprising that many house large numbers of patients (sometimes a hundred or more). Some are unsanitary and unsafe and fail to serve decent food and to provide even minimal services. Priscilla Allen, once a resident of such a home, recalls that there were more people around her who were hallucinating and feeling tormented by those experiences than there were when she lived in a state mental hospital. "The pervasive atmosphere within most board-and-care homes, rather than being one of outgoing, homey warmth, is that of cautious, cool silence. Residents seem fearful—reluctant to speak; to express themselves; or when necessary, to protest."[21]

Those who are admitted to skilled nursing care facilities rarely encounter the array of special services that the mentally disabled need. Nursing homes also tend to rely on medication to control behavior. Although Medicaid regulations require a medical evaluation and a program plan for physical disabilities, there are no requirements for psychological evaluation, assessment of community living, training, and rehabilitation of skills. Rarely do staff members possess adequate training to work with psychiatric patients. Moreover, since most nursing homes in the United States are run for profit, the easiest way to keep earnings up is to keep the number of personnel down. When the staff is small and inadequately trained, administrators also tend to allow overuse of drugs to maintain a stable resident population. National studies indicate that in most instances the level of care provided for the mentally ill is not "the least restrictive setting"—the ideal of the deinstitutionalization movement.²² Preadmission screening processes are often inadequate, partly because for-profit nursing homes are eager to keep their beds filled. Most communities, too, have failed to fully develop alternatives to nursing homes.

When well supervised, small foster homes have provided a good alternative. Group homes and halfway houses, which require more highly trained personnel than foster homes, are also more costly. To staff such alternative living arrangements adequately takes money (although they are far less expensive than hospitals or nursing homes). In most parts of the United States, government and private sources have been unwilling to provide sufficient funding.

Many discharged patients are unable to get into vocational rehabilitation programs. When residents of board-and-care homes are admitted into such programs, they find that, although they are allowed to keep $85 a month of their earnings from sheltered work, $1 for every $2 of the remaining earnings is subtracted from the SSI check. Hence in order to avoid possible disagreement over rent payments, proprietors of the homes may discourage residents from participating in the rehabilitation programs. As a result, people are deterred from saving toward a better living situation, and a therapeutic work experience is seen as punitive.

Group homes and day treatment programs exist in the cities, but in smaller towns their services are likely to be limited. Wilmington, Ohio, with a population of ten thousand, is probably typical. The day program at the local mental health center offers only four hours of activities a week. The two extra-mural residences, each of which houses four patients, are essentially foster homes; they are not staffed by a professionally trained person as would be required for a group home.

The structure of rehabilitation programs is often inappropriate for the severely disabled. Most cannot work a full day or tolerate the stress of certain expectations. Another problem is transportation. In a country that deifies the private automobile and tends to ignore the need for public transportation, the chronically mentally ill are frequently cut off from attending good rehabilitation programs, particularly those scheduled in the evening.

Hardest hit are those trying to live independently in SRO-type accommodations or with their families or who rotate via the revolving door between SROs and the hospitality of family or friends. An implicit assumption of those who originally framed deinstitutionalization policy was that the decarcerated would voluntarily assume responsibility for taking their medication. Yet it was well-known that antipsychotic drugs generally have unpleasant side effects; it would be natural to take them only sporadically or to cease taking them altogether in the absence of someone to supervise the regime. Even if a patient does make a monthly visit to a clinic, this does not ensure that she or he will take medication regularly, which is considered essential since drugs have proved more effective than psychotherapy in the treatment of severe chronic disorders such as schizophrenia.

Ironically, mentally disabled persons who become homeless are exposed to medications their physicians have never prescribed: street drugs. Increasing numbers of the homeless have been diagnosed as suffering from both chronic mental and substance abuse. Yet mentally ill people with substance abuse problems find it particularly difficult to find adequate service because they often fail to meet admission criteria for either mental health or substance-abuse treatment programs.

Even prescribed medications can cause psychological problems as well as alleviate them, especially for persons dependent on outpatient clinics. Psychiatrist Nathaniel Lehrman points out that although the psychotropic drugs given to almost all patients hospitalized today may help substitute for a solid doctor–patient relationship in reducing the short-term danger of explosion, they also produce long-term emotional blunting. This interferes with the patient's ability to function, aggravating demoralization and fostering chronicity. "But medication," says Lehrman, "can only be reduced by doctors who know their patients over time. It cannot be done when the system confronts that patient with a new doctor, and a new 'treatment team,' almost every time his condition, need, or status change."[23]

Like John Jones, many of the mentally ill find it difficult to negotiate the welfare system. The intricate and sometimes conflicting rules and eligibility criteria confuse even workers in the system. (In our explorations into homelessness, we were constantly referred from one employee to another with the comment: "Good question. Maybe Mr. X in Y Department can help you.") Doctors consulted by the Social Security Administration to determine eligibility for disability pensions may disagree. It is hardly surprising, then, that the obstacles in the so-called service systems often confuse and defeat the fragile mentally ill.

Since the VA offers an array of services, including the domiciliary care program, the community care program, VA hospitals, service-connected disability compensation, and pensions based on financial need for disabilities not related to military service, one might have expected veterans to fare better. This has not been the case. In San Francisco, for instance, a recent survey of homeless shelters indicated that nearly half of the residents were veterans and fully one-fifth were Vietnam veterans.[24]

The VA does not actively recruit clients. Hence it is usually middle-class veterans aware of their right who take advantage of benefits, whereas the poor, less educated, or mentally ill do not. Considering the low income as well as the poor physical and mental health of veterans who are homeless, most are probably eligible for pensions. Yet VA officials in New York and many other cities claim that the small number of homeless vets receiving pensions can be explained by their unstable lifestyles and their inability to document military service.

During the first Reagan administration, many of the mentally disabled were faced with still another obstacle. After reviewing 1.2 million cases on disability rolls, the Social Security Administration found 491,300 persons ineligible for benefits because they were deemed able to work.[25] The mentally disabled were particularly hard hit; only about 11 percent of all disability checks went to them, but nearly a third of the discontinued cases were psychiatrically impaired.[26] The rationale of the review board was that, although they might not be able to return to their usual jobs, there were many other jobs they could do. (It has never been considered the responsibility of the review board to consider whether there actually are many other suitable jobs available.) Among those rejected on these grounds were an incontinent man who wore seven pairs of pants at once and a woman who believed that she was a Vietnam War orphan.[27]

Fortunately for some, 60 percent of those who appealed a denial were subsequently reinstated. The irony is that the intended savings were offset by the administrative costs of the appeal process and of reinstatement. Moreover, when those who were purged from the rolls returned to nursing homes or hospitals—as many of the disabled did when their means of survival disappeared—the cost was transferred to the states. Institutionalization is obviously more expensive than community living. The Reagan administration's promise to ease the taxpayer's burden became an exercise in passing the buck.

Eventually public protests over the disability reviews reached such a pitch that several states unilaterally declared moratoriums on cutting people off the rolls. Congress was roused to study new legislation, and HHS finally declared a national moratorium on termination of benefits to people with administrative appeals pending. However, the moratorium did nothing to reinstate people who had appeals pending in federal court. Nor did it help people who did not appeal termination. Some failed to do so because they were too demoralized by the prospect of prolonged litigation. A few had committed suicide. Ultimately, Congress passed legislation establishing that a beneficiary's entitlement to SSD or SSI benefits could be terminated only if there is solid evidence that the person is now able to engage in substantial gainful employment.[28]

Many of those dropped from disability rolls end up on GA, a program that varies from state to state, even county to county. A community that grants an individual as much as $200 a month is considered a liberal one. In about a third of the states, GA does not exist at all.

The Never-Institutionalized Mentally Ill

Deinstitutionalization has generated highly restrictive admission policies, which have resulted in a shift in the locus of care. Most of the chronically mentally ill persons who would have been cared for as patients of state mental hospitals in the past are now treated on a short-term outpatient basis or not at all. The younger members of the chronically mentally ill population have lived their entire lives in an era of deinstitutionalization.

A significant proportion of this new group of young chronics are hard to treat. According to Sgro, "They go in and out of clinics and acute care hospitals with great frequency. But services that are available are usually not suited to their needs. Unlike many passive chronic street-dwellers, who typically are deinstitutionalized people, these episodic patients do request service, and then proceed not to cooperate. They resist efforts to involve them in rehabilitation programs. They are also likely to refuse hospitalization even if it is offered. They *are* difficult. Hospital and boarding home personnel become exasperated and find ways to keep them out.

"Many have a drinking or a drug problem in addition to the underlying mental pathology. Of course this exacerbates the illness. It also makes them even less welcome to their families, who often find it impossible to put up with them and finally force them to leave.

"Since they are likely to be young and apparently able-bodied, it is hard for them to obtain Medicaid and SSI. For all these reasons, they often end up on the streets."

Mary Rose Goeckle, program director of Cincinnati Restoration, Inc., describes a similar group of new chronic patients. "Their aggressive behavior and unpredictability frustrate the plans of mental health workers. If they do get to a day center or halfway house-type of living arrangement, they are often asked to leave because they are so disruptive. Some may live in a shelter temporarily, then return to their families, then get shoved into the streets. And no one has been consistently supervising their medications."

Not all the severely disabled young chronics are aggressive, of course. Even the passive ones, however, find that community programs are often targeted toward the higher functioning mentally ill, not those who need them most.

The Crazy Quilt of Responsibility

In this tangled web of bureaucracies, thousands of the deinstitutionalized and never-institutionalized mentally ill are shunted from one agency to another. Responsibility for supporting them is shifted from one level of government to another. Many receive no treatment and virtually no assistance with housing, employment, and financial support. Some receive inappropriate care. One might ask if the mental health system is not characterized by contradictions almost as illogical as the fragmentary, disconnected thinking of the patients it purportedly treats.

Take Medicaid, for example. For all the talk of the need for community-based programs in the last two decades, admission to an inpatient setting, which is a higher and more expensive level of care, is reimbursable under Medicaid, whereas room and board in foster homes, emergency residences, and halfway houses are not. Both Medicaid and Medicare currently operate on a medical service bias, which prevents them from embracing most social supports. In some states—Ohio, for example—Medicaid funds are available for group homes if they are operated by trained personnel, are accredited, and are supervised by a local board. Rehabilitation of mental health needs can be paid for through Medicaid, but only if the program is classified as partial hospitalization, meets rigorous standards, and is operated by qualified professionals. Medicaid will not pay for socialization programs, although the line between them and partial hospitalization programs often is very fine indeed. Socialization programs at CMHCs are paid for through a variety of other funding sources.

As for vocational rehabilitation of the mentally ill, local programs in Ohio use funds from the state Bureau of Vocational Rehabilitation, worker's compensation, and a state fund for mental health programs. Few use monies from Title 20 (the part of the Social Security Act that funds social services), however, because of the complicated regulations involved. Yet CMHCs regularly use Title 20 to fund treatment. Moreover, Title 20 funds are more readily available for vocational rehab programs for the mentally retarded and/or developmentally disabled.

Lamb says that in general, if one compares funding for similar resources for the mentally ill and the developmentally disabled, the latter have fared better. As of 1984, California pays operators of board-and-care facilities for the developmentally disabled a rate varying from a minimum of $525 a month for easily manageable residents to $840 a month for intensive treatment. For the mentally ill there is only one rate of $476 per month, regardless of the severity of the problem and the need for intensive care.[29]

The fact that the mentally ill have generally fared worse may also be due to the greater fear among the public of "crazies" who "will go wild in the neighborhood." It is significant that since mental health and mental retardation programs have split off from each other, the latter seem to have benefited in many states. In any case, the situation represents a gross inequity.

Decentralization of responsibility, so often lauded as an expression of the American way, has meant that policies vary from state to state, community to community. Authorities use different criteria for discharging patients or admitting them to institutions. Medicaid policies also vary considerably, since the program is predicated on a federal–state partnership, and in the 1980s states have had increasing discretion. In some states Medicaid payments are very low, in others fairly generous. Some states allow Medicaid funds to be used for a variety of programs, whereas in other states few are funded.

Local officials tend to segregate responsibility for the mentally ill. For example, the latest (1981) five-year plan of the New York State Mental Health Office asserts that the "basic needs" of the "street people"—food, shelter, clothing, and the like—are the responsibility of the "social welfare system."[30] Thus clinical problems are assumed to fall into the province of the mental health system, whereas basic needs fall into another.

There is still little coordination among agencies. The policies of each agency force workers to fit patients into categories rather than respond to their individual needs. Fragmentation of service is the rule.

Politicians, policymakers, and administrators seldom perceive or act on the "connectedness of things." The Federal Omnibus Act of 1981 resulted in economies for the federal government, but it also shifted financial burdens to other levels of government. Indeed, the overall omnibus cutbacks in social programs contributed to the growth in the need for mental health services at the same time that federal funds for them were being reduced; emotional problems always increase during periods of economic stress.[31]

In the past, state mental health agencies had clear responsibility for organizing and financing long-term care of the seriously disabled. In recent years some of these responsibilities have been shifting from the mental health system to the welfare system and from state to more diversified sources of funding, including the private sector. In most states today, no one agency at any state or local level has been clearly charged with responsibility for comprehensive appraisal of mental health and community support needs of the mentally disabled, for planning and implementing a system to assure that those needs will be met, and for monitoring the quality of both institutional and community support programs.[32]

On the local level, responsibility for building and/or operating group homes is sometimes split between the public sector and the private; the latter can include churches, consortia of churches, and profit-making entrepreneurs.

That the federal government would assume leadership in creating a network of services was the vision of the 1963 Comprehensive Mental Health Centers Act. This has not occurred. It would seem logical that NIMH take a leadership role. At present its functions include research, collaborating with state authorities, supporting state and community efforts, and encouraging organizations at all levels to promote mental health. It also conducts demonstration programs. However, NIMH contributes only a small portion of the funds needed to develop community support systems and has no authority to operate ongoing programs, set nationwide policy, or even monitor and enforce standards in state mental health programs.

Thus no clear pattern of responsibility for the mentally ill has emerged. The tendency to pass the buck to another agency or some other level of government and to jealously guard one's jurisdiction is related, of course, to competition for the scarce resources that have been allotted.

Here it seems relevant to make a point that appears obvious but is too rarely emphasized. The much-discussed failure of deinstitutionalization has really been a failure for low-income and moderate-income deinstitutionalized people. Excellent mental health care and supportive services, as well as adequate housing, exist in this country—for those who can afford to pay for them. This is not to deny that many communities do offer good care and supports, regardless of ability to pay. But the crux of the problem is the unwillingness of society to pay for good services for all who need them. In the market system that prevails in the United States, mental health care is seen as a commodity, not a right.

The plight of the homeless mentally ill is the most visible symptom of the malfunctioning of this system. In some communities they are offered "Greyhound therapy": a one-way bus ticket out of town. In less penurious communities they are committed to shelters, which are obviously cheaper to support than mental health services and low-income housing. The shelters have come to be known as the asylums of the 1980s, yet they do not even offer the treatment that exists (however inadequate it may be) in state asylums. Relatively few of the shelters make persistent efforts to connect residents with mental health services and to ascertain that there is follow-through. Although most of the mentally disabled would benefit more from services established on a regular basis in the shelter itself, outpatient clinics rarely take the initiative to set up such programs. The common rationalization for this and similar failures is that there isn't enough money.

The Search for Solutions

Is the answer to this complex array of problems reinstitutionalization? Krauthammer, whose proposal that the homeless mentally ill return to asylums was described in chapter 1, is by no means a lone voice today. Psychiatrist Robert Lampke, for example, has buttressed the same suggestion with the argument that "if we were to divide the truly homeless [sic] and the homeless mentally ill into two groups, we would obviously find a much smaller segment of truly homeless people, more manageable than the present chaos."[33]

Such voices do not express the majority opinion in the psychiatric community, however. The Task Force on the Homeless Mentally Ill of the APA asserts that those who talk of sending all patients back to state hospitals are exaggerating and romanticizing the care patients are said to receive there. The concept of deinstitutionalization was clinically sound and economically feasible; it was the implementation that was flawed.

Deinstitutionalization has worked successfully when alternatives are implemented under ideal circumstances. Talbott cites a number of community initiatives that have shown positive results.[34] A report by the Cleveland Federation of Community Planning found that deinstitutionalized patients who got more extensive and more varied services tended to remain in the community longer and to have fewer rehospitalizations.[35] A study, conducted by the Hamilton County (Ohio) Community Mental Health Board, of publicly funded residential programs in the county revealed that only 6 percent of the residents return to the hospital directly from a residential program and that only 27 percent of these clients were rehospitalized within eighteen months of beginning a residential program. This rate is substantially lower than the national rehospitalization norm of 40 to 50 percent at eighteen months.[36]

The authors of the APA report on the homeless mentally ill do not believe that there is a simple either-or answer to the issue of deinstitutionalization versus reinstitutionalization. The report does recommend that for the small proportion of the chronically mentally ill who do not respond to current methods of treatment and rehabilitation, ongoing asylum and sanctuary should be available, whether in hospitals or in locked skilled-nursing facilities that have special programs for the mentally ill.

This line of reasoning was set forth by Detzer, a psychiatric social worker with many years experience in the inpatient treatment of chronic schizophrenics. It is true that for some schizophrenics whose illness is under sufficient control, halfway houses, day treatment programs, sheltered workshops, even solitary apartments may be appropriate, he says. However, for the

Severe, chronic schizophrenic who experiences frequent exacerbation of psychotic symptoms (and there are thousands of such persons nationwide), there is no acceptable alternative to institutionalization for an indefinite period. . . . Chronically mentally ill individuals must be supervised, directed, and protected in a way which is not possible in community programs.[37]

What about the danger of institutionalization—the process by which patients can lose a sense of themselves as self-directed human beings? Although Detzer points up the positive aspects of hospitalization (food, shelter, clothing, medical and psychiatric care, a safe environment, even a community of sorts), he is well aware of the drawbacks. Few institutions, he says, provide opportunities for meaningful labor, earning money, and some participation in decision making. *All* these characteristics are essential in the *benign* institution Detzer envisions.[38]

If reinstitutionalization (even into improved facilities) is not appropriate for the majority of the discharged mentally ill, then the challenge is to upgrade and extend community services. Those services should meet the needs of both the homeless and those who may now be domiciled but are poorly served by the system. A comprehensive system should help prevent homelessness.

As Talbott points out, the problem is not the setting. Moving the locus of care will not in itself provide a solution. We must begin, he emphasizes, by focusing on the individual patient and his or her needs. In the past, we have concentrated on the needs of the system or on the politician's problem of selling whatever programs are proposed. Changing focus will not be easy.[39]

The paramount need is for systems based on continuity of care, perhaps modeled on those in England. Talbott stresses the necessity for a range of graded treatment services and housing alternatives that progress from inpatient facilities to community care programs. Ideally, treatment opportunities would extend from prehospital services (such as round-the-clock crisis intervention) through inpatient services to aftercare and rehabilitation. Living situations would range from prehospital facilities (crisis hostel or partial hospitalization) through inpatient settings to partial hospitalization (day, night, or weekend), the quarterway house, the halfway house, the hotel ward, Fairweather Lodge (a facility intermediary between the hospital and a community setting), group living, communal apartment, foster care, and individual home or apartment living (including homeshare programs). Wherever appropriate, housing would be linked to supportive services. The task of preparing patients for life in the community would, of course, start in the hospital. This spectrum of services would mean a single system of care with tracking of patients throughout the system.[40]

What planning principles could implement such a system? Among those described by Bachrach are:

Precise goals. Objectives should be reasonable and consistent with the resources of the target population.

Individualized programming. Certain treatment and/or living settings are appropriate for the chronically mentally ill, others for episodic patients. Within these broad categories, too, individual patients vary a great deal. Hence they should be placed in programs compatible with their current level of functioning. Some will need structured treatment settings; others will reject them. Some can respond to skill training; others cannot. Some may require supportive services that last indefinitely.

Flexibility. Program formats should be responsive to ever-changing needs. It seems generally inappropriate to think in terms of linear progress.

Interagency cooperation. The ideal would be to unify services, so that all agencies offering treatment and support come under a single planning and coordinating authority. At the same time, participating agencies should be allowed to maintain their unique identities.[41]

Such a framework represents a long-term goal. It will mean new approaches in housing, treatment, supportive services, and funding. Meanwhile, attempts are being made to incorporate at least some pieces of the system envisioned.

Some Efforts in Comprehensive Care

Some segments of the comprehensive concept are present in the approach of New York's Fountain House. Its clubhouse model has been adopted by many states across the nation and many cities around the world. The clubhouse is an intentional community designed to help deinstitutionalized persons raise their level of effective participation in interpersonal groups. All members who attend are unemployed; most have been without work for many years or have been unsuccessful in holding a job for long. Almost all have experienced long-term or multiple psychiatric hospitalizations.

Clubhouse programs do not deal directly with their members' mental illness, but instead provide rehabilitation through participation in day activities that range from menu planning to writing and editing a daily newspaper. The Fountain House program also includes transitional employment, a horticultural program, work on the Fountain House farm, and housing in the community for those who have no suitable home. Of special significance is a service providing more intensive care, both medical and psychiatric, to those unable to participate effectively in the day program. On average about three hundred members attend the clubhouse each day. Thus, for a very limited number of patients, social, medical, psychiatric, housing, and employment needs can be met under the aegis of one structure.

Some communities are moving toward a more integrated system. In Cincinnati, for instance, six levels of transitional rehabilitative living are offered to patients who have been discharged or never hospitalized: halfway houses, group homes, supervised apartments, coordinated apartments, day centers (for those who stay with their families as well as patients in group homes or in apartments), and independent living that can include some contact with the program. Yet the community-based program serves perhaps a third of the mentally disabled in the community. Others fall through the cracks because they drop out, are too disruptive to fit into existing programs, or, more commonly, because there are not enough funds to create sufficient treatment or supportive services.

As long ago as 1977 NIMH launched a demonstration project known as the Community Support Program to improve services for adults with chronic mental illness. The basic idea was to widen the scope of the mental health system to include leadership responsibility for securing not only mental health services but also support and rehabilitation services in the community. A Community Support System (CSS) was defined as a network of caring and responsible people (family, friends, and community members as well as service providers) who were committed to helping mentally disabled adults meet their needs and develop their potential without being unnecessarily excluded from the community. Central to implementing this concept was use of a case manager to coordinate the varied functions of the network serving each patient's needs. Support included assistance in applying for entitlements, crisis stabilization services, psychosocial rehabilitation, supportive living and working arrangements, medical and mental health care, and backup support to families, friends, and community members.

In 1978 HUD and HHS collaborated to broaden the demonstration program. HUD provided low-interest loans for housing development through the Section 202 Direct Loan Program and rental subsidies for housing units through the Section 8 program, and HHS allowed certain Medicaid regulations to be temporarily waived at state option. These financing mechanisms were used for construction or rehabilitation of either group homes or independent living apartments, linked to a range of supportive services.

The project was successful in stimulating most of the nineteen states involved to earmark increased proportions of state mental health budgets for community services for the chronically mentally ill, in securing set-asides at the state level of Section 8 subsidies, and in proving that comprehensive services linked with improved housing are effective in reducing the need for hospitalization.[42]

New York, one of the states involved in the demonstration, has applied the CSS concept in many parts of the state. William Goldberg, program supervisor for Rehabilitative Services at Rockland County Community Mental Health Center, describes his program:

> In Rockland County, our community support system provides these same individuals with a treatment program seven days and five evenings each week. Our case managers help formerly institutionalized people to find treatment programs and to travel to them; they provide assistance in finding proper housing and help their clients negotiate the systems which they encounter in the community. Our crisis service is open twenty-four hours a day, seven days a week, so help is always a telephone call away. In Rockland County we have proven that formerly insti-

tutionalized people can maintain their freedom in the community at less cost than in a state institution so long as proper support services are available to them.[43]

CSSs have not always lived up to their promise, however. Baxter and Hopper report that

> the experience of New York City—where thousands of homeless mentally ill cases are managed by three outreach programs, mental health evaluation and referral teams, and two community support teams in the public shelters—has shown limited substantive returns. Most individuals remain on the streets or in emergency shelters indefinitely. During two years of operation, a Community Support System in the Men's Shelter assessed several hundred chronically mentally ill persons, but succeeded in placing only fifteen men in residences off the Bowery.[44]

Baxter and Hopper stress that the problem is not primarily large caseloads, but that little can actually be done in the absence of supportive shelter or housing resources.

Nor has there been federal financial support to sustain the CSSs. The spotty success of the endeavor in New York illustrates the interdependence of new approaches in housing, treatment, supportive services, and funding.

Toward an Integrated Policy

It is not within our province to delineate a new system and its interlocking components. Nevertheless, we can make some obervations about what it would look like.

Housing. The need for appropriate shelter must be met before anything else. As one homeless patient put it: "The most important thing in every man's life is shelter. Once you have shelter, then you are able to get yourself together, then you are able to develop the idea of how you can get yourself out of the trouble you are in."[45] Those who work with the homeless have observed that often debilitating symptoms are markedly reduced once basic needs for food and shelter are met.

The general shortage of low-income housing is obviously the underlying problem. In the end, only the federal government can remedy this. HUD should be taking more responsibility in pushing for a strong housing policy that would meet the needs of all low-income Americans. It should also be pressing for more Section 202 housing for the mentally ill. The program, which offers nonprofit sponsors the opportunity to obtain forty-year loans at favorable interest rates while the Section 8 rental subsidies available to residents of the projects provide federal assistance to repay the loan, has served a tiny fraction of those who need it. HUD could also promote legislation making it illegal to use zoning codes to discriminate against the physically and mentally disabled.

States, too, can develop housing for the chronically mentally ill through state housing finance and development agencies. On the city level, government can do a great deal to create new housing for the mentally disabled. Bellamy advocates selling surplus land and buildings to the private sector for housing and economic development ventures, which could provide capital funds to nonprofit agencies that sponsor group housing for the mentally ill and other poor, locating *in rem* buildings appropriate for group housing, helping charitable organizations to acquire the property at low cost,[b] and developing homeshare programs that would match low-income homeowners who need extra funds with elderly and handicapped persons evicted from SROs.[46]

The three-tiered approach to housing advocated by the National Coalition for the Homeless (basic emergency shelter, transitional accommodations providing for some differentiation of the homeless, long-term housing) has particular significance for the mentally ill, the most vulnerable of the homeless. Long-term supportive residences that bring housing and treatment together are crucial if the mentally disabled are to relearn the skills necessary for everyday living. To date the most successful residences of this type seem to be those operated by religious or other voluntary groups, usually with partial support from government.

Treatment. For the mentally ill persons who are already homeless and living in shelters, there is urgent need for the services of psychiatrists, psychiatric social workers, and other mental health professionals who can provide treatment in the shelters. In Washington, D.C. the Health Research Group conducted a survey that revealed that, although there were thirteen hundred psychiatrists in the city, only two worked in shelters, providing just twenty-five hours a week between them to meet all the needs of the city's homeless. The group recommended that the city require every psychiatrist to donate two hours a week as a condition of holding a license. It also asked that fifteen psychiatrists from St. Elizabeths and fifteen from NIMH with only administrative duties work in shelters part-time—a proposal that immediately drew fire from psychiatrists and administrators.[47]

In Phoenix, Philadelphia, and a number of other cities, mental health teams have been working in shelters for some time. Sgro of the Hall-Mercer Center in Philadelphia says that the center now has five staff members who spend most of their time working with the chronically mentally ill homeless at Mercy Hospice (a shelter, long-term residence, and day center for women), at the Women of Hope Residence (designed for particularly reluctant street women), or in the Mobile Outreach Team. Workers on the team also spend a good deal of time in shelters, especially two run by Horizon House. All of these services are funded by the County Office of Mental Health/Mental Retardation.

For the homeless, outreach services are an essential part of the continuum needed. In some cities mental health workers and volunteers make the rounds of the city,

---

[b]Recently New York City has located such buildings for the Partnership for the Homeless, a church group that is renovating them.

offering sandwiches, coffee, hygiene kits, and blankets. Eventually, a team member who is willing to listen and can spend months working with street people may find that enough trust is built up to permit some to master their fears and come inside. Some teams have been vested with authority to transport people for psychiatric evaluation even against their will. One goal is to refer those on the streets for shelter, public assistance, or mental health treatment. Not all programs can be called completely successful. For example, although almost five hundred of the new clients contacted by New York City's Project Reach Out during one year were diagnosed as psychiatrically disabled, the staff made only twenty-six referrals to mental health services.[48] On the other hand, says Sgro, in one year alone the Mobile Outreach Team in Philadelphia identified over eleven hundred chronically mentally ill persons in the central city; over nine hundred accepted shelter at least once. Most accepted it consistently, and many of these agreed to psychiatric evaluations, medications, and day programming. The big stumbling block has been the paucity of further facilities in the continuum: interim housing, special care facilities, and longer-term treatment-oriented rehabilitation residences supervised by specially trained workers.

At the Fenwood Inn/Massachusetts Mental Health Center in Roxbury, the state mental health authority has made it possible to offer a continuum of supportive and rehabilitative services, including two day hospitals, a twenty-four hour intensive-care unit, and a dormitory facility.

A more complex innovative approach, proposed by Arce et al., would involve three interlocking facilities. The first would be a drop-in shelter, an open-access food and shelter program for anyone needing lodging. No demands would be made on clients to accept further placement or treatment since the goal is to ensure the survival of the most alienated street people who can accept only minimal human contact and no structured program. The second facility, an adult emergency shelter, would provide a five-day evaluation and referrals for clients willing to accept permanent housing as well as any necessary psychiatric or psychosocial help. The third, a personal care home with psychiatric supports, would offer short-term residence to clients who are not so ill as to be committed to inpatient psychiatric hospitalization but are too disturbed to be manageable in boarding homes. It would feature on-site partial hospitalization and individualized programming as well as mental health professionals on call twenty-four hours a day.[49]

Supportive Services. *Supportive* can describe a wide range of services to the mentally ill, for example, transportation, outreach, back-up support to family and friends, assistance with living skills in transitional residences, socialization programs, chore service, assistance in obtaining social benefits, conservatorship, and medical care. We comment on only a few of them.

Improved transportation is a precondition for achieving a more adequate mental health system. Good facilities are an abstraction unless they can be reached.

Outreach programs to seek out persons who are uninformed or fearful of existing services should be far more extensive and aggressive than in the past. They can be linked with drop-in day centers, which are loosely structured and make few demands on people who have had unpleasant experiences with bureaucracy or fear that they will be reinstitutionalized. Such centers offer food, refuge from the elements, protection from attack on the streets, and sometimes day programs and referral services. A few are desolate-looking places, but many are staffed by tolerant, sensitive people who offer warm emotional support.

Since more than half of the chronically mentally ill do live at home, straining the emotional resources of their families, the latter will need ongoing support to help them cope with problems as they arise. This can take the form of counseling from professionals and/or support from self-help groups in which family members share experiences and ideas. Perhaps even more important is respite care, which provides a chance for families to take a much-needed vacation. This concept is already an integral part of the Swedish health care system.

Mentally ill people who are homeless or living on the brink of homelessness can benefit from the assistance of a conservator or payee, someone in the community who takes personal responsibility for overseeing the patient's finances and other aspects of his or her welfare. In Cincinnati, Jane Jansak of the Prince of Peace Church and Catholic priest Father Chris Hall have volunteered to assume such responsibility for several dozen SSI recipients who otherwise might be exploited or simply might be too confused to manage their own affairs. People like Jansak and Hall are more than payees; they are friends. Washington's John Steinbruck describes the mentally disabled without such a bridge to the rest of humanity: "They have no one to look over them. No 'support system.' Consequently they begin to deteriorate and that cloud comes over them. It's like night suddenly falls upon them, and they end up on the streets unable to cope."

Socialization programs that focus on daily living skills can often be handled by a staff that includes only a few highly trained workers. Perhaps we need to get away from too much emphasis on professionalization of staff and bureaucratic regulation of facilities. The stress in our society on expertise and certification of programs can certainly create standards that help to avoid mediocrity of care. Sometimes, however, a perfectly good program does not get off the ground because it fails to meet detailed bureaucratic standards or because its originators do not have the time or money to spend a year or two in efforts to meet regulations. Overemphasis on professionalization of staff, too, can sometimes present a handicap for the mentally handicapped. Mental health workers, professionals themselves, have told us that when a program includes a higher proportion of degreed staff, the tendency is for the program to become regimented and for the staff workers to "do for" the clients rather than to help them help themselves.

This is not to say that a quality program can be run on good will alone, or that volunteers can substitute for thoroughly trained staff. Volunteers and so-called paraprofessionals can perform an invaluable—and sometimes irreplaceable—supplementary role, however. Somehow, we must strike a balance.

More attention needs to be paid to the physical as well as the psychological ailments of the mentally ill. Medical teams supported by the Robert Wood Johnson

Foundation and the Pew Memorial Trust to treat homeless people in shelters have discovered an unusually high frequency of acute upper respiratory disease, edema, skin ulcers, colitis, abrasions, lacerations, head injuries, substance abuse, and many other health problems. They have also found that the homeless suffer from tuberculosis at an astonishingly high rate. (One study, prepared for the Johnson Foundation, showed an incidence rate of active tuberculosis 130 times higher than in the general population.)[50]

If these findings describe the homeless in shelters, one can speculate that homeless people living on the streets or in a variety of other situations suffer the same disorders. There are also thousands of mentally ill persons who are not homeless and may even be attending a mental health clinic, yet have not been able to hook up with the medical care system because the need for ongoing treatment has never been explained clearly enough, they find the red tape involved in securing Medicaid too complicated, or hospitals either refuse to treat Medicaid patients or give them second-class treatment. Although growing acceptance of the case-manager concept has brought some improvement in focusing responsibility, it is still true that workers in the mental health system often fail to see that patients get medical care. It should not be surprising, then, that the chronically mentally ill have three times the morbidity and mortality of their counterparts of the same age in the general population and the homeless even higher rates.[51]

Physicians and psychiatrists know that one cannot neatly separate the physical and the psychological when diagnosing a patient. It is artificial—perhaps schizoid— to isolate the functions of the physical health and the mental health systems.

Doctors who treat the homeless commonly cite life on the streets as a breeder of injury and disease. They tend to overlook the fact that many of the physical disorders from which the homeless and potentially homeless are suffering are directly linked to the poor nutrition and living conditions that the patient endured even before sliding into the streets. Tuberculosis, for example, is known as a poor man's disease, related to malnutrition and crowded, unsanitary housing. Such factors are seldom recognized as concerns of the mental health or the physical health systems. They may be shifted to the welfare system instead. Moreover, relatively few physicians and psychiatrists have adequate working knowledge of the structure and functioning of social welfare or the level of benefits that people on public assistance receive. (Many physicians prescribe diets poor patients cannot afford, for example.)

The point is not so much that systems tend to pass on responsibility to another as that a more holistic approach is needed. At the same time, the mental health field, or some umbrella agency, should assume leadership for coordinating the functions of each agency serving the patient's needs.

The responsibilities of the social welfare system are crucial to this holistic approach. On the local service level, they include, at a minimum, outreach work informing people of benefits for which they may be eligible, simplifying procedures of applying for benefits, and working closely with mental health agencies to secure adequate housing. On the policy-making level, they include collaborating with policy makers in other fields and working toward a social welfare system that is more comprehensive, equitable, and preventive. These issues will be explored more fully in chapter 7. Perhaps the most basic new approach in supportive services would be to provide social benefits that can support human beings in decent fashion.

Patients' Rights.   In the current debate over the rights of mental patients, one side speaks ardently of the need to commit a mentally disabled person even against his or her will, when the circumstances in which that person is living pose a danger to his or her welfare. Some mayors have ordered police to take homeless people off the streets during extremely cold weather and put them into shelters, whether they want to go or not. Since the present law allows involuntary commitment to a state hospital when a person presents an immediate danger to self or others, such actions can be seen as an extension of this principle.

The other side places greater emphasis on the right of every individual to make his or her own decisions.

Such a neat dichotomy is misleading. Many of those reading editorials on the subject might conclude that state hospitals would welcome thousands of patients, but for their adamant refusal to accept treatment. As we have seen, this is not the case. Indeed, psychiatrists in hospitals often refuse entry to patients or discharge them within a few days because they do not agree with the diagnosis of psychiatrists who probated the admission. Perhaps the more serious issue is that many mentally ill people have sought hospitalization and have been turned away. Behind the issue lies the reality that in many communities there is a serious shortage of hospital beds as well as community facilities. Today hospitalization is more expensive than ever before because deinstitutionalization has meant more acute treatment and less custodial care for those patients who are admitted.

Then again, committing to hospital or shelter those who seem to be in danger of dying can result in a glow of satisfaction that we have done the right thing, thus evading the challenge of creating a system of alternatives in the community. If such a system existed, there would be far fewer people in need of commitment.

The dichotomy is more theoretical than real, of course. Most of those who argue passionately for patients' rights agree that when the mentally ill person is unable to care for self or make reasoned decisions, he or she should be subject to involuntary commitment. Talbott has testified that grave disability should be added as a standard. At the same time, he champions the right of patients to high-quality comprehensive outpatient care.

Should not the issue be the right to the most appropriate service? That criterion could mean quality community-based care for the great majority who can benefit from it and the right to institutional care. Some psychiatrists and other people who work with the mentally ill believe that anyone who *wants* a psychiatric hospitalization should have one. Is this not a sufficient indicator of pain?

In any event, the 1975 *Dixon* v. *Weinberger* case brought by the Mental Health Law Project, which resulted in establishing the right of those mentally disabled patients of St. Elizabeths Hospital who do not need institutionalization to receive suitable services in the community represents a landmark decision. In a 1980 consent decree the federal government and the District government agreed to follow a detailed plan for creating needed programs in the community. Some state legislatures have already adopted as law the community care guidelines set forth in the two decisions. The next step is likely to be a series of court battles to force states and even the federal government to guarantee the right to treatment by providing care to the mentally disabled in the community.

The *right* to treatment?

The report of APA's Task Force on the Homeless asserts that the chronically mentally ill have a "right to treatment" and "a right equal to that of other groups" to fulfillment of basic needs for food, shelter, and clothing. As Joan Walsh has observed, the APA seems unaware that our market-oriented society has not recognized such a right for other groups, either.[52]

The APA task force recommendations are thoughtful and provocative. They envision, for example, a range of graded housing settings in the community, general medical assessment and care, crisis services, a system of coordination among funding sources, comprehensive psychiatric and rehabilitative services, a system ensuring that each patient have one person in the community who is responsible for his or her care, ongoing asylum for those who cannot live in the community, and changes in legal procedures to ensure continuing community care for the chronically mentally ill. The bulk of the report discusses the manifold problems in creating better services for the homeless mentally ill and contributes many valuable insights.

Unfortunately, the recommendations do not go deeply enough into the heart of the problem, particularly its political aspects. Although the report lists an impressive array of steps that "must" be taken, it does not indicate which service systems or which levels of government should assume leadership. It does not delineate a structure of responsibility. It speaks of the need for additional monies for longer-term solutions but does not suggest where those monies should come from or what the total cost might be. It omits, for example, any definitive discussion of the federal role. Thus the recommendation for a system of coordination among funding sources remains an abstract ideal at best. Indeed, the overall tenor of the APA task force proposals seems to be one of repairing the existing system.

Perhaps patchwork reforms are as much as we can hope for in the next few years. In the final analysis, however, it is hard to see how these recommendations can be fully realized without a fundamental overhauling of the entire health care system.

All Americans might profit from a wider debate, one that focuses on the kind of mental health system they want in their country. It is not only the poor or the chronics who fail to get adequate mental health care in America. Some physicians say that 60 percent of their patients could benefit from counseling or psychotherapy. A 1984 study sponsored by NIMH concluded that one out of every five Americans is the victim of mental disorders (substance abuse, mood disorders, anxiety, schizophrenia, and antisocial personality). Fewer than one out of five of the respondents with psychiatric problems received any treatment during the six-month survey.[53]

Yet many middle-class Americans are reluctant to seek treatment at community mental health clinics because waiting lists are often long or because they feel there is a stigma attached to public agencies or to the phrase *mental health*. Most cannot afford a private psychiatrist, however. Many insurance policies pay for counseling and psychotherapy, but most place a stringent ceiling on fees and a limit on visits. They usually exclude direct reimbursement of social workers and counselors who have only master's degree training. Their services are reimbursed indirectly, since public or private insurance bodies will make direct payment only to a group where a psychiatrist or licensed clinical psychologist reviews the records. (A psychiatrist must review all cases involving medication.)

Encouraging, however, is the June 1985 U.S. Supreme Court ruling that states may require group health insurance plans for private employees to cover specific types of medical care. In this instance, the court upheld a Massachusetts law requiring all such policies in the state to cover sixty days of inpatient treatment in a mental hospital and at least $500 worth of outpatient treatment a year. Eleven other states have similar laws.[54]

We suggest that *all* Americans have a right to mental health care. It should be provided on a comprehensive scale to cover counseling, psychotherapy, drug therapy, somatic treatment, rehabilitation, and related services.

To be truly comprehensive, a mental health system should stress well care as well as sick care; it should be preventive as well as remediative. If intervention or education reaches a person early enough in life, a great deal of needless suffering and expenditure can be averted. The community education function of CMHCs represents a good effort in this direction, but there is not enough funding to realize all its potential. Moreover, present funding mechanisms for mental health reward treatment rather than prevention. Indeed, during the Reagan years some centers have cut down on the preventive component because it is not seen as profitable.

Medical care in the United States also fails to meet the needs of many Americans. It has been reported that some 35 million have no health coverage of any kind.[55] The American framework is the least equitable and comprehensive medical care system among the industrialized nations.

In a later chapter we argue the case for a national health system, federally financed but with some provisions for local control. At this point we are suggesting that all Americans would benefit from comprehensive national health care—and that mental health forms a logical component of such a plan. In many other countries—France and Sweden, for example—mental health is included in the national health system.

Chronic patients and others with severe mental problems who require drug therapy should be cared for under the mental health system, which incorporates a medical model. Most of those with problems in living (such as family conflicts) would probably do as well, or better, in the personal social services system, that is, with social workers or counselors who could also be reimbursed by the national health care plan. Frequently, the latter are more adept than psychiatrists at establishing rapport with troubled people. Their services are also less costly. Social workers or counselors can work either at social service agencies or under the auspices of the mental health system (as they do today at CMHCs). Adoption of an umbrella agency incorporating the mental health and personal social services systems would simplify coordination.

We see these as universal services in the sense that they should be made available to everyone who needs them. This does not mean that they should necessarily be free. A sliding scale similar to that used by community health centers could be used. Those who are indigent would pay nothing, whereas others would make a co-payment.

Universal health care, based on acknowledgment of the *right* to care, is probably a long way off. The ideology of the Reagan administration is hardly conducive to optimism among those who share this goal. Yet it is important to have long-term objectives in order to begin framing workable strategies. Since the need for adequate and well-coordinated care is urgent, particularly for the homeless, it is equally imperative to have concrete intermediate goals.

Funding. Unless new approaches to mental health care are accompanied by improvement in funding, substantive progress will remain an abstraction.

At the same time that there are calls to reexamine deinstitutionalization and devise new policies, funding of services has become even more difficult in many parts of the country. At one CMHC we have encountered in our travels, the initial operations funding originally guaranteed by the Community Mental Health Centers Act and earmarked for that purpose by the state, even after CMHC funds were collapsed into ADM block grants, will soon cease because the eight-year "spending down" funding span will have been phased out. The center has been searching for ways to survive. It has been contracting with companies that furnish health insurance to their employees. It also has been putting subtle pressure on its day-treatment program personnel to release chronic patients within two years after starting the program, even though some of them will need treatment indefinitely. Anticipating the end of that funding, administrators had a spacious new air-conditioned building erected in order to attract middle-class clientele. Therapists are told to ask their paying or insured clients to come two or three times a week even though they may not need more than a once-weekly visit. At staff meetings the big issue has become: "What can the staff do to get people to pay?" Therapists are even expected to bring this up in their sessions with clients. To therapists who object, the answer is: "You've got to help us collect money. Go with the system, or lose your job. You have to learn how to make their pockets jingle."

As pointed out earlier, other sources of federal support have also been dwindling. Even NIMH, which has never been adequately funded and does not provide financial support for ongoing programs, has been subjected to budget slashing.

(Significantly, in the same year that the Robert Wood Johnson Foundation spent $25 million in eighteen cities for model health care programs for the homeless—programs that include mental health care—NIMH allotted only one-fiftieth of that amount for demonstration programs on treating the homeless.) Title 19 funds (Medicaid) and Title 20 funds (Social Services) have been cut. Some mental health programs have managed to find income from other sources. Most community health centers, however, have suffered from the decline in federal monies and increasingly are turning to the private sector. As a result, what one therapist calls an elite system is emerging. One of the original purposes of CMHCs—to bring psychological services within reach of all Americans—is being frustrated. If we are to have a more equitable, coordinated, and preventive system, there is no substitute for federal funds.

Until a universal health care system becomes a reality in this country, one step toward implementing a preventive approach would be to expand the network of Health Maintenance Organizations (HMOs; organized systems of health care providing comprehensive services for members at a prepaid annual fee). At present most cover a certain amount of counseling and psychotherapy services but only with provisions for co-payment. A serious drawback is that current regulations allow such group plans to make profits and to ignore any responsibility for low-income neighborhoods that cannot contain costs.[56] As presently structured, HMOs have a built-in financial incentive to provide as little care as possible. They also make great efforts to limit their membership to healthier sectors of the population.[57] If federal and/or state governments increased financial support for HMOs, and doctors were required to accept Medicaid recipients, HMOs could serve more low-income as well as middle-class people.

Comprehensive service provided along a spectrum of graded treatment programs and housing alternatives means that we need tracking of patients throughout the system. Financial support should take into account the patient's needs for treatment, housing, rehabilitation, and social supports. Funds should follow the patient and not be tied to a program.

It is much simpler to declare these principles than to incorporate them into a viable model for practice. Since long before the era of deinstitutionalization, there has been ongoing rivalry and overlapping among the mental health, social service, medical care, and employment sectors as well as among various subsectors within them. The issues have become politicized.

A single delivery structure to channel services from funder through provider to patient would require clarifying ultimate responsibility for the patient's welfare. To coordinate the functions of agencies in the structure, we need a planning system that has adequate sanction. Kamerman and Kahn suggest that one way to achieve this is to set up a human resource administration authority at the state level with legal authority and real fiscal power.[58] It would coordinate categorical funding from federal and state sources and oversee the functions of each relevant agency in the state.

The question remains as to which system should carry ultimate responsibility for the severely mentally ill. Since these are patients who generally require medication, the logical answer would seem to be the mental health system. Indeed, this is the tacit inference from the fact that the growing number of case managers (who carry coordinating responsibility in the interdisciplinary teams working with the severely mentally disabled) have generally been placed in the mental health system.

This is not to say that it is the only possible model. According to Kahn and Kamerman,

> In the United Kingdom each neighborhood has its assigned local authority, on duty constantly for response to psychiatric emergencies, clearly charged with aftercare for the physically and mentally ill, and for the frail aged, thus incorporating what was previously 'mental welfare.' In such a system there is no question but that social care and accountability for cases on a community care status belong in the local social services office. There is a clearly defined, cooperative mechanism for movement into and out of psychiatric facilities. Where ongoing psychiatric treatment and surveillance are essential, there is no problem with defining the domains of day hospitals, psychiatric rehabilitation programs, and psychiatrically operated transitional community residences.[59]

In the United States, however, psychiatrists and medical doctors have so much status in society that it may be more practical to have the mental health system take the lead.

Summing Up

Excellent services exist in many parts of the United States. However, they lack the coordination necessary to render them truly effective. In most cities they also are underfunded. The accident of birth can determine the quality of treatment and supportive services a person receives. No nationwide standards exist.

What we have now is a competitive, inefficient, inequitable, uncoordinated, nonsystem of state mental hospitals, VA hospitals and outpatient facilities, public clinics, clinics sponsored by voluntary agencies, private sanitariums, city hospitals with psychiatric wings, community mental health centers, private psychiatrists, halfway houses, group homes, and rehabilitation programs—all of which are intended to offer some kind of treatment. Community-based housing ranges from luxuriously appointed group homes for affluent patients, to for-profit nursing homes, nonprofit nursing homes, foster homes, county poorhouses, jails, flophouses, SROs, emergency shelters—and the asylum of the streets. Treatment services have widely differing admission policies, modes of payment, therapeutic approaches, and quality of personnel. Indeed, a two-tiered system is emerging. Those who can pay privately, or have insurance, get one level of treatment. The poor get another; they are more likely to go to a public hospital, or an outpatient clinic, or to have their services terminated. They also are more likely to get no treatment or services at all.

To remedy this situation will take money. By now it should be clear to policy makers and the public that it is an illusion to believe that good community-based care will be cheap. To be sure, if we continue to use shelters as the asylums of the 1980s, as seems to be the case in some parts of the country, then this community care could indeed be called cheap. The cost of ongoing psychiatric care in a state hospital ranges from $100 to $300 a day. The per diem cost of shelters runs from $2 to about $30.

On the other hand, when a homeless person receives no shelter at all and eventually falls ill or seems to be on the point of freezing to death, the police may pick him up (as they did in the case of Franz, the elderly gentleman we met near the United Nations complex in New York) and take him to a general hospital where the tab runs $300 to $400 a day. This is hardly cheap care. The more preventive measure of domiciling him in community-based facilities such as a halfway house or foster home can cost anywhere from $20 to $40 a day. Prevention takes money. Assessment of the hidden social costs involved reveals, however, that lack of prevention is even more expensive.

The diversity of funding sources is both a cause and an effect of the pervading fragmentation of responsibility. It is also a cause of confusion. Some CMHC directors with whom we have talked cannot name all the original soucres of their support. One reason is that they usually contract with a state funding agency that derives its monies from a wide variety of direct and indirect sources. In Cincinnati one service is supported by thirty-four funding sources, ranging from the county levy and United Way, to those in federal, state, and city governments. A smaller town depends much more on the county levy, which is often not supported by voters, especially during hard times.

Tony Datillo, executive director of Cincinnati Restoration, Inc., says that if support came from one source alone, he could cut his administrative staff from five to two. Clearly, simplifying funding mechanisms could cut bureaucratic costs.

For many years the United States has had a fairly well-coordinated system providing a wide spectrum of services: medical care, mental health care, supportive housing, personal social services, vocational rehabilitation, employment assistance, nursing homes, outpatient care, education, and pensions. It is comprehensive. It is equitable in that it is available on equal terms to citizens in all parts of the country. Most of its services are free or obtainable for a low fee. We do not call the overall structure socialism, nor its medical component socialized medicine. We have another name for it: the Veterans' Administration.

In terms of quality, the VA leaves much to be desired. Certainly, the average discharged enlisted man does not receive the same level of care at the nearest regional hospital that the president or generals do at Walter Reed Hospital. The fact that many of the homeless are veterans betrays a failure to develop an effective outreach program and probably a failure to provide optimal services. Nevertheless, the very fact that we have such a system suggests that national health care (including mental health care) is not quite so foreign to the American way of life as the American Medical Association and some politicians would have us believe. Its existence demonstrates that a spectrum of services is an attainable goal.

In the final analysis, the only way to prevent homelessness among the mentally ill is to create a full range of services. It would be a system that could serve not only the poor, but Americans from all walks of life.

Employment office.

7

Work, Welfare, and Well-Being

T he young man sitting with his three-year-old son in St. Anthony Dining
Room in San Francisco looked across the table at us and said bitterly,
"All I want is to get out of the system—the welfare system!"

He was tall and lean with a neat gray beard, handsome features, tanned skin,
and the rugged build of a sportsman. He had, indeed, been leading an outdoor
life: hitchhiking with his son from Seattle to San Francisco.

The boy, blond and curly-haired, with puffy blue eyes, tugged at his father's
elbow."Daddy, I'm tired."

"Just a few minutes, Sean," his father said gently. "These folks want to hear
what's happened to us."

His name was Dennis Hamill, he came from the state of Washington, and
he used to make $12 an hour as a dry-wall operative. "But the business began to
dry up, and I began drinking too much. For about six months after Sean was born,
I lived with his mother. She was alcoholic. Because of that, eventually the state
took away her kids—Sean, and a girl by another father.

"Children's Protective Services called and asked me to take Sean. After thinking about it a while, I said yes. During the next four months we lived in Seattle,
but I could find only hit-and-miss jobs. So we set out for California. Sometimes
we camped out under trees, sometimes we slept in truck stops. Some of the people
who gave us rides bought us meals. When we got to San Francisco, we camped
on the grounds of the Presidio, an old Army base. One day we met a very nice
lady who bought us breakfast and took us to a place where they made arrangements
for us to get into a hotel for the homeless. A lady in charge there suggested we
sign up for AFDC—you know, Aid to Families with Dependent Children."

At that moment a disheveled but pleasant-voiced woman, one of the regular
guests in the dining room, sat down at the table and began playing with the boy.
Dennis looked at her gratefully.

"At the welfare office they told me to apply for unemployment. I was sure
I hadn't worked enough in the last period to be eligible, but I went to the unemployment office. Sure enough, I didn't rate.

"Back to welfare. They tell me to come back with the right papers. I did— came with a whole stack of them. On my third trip to the welfare office, they say everything's in order, and I'll get the money in five days. Nine days later I get a letter saying I'm not eligible, because my name's not on Sean's birth certificate.

"I did have a paper from Children's Protective Services in the state of Washington saying I have custody. But welfare won't accept it—an official paper from a state agency! So I go to Legal Aid. They helped us get affidavits from people in Washington who knew us from the time Sean was born. You can imagine what a long hassle *that* was, writing back and forth between states.

"In the meantime, we have nothing to live on. I try for General Assistance. They tell me I'm not eligible because GA is for single people or couples without kids, and Sean and me, we're a family unit. After I've been told we can't get AFDC because we *aren't* a family!

"This flea-bag hotel for the homeless is a disaster. The room's eight by ten. They won't let Sean play in the hall. I've been taking him everywhere. Didn't have enough money for the bus, so we walked. He's a good little walker for a three-year-old. We'd walk forty-five minutes to the dining room here, then back. We'd walk to Glide Memorial Church for supper. I figure we spent five hours a day just to get food. Plus three to four hours a day doing something else for the system. What a waste! And it was too much for Sean."

Because Dennis had not yet received food stamps, he went to the Salvation Army. The people there were very kind and supplied him with a bag of food and some food vouchers. He could not cook in the hotel, however; hence father and son continued to walk to the St. Anthony Dining Room for their noon meal.

Dennis had not given up hope for AFDC. Finally, he received a letter, dated July 17, saying that his case was being reconsidered, but that if the welfare office did not receive an answer by the next day (the 18th), his benefits would be delayed. The letter arrived on the 19th. "I was furious. I felt, What's going to hit us next?"

In his quest for assistance, Dennis was helped by an unexpected stroke of luck: appearing on the *Today* Show. Mel Torme had heard of his plight and turned it into a story that moved thousands of watchers. Dennis received sympathetic letters, small checks, and even job offers. Then his application for AFDC was approved, an event that Dennis feels was influenced by the publicity.

He was unable to accept the job offers, however, because he could find no day care for Sean. "Sure, there were places where they'd accept you according to your ability to pay. But the waiting lists were two months up to a year long.

"I'm *still* in the system. But if I find a job, can I go to work? Welfare provides nothing to get you started. No money for tools. No baby sitter. No day care. It'll make you *eligible* for free day care, but that doesn't mean a thing if there are no places available. Welfare doesn't give clothing. Our shoes were falling apart. Sean's were too small. His little feet were hurting. At the free clothing store, the shoes and most of the other things wouldn't fit. In the end, I was luckier than other people on welfare because the checks a few people sent helped buy some clothes.

"But look at the *system*. Like I said, welfare doesn't provide tools, day care, clothing. Or money for transportation. The stipend's so small that you can't spend much on transportation or planning. So how are you supposed to go to a job interview? Or make all the phone calls you've got to make when you're looking for work? Welfare doesn't give you enough to set up an apartment. Here it's *at least* $350 a month for a little studio apartment, and on top of that you have to pay the last month's rent *and* a security deposit. In this country they tell you, you'd better work. But they don't make it possible. Welfare can't produce the things I need to get out of the system."

Sean turned from the woman who had been playing with him, and again tugged at his father's elbow. Dennis looked down, rumpled the boy's blond hair, and sighed. "We've grown so close through this whole thing. It *has* been hard to care for him twenty-four hours a day, that's for sure. Still, I wouldn't trade it for anything.

"But what am I going to do now? I feel trapped. It's degrading. This is a useless system."

Dennis had far more options than most other people on welfare. He had marketable skills, a high school education, good looks, and a story that touched the hearts of television watchers. When Americans hear a dramatic personal story of hard luck, they respond warmly. But what kind of response do they make to the millions of invisible people in similar or worse situations?

To most Americans, "welfare" means a hand-out at the county welfare office. They are likely to associate the word with chiseler, Cadillac, fraud, blacks, or do-nothings. Rarely do they associate it with bail-outs to ailing banks or disabled defense industries.

To most Europeans, "welfare" (or more properly, "social welfare") carries a different connotation. They are likely to associate it with maternity benefits, low-cost or free medical service, child care, comprehensive unemployment compensation, and decent housing—benefits for all, not for the poor alone.

Even in our own country, welfare is defined in *Webster's New World Dictionary of the American Language* as "the state of being or doing well; condition of health, happiness, and prosperity; well-being."

In the following pages we show that the welfare system in the United States today not only fails to promote conditions of health, happiness, and well-being but actually seems designed to defeat such goals. America has a growing underclass of chronically poor people because of weaknesses in the economy and fundamental flaws in the welfare system. Those flaws reflect the biases of our public philosophy, which are rooted in our trust in rugged individualism and free enterprise, our deep suspicion of big government, and our devout faith in local responsibility. These values may have served us well in the past, but today they only serve to mystify reality.

Viewing the Poor

Americans tend to divide society into those who succeed and those who fail. The successful survive within a market system called free enterprise. The failures are contemptuously consigned to the subsystem, welfare. They are seen as idlers, and idleness is seen as a moral evil, the result of individual character defects, not of flaws in the socioeconomic system.

"We still want to believe that America is the land of unlimited opportunity, and that anyone who wants to escape poverty can do so with a little effort," observes Rodgers. "In homage to this myth we have designed our welfare programs with a punitive soul."[1] The poor must be made to suffer because only stingy handouts will force them to greater efforts. Assistance must be made degrading to remind recipients that they are dependent and to discourage poor people from applying.

Most Americans grow up with these attitudes; they are the heritage of nineteenth-century Social Darwinism, with its stress on survival of the fittest, and the Puritan ethic, which emphasizes material success as proof of salvation. These values are reinforced daily by the media and politicians.

Even some of the homeless poor share in these beliefs. Many of the wandering new poor we have met in our travels expressed the conviction that they would surely find that good job—it was only a matter of keeping on trying. They stayed in shelters only when necessary and looked down on chronically homeless persons who moved from one mission to another. Many so-called bag ladies, too, share the Puritan emphasis on the value of work and money. We remember meeting a distraught-looking woman in New York's Port Authority Bus Terminal who kept moving herself and her few bundles of possessions from one bench to another. Finally consenting to talk with us, she confided that Port Authority police would be after her because she did not have a bus ticket. When we sympathized with her, and said we considered that unjust, her eyes widened in surprise. Almost belligerently, she declared that this was the way it should be. "You pay for your ticket, you can sit in this place. You don't pay, you got no right to be here." When we pointed out that the terminal was largely supported by public funds, and she had been a taxpayer, she looked taken aback. "I never thought of it that way," she said slowly,

Because of our need to denigrate the poor, we fail to recognize the functions they serve in our society. As sociologist Herbert Gans points out, the existence of poverty assures that dirty work is done, and that there will always be a low-wage labor pool to do it. The poor subsidize, directly or indirectly, many activities that benefit the affluent. For example, domestics subsidize the well-situated, and the low income of poorly paid workers helps the affluent direct more of *their* income into savings and investment. Poverty also creates jobs for a number of occupations such as social work, penology, police work, and poverty research. Defenders of the desirability of hard work, thrift, and monogamy need people who can be accused of being lazy, wasteful, and promiscuous. In a society where class boundaries are fuzzy, the poor provide a way to measure where people stand. Conservative groups need "welfare chiselers" to justify their demands for reductions in benefits. Alternatives like redistribution of income can be made to look quite unappealing if those who would benefit most are seen as lazy, spendthrift, dishonest, and promiscuous.[2]

In the long run, of course, poverty is dysfunctional not only for the poor themselves but for others as well. It creates social problems such as crime and political protest, which upset the social order. The poor have a far higher incidence of mental [and physical] disease than the affluent.[3] Those poor who cannot be economically productive become dependent on other members of society. Crime, illness, malnutrition, and unemployment are social diseases for which the body politic ultimately must pay a price. The welfare system as it exists now does virtually nothing to cure them.

The homeless are the latest victims of this ill-conceived system. Thousands have taken to the streets because they lost their eligibility for welfare supports or have suffered from cuts in benefits. Others have been forced out of their homes simply because living costs have risen—welfare stipends were insufficient in the first place. Still others move closer each day to the brink of homelessness. To understand why this happens, let us look briefly at the characteristics of the major social welfare programs.

How Social Welfare Programs Work

The United States did not begin to develop a welfare state until 1935, with the passage of the Social Security Act. Its five titles provided for the Social Security system, the federal–state program known as Aid to Dependent Children (now Aid to Families with Dependent Children), and grants to the states for assistance to the aged, the blind, and the unemployed. Rodgers observes that the compromise in Congress that produced the 1935 act had an impact on American poverty programs that persists to this day.

> The powerful block of congressmen from the South insisted that assistance be narrowly oriented toward select groups of the poor, that the programs be administered by the states, and that the states be allowed to determine who would get assistance and how much they would receive. The Southern members insisted on these features because they did not want benefits under the programs to be generous enough to undercut the South's low wage structure, and they wanted to restrict benefits to their black constituents so as not to disrupt the South's caste system.[4]

Despite traditional American distrust of big government, public programs have greatly expanded since the 1960s. The "universal" programs, however, have grown much faster than the "means-tested" ones.

Universal in this context does not mean that everyone receives each benefit, but simply that everyone within a designated population group (children, the aged, the unemployed, college students) may receive a benefit, without regard to income. Universal programs, in general, embody what has been called the *institutional* concept of social welfare: the twentieth-century idea that welfare services should be seen as normal first-line functions of modern society. By contrast, the *residual* approach holds that social welfare institutions should come into play only when normal structures of supply, the family and the market, break down. The residual orientation reflects the way that we have traditionally tended to think of helping the needy. Today the American system reflects both concepts, and they are frequently in conflict.

The chief universal programs are the social insurances: Social Security pensions for retired workers, their spouses, and their survivors; Social Security Disability (SSD); Medicare; worker's compensation; unemployment compensation; college assistance for veterans. Since (except for the veterans programs) workers and/or employers pay into a so-called trust fund, these programs operate along the lines of pooled insurance, and workers feel that whatever they receive is an entitlement. Benefits go to comfortably situated people as well as the poor.

Means-tested programs are available in relation to financial need. One must prove poverty in order to be eligible; assets must be listed on a complicated form. These services include AFDC; GA; food stamps; Medicaid; Head Start; the Special Supplemental Food Program for Women, Infants and Children (WIC); SSI; public housing; Section 8 housing; low-income energy assistance; many day care programs; certain health clinics; pensions based on financial need for veterans who are over sixty-five or totally disabled from conditions other than military service; and student assistance.

Although average Americans do not consciously make the distinction, they tend to have very different attitudes toward clients of universal services and those who obtain benefits through means tests. The former recipients are seen as deserving; the latter are likely to be considered the undeserving poor. Greater acceptance, of course, is shown toward indigent veterans, students, and disabled or elderly persons. Lack of sufficient skills to find work during periods of high unemployment, however, is never perceived as a disability. On a conscious level Americans perceive children as the deserving poor since their poverty is the result of misfortune beyond their control. In practice, however, the children in families receiving AFDC—and youngsters have made up two-thirds of the clients in that program—are identified with their mothers, who tend to be seen as immoral, lazy ladies, if not outright cheats.

It is no accident that universal and means-tested programs enjoy very different spending levels. When Americans are told that X billion dollars have been allocated to social welfare, they tend to picture AFDC and other programs for the poor. Yet social insurances, which include well-off beneficiaries, are far more expensive. For fiscal 1986, for example, the social insurance programs were projected at $309.5 billion or 31.8 percent of the federal budget, whereas means-tested benefits were limited to $69.1 billion or 7.1 percent of the budget. Of the $69.1 billion in means-tested programs, AFDC amounts to only $7.1 billion.[5]

Social Security payments usually are far more generous than those for means-tested cash assistance. Indeed, since any retiree who paid into the Social Security program can apply even if he or she has significant assets and a good pension plan, many persons receive benefits even though they could get along without them. Yet it is the programs with a strong middle-class and upper working-class constituency (Social Security pensions, Medicare, unemployment compensation) that are least subject to the politicians' hatchets, even during periods when benefit-cutting is in vogue. Moreover, Social Security benefits have automatically increased according to the rate of inflation shown by the Consumer Price Index; AFDC and GA payments do not. Unemployment benefits are not indexed. Helen Ginsburg suggests that the unemployed are probably regarded as being a notch below the aged, who are seen as more worthy. The jobless are suspected of being out of work because of laziness. Although politicians have not eliminated unemployment benefits, the fact that they are not indexed has eroded their value in many states, which set the rules.[6]

Applying for means-tested benefits bears a stigma. Application forms are far longer than for Social Security. Minute details about persons living in the same household are required, as well as birth certificates, death certificates, utility bills, wage stubs, rent receipts, bank books, health and life insurance policies, and other documents. Many clients report that they feel as if the caseworker were a detective seeking to find some loophole in their stories. There is no doubt that most caseworkers are trained to be suspicious and to ferret out any conceivable sign of fraud. Indeed, their jobs hinge partly on this ability. Yet Huttman says that studies of AFDC caseloads have repeatedly shown low ineligibility rates and reports that a study by HEW (now HHS) of fraud revealed that 51 percent of the errors were made by welfare agencies or social workers.[7] Many errors also unjustly prevent poor people from getting benefits since they may be wrongly disqualified. A study by the Downtown Welfare Advocate Center revealed that New York saves about $7 million a month in erroneously withheld payments. The study also showed that more than half of the 15,000 to 30,000 persons who are wrongly dropped from the rolls are children.[8] Yet the welfare bureaucracy continues to focus on fraud instead of directing its efforts to seeing that all those in need do apply for help rather than go hungry and without shelter.

By contrast, applicants for old-age pensions and survivors' benefits through Social Security do not have to submit to interviews. They can apply by mail, supplying only completed application forms, a birth certificate, and W-2 withholding forms for the past two years. Should any questions arise, applicants can call Social Security workers toll-free; workers often take the initiative to phone applicants and courteously explain what is still required.

As we have seen in chapter 6, SSD beneficiaries do not fare as well as the aged or survivors on Social Security. Between 1981 and 1984, 491,300 disabled Americans were dropped from the rolls until Congress (after considerable pressure) passed legislation in 1984 that reinstated most of them. Thus even a universal program such as SSD can become distorted because of widespread suspicion that working-age disabled people are not really incapacitated.

The benefits of Social Security are sometimes advertised in post offices, subways, and buses. AFDC programs are rarely publicized. In fact, many clients report that welfare workers fail to tell them some of the programs for which they are eligible. Piven and Cloward maintain that this apparent oversight is structured into the system as part of the effort to keep costs to a minimum.[9]

An interesting insight into the two-class nature of our social welfare system is provided by a look at the SSI program for the indigent aged, blind, and disabled. Until 1974 these groups were covered by Old Age Assistance, Aid to the Blind, and Aid to the Disabled, and the programs were administered by the local welfare office. Many elderly and disabled persons were unwilling to apply because they associated it with charity. In 1974 the programs acquired a much more dignified name, nationwide minimum floors were established, and the delivery of service was transferred to the Social Security Administration. As a result, many more eligible persons were willing to apply. The programs still fell under the category of public assistance, but placing them under the aegis of a universal system conferred respectability. Unlike AFDC and GA, the SSI program is clearly explained in federal brochures. Criteria for eligibility are generally less restrictive, and the procedure, often called the eligibility confrontation, is usually conducted only every three years, not every six months. (Even so, there is still substantially less take up of SSI than of Social Security. According to some estimates, at least 33 percent of those eligible for SSI are not reached.)

The same procedure might have been adopted with AFDC and GA. Federalization of these programs would also have been cost effective, because administration expenditures would have been cut. Such a proposal always encounters strong opposition, however, because politicians and citizens seem to have a need to demean the "unworthy" poor and to draw a sharp distinction between them and the "deserving" poor.

A Closer Look at AFDC

The defects of AFDC offer some insight into the contradictions of the welfare non-system as a whole.

Ironically, when the program was approved in the midst of the Great Depression, it was designed to keep mothers at home with their children and out of the market where they might compete for scarce jobs. Today the thrust—the proclaimed one—is to get welfare mothers out of the home and into paid work. Seldom do politicians and welfare planners seriously address the question of whether appropriate jobs exist. Appeals to put welfare clients to work do serve a political function, however. It is instructive to note that stories about a life of ease on the dole emerge most frequently at election time.

The federal government usually contributes the lion's share to the program. Its portion ranges from 50 to 65 percent, depending on the state's per capita income. The state sets the payment and many other criteria. Rules vary so widely that in the last quarter of 1982, 82 percent of applicants were accepted in Wisconsin but only 52 percent in oil-rich Texas.[10]

Deserted or divorced women and their children make up the largest group of AFDC clients. In less than two-thirds of the states are families with unemployed fathers eligible, although federal guidelines allow their inclusion. Even in states that do have AFDC-Unemployed Fathers (AFDC-UF, sometimes referred to as AFDC-UP, Unemployed Parent), few families with an unemployed man become eligible. The father must have a waiting period without employment before applying, as well as a substantial work history, and no man who works more than one hundred hours a month can receive benefits even if his earnings are very small. In September 1983 male-headed families qualifying for assistance in that month constituted less than 8 percent of all families on AFDC.[11] Thus, although it is always difficult to obtain AFDC, it is even harder for families in which a father is present. Ironically, counseling is offered to the "normal" family, where it is considered important for the child to have a male figure present, yet a program for the poor is countenanced that can actually break up families.

The public tends to view AFDC families as large, mostly black, able but unwilling to work, and headed by immoral women who have children in order to get on or stay on welfare. All these beliefs are myths. The size of the typical AFDC family has been declining rapidly. Between 1969 and 1982 the average welfare household decreased by two people; in September 1983, the average number of children was just under 2.0.[12] Although black women do represent a high proportion of AFDC mothers (43.9 percent in 1979), white households still constitute the majority (51.7 percent in 1979).[13] A large proportion of women (60 percent in one study) find it difficult to work because at least one child is not yet in school. Two-thirds of the AFDC population—children—are not candidates for employment. As for having more children in order to stay on welfare, several studies reveal that there is little evidence that this is the reason AFDC clients have illegitimate children. There is hardly an incentive to do so; the increase in benefits is too small (often no more than $50 a month) to offset the additional costs of a child. On the contrary, Cutright found that women were more likely to use contraceptives when they were on welfare.[14]

Unlike AFDC, Social Security permits a sizeable proportion of Americans to move out of poverty. In 1959, 35.2 percent of people over 65 were poor; in 1980, 15.7 percent. Between 1970 and 1983 the income of older Americans went up faster than that of those under sixty-five. One reason is that Social Security was extended from 60 percent of the aging in 1960 to 92 percent in 1981. Another reason is that benefit levels were increased and then indexed.[15]

Why is it that AFDC rarely boosts recipients above the poverty level?

1. Benefits are inadequate. They are calculated according to an estimate of need determined separately by each state. Variations in such estimates are enormous. In October 1982 Texas's computation of the cash need for an AFDC family of one needy adult and two children with no countable income was $168; in Washington (state) it was $692. Although most estimates are decidedly low, only twenty-three

states, as of 1982, sought to provide enough assistance to bridge the gap between a poor family's income and the estimated cash need. Alabama, for instance, estimated that the minimum need for such a three-person family was $384, but actually budgeted $118.[16]

As mentioned earlier, AFDC benefits do not rise with the cost of living. In Ohio, for example, there were no increases between July 1979 and 1984. Effective 1 January 1984, a 5-percent increase was voted by the legislature. During those five years, the cost of living rose approximately 45 percent. Indeed, nationwide there has been a very significant *decrease* in the level of AFDC assistance. In 1975 the average stipend per person amounted to $72.40. When adjusted for inflation in 1967 dollars, that sum would equal $44.89. By 1983 the average rose to $106.38—only $35.31 when computed in 1967 dollars.[17]

Because there is no national minimum and stipends vary widely from state to state, some recipients are mired in abject poverty. For example, in 1983 Mississippi (traditionally the state with the lowest benefits) granted $91.02 a month to a penniless family of one adult and two children.[18]

2. Millions of needy people are excluded. Because of the categorical nature of the welfare system, an individual's *need* for assistance or services is not the primary criterion, but rather his or her eligibility within certain guidelines (age, disability, family status, veteran status, and as well as financial want). The only assistance for which one can become eligible simply by being poor (providing that one has few assets) is the food stamp program. Some needy people do not fit into the right categories. Of the poor households in 1982, fully 40.2 percent received no noncash benefits, such as food stamps, public housing, Medicaid, and school lunches.[19]

3. Although there has been a constant flow of rhetoric announcing intentions to get AFDC mothers into jobs, actual policies have been so ill-designed and so inconsistent with one another that they defeat such a goal.

In the late 1960s a work-incentive program called WIN was set up for all welfare mothers (including those with school-aged children) considered suitable for employment. A much higher proportion of welfare recipients applied for training than expected; in California, for example, 80,000 applied for 16,000 openings.[20]

The program has been beset with problems. First, despite politicians' claims that many, if not most, welfare recipients are capable of work, the reality is that many are unemployable. Second, many are not trainable or have been trained for dead-end jobs. Third, in some areas the only work available is that for very low wages. Pearce observes that by taking a group of women with low educational levels, low skills, and low occupational status and giving them no training or minimal training in fields that do not pay a living wage, then forcing them to work, WIN created for many women a no-win situation.[21]

Another problem is that, although day care is authorized, there is widespread lack of adequate funding for it. Rodgers says that in the early 1980s there were funds to provide day care for only about 115,000 AFDC families (or some 200,000 children); he adds that between 4 million and 7 million children would have to receive full- or part-time supervision to allow all potentially employable AFDC mothers to join the job force.[22] Piven and Cloward maintain that, since the day-care facilties to free AFDC mothers for work or work-training are very expensive [In 1984 real costs were calculated $5,000 per child,][23] officials do not seriously believe they will be developed on any scale. They persist in emphasizing such programs, however, to appease public criticism by portraying the relief agency as exorcising the moral and personal defects that are the presumed source of poverty.[24]

Although AFDC rules permit a working head of household to receive a standard reduction (disregard) of $75 for job-related expenses (as well as a $30-plus-one-third-of-earnings exemption during the first four months of employment), the cost of transportation and other expenses (including day care in many cases) can total well over $75. Even with the disregards, each state has some cutoff point beyond which even $1 in earnings can bring about the loss of all in-kind benefits. Even working mothers who get only minimum wages almost always earn somewhat more than the welfare stipend. Hence after four months they lose their precious Medicaid card. When they or their children become ill, they refrain from getting treatment, or amass heavy bills, or hope that some hospital and physician will give them charity care. Women who have had medical problems will seek to avoid being forced into the WIN program for fear of losing Medicaid coverage.

The workfare programs advocated by the Reagan administration provide no real incentive to struggle for a more rewarding future. Workfare is a system in which recipients of public assistance are required to work off their benefits in public or private job assignments. The American Friends Service Committee cites an example of a woman in Georgia assigned to clean pots and pans in a school lunchroom. The time slot—1:00 P.M. to 2:30 P.M.—would prevent her from being home when her retarded child came home from school. For this reason she refused to participate. Her welfare check was cut from $162 to $82 a month.

Workfare participants are almost always placed in menial, dead-end jobs. They are not considered employees and do not have protections or opportunities that regular employees enjoy. They receive no wages and get no sick time or vacation. Even some prominent conservatives, such as George Gilder, consider workfare programs for welfare mothers to be an administrative nightmare, requiring large day-care expenses and accomplishing little of value. Workfare also introduces a substandard forced labor group into a crowded labor market, and thus threatens everyone's work standards. For this reason unions oppose it.

If workfare were well designed, with meaningful training, fringe benefits, work experiences that led to full-time unsubsidized employment, and adequate provisions for child care, it might be valuable to both client and community. However, if that much effort is to be expended in developing a practicable plan, why not expend it on comprehensive programs for job training and full employment? On programs that do not segregate "welfare people" from others, but on the contrary unite all jobless Americans who are ready and able to work?

Down, and Outside the System

Most Americans assume that, although the welfare system in the wealthiest country in the world may be inadequate, it does provide assistance to anyone in need. As we have seen, this is not the case. In many states, notably in the South and West, indigent single persons and childless couples who are under sixty-five and without measurable physical or mental disability are eligible for no cash benefits whatsoever. The only assistance they may receive is food stamps. The reason for this anomaly is that legislation setting up the food-stamp program provided that it be noncategorical and run by the federal government. Hence it imposes no burden on local and state governments (except for some administrative costs).

The federal government provides no cash benefits to these indigent individuals and childless couples. Approximately three-quarters of the states do have GA (or sometimes General Relief or Home Relief). The use of the word *relief* conveys the stigma attached. It is the lowest of the low among the welfare programs. In June 1980 (the latest date for which nationwide figures are available) monthly benefits to a couple averaged $157.13 and those to an individual, $126.58.[25] Out of this recipients are expected to pay for rent, furniture, clothing, transportation, nonprescription medicines, soap, toilet paper, entertainment, gifts, repairs, and the like, that is, all expenses except those covered by food stamps and a medical card. GA varies from state to state. Because it is purely a state and/or county program, it can even vary within states. A standard allowance can be established by local county commissioners within a range set by the state. Some states, however, allow counties to decide if they will offer GA, and if so, how much. Hence some counties elect to offer nothing, whereas others provide assistance for only a temporary period, perhaps two or three weeks. The accident of residence can determine a person's chances for survival. In 1985 an indigent single person could receive up to $272 a month in San Francisco, in Cincinnati, $128, and in Louisville, nothing.

Some states permit an unemployed father to apply if he has been disqualified for AFDC–UP because his work history was not substantial enough. In Ohio the maximum stipend for a family of four on GA was $270 in 1985.

The Weaknesses of the System

The other principal means-tested programs—food stamps, Medicaid, SSI, public housing, low-income energy assistance, the WIC feeding program—share many of the defects of GA and AFDC. To summarize:

1. The organization of the system is illogical. It is complex and ineffective. It lacks the indispensible element of far-sighted planning. Funding levels vary from year to year, depending on the political needs of legislators.

2. It lacks coordination. There are too many individual programs administered by different agencies and at different levels of government. For example, AFDC

is administered by HHS and the states, the food-stamp program is operated by the Department of Agriculture, unemployment compensation comes under the aegis of the Department of Labor and the states, workers' compensation is implemented solely by the states, and veterans benefits come under the VA. Each program has different standards of eligibility. For example, one may qualify for food stamps but not for Medicaid, for Section 8 housing but not SSI.

In the mid-1970s, the two dozen largest federally funded income support programs were under the jurisdiction of eleven agencies, and ten House and nine Senate subcommittees as well as innumerable state and local administrative authorities. In 1973 the secretary of HEW (now HHS) described the situation in his department alone:

> Since 1961, the number of different HEW programs has tripled, and now exceeds 300. Fifty-four of these programs overlap each other; 36 overlap programs of other departments. . . . Although studies indicate that more than 85 percent of all HEW clients have multiple problems, that single services provided independently of one another are unlikely to result in changes in clients' dependency status and that chances are less than one in five that a client referred from one service center to another will ever get there, the present maze encourages fragmentation.[26]

This picture has not changed substantially. As Kamerman and Kahn note, "There is no single delivery structure which channels services from funder through provider to consumer."[27]

3. Benefits are almost always inadequate. In 1984 the Center for Budget and Policy Priorities revealed that AFDC benefits for an impoverished mother with no other income were less than $3,000 a year in fourteen states and below *half* the poverty line in thirty states.[28] In 1982 Medicaid covered only 39.2 percent of all poor households.[29] Even Medicare, which includes middle- and upper-class recipients, pays only about 44 percent of the health costs of the aged.[30]

4. The system is very inequitable. Wide variations from state to state are evident in AFDC and even SSI and unemployment compensation, with the greatest inequity in GA.

The system also lacks vertical equity: those with the greatest need do not necessarily receive assistance before those with less severe needs. Comfortably situated persons on Medicare, for example, may receive health benefits, whereas millions below the poverty level are ineligible for Medicaid.

5. The categorical nature of the system means that eligibility has less to do with actual need than with fitting certain requirements. If a jobless person is neither over sixty-five nor permanently disabled, nor female and charged with responsibility of children, nor of veteran status, he or she may well have no alternative but the streets.

6. The system is wasteful in a variety of ways. Programs overlap (Medicare and Medicaid, veterans' pensions and Social Security, workers' compensation and disability benefits, etc.). There have been cases of men receiving veteran's compensation for

service-connected disability, SSD, and a railroad workers' pension at the same time. Abuse has been extensive in the Medicare and Medicaid programs, largely because the medical profession and other sectors of the heatlh care industry have successfully fought against comprehensive controls. Ginsburg stresses that even without any fraud, costs can go sky-high simply because of the way the programs have been structured. It can be all neatly legal but gluttonous, she says.[31]

Most important, the system is wasteful because it is not oriented to prevention. Americans tend to believe, says Rodgers, "that if we give each welfare recipient as little help as possible, welfare costs will be held down. Nothing could be further from the truth. Any program, whether for the poor or rich, that does not solve a problem or achieve desirable goals is wasteful.[32]

The system is not preventive because benefits are too low to keep the poor out of poverty. Nor is it designed to make certain that children born in poverty shall have—through the provision of good nutrition, health programs, adequate education, and decent income—genuine opportunities to live a more dignified and productive life. True, family planning and early periodic screening diagnosis for recipients under twenty-one are available. However, the general thrust of Medicaid and Medicare is not preventive. The programs are not planned to provide care, education, and services that prevent hospitalization. Various estimates indicate that between 25 percent and 40 percent of all nursing home residents would not have to be there if they could receive home health care, which Medicaid and Medicare fail to provide in any comprehensive way.

The system is not preventive because it is not based on a strategy that would move people into jobs. The problems that handicap them—unemployment, subemployment, lack of job skills, inadequate education, and low self-confidence— are rarely addressed.

Training for Work

The Comprehensive Employment and Training Act (CETA) program, to be sure, was an attempt to break the vicious cycle of poverty. Ginsburg points out that CETA was too small to serve all those who might have benefited. In 1977, when there were about 7 million officially jobless, the Carter administration authorized an expansion of the public service component of CETA; as a result, the number of such job slots grew from about 300,000 to a peak of 725,000 in 1978 when there were still 6 million officially and many more unofficially jobless.[33]

Instead of expanding the program or remedying its much-criticized weaknesses, the Reagan administration replaced it with a far smaller one, the Job Training Partnership Act (JTPA). It has focused almost entirely on the private sector. In contrast to the CETA program, some service areas give trainees only gas money while training. Employers get free labor during the apprenticeship period. Any trainees they later hire also constitute cheap labor since the government pays half the wage, through tax breaks, for the first year. Unlike the Job Corps, JTPA screens out hard-core unemployed persons with few or no skills, those who most need the program. Prospective employers also want candidates with work experience.

The program has encountered considerable criticism. Observers have charged that in some parts of the country it was failing to serve drop-outs, youth, and minorities, and that government officials violated regulations by counting JTPA training allowances as income in calculating food-stamp benefits. Other critics pointed out that some communities used JTPA funds to displace county welfare expenditures. In Los Angeles County, for example, the County Board of Supervisors abolished its general relief program and replaced it by focusing all the available JTPA funds on work experience for the county's fourteen thousand welfare recipients. One Los Angeles County official lamented,

> JTPA participation could become just one more barrier to the receipt of aid by a group of destitute people who already have to pass over a number of hurdles before receiving assistance. These people are in despair. . . . But they are not going to just disappear if they are forced to drop out of the program, or once they complete the short-term JTPA training now being provided in place of general relief. If they don't receive assistance because of the way the county is manipulating the program for its own benefit, then we will end up with a lot more homeless people, or worse.[34]

An even more fundamental criticism was leveled by the chair of Los Angeles County's Private Industry Council.

> If I had my way, I'd tell them to draft a law that made more sense. One that provides real incentives to employers to create *new* job opportunities instead of one that pits one needy group against another for limited training projects that can't do anything to change the basic fact that there are not enough jobs available. *All we are doing now is training some people to take jobs away from others who then become unemployed.* . . . [italics ours] JTPA's biggest problem is that it is a training act, not a jobs act. . . . [the industrialists'] goal is not really training. It's cost cutting.[35]

The program was expected to reach seventy thousand jobless during fiscal year 1984—a time when the number of unemployed persons averaged between 8 million and 9 million. This is a far cry from the original goal of the Humphrey–Hawkins Full Employment Act: "to translate into practical reality the right of all Americans who are able, willing, and seeking to work, to full opportunity for useful paid employment at fair rates of compensation."[36]

A Downward Spiral

Unemployment

In January 1981, when Ronald Reagan took office, unemployment stood at 7.4 percent. By March 1984, after a steep rise in unemployment followed by a recovery, the Reagan administration was proclaiming the good news that unemployment was down to 8.772 million, or 7.8 percent—a rate that would have been considered intolerable in the 1960s. Moreover, despite the Reagan rhetoric of rescuing the economy, the record shows that the average civilian unemployment rate during the Carter term was 6.5 percent, and during the first Reagan term through mid-1984, 8.5 percent.[37]

These figures do not tell the whole story, for they refer only to the officially jobless. In March 1984 there were also 1.353 million discouraged jobless, people who had found employment prospects so dim that they had stopped looking for work. Moreover, official unemployment counts do not include people who wanted to work full-time but had to settle for part-time jobs. Those who work for one or more hours for profit during a survey period are counted as employed even if they want to work much longer. In March 1984 those working part-time for economic reasons numbered 5.463 million.[38] If one adds all these figures, for March 1984, then 15.588 million Americans were partly or fully unemployed during that month.

Finally, there are hundreds of thousands of workers who once held well-paid jobs ($15 an hour as steelworkers, for instance) but now must eke out an existence at $4 or $5 an hour or fail to find new employment.

Ginsburg notes that millions of others outside the civilian labor force probably would become employed if jobs were available. Such persons include many students, disabled persons (often prevented from job-seeking by lack of transportation), housewives (frequently left outside the job market because child-care facilities are lacking), and retirees (who may have lost their jobs, given up, and applied for Social Security). All labor force figures exclude the institutionalized population (although offenders do perform work). If the prison population is to be reduced and ex-offenders are to become productive members of society, more jobs will have to become available.[39]

Other factors, too, darken the rosy picture painted by the Reagan administration. The minimum wage has been eroding relative to the cost of living. Periods of unemployment, too, last longer. In June 1983, well after the recovery began, average duration of unemployment was twenty-two weeks, seven weeks longer than at the low point of the 1973–75 recession. Yet unemployment compensation also has been eroding in the 1980s. By October 1985 the percentage of unemployed receiving benefits had fallen to 25.8 percent, the lowest percentage recorded in the history of the unemployment insurance program.[40]

Reasons for the decline include longer periods of joblessness, tighter state eligibility requirements, and profound changes wrought by the Reagan administration in the unemployment compensation system. Traditionally it has consisted of three pieces: a regular state unemployment insurance program, a joint federal–state extended unemployment benefits program, and a federal supplemental compensation program. The regular state program pays benefits (up to twenty-six weeks in most states) as long as the jobless person is still looking for work. In addition, in the past the federal–state extended benefit program was activated when unemployment rates became relatively high in a particular state. It provided up to thirteen additional weeks to those who had exhausted their twenty-six weeks of regular benefits and continued to look for work. However, in 1981 changes were made that resulted in the virtual elimination of that program.

Federal supplemental compensation, a temporary program, has generally been used by Congress during times of high unemployment to supplement regular and extended benefits when these are exhausted. In 1975, for example, unemployed workers received up to sixty-five weeks of coverage. Under the Reagan administration federal supplemental compensation became little more than a replacement for the extended-benefits program that was almost dismantled by the 1981 budget. Hence, during the year 1983, forty-three states provided a total of only thirty-four to forty weeks of unemployment benefits, although unemployment levels were higher than in 1975.[41] On March 31, 1985, with official unemployment at 7.3 percent, federal supplemental compensation was terminated.

Finally, since rules vary considerably among the states and the duration of benefits usually reflects the individual's earnings history, many jobless workers are actually paid benefits for a period considerably shorter than the maximum. Tom Joe estimates that in mid-1984 the average length of time for all benefits (counting the three types) was only fourteen to sixteen weeks.[42]

What about black workers? In 1975 (the high point for unemployment in the 1970s, partly because of the oil crisis) official joblessness for whites ran 7.8 percent and for blacks 13.9 percent. Under the Reagan administration the gap has widened. In December 1985, joblessness for whites was 5.9 percent; for blacks, 14.7 percent. For black youth the rate was 41.6 percent. Even those figures do not tell the whole story. Joe calculates that in 1960, nearly three-quarters of all black men included in the census data were working; by 1982 only 54 percent were employed. In 1982, 20 percent of all working-age black men (aged sixteen to sixty-four) or nearly 2 million people were classified as out of the labor force. Moreover, by that year there were an estimated 925,000 working-age black men whose labor force status could not be determined because they were not even counted in the census. In toto *46 percent* of the 9 million working-age men were jobless—officially unemployed, not participating in the labor force, or simply unaccounted for.[43] It is hardly surprising that blacks constitute such a high proportion of the homeless.

Although official unemployment has been dropping slowly since 1983, the problem of the discouraged jobless is becoming more and more serious. A study by Youngstown State University revealed that federal unemployment rates calculated for the Youngstown–Warren area greatly underestimated the number of jobless. The local unemployment rate for June 1984 was found to be 16.5 percent, as compared with the U.S. Bureau of Labor Statistics rate of 10.7 percent. According to Dr. Terry Buss, who supervised the study, even these figures do not tell the whole story; if unemployed people who have given up looking for work, together with individuals forced into early retirement and part-time workers seeking full-time jobs are included, the unemployment rate would be 32.9 percent.[44]

Discouraged workers have sometimes been called the phantom jobless. Some of these phantoms are among those forced to take to the streets.

Poverty

In 1980 Americans living under the poverty level constituted 13 percent of the population. Three years later their numbers had grown by 6 million to 35.3 million or 15.2 percent.

By 1984 the figure had dropped slightly to 14.4 percent. The modest decline, just eight-tenths of one percentage point, was hailed by the administration as a triumph for Reaganomics. Nevertheless, the result was still the highest poverty rate for any nonrecession year since 1966—and higher than during the 1974–75 recession as well. The rate for black children under the age of six actually rose from 1983 to 1984, arriving at a new record high of 51.1 percent. The poverty rate for Hispanic children under 18 also rose from 1983 to 1984 to a peak of 39 percent.[45]

A cardinal reason for the overall rise in poverty has been the drastic cut in social programs. Murden and Meier have shown that the poverty rate of the entire population based solely on income rose 28 percent from 1979 to 1982, mostly because of inflation and unemployment. The poverty rate based on income and the cost of entitlements such as Medicare and food stamps, however, rose 47 percent between 1979 and 1982. Almost half of the true rise in poverty, they say, was due to cuts in social benefits under the Reagan administration and not merely to inflation.[46]

Let us compare entitlements accruing to the affluent and to the poor under the Reagan administration.

A study by the Congressional Budget Office (CBO) showed that the combined effect of budget and tax policies in the Reagan administration's first three years was to increase the income of individual taxpayers with incomes over $80,000 a year by an average of $8,000 a year. By contrast, those with incomes below $10,000 would suffer an average loss of $1,100 from 1983 to 1985.[47]

The CBO study revealed that the tax cuts (which benefited the wealthy) would cause the federal government to lose far more money ($90.8 billion in calendar year 1984) than it would save from all the changes in cash and noncash benefits programs ($26.1 billion). The disparity was one of the principal causes of the alarming growth in the federal deficit.[48] (Reagan had argued that his tax cuts would stimulate so much new investment and economic growth that revenues would actually be higher than before the tax reductions.)

The poor not only failed to benefit from tax cuts; their tax burden actually increased. According to the Urban Institute, between 1980 and 1984 an average family of four at the poverty level saw its taxes double from $460 to $1,076.[49]

It is worth adding that the average chief executive's salary leaped form $552,000 in 1980 to $775,000 in 1984.[50] The number of millionaires nearly doubled from 1980 to 1983 from 4,414 to 8,408.[51]

By contrast, the entitlements of the poor were slashed. During the first Reagan administration, SSD payments were stopped for 491,300 people, many of whom had serious mental or physical handicaps. Seven hundred thousand families lost all or part of their AFDC benefits, and the administration cut spending for that program by 13 percent.[52] Although the New Federalism announced by the administration allowed states the privilege of assuming more responsiblity for the poor, most respectfully declined the offer. Instead, between 1979 and 1983 states lowered cash welfare benefits by 17 percent.[53] Yet nationwide funding for nonmeans-tested programs increased 24.5 percent.[54]

One must also ask which of the population groups among the poor have suffered most. The answer is women, children, and minorities.

In 1982 the median income for all full-time women workers was $13,663 a year, as against a white male median of $21,655.[55] In 1984 the poverty rate was 34.5 for all families headed by women and 51.7 for those headed by black women.[56]

In the 1980s children have come first in budget sacrifice, according to the Children's Defense Fund. Between 1980 and 1984 they lost $1 of every $10 previously provided by their national government for critical preventive children's and family support programs. More than 3.1 million children fell into poverty between 1979 and 1984. The 31-percent increase during these years represents the sharpest rise in child poverty since poverty statistics have been collected.[57]

By 1984, 24 percent of all children under six and 51 percent of black children were poor.[58] In the same year black family income was only 56 percent of white family income.[59]

An Urban Institute study of the 1981 budget cuts found that, although the average black family lost more than three times as much in benefit reductions as did the average white family, the average Hispanic family also bore heavy costs—indeed, twice as large as those for the average white family.[60] The number of Hispanics living in poverty rose 45 percent from 1979 to 1983, an increase greater than that for either whites or blacks.[61]

If an adult is female, black, and head of family, she is hit by a triple whammy. The Center for the Study of Social Policy points out that more than 60 percent of black female-headed families with children live in poverty.

> In the last seven years alone, the number of black families headed by women has risen by 700,000 and the ranks of black men out of the labor force or unemployed has increased by the same number. The rise in black female-headed families is the result of multiple forces, and these data suggest that the increase is due at least in part to the increasing anomie of black men. If 46 percent of all black men are jobless—either unemployed, not looking for work, in correctional facilities, or unaccounted for—it is little wonder that an increasing number of black women are raising families alone.[62]

Slashes in social welfare programs cannot be measured in income alone. Cuts in health programs and AFDC cutbacks resulting in loss of eligibility for Medicaid have also taken their toll. In 1980 the percentage of children in poverty served by Medicaid was 83.5; by 1983 the percentage had dropped to 70.7.[63] According to David Nexon, senior health policy advisor for the U.S. Senate Committee on Labor and Human Resources, by 1985 the number of Americans not covered by any form of health insurance had reached 35 million, and the proportion of the poor and near-poor covered by Medicaid had declined from 63 percent to about 50 percent.[64]

Between 1980 and 1984 the proportion of those eligible to receive food stamps who actually got them had dropped from 65 percent to 55 percent.[65] By 1984 the average stipend amounted to only forty-seven cents per person per meal.[66] Studies have shown that poor Americans have to pay 26 percent to 54 percent more than what they receive under the food stamp program to obtain a nutritious diet.[67] Although Congress resisted the administration's efforts to cut the WIC nutrition program and even expanded it, WIC still reaches only about one-third of the mothers and children who need it.[68] The child nutrition programs were reduced $5 billion over fiscal years 1982 to 1985.[69]

The 1981 Federal Omnibus Act eliminated welfare benefits for many working poor. A 1984 General Accounting Office study showed that the administration's hope of cutting caseloads had been fulfilled since they had dropped 13.7 percent; there were now 493,000 fewer cases than there would have been in the absence of the 1981 cutbacks. The people eliminated had generally increased their work efforts but still suffered large losses of real income. Many families ran out of food; many others could not pay their rent.[70]

Such programs—merely a sampling of those cut by the Reagan administration—are preventive ones. They could avert disasters that are costly in terms not only of money but of damage to the human spirit.

What other factors besides the tax and program cuts have contributed to the growth of poverty in the richest country in the world? It is beyond the scope of this book to explore them all, but we can point up some of the most prominent factors.

Competition from countries where labor is cheaper and/or output per hour is higher continues to grow. The trade deficit, resulting partly from rise of the dollar since 1980, has meant the loss of millions of jobs. The technological revolution is replacing high-paying jobs with low-wage nonunion work, and substituting automation and robotics for human labor.

Harrington observes that as manufacturing jobs disappear, large numbers of workers are dislocated and cites Congressional Budget Office estimates that by the year 2000 the dislocated will number 7 million. Many are finding new jobs but in another line of work at lower pay. When a worker slides from the primary-metals industry to the electronic-components industry, his or her new salary is only 61 percent of the old, says Harrington. At the same time, new entrants into the labor force find more openings in low-paid service work than in skilled crafts or industries. The lower-income class grows as a result of such skidding, the upperclass is sustained through favorable tax treatment and other measures, and the middle-class, the backbone of America, shrinks.[71]

Other factors, such as the expanded supply of potential workers resulting from the baby boom and the entry of more women into the labor market, have also affected the growth of poverty. Moreover, the minimum wage has not been adjusted for inflation since 1980, and earnings from a full-time, year-round minimum wage job are $4,000 below the poverty line for a family of four.[72] Thus people can work hard all year long and still be mired in poverty.

Another reason that high unemployment continues is that no concerted efforts have been made to address the problem. Although automation has been a topic of concern since the 1960s, as a society we seem to be avoiding the issue. Americans have almost come to accept the existence of a permanent underclass of expendable people. As Willhelm observes,

> Blacks have become victims of neglect as they become useless to an emerging economy of automation. . . . Blacks are not needed; they are not so much oppressed, as unwanted; not so much unwanted as unnecessary; not so much abused as ignored. . . . The resulting anguish arises not only out of memory of past oppression but now, more than ever before, from the realization of being discarded as a waste product of the new technological mode of production.[73]

The end result of this complex interplay of causes is that in 1984, according to Bickerman and Greenstein, "the wealthiest two-fifths of American families received more than two-thirds of all national income (67.1 percent—the highest percentage ever recorded). The poorest two-fifths of U.S. families received 15.7 percent of all income, the lowest ever recorded."[74]

Clearly European countries have been suffering from inflation and unemployment. Most Americans, fed by remarkably consistent messages form the media, tend to attribute European economic problems to the high costs of the welfare state. They overlook several factors: (1) the effects of the oil crisis, which hit European countries to a far greater degree than the United States, a nation with its own oil reserves; Europeans have been paying for OPEC oil in dollars, until recently overvalued; (2) competition with third-world countries; (3) growing military expenditures in response to U.S. insistence; (4) high interest rates (attributable in large part to high U.S. rates, since to prevent flight of capital to the U.S., Europeans must raise their own rates).

Certain cuts in services and benefits have indeed occurred throughout Europe. All Western countries have been challenged with tough choices. All must deal with the necessity of supporting growing numbers of unemployed workers. All must face the problem of aging populations. In the United States nearly 12 percent of its citizens are over 65. In Sweden the corresponding figure is *17 percent*. The expense of sustaining dependent members of a society has far less to do with the excesses of the welfare state than with changes in the economy and demography of that society.

In Britain, as in many other nations (including the United States), the largest
increase in social spending, in absolute terms, has been on pensions. The fastest
growth in British social spending, however, has been on means-tested benefits. The
reason, says *The Economist*, is the rise in unemployment, particularly long-term
unemployment. Those out of work for more than one year are not entitled to the
unified national insurance benefit; instead, they get a means-tested supplementary
benefit. The Conservative government has responded in several ways. Although
the number of people receiving unemployment benefits doubled between 1979 and
1985, the cost has been cut because the link between benefit and previous earnings was severed and recipients were put on a flat rate. To restrain the future growth
of social security, the British government now uprates benefits in line with prices,
not wages, and taxes all national insurance benefits.[75]

In France, the Socialist government in 1983 ordered what some American
observers called sweeping cuts in jobless benefits. The new measures reduced from
90 to 80 percent the amount of their salaries that workers had received while
employed. Rules were also changed so that some young people with little work
experience were left without protection. West Germany has reduced child allowances
and length of maternity leave. Denmark has cut unemployment insurance and
workers' compensation, and reduced block grants to local governments. The Swedes
have made modest cuts, for example, by requiring more elderly people receiving
home helper service to contribute to the cost. Italy has introduced stricter guidelines
for welfare payments and has reduced allowances for children of higher income
families. Holland has imposed across-the-board 3-percent cuts in public sector
payments and welfare stipends.

As we shall see, most Western European countries offer social benefits more
comprehensive than does the United States. Hence some of these cuts occurred
in programs that do not even exist in the United States.

Despite the trend toward cost-cutting, even the conservative elements in most
of these countries have been unwilling to perform radical surgery on social programs because the average citizen has come to see them as rights—rights for all,
not for the poor alone.

In Britain, when unemployment peaked at 14 percent in 1982, most of the
jobless were maintaining nearly the same living standards they had when working.
No families were known to have been turned out of their homes or to have had
to sell their possessions.[76] The sweeping cuts reducing French jobless benefits
from 90 to 80 percent of former wages would hardly seem sweeping to many
unemployed people in America (where in 1984, the ratio of average weekly
unemployment benefits to wages previously received was 35 percent).[77]

In some countries, social expenditures actually rose. In Finland, for example,
outlays for all forms of social welfare went up (in constant Finnish marks) between
1981 and 1982. In the fall of 1982 Sweden's newly elected Social Democratic government moved—in the face of economic problems and opposition from conservative
parties—to restore the indexing of pensions, to increase child allowances, and to

double the supplement for the third subsequent child. In addition, old-age pensioners were awarded an extra yearly stipend of 426 kronor (about $80 in 1983) to provide some compensation for expected price increases, and regulations for the allowance to help parents care for a disabled child were amended so that part of the allowance could be treated as tax-free compensation for the family's additonal costs.[78] In Norway, the Conservative–Christian–Center coalition government presented a draft budget proposal for fiscal year 1985 that cut taxes but also allocated record funds for health and welfare—an increase of 10 percent over the 1984 budget.[79] In Denmark, the new Conservative government in 1983 proposed eliminating medical subsidies for the wealthy. This was quickly turned down, so the government proposed that all Danes, regardless of income, should pay $2.35 per doctor's visit. This, too, proved unacceptable, and the idea was quickly shelved. Although Danes complain about big government spending, polls show that few want their social benefits cut.[80]

Europeans admit that the cost of extensive social programs is high, but as Danish social planner Paul Vorre put it in a conversation with us: "so is their absence. What is the price of illness, pollution, drug abuse, slums, loss of productivity?"

There are three foundation blocks in European programs: viable income maintenance level, basic health provision, and access to adequate housing, say Kahn and Kamerman. Although European countries have problems and gaps in their services, government is expected to play a central role in creating adequate provision in these fields for all classes of society.[81]

Historically, the United States has lagged far behind European nations in the development of government-sponsored programs. In 1883, 1884, and 1889, Germany passed laws establishing compulsory sickness, accident, old-age, and disability insurance programs for wage earners. Chancellor Otto von Bismarck, the architect of these laws, was motivated by a determination to maintain the loyalty of German workers while softening the thrust of the socialist movement. In the 1890s Denmark passed similar laws for its workers, while France, Italy, and the United Kingdom set up occupational hazard programs. By the second decade of the twentieth century, most European nations had created a fairly comprehensive range of programs for workers and sometimes for other citizens. In 1913 Sweden took a major step by setting up the first comprehensive social insurance program, one that provided not only for laborers but for the whole population.[82]

It was not until 1935—forty-six years after the German retirement pension plan was established—that the United States passed the Social Security Act. It was not until 1965—eighty-two years after Germany had created its health insurance program—that Congress approved Medicare and Medicaid. Christopher Leman observes that in the United States, progress in social policy has occurred only under conditions of crisis and calls this innovation by the "big bang."[83]

Today the United States still lags far behind most European nations in the extent and comprehensiveness of social programs. Its philosophical approach to poverty is also less progressive. For example, in the United States social insurance benefits are closely tied to past earnings, whereas Europeans tend to believe that the aged, the disabled, and the involuntarily unemployed deserve to live in dignity, whatever their past earnings.

The United States is the only major industrialized nation without children's or family allowances, measures that are designed to promote healthy family environments by paying part of the cost of child support. Even many poor countries in Africa and Asia provide such allowances. Seventy-five other nations, including Canada, France, and West Germany, guarantee women the right to leave work for a specified period of time to care for a baby without losing their jobs. The United States also is the only industrialized country that does not provide a national health care system. Even Japan, our biggest rival in free enterprise, has had a successful national health insurance plan since 1961.

The approach to social welfare in Europe embraces a philosophy of comprehensiveness. According to Rodgers, this comprehensiveness rests on five major principles: prevention, universality, public financing of minimum income, the welfare state philosophy, and labor market strategy.

1. *Prevention.* Family policy, for example, includes paid maternity leaves for working women, prenatal and postnatal mother and child care, and family allowances. The prenatal and postnatal care is part of national health insurance. Even Italy, a poor country by U.S. standards, provides maternity benefits amounting to 80 percent of earnings for two months before and three months after confinement.[84] France, West Germany, Great Britain, and the Scandinavian countries, among others, have maternity centers for periodic checkups. In some countries, health visitors (trained nurses) make home visits to mothers who cannot travel to centers.

Most nations in both Western Europe and Eastern Europe also have a wide network of child-care centers, subsidized and sometimes administered by the state. They are not merely custodial; the children receive educational, nutritional, and medical care. This commitment to supportive services has been aptly summarized by Kahn and Kamerman:

> What Europeans apparently know but what many Americans do not yet perceive is that social services may support, strengthen, and enhance the normal family—and that failures in social provision may undermine our most precious institutions and relationships. The issue is not whether or not government will intervene. It will. The question is, will it intervene for enhancement and prevention or to respond to breakdown, problems, and deviance alone.[85]

Most of the industrialized nations make sickness insurance available as part of the social insurance system; the United States does not. The benefit is increased when the wage earner has dependent children. Sickness allowances are often paid when working mothers are needed at home to care for sick children. Such services are widespread not only in Western Europe, but also in Bulgaria, Hungary, East Germany, the Soviet Union, and other socialist countries.

Housing policy is also based on a belief in prevention. Recognizing the social and economic costs of crowded, unsanitary, oppressive slum living, European nations have tried, albeit imperfectly, to assure every citizen access to adequate housing.

European nations have health policies that are predicated on extending medical services to all citizens. Services include hospitalization, physician's charges, prescriptions, medical appliances, nursing, and often dentistry, as well as maternity and sickness allowances and prenatal–postnatal care. In most countries these programs are financed by a tax on workers and employers but also are subsidized by general tax revenues. Usually the patient must share in the cost by paying a modest fee for certain types of service. In many countries, the plan includes not only medical expenses but also a household allowance to enable families to hire assistance during an illness, a lump sum maternity payment, and a cash grant to cover funeral expenses. Clearly such programs help prevent poverty by avoiding bankruptcy from medical expenses and promoting good health.

2. *Greater universality.* Programs in Europe are generally less categorical than in America. Families are not excluded from assistance simply because they are intact or in the work force or because the family is headed by a male. In general, working-age males are not excluded because they appear able-bodied. These differences from the U.S. system seem to result from a greater willingness to believe that most economic hardship is rooted in factors beyond the individual's control, and that it is in the interest of the larger society to see that none of its citizens sink into desperate poverty.

European benefits more often are intended to cover all citzens. This is particularly true of health care programs and to a lesser extent of housing programs (since people from all walks of life may live in the same housing project, paying according to income). Home help service is usually available to all, although those who can afford it may pay on a sliding-fee scale, while coverage on a means-tested basis is provided for those who can pay nothing at all. In Sweden even eligibility for public service relief jobs is not contingent on low income, disadvantaged status, or receipt of public assistance. If a person is jobless, Swedes reason, he or she may require help, regardless of income or skill level. Such relief jobs always pay regular wages and fringe benefits.[86]

In most European countries (as well as Canada, Australia, and Japan) the children's allowance is a truly universal (nonmeans-tested) program. Some countries pay allowances only to families with two or more children, or give smaller allowances to better-off families. In any case, progressive tax systems tend to cancel out the benefits for families who might be said not to need them. Kamerman reports that these benefits represent a significant percentage of median wages, 5 to 10 percent when there is one chiild and substantially higher for single mothers and families with several children.[87] Schorr points out that because the United States provides no children's allowances, it spends more on such means-tested programs as AFDC, in dollars as a proportion of social benefits, than any other industrial country.[88]

3. *Public financing of minimum incomes.* Many countries have decided that all aging citizens deserve a guaranteed minimum income. Public pensions still reflect contributions and wages but not as directly as in the United States. In Sweden, the guaranteed minimum takes the form of a basic pension that goes to everyone at age sixty-five. In addition, a person who has earned income from employment in

excess of the base amount for at least three years receives graduated earnings-related benefits on top of the basic pension.[89]

As they faced the problem of what to do if benefits paid out were larger than contributions (Should they raise contributions, or reduce benefits, or seek other sources of income?), some countries decided to finance pensions entirely from tax revenues. Most have dealt with the problem by subsidizing the social insurance fund from general revenues—an idea proposed by several U.S. policy analysts and investigative commissions but always firmly rejected. In addition, some nations have a unified insurance system for all citizens, not only the retired. It covers workers, who make regular contributions, as well as spouses and dependent children. Benefits are paid out for sickness, invalidism, industrial injury, maternity, widowhood, unemployment, and retirement.

4. *The welfare state philosophy.* Rodgers observes that even in Europe welfare programs have rarely been guided by a clear and comprehensive philosophy of the state's goals or obligations to its citizens. A major exception, he says, is Sweden. There the political parties, academics, and unions have promoted a rather specific idea of the society they would like to create and have formulated social policies necessary to achieve it. The philosophy is that every citizen has a right to live in a democratic society. Since equality assumes that the society be as free as possible of class barriers, Swedish unions have tried to reduce differences in income by implementing solidaristic wage policies. Wage negotiations are designed to reduce as much as possible the range between the lowest- and the highest-paid workers. Sweden also uses the income tax to narrow the discrepancy between incomes. Finally, the Swedes believe that the state should assume the responsibilty for seeing that all citizens have a dignified life style. This belief orients policy toward prevention of social problems rather than crisis relief. To be really preventive, Swedes believe, social policy must be comprehensive.[90]

5. *Labor market strategy.* Sweden comes closest to actualizing the philosophy that the market should be used to promote public well-being. This embraces three goals: full employment, economic efficiency, and public control of the economy. Full employment would mean that every citizen who wants a job should have one. Sweden has never quite achieved this goal, but between 1974 and 1980 (oil crisis years) the open unemployment rate averaged only 1.9 percent. Between 1980 and 1984 (when official unemployment ranged from 6.3 percent to 10.7 percent in the United States) open unemployment in Sweden varied between 2.0 and 3.5 percent.[91]

Sweden does count as employed those persons in labor market training and on relief jobs—a figure that represented 2.9 percent of the 4.3 million persons in the labor force in May 1984. (The United States counts trainees receiving a wage as employed: however, it counts those receiving no wage while training not as unemployed but as out of the labor force.)[92] Indeed, training is an important part of the labor market strategy, for it not only furnishes worthwhile occupation and a future for the individual but also promotes efficiency and productivity. That is to say, workers, and unions do not have to protect obsolete jobs because, if the latter are abolished, workers are assured of jobs that pay equally well. The goal is to create enterprises that can successfully compete in international markets.

Sweden's economy has clearly become more competitive. In the late 1970s and early 1980s the budget deficit grew and productivity showed a severe decline. In fiscal 1983–84, however, the deficit was 6 billion kronor less than the deficit the previous fiscal year. Moreover, after a weak 0.5 percent average increase in 1981 and 1982, productivity shot up by nearly 8 percent in 1983 and showed a continued rapid rise—5.5 percent—in 1984.[93]

Swedes believe that the public should run the economy, not be run by it. Public control does not mean that most industries are nationalized. On the contrary, 90 percent of the Swedish economy is privately owned. Fewer industries are nationalized than in Italy, France, South Africa, and Britain, where in the past two decades conservative governments have been the rule. Public control does mean that the state makes some critical decisions about when, where, and what industry produces. Moreover, the government also guides negotiations between the Swedish Employers Association and the Swedish Labor Union Confederation, with the result that very few major strikes have occurred since World War II.

Toward a New System

Today the question is not whether the United States should become a welfare state. It is already a welfare state. Government provides means-tested stipends to the poor (providing that they fit certain categories); Social Security and Medicare to members of the middle class as well as less fortunate citizens; subsidies (tax breaks) to wealthy corporations and individuals; and grants to "deserving poor" clients such as Boeing, Chrysler, and the Continental Bank. Tax deductions for expense account lunches and dinners represent the government's largest food program.

The question is whether the United States can develop a comprehensive social welfare system that will make it possible for all Americans to enjoy basic security, live in decency, and have an opportunity to fulfill their potential. Can we create a system that could avert the drift toward a potentially explosive two-class society? The glimpses of European programs offered here should suggest that such a goal is attainable. Indeed, starting with Bismarck, these programs in Western Europe have often been legislated and/or preserved under conservative governments.

A more viable system would be comprehensive, would seek to prevent citizens from becoming poor, would be more nearly universal by seeking to serve all the public, and would be better coordinated. Specific changes would include:

1. *Comprehensive family policy.* Such a policy would assure not only adequate income (primarily through child allowances) but also family planning, child care, preschool education, and maternity and health benefits. This would not only help poor families but also contribute to greater equality for women. Obviously, it would promote better health and productivity, results that benefit society at large.

2. *Comprehensive personal social services.* These include a broad scope of services, ranging from senior citizens' centers and family-planning clinics to programs for abused children and nursing homes for the disabled. At present some require a means test, whereas others are universal, although they may impose fees determined by income. Since personal social services are important to average people, such services should be available on a universal basis. Creating a national network of responsive multipurpose neighborhood service centers would go far in making these programs available to everyone.

3. *National health care.* The United States has the world's most expensive health care system, yet ranks fourteenth in infant mortality and only eighth in life expectancy. Twenty other nations, including Argentina, Portugal, Poland, and Mongolia, have a better population–physician ratio.[94] Two Baltimore census tracts show infant deaths as high as 59.5 per thousand live births. This rate exceeds 1981 infant deaths in poor countries such as Costa Rica, Panama, Guyana, Trinidad, and Tobago and is more than double the rate in the Soviet Union.[95]

Americans are always being told that national health care would be even more expensive. Yet it is interesting to note that the proportion of gross national product (GNP) that Americans spend on health (an estimated 10.8 percent in 1985)[96] is roughly the same as that spent by Swedes. However, Americans get much less in return. The Danes spend a much lower proportion of their GNP than we do (an estimated 6.1 percent in 1984[97] for care that is more comprehensive. Health care systems in Europe, of course, are financed largely through taxes, ours through the market. Our privatized system allows for more overlap, waste, and excess profits. A good national health care system would be universal, finance cost on a progressive basis, be oriented to prevention, provide quality control, limit increases in cost, and offer comprehensive benefits.

4. *A multifaceted housing policy.* In the long run, two of the best ways to alleviate housing problems are to get low-income people into the job market and to provide a decent income to those unable to work. These are not the only strategies, of course, for they do not directly produce the units needed. Moreover, middle-class people need a housing policy almost as much as the poor. Specific proposals to ameliorate the U.S. housing problem are set forth in chapter 5.

5. *A more equitable income policy.* All income support programs should be administered at the federal level. This could include integrating worker's compensation and unemployment compensation with Social Security, thus creating a unified national insurance system. Following the example of other countries, this comprehensive insurance could also include components such as sickness benefit, parental benefit, and housing allowance. At the very least, the federal government should establish a basic guarantee in both the assistance and insurance programs as well as uniform nationwide standards of eligibility. As we have seen, federally directed programs are far more equitable, generous, and cost efficient. According to Prigmore

and Atherton, the Social Security Administration administers its vast programs for an administrative cost of no more than 3 percent.[98]

For the elderly, the federal government could institute a two-tiered system long advocated by Alvin Schorr and already practiced in Sweden. The basic benefit would be an equal subsidy, which would mean that lower-income retired workers would gain. The second tier would be related to past contributions. Pensions would be financed by both payroll taxes and general revenues. They would be fully subject to taxation as in Sweden. (In 1983 Congress made one step in this direction by voting to make half the benefits for people above certain income levels subject to federal income tax, with revenues flowing back to Social Security trust funds.) Since income taxes are progressive, this would be an effective way of both financing the Social Security system and redistributing income, without converting Social Security into a welfare program.

A more radical solution (favored by many conservative economists) would be implementation of guaranteed income and negative income tax proposals to take the place of most existing means-tested cash maintenance programs. They would assist all poor persons and avoid penalizing work or marriage. A modest but adequate guaranteed income could replace Social Security, SSI, GA, and AFDC in those cases in which the family head could not be expected to work. In the negative income tax, a cash floor is provided for poor persons, but work incentives are also built in. A floor (say, $9,000 for a family of four) is agreed on. Those who earn less would receive enough to bring them up to the floor. Those who earn more would receive some matching aid for earnings above the floor, up to a certain cutoff point (say, $13,000). A family earning $10,000 would receive some proportion of the deficit between earnings and the break-even point. If this were 50 percent, the payment would be $1,500, for a total income of $11,500. Such a policy would have to be integrated with a family policy (assuring child care, for example) and with an employment policy guaranteeing the right of all who can work to paid employment.[99]

Schorr opposes the negative income tax. He argues that there are inherent conflicts among its objectives: providing adequate payment to families that earn little; building in a strong incentive to earn more; and limiting costs by avoiding payments to those who do not need them. Either the rate of payment pushes downward and many people receive inadequate income, or it moves upward and people with comparatively decent incomes receive assistance. From a political point of view, a small, inadequate program is likely to be attractive to Congress, whereas a plan with decent payment levels raises irresolvable conflicts. In lieu of the negative income tax, Schorr advocates improving and expanding Social Security programs, unemployment compensation, workers' compensation, and Medicaid. To replace income tax exemptions for children, he proposes children's allowances, financed out of general revenues and subject to progressive taxation.[100]

6. *Full employment.* This sounds utopian in the United States, and it may well be that the forces against the idea—ranging from organizations such as the National Association of Manufacturers and the Chamber of Commerce to traditional American values such as competitive individualism—are too powerful at present. Nevertheless, it can be a long-term goal.

If the Swedes can keep their unemployment rate so low (between 1.8 and 3.3 percent from 1979 to 1984), Americans can achieve a rate in the range of 3 to 4 percent, providing that they set this as a high priority. As Ginsburg notes, "Studying full employment in Sweden makes it clear that the engine that propels the system is political commitment.[101] Strategies to achieve full employment will be discussed in chapter 10.

Rational restructuring of our social welfare system and implementation of a full employment policy would require genuine tax reforms. A large part of the current deficit can be attributed to tax breaks favoring the rich. The Swedes, says Ginsburg, are more willing to support high taxes because they feel they get a great deal in return. A more equitable tax system might make Americans more willing to support public expenditures.[102] Moreover, when incomes are more equal, the number of workers with wages so low as to leave their needs unmet is greatly reduced, and there is less need for social welfare expenditures.

The plight of the chronically poor—those most likely to become homeless— should be a major focus of attention. If there are no radical changes in the social welfare and labor market systems, the chronically poor will remain an underclass, a faceless mass of human beings with no future. Many of today's old poor are yesterday's new poor. Many of today's new poor will be the old poor we encounter tomorrow.

The key to their future, and to that of their fellow citizens in this bountiful land, is planning. Americans have evidenced a talent for short-term programming. To plan for the future decades from now seems difficult for a people reared in the nineteenth-century ethos of rugged individualism and the vision of a constantly expanding frontier. Our piecemeal, crisis-oriented welfare programs demonstrate our tendency to think in terms of immediate costs and our failure to take long-range social costs into account.

Planning, public enterprise, and social contracts have been used successfully by other democratic countries, notably West Germany, France, Sweden, and Japan. Planning techniques vary, as do degrees of success. In each of these nations, far greater efforts are made to develop cooperative partnerships between business, labor, and government than in the United States.

As a beginning, Americans could engage in a nationwide debate on full employment, and on the kind of social welfare system they want. Citizens at the grassroots have never taken part in a discussion of the goals and principles that should guide public welfare; like Topsy, the system just grew.

In America, such a debate could take place not only in the chambers of Congress, but in town halls, unions, Rotary Clubs, community councils, state legislatures, colleges, universities, church or synagogue halls, women's clubs, and precinct halls and through newspaper, radio, and television. Social welfare means the well-being of all citizens.

Photo by Nancy Miller Elliott

Part IV
Looking at the Future

Chris Sprowal, president of the National Union of the Homeless.

8
Work with the Homeless: Emerging Trends

H omelessness has become a nagging issue for politicians and the general public. In 1980 few Americans believed that it could develop into a large-scale persisting problem. *Ad hoc* organizations sprang up to meet the need. Today that handful of groups has grown and matured into a movement. Advocates today are more unified and sophisticated; they are making long-term plans for the future. Let us look at some of the directions that the movement is taking.

Differentiating the Homeless

There is a growing sensitivity to the wide diversity of backgrounds and needs of the homeless. Chronic alcoholics and narcotics abusers, for example, are not the best roommates for young children. The mentally disabled have needs different from those of families unable to pay their rent or spouses who are victims of domestic violence. Whenever possible, perceptive and experienced shelter providers seek to differentiate the homeless by age, family status, and type of problem. In some cities small shelters and residences are being set up to meet the needs of special groups such as Hispanic men, the elderly, and the mentally or physically disabled. In a few communities there are special hostels for homeless people who do not necessarily require hospitalization, but need treatment for leg ulcers, skin diseases, or other maladies brought on by street living. Washington D.C.'s CCNV has opened a home where street people released from hospitals can recover in a quiet, dignified atmosphere. All over the United States one can observe efforts to sort out families with chronic problems from those who can make good use of intensive short-term counseling and then to direct them into different programs.

Diversifying Facilities: The Three-Tiered Approach

A broader range of accommodations is also beginning to evolve in response to varying needs within these population groups. To some degree these facilities reflect the three-tiered approach advocated by the National Coalition for the Homeless.

Tier 1: Emergency Shelters

Emergency shelters, of course, respond to the basic need for asylum. For virtually every homeless person, they are a port of entry into the system. They provide or ought to provide clean bedding, wholesome food, adequate security, and supervision. In addition, says the coalition, regular clinical attention should be made available. Armories, church basements, school buildings, and athletic facilities are all used for such purposes.

Some homeless people—those who fear large overnight shelters or who are turned away for lack of space—find refuge in a drop-in center, where (ideally) showers, laundry facilities, television, simple recreational activities, and comfortable chairs are available for resting, snoozing in the day, and sleeping at night.

Since most night shelters close at breakfast time, in practice many shelter clients use drop-in centers during the day for protection and to get themselves together. Hence the two kinds of facilities can supplement each other. At this point in time the reality of the situation is that there are neither enough overnight shelters nor enough drop-in centers.

Tier 2: Transitional Accommodations

In some cities emergency shelters are becoming semipermanent simply because individuals and families have nowhere else to go. (In New York's public shelters, according to a 1984 survey, the average stay is more than a year.)[1] This, of course, means that others will have no roof at all. Moreover, many homeless people need services that can facilitate re-entry into normal life. In response to this situation, concerned groups have set up relatively small facilities where intensified efforts are made to secure varied kinds of assistance that help clients frame long-term solutions. At the same time, more demands are made on transitional clients than on those in emergency shelters; they are expected to assume responsibility for seeking a job, utilizing any training they receive, and making plans for reunification of their families.

An excellent example is the innovative program developed by Sister Kathleen Toner of Samaritan House in New York. Part of the support comes from a grant made by the J. M. Kaplan Fund, which enabled the group to begin rehabilitation of an abandoned building that had been owned by CHIPS—Christians Help in Park Slope—for several years. The project is also financed by proceeds from Emergency Assistance for Families, a social welfare program in which proceeds generally go to welfare hotel operators. Instead, Samaritan House is paying back a conventional Citibank mortgage, using Emergency Assistance funds for part of the financing. An escrow account has also been set up to reestablish the Kaplan Fund equity with these payments from the welfare office. The funds are earmarked for the construction of additional residence beds. Support services are integral to the plan; the goal is to relocate families into permanent housing and help them stabilize their lives.

Tier 3: Long-Term or Permanent Supportive Residences

The National Coalition for the Homeless describes long-term or permanent supportive residences as homes with services built in as part of the structure of everyday life. They are particularly appropriate for some of the chronically mentally ill.

The St. Francis residences, two old New York SRO hotels converted into homes for deinstitutionalized mental patients, are often cited as outstanding examples. They also represent a successful partnership between the private and public sectors. In 1980, the Franciscan Friars converted the first SRO, the Beechwood, into a ninety-nine room home for 104 deinstitutionalized patients. Today it is an informal, friendly place. In the small office an elderly man sits smoking, nodding an "official" welcome to every visitor, while another resident sits chewing his fingers. A woman leans against the desk, shrieking into the phone: "He's the sickest! He's the sickest! And he's after me!" Rev. John Felice and social worker John Gaines explain to us that St. Francis is able to operate at the low cost of $13 per day. This covers maintaining the place and paying the salaries of social workers. Salaries of the activities therapists and the nurse practitioner (who supervises medications) are provided from the state's Community Support System. The staff is not as large as in some city-run shelters, but it is adequate, we are told. Another reason that the residence can operate at low cost is that St. Francis's Friends of the Poor bought the hotel outright since they were able to raise the cash from contributions. The major reason for the economy of the operation is that all residents pay rent, contributing a portion of their income from GA, SSI, SSD, or pensions. The rent varies from $145 to $225, depending on the size of the room and the guest's ability to pay. Breakfast costs twenty-five cents, lunch fifty cents; at dinner residents are on their own. Some of the men and women at St. Francis do various paid jobs.

Although the rooms are tiny and sparsely furnished, they are clean and noninstitutional in appearance; each room reflects the personality of its occupant. A few residents are allowed to keep pets since some withdrawn people can respond more to animals than to humans. In a large room, an art therapist is showing members of a small group how to express themselves in painting; colorful samples of their work hang on the walls. In the recreation area several men and women are playing cards and watching television. Two residents, who are in charge of the coffee lounge, are setting out cups. Every effort is made to help these cast-asides of our society to assume responsibilities. Many rise to the challenge very well, perhaps because, for once in their lives, they are treated with respect and affection.

In 1986 St. Francis's Friends of the Poor was converting a third SRO, using its own funds and money paid in an out-of-court settlement by a developer who had demolished a welfare hotel without a permit.

In other parts of the country, residences (such as Tender Mercies in Cincinnati) are running on similar lines. They are still few in number, however, because even when municipal governments do face the homeless issue they generally think only in the framework of emergency solutions, solutions that often become more expensive than long-term arrangements.

Beyond Shelter: Permanent Housing

Only a few private groups have had the time, trained personnel, and financial resources to move people into permanent housing, although the work of the St. Louis Relocation Clearinghouse, New York's Partnership for the Homeless, and the Community of Hope in Washington D.C. demonstrates that it can be accomplished on a small scale.

By the mid-1980s it had become increasingly evident that, even if the current economic recovery lasts, homelessness will not ebb unless the low-income housing shortage is alleviated. Hence growing numbers of advocates are shifting their focus. What any human being needs, they say, is not mere shelter but a home.

The lack of decent low-cost housing is a political problem, requiring a political solution. Today the most significant trend in work with the homeless is the thrust to pressure all levels of government to assume more responsibility. The 1983 conference of the National Coalition for the Homeless spelled this out clearly as it declared that more advocates should be engaging in propaganda and protest, legislative lobbying, administrative lobbying, and litigation.

Political Action

Action on the City Level

In many cities advocacy groups have prodded the municipal government to furnish basic shelter through providing facilities outright, offering financial support to nonprofit projects, or vouchering the homeless into hotels.

The first step is to confront officials. If they refuse to recognize that a crucial need exists, the groups may move to a second step: conducting a survey of people living on the street and in makeshift homes. In Denver, where the law mandated that the only single persons eligible for public assistance were the handicapped, the Citizens Coalition for Shelter decided to interview 769 homeless people. The coalition discovered that 80 percent had a physical or mental condition meeting the criteria of handicapped as defined by the state's rehabilitation act. Confronted with this evidence and the coalition's threat to sue the city, the welfare department director promised to change the interpretation of the law.[2]

Another step may be demonstrations before city hall; those in Chicago, Denver, San Francisco, and Washington, D.C. have been especially successful in publicizing the need for shelter and convincing the city to open shelters or fund private ones. Other tactics include involving the media, engaging in lawsuits (or threats of a lawsuit), and carrying the right-to-shelter issue directly to the voters.

In San Francisco, the Central City Shelter Network (CCSN) used a variety of actions in a campaign to press the city to take responsibility for the homeless, including a survey of street people, public hearings, importing leaders of the National Coalition for the Homeless to address a hearing, sending Mayor Dianne Feinstein a well-documented fact sheet, and, together with the Homeless Caucus (the first political group organized by street people themselves), organizing mass demonstrations before city hall. Mayor Feinstein listened. The city devised a new system, offering vouchers into seven private shelters. A mayor's task force on homelessness was set up.

Eventually, the city changed tactics. Instead of supporting a network of emergency shelters, it liberalized procedures for getting GA, gave all homeless persons soupline tickets, and vouchered them into cheap hotels during the application process.

Advocates such as Sara Colm of the North of Market Planning Coalition were pleased, but also disappointed. "The entire GA stipend of $258 a month is barely more than rent for an SRO room in San Francisco. And we knew that GA's policy has consistently been to cut its rolls. So we insisted on a monitoring committee."

Discovering that conditions in the hotels were often deplorable, the committee confronted the city. Although the administration did little to remedy the situation, it did make some improvements in GA procedures. The CCSN has also pressed the city to authorize more space in the hotels and backed a lawsuit to guarantee every citizen's right to GA. CCSN has done a great deal to publicize the plight of the homeless. It has sponsored TV public service announcements and memorial services for people who have died on the streets; its past chairman, Steve Whitney-Wise, has appeared on the *Today* show; and it sponsored a play, *The Rains Are Coming*, in which half the players were homeless people.

Across the country advocates have stepped up pressure on local governments to provide or preserve low-income housing. In Seattle, for instance, they scored a victory when the City Council passed a Housing Maintenance Ordinance requiring that all habitable rental units be offered to prospective tenants for rent. The measure was designed to counteract deliberate refusals to offer units for rent in order to speculate in future conversion. A Preservation Ordinance also regulates all demolition, requires owners to replace the residential area with an equal number of net square feet of replacement housing, provides that tenants may not be evicted for 180 days prior to application for a housing demolition license, and stipulates that tenants below 80 percent of the area median income must also receive relocation assistance of up to $2,000.

Legal actions to establish the right to decent shelter have enjoyed remarkable success in many parts of the country. This marks an evolutionary change in recognition of rights of the poor. Traditionally, as Hopper and Cox point out, "the claim of the homeless poor on public resources had no legitimacy other than that gratuitously extended by officials of the state. What was popularly and officially perceived as a plea became, through the agency of the court, endowed with the dignity of a right."[3]

The first successful litigation occurred in December 1979, when Robert Hayes, then a legal services lawyer and now counsel to the New York Coalition for the Homeless, brought suit on behalf of Men's Shelter residents against New York City and New York State, and eventually won a consent decree in which the defendants agreed to provide clean safe shelter to any man who sought it. Since 1983 orders have been entered by New York Courts protecting the rights of homeless women and homeless families to decent shelter.

In Boston, threats of the Emergency Lawyers Committee for Shelter to bring a similar suit were instrumental in the expansion of bed-space and creation of an Office of Human Resources to coordinate human services and housing. In Philadelphia, the Committee for Dignity and Fairness took the city to court and won a consent decree stipulating that the city make shelter available to all homeless persons not otherwise provided for and that shelter not be denied simply because a person is inebriated or under the influence of drugs. By early 1986 the cities of Los Angeles, Atlantic City, and St. Louis also had recognized the right to shelter for the homeless.

Concerned citizens in many parts of the country also have been prodding the courts to recognize the right of homeless men and women to vote. The usual prerequisite has been that a voter must have a fixed address. In some cities a shelter is not regarded as fulfiling that requirement. In Washington, D.C. the Board of Elections ruled that homeless individuals staying at overnight shelters may register to vote, but those living on the streets may not. CCNV, pointing out that the irony of the ruling was that some people could be in a shelter for one week and register to vote, whereas others could be living on the same grate for years and be unable to register, mounted a challenge. The Board of Elections reversed its original decree and ruled that a homeless person may vote so long as she or he has some place to pick up mail.

In Phoenix, the county recorder declared that "such a person attempting to vote would violate the law. If I became aware of it, they may have a temporary shelter—and may it be jail." When the staff attorney for the Arizona Center for Law in the Public Interest consulted the county elections director, it turned out that the county recorder was wrong. Similar cases have been fought successfully in a number of other cities, including Philadelphia, New York, Minneapolis, and St. Paul.

The case of New York provides a good insight into the successes and unresolved difficulties of advocates working on the political level. The city has changed since we tried to help Franz find refuge in 1977. As the numbers of homeless have risen (to an estimated 60,000 in early 1986), the city has increased its facilities. Today it has four emergency assistance units, runs some twenty shelters for men and women, contracts with hotels and social agencies to house families, works with church groups that offer shelter to individuals and families, and sponsors outreach patrols. A great deal of this progress can be attributed to pressure from the New York Coalition for the Homeless, which, among other things, has sponsored lawsuits to force city and state to offer shelter to all who seek it and continues to criticize the pace and quality of the city's efforts. It has also conducted a study that showed that pregnant women have had to sleep in welfare offices because there was no room for them, that children have slept on the floors in welfare offices, and that life-threatening situations had caused three infant deaths in city-run facilities.

On a recent visit to New York, we returned to the Men's Shelter and the Emergency Assistance Unit on Church Street. At Emergency Assistance, Marjorie posed as a homeless woman seeking shelter. Following is a brief account of her experience.

In Cincinnati, on three different occasions, I had passed as a homeless woman, and although I was quizzed in some detail each time, the process of admission had gone fairly quickly. When I first entered Emergency Assistance at 9:30 P.M., I had the impression that here, too, admission would not be difficult. There were many improvements since we had first come here with Franz. The place was now painted in bright colors, institutional carpet covered the floors, partial partitions had been erected to provide a few bunks, and signs in both English and Spanish informed clients that juice, diapers, and milk for infants were available and that clients had the privilege to protest if they believed that their rights were violated.

If the clients felt dissatisfied, they did not show it. Some thirty people sat mutely waiting. One child was sleeping on the floor while other youngsters chased one another. I was the only white person in that room.

An hour passed. There were three staff people at the reception window in the hall, apparently doing nothing, but none of the clients had been admitted to a social worker's office. A half hour later, at 11:00 P.M., a young mother said with a shrug: "I been here since nine." I approached a guard. "The staff won't see nobody till after midnight," he said curtly. Since it would be hours till my turn came up, it seemed more worthwhile to join my husband, who was asleep in the car and with him visit the Men's Shelter.

The Men's Shelter, too, had undergone cosmetic surgery. The entrance was now divided, with a clear IN to the right and OUT to the left. Inside, the floors were slightly cleaner than in 1977, the walls were painted, the registration booths boasted shining new glass windows and a battery of locked steel files, and the Big Room had been transformed into a holding area.

As a friendly staff member enthusiastically described the improvements, we kept looking at the men on plastic chairs waiting to be processed to the buses that would carry them in the middle of the night to huge armories and other dormitorylike facilities. Like the men waiting for supper in the Pierce School basement in Washington, they sat there in vacant silence.

As Franz might have put it, *"Plus ça change, plus c'est la même chose."*

Action on the State Level

Every year since 1980 there have been more statewide conferences on the homeless where advocates can exchange ideas and campaign stories. Since some bureaucrats and legislators are usually present, these meetings also give shelter providers opportunities to meet politicians and kindle their awareness of the problem. Every year more state legislatures hold hearings on the topic.

In some cases the lawmakers' discussion eventuates in little more than an inspiring flow of rhetoric. In other cases, however, real change has resulted. In 1985 the state of Washington set aside $1.9 million for emergency shelters. Missouri and Ohio passed bills requiring that part of each marriage license fee go to support shelters for battered women. Not content with this step, Missouri advocates pressed the legislature to pass a law allowing the abused wife to stay in her own home, so that the husband becomes the homeless person who must cope with the situation on the outside.

Most activity on the state level has focused on the right to shelter, social welfare entitlements, services for the mentally ill, and housing. We cite only a few examples to illustrate the directions the movement is taking.

As a result of prolonged litigation, New York and West Virginia became the first states to explicitly affirm the right to shelter. Advocates in other states have been pressing their legislatures to do the same. In Illinois, for example, a bill that would have insured shelter, food, and clothing for every homeless person in the state passed the House Committee on Human Services but then encountered opposition in the full house. In the end, instead of declaring an open-ended entitlement to shelter, the bill authorized the Illinois Department of Public Aid to administer food and shelter programs, distribute funds, and cooperate with local governments and nonprofit agencies to develop plans for temporary shelters. More importantly, the state administration's proposal that $300,000 be appropriated for emergency food and shelter was replaced by approval of $800,000. The Department of Public Aid was also enjoined to furnish emergency housing assistance to abused women and children and to provide assistance in cases where deprivation of shelter exists for reasons other than nonpayment of rent. In other words, Illinois was moving toward a more explicit admission of responsiblity for providing not only emergency shelter but transitional housing.

In many states advocates are seeking to liberalize laws that limit social benefits. Restrictions on GA have become a special target of such efforts. People living in abandoned cars have been known to pay as much as $40 for an address so they can receive the meager benefits of such programs. In the face of stubborn campaigns launched by supporters of the homeless, Massachusetts and Ohio have changed welfare regulations so that people without permanent addresses can receive benefits. In Pennsylvania, advocacy groups have been fighting the law that cut off GA for nine months of the year to 100,000 Pennsylvanians between the ages of eighteen and forty-five, a law that turned thousands of people into the streets.

As a result of vigorous pressure, many states have expanded services for the mentally disabled. The Ohio Department of Mental Health is now funding more psychosocial rehabilitation programs that include living skills and occupational therapy. New York opened community residences for approximately 800 mentally ill persons in 1984 and planned homes for another 800 in 1985; western Massachusetts has introduced a spectrum of services, ranging from twenty-four-hour-a-day supervision in small residences to social clubs, emergency psychiatric crisis teams, and walk-in clinics.

Most states have provided services to the homeless by passing through to local governments funds that come from federal sources such as Community Service Block Grants, and Social Services Block Grants. Only rarely do they use their own revenues for emergency services for the homeless or the potentially homeless. Some states, however, make vacant buildings available to private shelter providers.

A few far-sighted states are making long-range plans not only for emergency shelters but also for transitional accommodations and permanent housing. In New York State, as a result of Governor Mario Cuomo's pledge to spend $50 million on the homeless, a Homeless Housing Assistance Program has been set up. In addition, the state has increased the portion of public assistance payments that may be used for rent. Minnesota has taken a somewhat different route, with a demonstration program that awards grants to nonprofit agencies for the start-up, expansion, and operation of temporary housing.

It was largely because of pressure mobilized by the Massachusetts Coalition for the Homeless and other advocacy groups that the state moved ahead to expand welfare and mental health services and to provide certain kinds of financial assistance for housing to prevent homelessness. The coalition, however, has been highly dissatisfied with the lack of progress in planning long-term housing. Advocates point out that public housing authorities have refused to assign priority to homeless families, let alone single people, that the real need is for affordable housing, and that the supposedly tough new law on condominium conversion has been implemented in a half-hearted way. Hence fighting for long-term low-income housing has become a top item on the coalition's agenda.

Action on the National Level

During the 1980s conference committees and coalitions have mushroomed throughout the country. The first to emerge were citywide coalitions such as the Chicago Coalition for the Homeless and San Francisco's Central City Shelter Network. Then advocates began to gather for statewide conferences and to form state coalitions. "Linking up with other groups gives you moral support, new ideas, and more clout," says Cincinnati Drop-Inn Center's Buddy Gray, who was instrumental in founding the Ohio coalition.

The formation of the National Coalition for the Homeless in 1982 signaled the scope of the problem and the intensity of feeling among those seeking change. The coalition serves as an advocacy voice and a clearinghouse to share information about strategies and resources. With headquarters in New York, its membership includes representatives from church groups and community agencies as well as concerned individuals and homeless persons from more than forty cities and regions throughout the country. The coalition convenes conferences on homelessness, publishes a monthly newsletter entitled *Safety Network*, and occasionally co-sponsors conferences with like-minded groups such as the National Low-Income Housing Coalition. Its announced objectives include increasing the quantity and altering the character of resources available to the homeless, challenging the institutional mechanisms that contribute to homelessness, and empowering the homeless themselves.

A prime objective of all these coalitions is to put pressure on the federal government to acknowledge responsibility for citizens who have no roof of their own. The reasoning is basically simple: if the homeless are a national problem, then action must be taken on a national level. At the 1983 conference of the National Coalition for the Homeless, delegates overwhelmingly agreed that the federal government must support a *right* to shelter and that a program priority should be national hearings on such a right. They also pushed the idea of voter registration drives in alliance with the National Council of Churches, formulated plans to send a team of experienced shelter providers to the next congressional hearings on homelessness, and endorsed a plan for legislative watchdog groups at all levels of government.

On the surface, at least, there was a burst of activity on the federal level between 1982 and 1986:

After a long struggle by advocates to bring the plight of the homeless to the attention of Congress, in December 1982 the House Subcommittee on Housing and Community Development convened a hearing on the topic. Fifty-one witnesses, ranging from public officials to shelter providers and homeless people, presented vivid and clear-cut testimony. The following month, a Senate Subcommittee on Appropriations opened a hearing with a narrower focus: the chronic mentally ill living on the streets. On 25 January 1984 the House Subcommittee on Housing and Community development held a second hearing, this one at a federal community college converted by CCNV into a shelter. In the fall of 1984, the House Subcommittee on Intergovernmental Relations and Human Resources held hearings in three cities to determine the effectiveness of the Federal Interagency Task Force on Homelessness.

NIMH funded eight studies on psychiatric problems of the homeless. It sponsored meetings of the National Association of State Mental Health Program Directors and of the American Public Health Association and planned demonstration programs in several cities.

GAO conducted a study of the problem of homelessness and the federal government's response.

HHS set up a study commission known as the HHS Working Group on the Homeless, and also initiated the Federal Interagency Task Force on the Homeless, designed to augment the efforts of existing public and private groups.

HUD released its oft-criticized report on the homeless.

Out of this profusion of studies, surveys, oral testimony, discussion, and written reports, very little funding has emerged. The congressional hearings did result in appropriations for emergency services for fiscal 1983 and fiscal 1984, both administered by FEMA. As we have seen, the Housing Act of 1983 authorized $60 million for rehabilitating and operating shelters, but President Reagan declared he would veto the appropriation because enough had been done for the homeless. (A few months later HUD released its controversial study, declaring that there were only 250,000 to 350,000 Americans without a place to live.) Because HUD refused to set up a program, Congress instead appropriated $70 million to FEMA. In fiscal 1985 Congress appropriated $90 million to FEMA, and in fiscal 1986 $70 million. By 1986 all FEMA appropriations totaled only $300 million.

Although frustrated by the slow pace of progress in Washington, advocates have continued their work at the national level. Their efforts bore fruit at the 1984 Democratic Convention. For months preceding the conventions of the two major parties, members of the National Coalition for the Homeless worked on position papers to be considered for inclusion in the platforms. The topics included not only shelters and permanent housing but food, jobs, displacement, health care, rural and migratory homelessness, disability, the criminal justice system and homelessness, and federal funding mechanisms. The Republican National Convention ignored the issue.

The Democrats, however, responded. In the keynote address to the Democratic Convention, New York Governor Mario Cuomo spoke passionately of the two cities in the United States, one for the rich and one for the poor. "There are people who sleep in the city's streets, in the gutter, where the glitter doesn't show," he declared. In its platform the Democratic party pledged to develop short-range emergency responses to the problem of homelessness as well as long-range solutions to its causes. In particular, the Democrats pledged to support the expansion of publicly assisted housing.[4] For the first time in U.S. history, a pledge to the homeless had become a plank in a national platform.

Empowering the Powerless

Although the movement is only in its infancy, there is a growing impetus on the part of the homeless to speak and act for themselves.

At the January 1984 House hearings on homelessness, Leon Zecha, a street person and past president of the Homeless Caucus in San Francisco, spoke fervently to the issue.

> We need to organize because social workers and other professionals working in our behalf, no matter how well-meaning, do not understand our needs. For instance, some of our advocates, representatives of major provider agencies in San Francisco, in a proposal to the city on managing hotels for the homeless, wanted to remove all the doors from the rooms and separate couples because genders must not be mixed.[5]

Anyone who has worked with the homeless knows that they are not likely to organize well. They are usually physically exhausted, confused, and, at least on the surface, apathetic. Few have any experience in organizing, and many have little experience in cooperating on a group level. Lacking in self-confidence, they are full of fears, especially fear of authorities. Even more than other poor people, they are preoccupied with the task of getting through the next bout with the bureaucracy.

Yet Zecha could show that the Homeless Caucus in San Francisco had enjoyed considerable success. Within a year its membership grew from three to two hundred. In the first months it put together a constitution, elected leaders, drew up its own plan for housing the homeless, and was accepted into the Mayor's Task Force on Homelessness and the National Coalition for the Homeless. Partly because of the caucus's active cooperation with CCSN, the city agreed to pay the cost of seventeen hundred beds in shelters and welfare hotels.

When we met Zecha in San Francisco, he was sharply critical of the city. Conceding that it had done more than most other cities, he nevertheless pointed out that the municipally supported shelters were overflowing and that conditions in the hotels subsidized by the city for homeless families were often deplorable. Sometimes four hotel guests slept in one bed; sometimes more than one family occupied a room. Carpets were filthy, and incoming guests frequently had to sleep on dirty sheets.

Since early 1984 the Homeless Caucus, together with some advocates from the CCSN, has acted as watchdog on these welfare hotels. As a result, conditions have improved a little. So slight is the progress, however, that the caucus has mounted a stronger campaign to force the city to correct these abuses and to intervene to stop hotel owners from illegally evicting homeless people.

Other efforts have been more successful. It was the caucus that sparked a series of investigations that eventually forced an agency that administered three mental health programs in the Tenderloin District to withdraw from serving as the city's contractor for those services. The caucus also took a prominent part in the successful drive to defeat Proposition 41 in the November 1984 election campaign, a measure that would have slashed California's welfare spending nearly in half. The homeless activists sent a vocal delegation to Sacramento to demonstrate for a state bill providing $5 million to establish new shelters in California and $5 million to rehabilitate existing shelters; the legislature passed the so-called Waters bill into law. Together with other housing advocates, the caucus fought down an antirent control measure. Finally, says Zecha, the number of homeless people who attend the general meetings of the caucus has increased a great deal. This turn-out, as well as ongoing demonstrations, has created a growing awareness of the problem on the part of the public.

One abiding problem, according to Zecha, is that the great majority of the homeless people fail to become active in the organization. "They're so depressed that they feel 'What's the use?' Our steering committee has been trying to find incentives for participation. One idea is building up small businesses that would help support the caucus, and, what's more important, provide training for the homeless.

"Another problem is the mentally ill. The city supports a drop-in center for them, but it's not open twenty-four hours. We've succeeded in getting the city to increase the hours. But we're pressuring the city to make it round-the-clock. Plus provide 'street walkers' to go out and talk to these people, try to get them to come inside. Eventually some of them will accept counseling."

Homeless, Not Helpless

In Philadelphia a group of aroused homeless men and women have founded the first shelter to be run by the homeless themselves as well as the first union for homeless and other poor people.

As we entered the basement of the Spring Garden Methodist Church in Philadelphia, we became aware that this shelter was different. On one wall a sign proclaimed that the place was run by the Committee for Dignity and Fairness for the Homeless. On another wall (near a placard declaring No Foul Language) was the motto: Homeless Not Helpless.

Dignity, as the shelter has come to be known, is the fruit of the efforts of three men: Edward "Tex" Howard, a cook and ex-convict; Franklin Smith, an ex-gang leader; and William "Chris" Sprowal, a one-time community organizer.

Of the three, Sprowal is the most articulate, partly because of his college education and professional experience. He is a tall, huskily built, neatly dressed black man in his early fifties, with a well-trimmed moustache and watchful eyes. Despite the traumatic experience he has endured on the streets, his low, controlled voice conveys quiet self-confidence; he seems angry at the situations he is confronting, not hostile toward the world.

"How did this place happen? Well, in the first place you've got to understand that there are never enough beds in this city. It's been estimated that there are between 10,000 and 15,000 homeless people in Philadelphia. The number shot up when the state passed a law barring financial assistance to so-called able-bodied people between the ages of eighteen and forty-five, except for three months of the year. What's supposed to happen to unemployed people during those other nine months? What actually happens is that they live off friends, or go crazy, or get into crime, or end up on the streets. Or all these things.

"When I was homeless, I often stayed at the city's Drop-In Center, which is actually operated by the Diagnostic Rehabilitation Center, on contract with the city. You enter through an alley that has the stink of urine and garbage. It had only fifty beds, and if these got filled up you'd be sent down to the cellar where there were fifty chairs to sit on. You could stay just three nights on beds if you were one of the lucky few. People had to fight their way in. In exchange for showers, the staff began playing favorites for gifts like peaches and apples you'd get from fruit-picking work. With things like that going on, there was a lot of verbal abuse.

"When my two buddies and I tried to talk with the director and shift supervisors, the meeting became a personal attack on me. We walked out and decided to have a demonstration. Since we knew that a small group of homeless people were powerless alone, we went to service providers to get backing.

"The Drop-In Center staff ridiculed the demonstration, until they began to see that we had support. So they used a law firm and began to send out menacing letters. This did frighten some homeless people off. But the demo worked, in spite of the fact that officials were taking pictures and threatening that anyone participating would not be able to get into the center. Some of the conditions there have improved.

"But we wanted a shelter of our own. With the help and support of the Philadelphia Committee for the Homeless, we wrote a proposal and got a temporary FEMA grant. Actually, I'd found work as a counselor at Voyage House, a group home for kids, so for the first month, till the FEMA money came in, Dignity Shelter operated on my earnings.

"We wanted to be different from the other shelters. At almost all those places, *they* tell you what to do and when. You've already lost control over your own life, living on the streets. In shelters you lose whatever control and dignity you have left.

"We believe—we *know*—that homeless people have the capability to do things for themselves. So we demand that people who want to stay here make a comitment to stabilizing their lives. This is not a flophouse; it's a resurrection. The food is prepared and served by the residents. They are responsible for the upkeep of the entire facility. They pick up, distribute, and launder clothing. And we require all those who have incomes to save money for boarding rooms or apartments."

However, it did not make sense to talk about promoting responsiblity unless the basic means of realizing that goal were available, the three founders insisted. Hence, in addition to a social worker who helps the homeless register for employment, housing, income entitlement programs, child care, and health services, Dignity also provides emergency stipends to cover transportation and other expenses involved in the quest for work, housing, and social services. "I remember what it was like when I was homeless, looking for work," said Sprowal. "I'd walk five miles because I had no money for the bus. I'd arrive tired, and muddied up, too, if it had rained. All because they couldn't give us bus tokens!"

The shelter also runs a van that searches out people in railroad stations, on heat vents, and in abandoned buildings, distributing meals and the offer of a bed. "In other words, we meet people where *they're* at," said Tex. "We have peer support and self-help groups too, so people can help each other."

The three men felt that their idea had proved itself. At Dignity the cost for decent shelter was $6 per night; at the city's drop-in center, $17. Their group was represented on the city's Task Force on Homelessness. In the spring of 1984 they organized a day-long convention of 178 homeless men and women, where delegates developed strategies to ensure that homelessness remain in public awareness, cosponsored a protest rally asking the city to open additional shelters, and organized another rally calling for jobs, housing, education, and voting rights for homeless people.

"As a result, the Department of Public Assistance granted anyone living on the streets the right to food stamps," said Sprowal. "We also filed a suit asking the city to grant voting rights not just to people who could list a shelter as address, but also to those who consider the streets as their home. I told the court that we're citizens, our only crime is that we're homeless. In the end it was agreed that people who had some contact with a shelter in the past or present, or would use one in the future, were entitled to use a shelter address to vote."

Sprowal's skill in organizing might make one wonder why he became jobless and homeless. "A lot of people can't seem to believe I could have such a problem. I couldn't, either," he said. He has a bachelor's degree from the State University of New York at Westbury and thirty-seven credits toward a master's in social work. In the early 1960s, he left his native Philadelphia to work as an activist for the Congress of Racial Equality (CORE) in the South. In the late sixties and early seventies he had a succession of political jobs: as an organizer for the Health and Hospital Workers Union, Local 1199; as an assistant to Congressman Allard Lowenstein; and as an organizer for George McGovern's campaign. In the 1970s, he also worked with runaway, throwaway, and troubled youth, first as a child-care counselor and later as administrative supervisor for Edwin Gould Services for Children. Sprowal left this work in order to start his own business as a distributor of fresh seafood in New Orleans, but the recession of the early 1980s forced him to the wall. Then his second marriage fell apart. Returning to Philadelphia, he began looking for work. "But I ended up on the streets. I didn't have a drinking problem or a drug problem. I was just jobless. Everywhere they said I was overqualified. I still kept hunting. One day I looked in the mirror. The face that looked back at me was gaunt, terrible. When you're homeless looking for a job, there's no place to get clean, no money for carfare, no money to get resumes typed up properly. Even if an employer is interested, where's he going to call you?

"Once you realize you're homeless, it's a shock. Then it becomes a constant humiliation. You envy people going to work. You feel guilt—it must have been something *you* did that was wrong. One day I had an interview at a child-care agency, and the interviewer looked at me, and then at the resume, and then back at me. 'Are you *sure* you're William Sprowal?' he asked. That did it. I went out of there shaking. After that, the only work I dared apply for was day labor."

Sprowal's experience as a child-care worker has made him particularly sensitive to the plight of homeless children. "We often have as many as fifteen kids here, aged two to eleven. They usually sleep in the women's room. After the experience of living on the streets and in shelters, these kids need help in re-adjusting to society. In fact, any person who's spent over thirty days in a shelter needs it. When they go to school, homeless children are labeled as 'those kids who live in a shelter.' The parents lose their dignity, partly because staff take over and run the lives of the family, tell them when to get up, when to go to bed, where they can play, where they can't. Parents lose the respect of the child, who sees they don't have control of their lives.

Some kids withdraw. Some kids act out. They tell their parents, 'Who are *you* to tell me what to do?'

"We can't change this entirely, but we do what we can. We made this into the only co-ed shelter in Philadelphia. When the church objected, we said, 'We won't run it on any other terms.' It's ridiculous that the homeless should be segregated by sex. It's not that way in their homes. Why here? It's not good for adults, not good for kids. The presence of someone of the opposite sex is *natural*—it means something important to a person. And the laughter of a child is important.

"What happens? Men behave better, don't curse so much in the presence of women and children. We haven't had one incident of misusing a child or a woman in this place. Men become more concerned with their appearance. And children see their parents in natural roles—cooking, cleaning up, making decisions.

"Beyond that, we see ourselves as an extended family. Kids without fathers can find them here. Even those with fathers can get extra affection and support at a crucial time in their lives. We can all help each other in parenting, which is a hard task for anybody but especially for people who've been through the mill, the mill of the streets."

"We still have problems here," said Franklin. "But we *are* seeing progress. It comes from making people part of the process. Like we don't say we *service people*—sounds like servicing cars. We don't even like the word *client*. We say, 'brothers and sisters in residence.' Even when we use phrases like *case management*, we don't mean it like business management—we don't mean that *we* are managing their cases. Instead, we're here to help people manage their own lives. So we say, 'You and us together, we can make a program toward a better life.' They respond to that. They see there's dignity in doing for themselves."

"And for us, the good thing about all this is, it's changing our lives." said Tex. "We're standing back up as men. It's making us reach out to people."

In the future, the three leaders told us, they hoped to form cottage industries that use the skills of homeless people, skills such as tailoring, catering, handicrafts, appliance repair, and sewing. They also hoped to establish a multifaceted life support center that would incorporate their philosophy that emergency services alone cannot remedy the malignant effects of chronic homelessness; many people require intensive, sustained supports. Sprowal and his friends envisioned an eight-to-twelve month residential program for persons who have been homeless ninety days or longer, a program encompassing social services, counseling, job training, health care, and life-management skills workshops. The goal was to move residents from dependency and despair to some tangible measure of self-sufficiency within one year.

After our visit in the fall of 1984, events moved swiftly for the committee. Dignity launched two programs intended to provide homeless people with skills. In the first project, residents rehabilitated two houses to be used as transitional facilities. Men who felt useless have gained proficiency in a trade and new confidence in themselves.

The other program involved a partnership with the city to train homeless people in job skills and the basics of finding and keeping a job.

Long-simmering tensions with the Spring Garden Church congregation, however, culminated in a rift when church members voted to ask the homeless to leave. United Methodist Metro Ministries, the denomination's citywide administrative body, was faced with an uncomfortable choice: to evict either the homeless or the congregation. In the end it opted to lease (at no charge) the entire building to the committee, since the homeless's needs were greater. The congregation, it was suggested, could use nearby Sanctuary Methodist Church.

Thus the church building was transformed into a Life Transition Center in January of 1985. Sprowal, who had decided that he had no gifts or liking for administration, turned the center over to committee member Leona Smith. That left him free to do what he wanted to do most: organize a union for the homeless and other poor people. The only requirements would be that unemployed workers pay dues of $1 a month, that those with a job pay $5, and that all promise to register to vote, so that the union would have political leverage with the city. In a few months nearly forty-five hundred union cards had been signed.

On 6 April 1985, the Philadelphia/Delaware Valley Union of the Homeless was founded at a convention in the city that had witnessed the signing of the Declaration of Independence. These founding fathers and mothers pointed to a different kind of revolution today—" a revolution built on the principle of survival of the most wealthy at the expense of the most poor, of profit for the few earned by the sweat of the many, of the redistribution of wealth and opportunity and food and shelter away from those most in need and toward those living in comfort."[6]

To deal with that new revolution from the right, convention delegates passed a declaration of opposition to the trend, and ratified resolutions on a wide range of social issues. In his speech accepting the presidency of the new union, Chris Sprowal promised that the resolutions would be translated into marching orders.

Within a month of the convention, the Union of the Homeless met with the city's health commissioner to demand that fifty beds be set aside for the homeless and other poor, conducted a sit-in at the Transportation Authority to ask for reduced fares for the homeless and the poor, staged a sit-in at Temple University to demand that it convert a vacant armory it owned into a facility for the homeless, and pressured the University of Pennsylvania to furnish free health care to fifty union members.

The new union also began formulating plans to expand. Today the National Union of the Homeless embraces chapters in eight cities around the country, fulfilling a long-standing dream of Sprowal. "We need a broad movement that would include all kinds of groups that are working to change the priorities of this crazy government," he says. "There are millions of young people today who are functional illiterates. There's a whole generation growing up not knowing what it is to have a job. So we can't say we're successful till all Americans realize that food and shelter are *entitlements*. If they don't realize this, these problems will simply grow while we continue looking at symptoms and dabbing away at them with Band Aids."

Viewpoints

The View from the Top

Philip Abrams, senior HUD official: "No one is living in the streets."

—June 16, 1982

Edwin Meese, then Presidential advisor, now Attorney General: "[People go to soup kitchens] because the food is free . . . that's easier than paying for it."

—Christmas season, 1983

President Reagan: "What we have found in this country, and we're more aware of it now, is one problem that we've had, even in the best of times, and that is the people who are sleeping on the grates, the homeless who are homeless, you might say, by choice."

—January 31, 1984

The View from Below

A homeless woman in Grand Central Station, New York: "They must be conducting an experiment or something. They must be trying to see how long people can get along without food or shelter."

—Ash Wednesday, 1984

Then a woman gave an account of what happens when someone dies on the streets of Los Angeles. . . . If no one comes to claim the body, it is brought to the city Crematorium. The Crematorium is staffed by General Relief recipients, who burn the bodies as their work assignments. The bodies are burned for one hour, then swept into boxes like orange crates. Each box is marked with a paper tag with a case number and either a name or "John Doe # _____ " or "Jane Doe # _____ . . . ." If no one claims the body, the crate of bones and ashes is dumped without ceremony into a plywood covered pit outside the Crematorium. There are no names and no markers on the pit. Workers at the Crematorium say that they burn eight to twelve bodies a day.

—From the *Catholic Worker*, June/July 1984. Reprinted with permission.

The entrance to St. Patrick's Cathedral, New York City.

9
Prevention versus Containment: Conflicting Ideologies

When Michael Harrington published *The Other America* in 1962, the book shocked many citizens of the United States. In addition to the affluent society that many Americans had come to take for granted there was, said Harrington, a land of the invisible poor. The poor inhabited the miserable housing in the central city and in remote rural areas, but suburbanites rarely saw them. Second-hand or even new clothes were relatively so cheap that one could say that America had the best-dressed poverty that the world had ever known. Many poor people were too old or too young to be seen. Most important, the poor were politically invisible; they had no face, no voice.[1]

Today many of the poor are more visible. Those without homes have nowhere to hide. Although the police do their best to hustle them away from the Fountain Squares and Lafayette parks of this country, the guardians of law and order cannot cleanse all the avenues and byways of their presence. At some point, downtown developers, yuppies who have migrated from the suburbs, and millions of ordinary middle-class Americans find themselves disconcerted by the sight of a human being slumped in sleep on a sidewalk.

In some respects the picture that Harrington drew has changed very little. Nearly 34 million Americans still live under the poverty line, and some 20 million know hunger.[2] The number of long-term unemployed in June 1985 had risen nearly 80 percent over the level in January 1980.[3] As in the period that Harrington was describing, the vulnerable groups today are the industrial rejects, migrant workers, the aged, children, families with a female head, and people with little education. Disproportionate members of the poor still belong to nonwhite minorities.

In other respects the picture is bleaker. Millions of Americans read Harrington's book with a sense of outrage and pressed the government to take action. They took seriously his contention that there was only one institution capable of mustering the forces to meet the problems: the federal government.

During the following years, Lyndon Johnson projected a vision of the Great Society, one that would unite Americans as never before. The strategy to achieve it would be an unconditional war on poverty.

In theory, at least, the programs were designed not only to alleviate but also to prevent poverty. Job training, expanded educational opportunities for the disadvantaged members of society, and programs involving participation of the poor in controlling their own communities were an integral part of the war. The architects of the new vision seemed seized by the fervor of urgency and hope.

It was not because they were mere visionaries that the War on Poverty never achieved all they had hoped, Harrington tells us today. The rhetoric of the politicians and the expectations of the public were unrealistic, given the resources they were willing to devote to making the endeavor successful. When President Johnson declared that domestic war, the United States was the most limited welfare state in the industrialized world; it was the advanced capitalist nation where the poor had the fewest economic and social rights. More importantly, the basic reason for the so-called failure of the strategy was the war in Vietnam, which deflected resources and attention from the war at home. "It never cost even one percent of the federal budget and never reached the 'takeoff' point that is normal in most federal programs," Harrington says. Nevertheless, that domestic war did accomplish a great deal. Harrington cites analyses that show that, for all its faults, the job-training effort not only helped individuals but saved money for society as well.[4] Moreover, the poverty rate declined from 22.2 percent in 1960 to 11.6 in 1973. During the late 1960s and 1970s hunger was virtually eliminated and infant mortality declined. The life span of minorities increased, and their job opportunities, income, civil rights, and chances for quality education expanded significantly.

Saving the Poor from Themselves

Today the Great Society programs of the sixties have either dwindled or disappeared. Even the Democrats failed to make poverty a central issue in the 1984 campaign. Instead of a war on poverty, we witness a war to contain the forces, at home and abroad, that might upset the status quo.

During the sixties poverty increasingly came to be seen as caused not by some defect in the individual but by conditions in society and the economy. In the eighties we are witnessing organized efforts to locate the fault in the individual poor person, who presumedly would prefer to get handouts than to work, and in social programs that are seen as incentives to the poor to live gratuitously rather than toil for their bread.

Thus the Reagan administration's emphasis has been on what should *not* be done for the poor. More openly now, some ideologies of the Right articulate a life boat ethic: the productive strong shall survive, the useless weak shall sink or swim. The administration's new bible is Charles Murray's *Losing Ground: American Social Policy 1950–1980*, which argues that social programs are actually harmful to the poor themselves. The increasing unemployment among the young, the increased dropout from the labor force, and the growth of illegitimacy and welfare dependency in the 1960s and 1970s can all be explained by the rewards for not working that have accrued from expanded social welfare programs. (Murray conveniently stops at 1980.) He proposes abolishing the entire federal welfare and income support structure for working-aged persons, with the sole exception of unemployment insurance. AFDC, Medicaid, food stamps, worker's compensation, disability insurance, housing assistance for low-income families, nutrition supplements for poor pregnant women—all these and others would go, leaving the nonelderly poor with no resources whatsoever except the job market, family members, friends, locally funded services, and private charity.[5]

It is beyond the boundaries of this chapter to offer a full critique of Murray's thesis. This has been done skillfully by Robert Greenstein, director of the Center on Budget and Policy Priorities,[6] and by Michael Harrington,[7] among others. Both men demonstrate that Murray's thesis that federal programs have utterly failed simply does not hold up because he has consistently omitted or concealed crucial facts that do not support his case, juggling numbers in order to promote a radical political agenda.

Murray's ideological thrust reflects a nostalgia for the nineteenth century, when the poor could more readily fall back on family or the local community, and there was a western frontier beckoning with boundless opportunities. That world view takes no cognizance of the reality that our economy and our society have changed. Many of the jobs formerly available to the poor no longer exist.

As Harrington observes, Murray disregards technological change, stagflation, the multinationalization of corporate capital, rising levels of so-called normal unemployment, cultural shifts, the revolution in occupational structure, and other factors. Greenstein demonstrates that the social programs were actually helping people who otherwise would have been impoverished by the sluggish economy. In effect, he says, from 1968 to 1980 the slowing of the economy dropped people into poverty and the expansion of benefit programs lifted them out. When benefits were raised in the period 1960–80, poverty declined, and when benefits diminished, progress in reducing poverty halted. In other words, social welfare programs, with all their shortcomings, succeeded in preventing even greater poverty.

The slowing of the economy has also brought a growth in the number of young people who have *never* had jobs, although they have desperately sought them. Together with other long-term unemployed people, they form the hard core of the homeless. A small but apparently permanent caste has been forming at the bottom of the economic ladder. How small? A study by the institute for Social Research at the University of Michigan arrives at the happy conclusion that contrary to popular belief, only 1 percent of the American population lives in long-term poverty. That statistic, a mere 1 percent, means 2.4 million human beings—2.4 million men, women, and children who live without hope.[8]

A high proportion of those who belong to this apparently permanent caste are the blacks whom Willhelm describes as "not so much oppressed as unwanted, not so much abused as ignored." Nothing, perhaps, is so devastating to the human spirit as indifference. Under such circumstances some seek what psychologists term negative strokes. In crime, hustling, prostitution, and a variety of other deviant activities they find some recognition, some affirmation of their aliveness. Others withdraw into flaccid resignation. All become human waste.

To be homeless means something more—or rather, something less—than to be poor. It means sinking to another level of precariousness, where there is nothing to hold on to. To be homeless means to be powerless.

Bahr, in his classic *Skid Row*, characterizes the homeless as powerless.[9] Nowhere, however, does he suggest that there are forces interested in keeping them impotent, or in Pentagonese, neutralized. Yet how else can one explain the resistance to efforts of homeless people to exercise the right to vote, to use public lavatories, or to sleep on heating grates in the nation's capital?

In *The Making of America's Homeless*, Hopper and Hamberg pose a provocative thesis. The desultory character of official relief efforts, the emphasis on crisis management, they argue, go beyond interest in keeping immediate costs down. The crisis of homelessness also serves unacknowledged latent functions. It is not that the crisis was planned, but that the situation and efforts to ease it may be put to subtle use. Thus the "spectacle of homelessness" serves a larger disciplinary function, one that extends far beyond candidates for immediate relief. "The prospect of a degraded life on the dole serves to steel otherwise recalcitrant workers to the rigors of the laboring world, to stifle demands for higher wages or better working conditions, and to cause those who do fall upon hard times to seek assistance elsewhere."[10]

Hence relief efforts must not cease entirely. They not only alleviate real suffering, but serve to neutralize the potential threat of discontent. They also help to enhance the legitimacy of the established order. "A judicious measure of deterrence is thus one that keeps alive the example of the wages of failure while not letting the exhibit get out of hand."[11] In other words, one that manages the situation through a careful balancing act.

Washington's Response to Homelessness

The federal government's reaction to homelessness is symbolized by the official attitude toward Mitch Snyder's well-publicized fifty-one day fast to get federal action on two fronts: rehabilitation of the huge facility that CCNV had converted from a community college into a shelter, and direct grants to other shelters across the country. Threatened with negative publicity, Reagan gave in just two days before the election and four hours before Snyder's fast was to be portrayed on CBS-TV's "60 Minutes." Reagan and administration officials agreed, on the one hand, to a dramatic one-shot measure: renovation of the CCNV shelter. At the same time, they balanced that concession with a declaration that in no way could this become a nationwide precedent.

The president had already made his oft-quoted genial observation that homeless people were sleeping on Washington's heating grates out of choice and had refused to appropriate the $60 million authorized by Congress for the rehabilitation of shelters on the grounds that the federal government had already done enough for the homeless. As Sidney Schanberg observed, Reagan seemed to be arguing that granting $60 million (to help up to 2 million people) would only be government imposing its will on Americans who would rather live alfresco.[12]

The one federal group designed to take some action on the problem has been the Federal Interagency Task Force on Food and Shelter for the Homeless, which was set up as a catalyst to supplement local efforts. A survey of the task force's effectiveness by the National Coalition for the Homeless in twelve cities revealed that although the task force did provide assistance to a few groups wishing to establish their own shelters, most of the vacant federal buildings offered by the task force were unsuitable for sheltering the homeless because of their size, dilapidated condition, or location. Some service providers found that the task force was simply unable to secure properties it said were available or to cut through bureaucratic red tape. The basic problem was that the task force had no money to distribute and no power to establish or administer any facility.[13]

Mr. Reagan has been less reluctant to fund inquiries into the problem. As previously noted, these have included studies by HUD, NIMH, GAO, several congressional committees, and the HHS Working Group on the Homeless.

Since the report of the HHS Working Group contains the greatest number of proposals, it is worth examining in some detail. The study describes forms of assistance now being provided, a strategy for "a public/private partnership to aid the homeless," and specific options. An impressively long list of in-place federal programs that could help people without homes is cited. The trouble is that they paint a highly misleading picture of the federal role. The programs administered by FEMA and by the Department of Agriculture are indubitably targeted to the homeless and hungry. However, the report also lists twelve *regular* programs, ranging from Community Services Block Grants and Social Services Block Grants, to low-income energy assistance, which are not specifically designed for the homeless. Most take the form of grants to states, which decide priorities for their use. In fact, most of these programs have suffered drastic cuts under the Reagan administration.

Had the report described them as preventive programs, which, if expanded, could have served to avert homelessness, their inclusion would have been relevant. The study did not do so; indeed, there was little evidence of interest in prevention.

A cost estimate was attached to each of the specific options in the HHS report. Most of those options would cost the federal government nothing at all, because the working group perceived the federal role as one of supporting private and local efforts. The federal government might do this in five ways: (1) provide leadership (including an executive order to direct all federal agencies to give top priority to efforts on behalf of the homeless, supporting White House Office of Private Sector Inititatives, and developing a public awareness campaign); (2) extend current outreach efforts to include not only SSD and SSI but also food stamps, AFDC, Medicare, Medicaid, and Veterans cash and medical benefits; (3) offer technical assistance such as workshops and a national clearinghouse of information; (4) provide resources such as surplus food, buildings, and equipment; and (5) set up facilities for research, demonstration, and training.[14]

Let us look briefly at these options and at how they have become translated into reality. No public awareness campaign nor executive order to give top priority to action for the homeless has emerged from the White House. Extending outreach programs obviously is a good idea. However, the project would not include state–local GA, the program with the lowest stipends. Nor would the project consider a more basic problem: payment levels which are generally too low to prevent homelessness. It would do nothing to relax the rigid (and inconsistent) rules that keep thousands of Americans from receiving modest benefits that could make the difference between living under a roof or on the streets. The report tends to attribute the failure of potential recipients to receive benefits not to the system but to the victim: mentally disabled persons "have difficulty applying for and managing their benefits"; "many homeless do not know how to access [*sic*] those programs for which they may be eligible." In any case, by early 1986 very little federally sponsored outreach had materialized.

The technical assistance provided through a federal clearinghouse would be redundant; the National Coalition for the Homeless already has a well-functioning service to meet this need. The one workshop sponsored by HHS, an effort to identify models for a proposed how-to reference manual, was a joke, according to disappointed participants. Most service providers also feel that, although research, demonstration, and training have their place, they are hardly priorities. Considerable research has already been done, and it is not—or, more precisely, should not be—a substitute for action. Very few surplus resources have been made available. In fact, most of an $8 million appropriation designated by Congress to transform surplus military buildings into shelters had been used for Defense Department maintenance. Rep. John Conyers declared that he was outraged that the Defense Department would use money set aside for the nation's poorest when it operated from a multibillion dollar budget.

Finally, although the study group made tentative proposals that urban homesteading units currently sold to cities by HUD also be sold to nonprofit organizations for use as shelters, FEMA-type grants for shelters be continued, and eligibility for Section 8 certificates and vouchers be extended, there were no suggestions that the *supply* of low-income housing be increased.

In sum, while there is obvious merit in all these ideas, they envision little federal funding and hardly make a dent in the problem.

It is interesting to note that the term longer-term solutions was used several times in the report. Indeed, a tentative suggestion was made that the federal government consider establishing a permanent office for the homeless. What could this mean? Have federal officials come to accept homelessness as a sad but inevitable feature of the American scene?

One could speculate further. Although the report spoke of longer-term solutions, all the steps actually proposed were stopgap measures. A contradiction? Or a well-contrived response? A permanent office for the rootless and roofless could indeed raise the spectacle of homelessness to deter poorly paid workers from demanding higher wages and better working conditions.

In both the HUD and HHS reports the message is plain: Federal government can play only the role of catalyst, supporting private and local efforts. Yet private groups have made it abundantly clear that they are unable to bear the brunt of the financial burden. Even the Catholic bishops in their *Pastoral Letter on Social Teaching and the U.S. Economy* have declared that "private voluntary action is not sufficient. The works of charity cannot and should not have to substitute for humane public policy."[15]

The cities have their own message: "Don't expect the *municipal* level of government to assume so much responsibility." In a survey sponsored by the U.S. Conference of Mayors, Boston officials describe the efforts of private agencies, organized labor, and state as stretched to the limit and emphasize the need for a national commitment.[16] Officials in virtually every city surveyed use almost the same words in stressing the need for federal resources to address the root causes of the problem.

There has been a shift, then, in the debate. To local officials and most advocates, the question is not whether the greater part of the fiscal burden shall be carried by the private or public sectors but which level in the public sector shall bear major responsibility.

Voluntaryism: Myth and Reality

The ideology positing the moral and practical superiority of voluntaryism persists in America. How well has it been working? A look at the situation in the 1980s suggests that a mantle of mythology has served to mystify the public.

A study by the Urban Institute's Nonprofit Sector Project substantiates what workers in the voluntary sector have known for a long time: in the 1980s, when nonprofits were called upon to do more, they have paradoxically found themselves in a position to do less.[17]

Actually, the study points out, over the years *government* has become the largest single source of income for nonprofits (defined as service organizations operating for the benefit of the public, excluding religious congregations and professional organizations, but including hospitals and universities, which together make up 70 percent of the sector's resources). That is to say, through direct grants, purchase of service contracts, and third-party payments like Medicare, government funds agencies that deliver the services. In many parts of the country, nonprofits deliver more government-funded services than do government agencies. In 1980, the federal level provided about $40 billion to support nonprofit agencies, whereas private charitable donations totaled only $26 billion.[18]

The most salient conclusion of the study is that government is moving away from this partnership. According to figures available in mid-1984, federal support to these organizations in fiscal 1984 would be an estimated $4.5 billion less than in fiscal 1980, a decline of 27 percent. Although private charitable (including corporate) giving increased significantly between 1980 and 1983, it did not fill the gap left by government cutbacks.[19]

Some nonprofits were able to offset cutbacks by turning to commercial sources of income, such as fees and sales of products. Almost half the agencies surveyed reported that the poor comprised less than 10 percent of their clientele. The organizations serving people in the greatest need (those engaged in social services, employment and training, and legal services and advocacy), together with multipurpose organizations, were least able to benefit from commercial income, hence ended up with overall losses. These are the agencies most oriented to serving the poor and hardest hit by the budget cuts.[20]

A significant sign of the trend toward commercialization is the growth of for-profit hospitals. It has been estimated that the cost per patient admission in such hospitals is 15 to 24 percent higher than in nonprofit facilities. Most for-profit chains increase their earnings by treating a lower percentage of Medicare, Medicaid, and uninsured patients than do nonprofit facilities. These patients are frequently denied admittance to for-profit hospitals and sent to public hospitals. As a result, public hospitals are threatened by their very mission: to serve all patients regardless of their ability to pay. Public hospitals are further jeopardized because they treat sicker patients. Today the population of public facilities is largely made up of transfers from other hospitals, refugees, illegal aliens, homeless people, and other groups not served by the expensive but inequitable health care system.[21]

In reducing public assistance programs the Reagan administration has already forced the public sector to adopt tighter eligibility criteria. Now its policies are forcing the nonprofits to go in the same direction or to shift toward commercialism. Either option excludes large numbers of poor people.

Although these developments do not extend so far as scrapping virtually the entire federal social welfare system, as Murray proposes, they do point in the same general direction. Is this creating a void, hence a demand, for serving the poor through charity?

Actually, charity is not synonymous with relief or alms. As the *Encyclopedia Britannica* points out, the word has many meanings. It can denote the impulse to give love, friendship, and service. It can represent individual acts of good works. It can signify organized philanthropy, which associates members of a community together for a purpose. The Greek word *charis* means not only dearness in the commercial sense, but also gratitude, grace, and kindness. In practice it has largely concerned itself with the poor. But it is also closely linked to the sense of obligation to one's fellow human beings as a whole, and to the belief that society, acting through its appropriate institutions, has a collective duty to ensure the well-being of all its members.[22]

Charity in the sense of alms-giving is an act that poses a barrier between benefactor and beneficiary, and reinforces the latter's low self-esteem and sense of helplessness. Partly because of these overtones, charity is a term that has fallen into a certain disrepute.

In the 1980s, however, it seems to be enjoying renewed respect. Charity in this sense underlies a current ideological thrust—a thrust that ties giving, voluntaryism, and private sector initiatives together. Voluntaryism becomes an expression of freedom, a value that by implication is prized in America as nowhere else in the world. Thus "voluntary" giving to the United Way is lauded as an act of free will—although it may be your boss who requests the donation, and you have little or no control over how it is spent. To give through government taxes is seen as denial of freedom. It is somehow more noble, more generous, and more American to give to a United Way drive than to ongoing government programs that can serve to *prevent* poverty. Free will is elevated above duty; the freedom of the donor, however ill-informed he may be, to satisfy his need to choose the mediary of his good works becomes more important than the collective duty to ensure the well-being of all members of society.

From a practical point of view, expansion of the voluntary sector leads to greater fragmentation of services. Reliance on that sector introduces a great deal of unpredictability. Moreover, the prevalent belief that government programs are *ipso facto* wasteful, those in the private sector efficient, simply is not based on fact. Many voluntary organizations spend up to 50 percent of their budget on administrative overhead; some spend even more. Social Security programs, which can prevent millions of people from becoming recipients of private philanthropy, devote approximately 3 percent of their budget to administration.

This is not to denigrate the voluntary sector. On the contrary, it should be evident that some of the finest work with the homeless and other rejected members of our society has been carried out by individuals, church groups, and other private organizations. Rather, we are suggesting that the elevation of voluntaryism serves to deflect attention from root causes and long-term solutions.

Consider an article on the homeless by influential conservative George Will. Describing in moving terms the plight of street people in Washington, D.C., he observes that "no social safety net, however tight its mesh, could prevent many such persons from falling through." Without arguing for the superiority of voluntaryism, he makes the same point by eulogizing "gloriously inexplicable" small organizations like a mobile food service that runs through Washington's streets, and its volunteers, who perform "little miracles" as they pass.[23]

One wonders whether the homeless need little miracles, or earthly changes in the society that excludes them.

Could the elevation of voluntaryism be useful in other ways? If it is an expression of freedom, perhaps we should ask, "Freedom for whom?" Charity in the sense of alms-giving can be a situation in which the giver, however unconsciously, confirms his position of power, while the recipient is expected to understand his inferiority.

The return to an emphasis on an older mode of charity, then, can function as one piece of a strategy of subtly controlling a troublesome population. Thus government may agree to fund one shelter but not set a precedent. To support studies of the homeless problem but not ongoing programs to feed the human beings experiencing the problem. To fund not long-term housing programs but emergency shelters, which ultimately become quasi-permanent for those who have nowhere else to go. To provide more jails, prisons, and workhouses but not work programs.

At the same time, labor unions are weakened, real wages decline, and the minimum wage is contained. Public assistance and unemployment compensation are cut. The demand for labor is reduced, thus making workers more competitive with each other.

As Hopper and Hamberg suggested, the spectacle of homelessness can serve as a threat to dissatisfied workers. The unstated objective becomes one of containing the homeless and the potentially homeless—of keeping them in their place.

We are reminded of a conversation with the manager of a small private shelter. "Sometimes I feel as if I'm playing into the authorities' hands," he sighed. "The more *we* do, the less willing government is to support programs that would prevent this mess."

We think of an observation by Steve Whitney-Wise as he reviewed his work with the homeless: "Maybe our charitable organizations *need* to have someone to serve. Maybe our society *needs* to have poor people."

Let us look briefly at the ways other societies deal with people who have no home.

A Glimpse of Homelessness around the World

It is tempting to assume that in other industrialized nations the number of roofless persons is comparable to the number in the United States and that in poor countries the problem is always worse.

It is true that homelessness is a worldwide phenomenon. Separately or together, we have visited or lived in seventy-four countries; all of them have rootless people. Indeed, the United Nations, which estimates that there are some 100,000,000 people in the world with no housing whatsoever,[24] has designated 1987 as the International Year of Shelter for the Homeless.

It is important to make some distinctions when using the term *homeless*. There are millions who have been uprooted by war and still live in refugee camps. There are others who have been dislocated by earthquakes, famine, floods, tornadoes, and fires. These people, however, are victims of war or natural disasters, not social policy.

The streets of Bombay, Calcutta, and Madras are home to millions of families. In Turkey, Mexico, Colombia, and many other poor countries, vagrant children roam the streets, begging in open air restaurants, singing for change in city buses, and bathing in public fountains.

The root causes of homelessness in both rich and poor countries are the societal changes resulting from industrialization and urbanization. In traditional societies—in Europe during the Middle Ages, and in less advanced countries until recently—patterns of mutual obligation in the community provided a certain basic security. Landlords, and even a few peasants, might be far better off than the great majority of poor toilers, yet except in times of famine or other natural disasters, everyone was accorded subsistence. Everyone, too, was expected to make some contribution to the community, although it was not called a job, an occupation with some arbitrary monetary value. The agricultural revolution eroded these patterns of community. By allowing smaller numbers of people to be engaged in the production of food and raw materials, it stimulated a great increase in the number of people engaged in nonagricultural occupations.

The industrial revolution moved the locus of production from the home or small shop to the factory. It also created a class of workers who labor for wages and submit their livelihood to the vagaries of the marketplace. The twin revolutions, then, created an influx of rural dwellers into the cities. Some found relatively secure jobs; others became victims of cyclical unemployment.

No country has been immune to these developments. Every nation belongs to the world capitalist system. The rules of the game for even those countries that call their guiding philosophies by some other name—be it communism, socialism, or theocracy—are ultimately shaped by the stronger forces of capitalism.

Nevertheless, Third World countries have responded to the mass emigration to the cities in different ways. Authorities in all these societies pin their primary hopes on the extended family network. Traditionally, the new arrival from the country has been able to knock on the door of his city cousin (who might be a third cousin, an uncle twice removed, or a godmother) and be invited to stay. As a Zambian schoolteacher who was supporting eighteen relatives once told us, "Your kinsman says he's come for two days, but you know it could be for two years."

In countries such as India, where millions exist in abject poverty, that family network has obviously been strained beyond the breaking point. In somewhat less impoverished countries, the government may do little if anything to build housing for the poor, but a cushion of sorts is fashioned from a variety of sources: family, neighbors, charity, government. The new migrants may set up shacks in the ubiquitous shanty-towns that surround the sprawling cities of the Third World. (Indeed, many developing countries use the term *homeless* to describe squatters.) Concocted of cardboard, straw, sticks, cast-off shingles, and beer cans, all mortared together by mud, the flimsy constructions often collapse in the wind or the rain. Yet, the next day neighbors are likely to band together to rebuild the house; the sense of community among squatters is strong. As time passes, those who find work make their own bricks and gradually build the walls for a more durable dwelling around the original core. Flimsy though their abode may be, the squatters have some sort of roof over their own.

To be sure, most governments in the Third World discourage squatting. In Zambia, Tanzania, and Kenya, for instance, authorities have attempted to dissuade rural dwellers from coming to the city through a mixture of threats, rewards for staying down on the farm, and measures such as rounding up unemployed youth and relocating them to rural camps where they are taught to work the land. From time to time authorities may even send in police to bulldoze illegal shanties as a warning to potential migrants in the countryside. Often the squatters find champions, however. Several times during the 1950s and 1960s in Peru, for example, university students locked arms, forming a barricade as they shouted, "Shoot them and you shoot us first!"

All these tough measures have been remarkably unsuccessful. In the end, the government usually accepts the squatters: a tacit acknowledgment that they have a right to a home. In some countries the government may even help them upgrade their shanties and provide water, roads, community halls, and schools. As their dwellings improve, the squatters are expected to reciprocate by paying taxes.

A few societies take authoritarian measures to avert such a situation. Communist China, for example, is well aware of the pathological problems that could be generated by homelessness. So acute is the housing shortage in its metropolitan areas that no citizen is allowed to live there without having first secured a job. With the job goes the assurance of housing, which is arranged by the union or employer. Much of the housing would seem pretty cheerless to most Americans. Almost everyone in the large cities lives in crowded quarters, sometimes three or four to a room. A youth we met in Beijing was living in one room of his company's offices. Any Chinese caught trying to evade the rule are ensconced in a dormitory until they return to their original communities. During our visit to the Chinese People's Republic we observed no one who did not have a place to call home. Yet in neighboring Hong Kong, that glittering monument to the efforts of Chinese who make it the free enterprise way, men and women sleep in the alleys beside luxury hotels and casinos.

To Americans the restrictions that the Chinese (and the Soviets) place on movement to cities is an intolerable infringement on freedom. In principle, Americans allow any citizens the freedom (if not the wherewithal) to seek their fortune on another frontier. Upon arrrival in the city of opportunity, however, American migrants encounter a variety of hurdles to discourage them from staying. Only a few communities have used police dogs or sprayed poison on garbage cans to spell out the welcome to squatters and vagabonds. Usually tactics are more subtle. The wandering poor discover that without addresses they have no rights to social benefits, that there are not enough beds, that shelters ask them to leave in a few days, and that many public accommodations resemble the poorhouses of Dickens's day. They are told to seek help from charitable organizations. The unspoken message is clear: MOVE ON. And Americans, citizens of the world's greatest democracy, have the freedom to do so.

Sister Marie Heinz, a Catholic nun who worked with the poor in Brazil's impoverished Northeast, observes: "The situation doesn't seem as bad there, because so many people are poor. Here, there's such a contrast between average Americans and those who have been unsuccessful in a society that expects any man who *is* a man to make it. In Brazil they're already at the bottom and can't go further. There's more informal support from others in the community. They can build shacks together. Or climb trees to pick fruit. Here that would be poaching on private property. So you have to buy food in supermarkets or steal; everything has a price. In America those who are down and out seem more isolated and rejected."

Although unemployment during the 1980s has been far worse in most European countries than in the United States, visitors to Europe will find, comparatively speaking, fewer homeless people in cities or rural areas. To the best of our knowledge, no definitive comparative census of the homeless populations in the industrialized countries exists. Estimates vary widely. Unofficial counts of the roofless in Paris, for example, range from 10,000 to 40,000. The problems in making an accurate survey would be legion. Take the problem of definition. When Gillian Cussen of Threshold, the National Voluntary Housing Advisory and Research Service, told us that there were 10,000 homeless women in Dublin, we discovered that she meant 384 women in hostels, over 600 squatting or living in cheap lodging houses, and 9000 hidden homeless. Threshold defined *homeless* as covering not only those who had no place of their own, but also people who were faced with deteriorating housing or rising rents and did not know how long they could continue in their present dwellings.

Simple observation in the course of walking through the streets in both Western and Eastern European cities can only lead to the conclusion that homelessness is not as widespread as in the United States. During our explorations of the problem and our talks with human service workers and ordinary citizens in a dozen countries, many Europeans have expressed shocked disbelief that the richest nation in the world should have so many destitute citizens. Radio and television programs in Europe have made much of America's homeless. A few Europeans have even come here to work with them.

It is true that there are some homeless people in every European city. Who are they? Our research and observations lead us to conclude that although the situation varies from country to country, it is probably fair to generalize that the majority are chronic alcoholics, many of them so accustomed to street life that they eschew shelters. Another important group would be illegal aliens, who obviously receive no entitlements. Comparatively few of the homeless are battered wives, runaway children, deinstitutionalized mentally ill persons, evicted tenants, relief recipients unable to survive on their stipends, or destitute citizens ineligible for any social benefits at all.

Martin Gittelman, who edited a series on the mentally ill in other countries for *Hospital and Community Psychiatry*, notes that in most developed nations one rarely finds a mental patient living in the streets.[25] Leif Öjesjö, who directs a psychiatric clinic in Linköping, Sweden, and has taken a keen interest in homelessness around the world, comments:

I do not (yet) have the impression that homelessness is growing [in Sweden]. There are two categories, or maybe three, of homeless people.

1. Alcoholics and drug abusers with *deviant* and *"noisy"* life styles. They do not fit in among the non-deviants, and they are not welcome anywhere (mainly an urban phenomenon, and the group is not very large, anyway.)

2. Mentally ill people, who do not accept any kind of home they are offered by the agencies (a negligible group so far, I believe.)

3. Finally, the new and probably increasing category of *refugees* from different parts of the world, Chile, Sudan, Iran, etc. Some of these unfortunate people are not accepted to stay, so they hide among friends and others—even in monasteries, would you believe that!?[26]

It is also true that homelessness among the new poor has grown in many European countries. Authorities have become alarmed. In 1985 twelve nations gathered at a summit meeting sponsored by the European Commission to discuss poverty and homelessness. Delegates from voluntary groups and government reported common problems: unemployment, housing shortages in the cities, declining social benefits, and growth in evictions. The most severely hit group seemed to be young people.

It is our impression that in Europe, homelessness has reached its greatest proportions in Great Britain, where social policies in the 1980s have most closely paralleled Reaganomics.

Let us look, then, at the worst case. Aside from their current similarities in political ideology, the two nations share other characteristics. Like the United States, Britain has an aging industrial society; mixed, often Darwinian, attitudes toward the poor; and a long tradition of private charity that conflicts with the welfare state philosophy.

In London, growing numbers of families have joined the hard core homeless, the chronic alcoholics who live in and out of dormitorylike hostels, bed-sitter lodging houses, and missions. (The Salvation Army was founded in London.) The chief factor in the rise of roofless families seems to be the decay of low-income housing under the Thatcher government. Public housing has been offered for private ownership, with tenants allowed first choice. An English House Condition Survey published in December 1982 revealed that the sharp rise in homeownership has been a major factor in the deterioration of city housing stock; owners cannot afford to keep it up.[27] At the same time, there have been cuts in housing benefits for low-income people. The result is that housing starts (public, private, and voluntary) in 1983 under the Conservative government were 50,000 less than the worst year under Labour in 1978.[28]

Nevertheless, the slashes in housing programs have not been so drastic as those wrought by the Reagan administration. In response to a series of damning reports on the effects of the cuts, the British government canceled some of them. For example, 300,000 families who were to have lost their benefits altogether managed to keep them. The national housing minister has put pressure on hostels for homeless men to stop some evictions. Members of Parliament have been working on legislation to upgrade the hostels. In other words, the central government—in sharp contrast to the Reagan administration—regards these actions as fulfilling its responsiblity.

Reporting on a trip to London, Peter Friedland, coordinator of Emergency Shelter of Greater Springfield (Massachusetts), says that many of the old hostels and bed-sitters are warehouse-type structures, and that, although conditions vary, these facilities are generally substandard and degrading. Yet he found significant differences between the responses of government in Britain and the United States. For example, in 1977 the central government in Britain passed the Homeless Persons Act. The goal of advocates was that all homeless people have priority for public housing. They succeeded only with families, the elderly, and the handicapped; single people and childless couples were excluded. Families considered intentionally homeless can be barred from priority government housing. Because of the shortage of dwellings, families can also be parked in hotels for a year or more. Nevertheless, says Friedland, at the end of the line some housing is available.[29]

In total contrast to the situation in the United States, he says, substantial funding for the Campaign for the Homeless and Rootless (CHAR), an aggressive critic of government policies, has come from government sources. CHAR has lobbied for the national homelessness law, legal rights for the homeless, higher standards for shelters, and expansion of low-income housing stock. Its attack on bed-sitters (which George Orwell described so eloquently in *Down and Out in Paris and London*) has been influential in development of far-reaching plans to tear down the worst examples. Government agencies as well as private ones are working on resettlement programs for single homeless people who were living in these condemned structures.

British advocates, who have a much more consistently left philosophical base than their American counterparts, fear that too much focus on shelters instead of housing and jobs will provide conservative governments with an excuse for human dumping grounds. Nevertheless, even though the private sector continues to play a major role, "England is way ahead of the United States in rejecting and moving away from the delusion that private charitable mechanisms suffice," according to Friedland. This, he says, reflects both a conscious strategic choice by advocates to push through a national legal framework, and Britain's broader social welfare experience.[28]

Alvin Schorr, who has been a United States government official and an advisor to British Labour governments, says that although convervative cutting of social benefits originated in the United Kingdom, cuts there have been modest compared with those in the United States. No British official has made a statement comparable to David Stockman's "I don't believe there is any entitlement," and no reordering has been as deep as America's new federalism.[30]

A visit we made to London in the summer of 1985 confirmed the impressions of these observers. Whatever their actual numbers, the English homeless were far less visible than their American counterparts. Even at the Embankment tube station, reputedly the central gathering place for London's homeless, there were less than forty street people at eight o'clock in the evening. Although many hostels were run-down, the Princess Beatrice, where we talked for several hours with a group of articulate and well-informed young residents, was clean and well-ordered and offered private rooms. What emerged from that lively discussion was a picture of government delays in rent subsidies, cuts in housing benefits for single unemployed people, a growth in illegal evictions, and a surge in gentrification, at the expense of low-income housing. Yet these dissatisfied young people were doing better than most of their counterparts in the United States because they all qualified for some housing benefit, however inadequate, as well as health care and a means-tested living stipend. There was no counterpart to the situation of young unemployed Americans living in states that do not even offer General Assistance.

If Britain's situation is closest to ours, what about other European countries? As noted in chapter 7, during the eighties they have made far less sweeping reductions in social programs than has the United States. A few countries have actually raised some benefits. In general, unemployment insurance still lasts longer than in the United States, represents a larger proportion of pay, and at termination is followed by some sort of assistance, although it may not be enough to live on. (At the Salvation Army houseboat in Paris, for example, we met a young man who was homeless because his unemployment insurance had run out after a year, and his welfare check amounted to only 1200 francs a month.)

Deinstitutionalization of mental patients has also proceeded at a more cautious pace in Europe. In contrast to the United States, where the number of resident patients at the end of the year dropped from 512,501 in 1950 to 137,810 in 1980, the Norwegian mental health patient population declined only from 7,915 in 1950 to 5,534 in 1980.[31] In England, the number fell from 104,638 in 1971 to 74,831 in 1980.[32] In Denmark, where the method of keeping statistics was changed in 1976 from showing the number of patients treated to showing the number of discharges, the latter rose only from 21,585 in 1976 to 22,019 in 1980.[33] In the Scandinavian countries, particularly, deinstitutionalized mental patients are offered a living stipend, housing ranging from quarterway houses to independent living arrangements, and ongoing treatment and rehabilitation services. Although coordination among all agencies serving the deinstitutionalized is far from perfect, strong efforts are made to this end.

As pointed out in chapter 5, European governments tend to take far more responsibility for low-income housing through combinations of various kinds of assistance. Many nations have far to go. Yet even in the countryside of Ireland, a poor nation by our standards, almost the only decaying dwellings one sees are thatched-roof farmhouses, which are being replaced by sturdy, attractive cottages built through generous government grants and loans. In the large cities many apartments are deteriorating, but even there government is struggling to replace them with decent multifamily structures.

The conviction that government bears ultimate responsibility for the well-being of its citizens was manifest in the resolutions reached by the 1985 conference on poverty and homelessness sponsored by the European Commission. The delegates agreed that all vagrancy laws should be repealed; funds thus freed should go to social services for the homeless; they should have the right to legal representation and the right to vote; they should not be discharged from health institutions without full arrangements for their housing; a guaranteed minimum income should be available.

Shelters, then, were not seen as the solution to homelessness. Perhaps most important was the resolution that housing is a fundamental human right that must be realized through progressive programs of construction and rehabilitation of housing for the poor.[34]

It has become somewhat fashionable to attribute Europe's economic problems to the largess of the welfare state. How, then, does one explain that in the postwar period Europeans spent far more than the United States on social programs, yet had lower rates of unemployment and inflation and high levels of investment?[35]

A closer look at the situation suggests that, on the contrary, the largess of the welfare state has provided a cushion against utter destitution. Comprehensive social planning means that, by and large, European countries have managed to prevent homelessness from erupting into a full-scale malignant problem.

We recall a conversation with a social worker in Stockholm. When we described the case of Franz, the elderly gentleman we encountered near the United Nations, and asked what his experience might have been in Sweden, she looked puzzled. "But we would never put old people out on the street. It practically never happens to *anyone.*" In the first place, she pointed out, an old person would have a basic pension, and in most cases a supplementary pension based on previous earnings; together the two would probably equal two-thirds of the average income during his fifteen best working years. Second, he would be eligible for a housing subsidy. Third, he could receive free or nearly free home helper services: housekeeping, transport, shopping, assistance in bathing, and a listening ear. Fourth, Home Service could place him in a collective home, then find him an apartment. In case he were evicted—highly unlikely, since laws concerning eviction and conversion are strict in Sweden—he could be furnished with a free lawyer. Finally, home helpers, who perform a valuable outreach function, would report any physical problems or mental confusion to Home Service.

It is easy to assume that because European countries are smaller and appear more homogeneous than ours, their experience is too different to allow fair comparisons. Many Americans—with a little help from the American Medical Association and the *Wall Street Journal*—view Sweden, particularly, as the embodiment of dangerous socialist–communist philosophies that have caused a wide range of pathologies: statism, free love, legitimized illegitimacy, alcoholism, and suicide, all because of the debilitating effects of socialism.

Those who take such arguments seriously can find comparative studies that demonstrate that most of these problems occur with equal or even higher frequency in the land of the Moral Majority. Here we only wish to point out a few of the similarities and dissimilarities between the two countries. Swedes share with Americans an attitude toward work that is based on the Protestant Ethic. The Swedes also possess a comparably high level of technology, a high standard of living, and a determination to protect them.

Socialism (in Sweden more accurately called social democracy) has not led to statism. As noted earlier, 90 percent of the Swedish economy is privately owned; it is the social programs that are socialized. The 1982 Swedish Law on Social Services, which was designed to establish an even more comprehensive approach to dealing with the individual's total situation, explicitly articulates the *right* of all Swedes (and immigrants) to financial assistance and other services. Yet it also emphasizes a principle with which Americans would agree: no service can ever replace the social bonds, the responsibility, and the solidarity that should exist between individual human beings.

Yet unlike the United States, which was founded on an essentially egalitarian philosophy, Sweden and other European countries have had to contend with a traditional class structure as they strove for more equal distribution of life chances.

This is not the place to describe how European nations got from there to here. The point is that instead of accepting the comforting maxim that the poor will always be with us, they have striven for greater social equity. Although all countries in Western Europe operate on primarily capitalist principles, they have attempted to soften the impact of rugged capitalism on the less fortunate members of society.

British social welfare scholar Richard Titmuss calls this "partial compensation for disservices, for social costs and social insecurities which are the product of a rapidly changing society."[36] Such compensation may be expensive in the short run but economical in the long term since it serves to prevent the costs of festering social problems. That is the pragmatic side of the story. The other, perhaps even more important side is the belief that some elements of life in the human community supersede the forces of the marketplace.

Fort Washington Armory, New York City.

10

Prospects and Proposals

O ver the years of studying homelessness in the United States and abroad, we have evolved or crystallized certain views and beliefs. Before summarizing our suggestions for dealing with homelessness, it might be well to share these views and beliefs with the reader.

We believe that, as the National Coalition for the Homeless puts it, "in any society of sufficient means, homelessness should be exceptional, a state of duress and deprivation befalling victims of catastrophe"[1]—not a condition that has become commonplace as it has in the United States.

We have arrived at an answer to a question posed in the opening chapter: Is homelessness the result of our capitalist system? Of course it is. We suspect that almost everyone who has thought long enough about the problem has come to the same conclusion, although it is not fashionable to criticize capitalism today. The core of the capitalist system is the drive for profit—the maximization of profit above all else. In a capitalist system the value of goods, services, and work is primarily decided by demand in the market place. Like Marxism, capitalism sees human behavior as determined by economic factors, an urge for accumulation of more goods, more wealth.

It has become abundantly clear that the very nature of the system has led to a short-term surplus of goods in many industrialized nations, side by side with crucial shortages of the same goods in other countries. For example, in a year when U.S. farmers were paid to take nearly 100 million acres of cropland out of production, 450 million people in the world were starving. Since some of these countries had shifted much of their production from subsistence to export crops that would reap profits for certain strata of the society, world capitalism contributed to the starvation. Exploitation of the environment for short-term gains continues, even as the world's natural resources are dwindling. As the system is rendered more efficient by computerized production, that surplus of goods is accompanied by a surplus of people—so-called unproductive human beings who eventually may have nowhere to go but the streets.

Still, having said that, what have we said? That capitalism takes the same form in all countries? That homelessness is an *inevitable* consequence of capitalism? We do not find this to be the case. Many other capitalist countries, notably Japan and those in Western Europe, have found it possible to mitigate the profit motive and to provide a cushion that can soften the impact of rugged capitalism. Government intervention assures better distribution of income, goods, and services to fulfill the basic needs of all citizens.

If homelessness is not inevitable and cannot be attributed to scarcity, then it is a result of choices—choices that place market forces above the fair distribution of social goods. Homelessness in our society, says the National Coalition, "betrays either a decision to exclude a certain class of people from the prevailing norm of what constitutes a decent share of social goods, or the tacit creation of a second and inferior standard for those who are destitute."[2]

We believe that the inalienable rights of life, liberty, and the pursuit of happiness are glorious but empty abstractions unless they are animated by more elemental rights: to housing, to sustenance, to health care, to social services, to work. Human beings dumped into the streets like yesterday's refuse hardly possess life or liberty, and do not know what the pursuit of happiness means.

We believe that just as the state has responsibility to guarantee the rights of free speech and a free press, it has the duty to insure these rights to subsistence. This does not exclude religious and other voluntary groups. On the contrary, they play an invaluable function. Operating on the front line, they can meet urgent emergency needs more quickly and more humanely than most government agencies. Wherever feasible, they should deliver services funded by government. They should never, however, be expected to take on the preventive functions of government, that institution to which we have assigned the role of overseeing the well-being of all citizens. Moreover, unless the material assistance and other services funded by government and delivered by voluntary groups are deemed rights, they are likely to be seen as handouts by both the recipient and the mediary of services. This dehumanizes both of them.

A true safety net should be a first step, a minimum goal. A more far-reaching goal should be a fairer distribution of all the resources in our society. Sometimes this will mean more than assuring equal access to services. As the Sidels emphasize in their discussion of health care, some people, because of illness, disability, or their social or economic circumstances may need far more than their equal share of access to services in order for equity to be achieved.[3]

American society seems to be moving toward greater division and greater inequality, not less. Yet the history of the United States has been based not only on competitive individualism and the survival of the strongest, but also on a fundamental egalitarianism. Cooperation and mutual aid helped America's founding fathers and mothers survive the rigors of the frontier. Our observations lead us to believe that despite the deep ambivalence in American society, these values are still very much alive. We think of volunteers such as the woman who offered to spend two evenings a week at Seattle's Downtown Emergency Center, and after one evening confided: "It's a jolt to realize these people are so much like us—the real difference is that I've been born lucky enough to have a roof over my head." We think of advocates such as Buddy Gray in Cincinnati and Sara Colm in San Francisco, who gave up lives of relative comfort in order to work not *for* the poor in the community but *with* them. We think of church groups such as the Community of Hope in Washington, whose members work alongside homeless people to rehabilitate apartments. We recall the quick response of individuals, groups, and even some officials to appeals to form advocacy networks. They all are inspired by a sense of anger that America's standards of justice have been violated. As Chicago Mayor Walter Washington put it: "This is the richest society in the world; and *one* person without a place to live is a tragedy; *100* homeless people are a scandal; but *25,000* people in just one city who have not even a ragged hut or camping tent to call their home is an indictment of us as a people. It is a hard condemnation of our standards of humanity and fair play."[4]

This outrage at the violation of American values gives us hope that there is a foundation for the changes needed to prevent the United States from drifting toward a two-class society.

Short-Term Proposals

Many of the following suggestions have been described at some length in previous chapters. Here we shall only summarize them briefly.

The Federal Role

Homelessness is clearly a national problem. Many of the Americans with no place to live are transients who move from state to state in search of jobs. It is unrealistic to expect state governments to assume major responsibility for them. It is even more unrealistic to expect local governments to take on most of the financial burden. Some cities are poorer, more overburdened, or less hospitable than others. It hardly makes sense for a citizen of this country to be offered a temporary roof in one city, not in another, to get voting rights or General Assistance in one community but not in one just fifty miles away. If Americans are to enjoy the equal rights guaranteed in their Constitution, the federal government bears ultimate responsibility for guaranteeing basic services, although it need not administer all of them.

Emergency Measures. It is interesting that even the HHS Working Group on the Homeless describes the federal government's role as that of leadership, although the same report depicts the role as one of supporting private and local efforts, and statements of many federal leaders have trivialized the problem. What would true leadership mean? First, enunciating the *right* to shelter. Second, funding emergency assistance to a far greater extent than at present. At a minimum, the administration needs to make an explicit commitment to funding food and shelter programs, to request Congress to increase appropriations, and to ask that they be on a sustained basis rather than a year-to-year basis. Funds should be included for emergency health care.

Although many surplus federal buildings are not suitable as shelters, wherever possible they should be used as emergency facilities.

The outreach functions of SSI and Social Security programs should be expanded, and proposals to extend outreach to include food stamps, AFDC, Medicare, Medicaid, and Veterans cash and medical benefits, should be implemented as quickly as possible.

If the federal role is to go further than taking emergency measures, however, it should encompass improving housing, welfare, and mental health programs.

Housing. As pointed out in chapter 5, despite the Reagan administration's policies of drastically reducing HUD and FmHA programs, the struggle for a strong federal role continues to be waged by some members of Congress—particularly Representatives Henry Gonzales, Bruce Vento, Barney Frank, Augustus Hawkins, and Mary Rose Oakar, as well as Senators Daniel Moynihan and Slade Gordon. They are fighting not only for the preservation of emergency projects and the federal housing programs described in chapter 5 but also for creating new programs in transitional housing. For many of these lawmakers, a driving concern is the growing number of families for whom emergency shelters or welfare hotel rooms have become a way of life. For thousands of children, home may mean living amid scenes of crime, drug dealing, and physical violence.

The HHS Working Group's proposals to waive the limit on the amount of Section 8 housing assistance funds that can be used by single, nonelderly clients, to issue Section 8 vouchers to emergency shelter providers, and to provide relatively independent mentally disabled people with Section 8 vouchers all deserve implementation. Cities could be given the option of selling urban homesteading units to nonprofit organizations for use as shelters.

There is a great need to coordinate the programs of HUD and FmHA with those of HHS. Social services should be included in housing development plans.

Social Welfare. The weaknesses of the welfare system, as we have seen, are many. Benefits are inadequate; they are inequitable; the system excludes needy people; it stigmatizes people; it does little to help them get jobs; it lacks coordination. Until the system can be overhauled, the following changes would go far to meet the needs of the homeless and potentially homeless.

Unemployment insurance, which presently covers only a minority of the unemployed and varies from state to state, should be expanded and made more equitable, so that it provides benefits to all unemployed and involuntary part-time workers. SSI benefits should be raised to at least the poverty level. Supplemental aid should be made available to Social Security recipients who are not eligible for SSI. At the same time, the qualifying conditions for disability under both SSI and SSD should be broadened.

Food stamp guidelines need to be simplified and clarified. Although it is a federal program, hence one that presumably would be uniformly administered in all fifty states, a study by the Physician Task Force on Hunger revealed that in 150 counties around the United States, food stamps reach less than one-third of those eligible.[5] Some authorities may deliberately withhold benefits. Others may be honestly confused by complex rules. For example, although federal rules state that the applicant must live in the political subdivision designated to administer the program, they do not require a fixed residence; a migratory campsite could satisfy the residency requirement. For food stamp purposes, people living on the street can be considered recipients of the project areas in which they live. Eligibility should also be restored to people who lost it through budget cutting, providing they meet the old guidelines. Many valid criticisms can be made of the food stamp program—that it is cumbersome and stigmatizes recipients, for example—but the fact remains that it is a cost-efficient way of relieving distress.

A more far-reaching proposal is that the federal government take the dominant role in financing, administering, and setting standards for the AFDC program. Although this may not be realizable during an administration bent on decentralizing and diminishing services, it is not too early to stimulate public discussion of the idea. Following its own example with SSI, Washington would guarantee a national floor, one that met minimum standards for dignified living. A reasonable standard would be a fully updated poverty level. As with SSI, states would have the option of supplementing the minimum guarantees, to adjust for differences in the cost of living. Such a reform would compensate for the unwillingness or inability of some states to support impoverished families adequately. At the same time, releasing states of this responsibility would enable them to take on the task of responding quickly and equitably to the needs of families and individuals for short-term emergency aid.

Another program that should be taken over by the federal government is General Assistance. A reasonable national minimum would be a guarantee equivalent to that for SSI. In the interests of equity, as well as reduction of waste, GA could be fused with SSI. Impoverished single persons and childless couples under sixty-five are as worthy as people who are elderly or disabled and should not be penalized for the inability of market forces to create jobs.

One immediate measure that would be particularly effective in preventing people from becoming clients for public assistance would be raising the minimum wage to its traditional level, 50 percent of the average hourly wage in the private sector.

Mental Health Policy. Chronically mentally ill people need comprehensive psychiatric and medical care, continuity of care, and individually designed treatment regimens. All of these assume the existence of diversified programs, including those that can serve the difficult patients largely overlooked by the present care system.

Until the time when the NIMH and its parent body, HHS, can assume an expanded, more preventive function, their present activities should be strengthened. For example, the Community Support Program that NIMH launched as a pilot project in 1978 provides a model for cooperation in improving services for severely disabled adult psychiatric patients.[6] NIMH has shown considerable interest in homelessness. It has convened meetings of professional associations to discuss the problem, sponsored research projects in several states on the interaction between homelessness and mental health problems and needs, and conducted demonstration programs on work with the homeless. The problem, however, is not a dearth of research, seminars, or pilot projects. Even in the 1970s, before the explosion of mentally ill persons to the streets, considerable research was being done on the unmet needs of chronic patients, and writers were warning that many were falling through the cracks. The problem is funding the sound ideas that already exist.

Federal block grants to the states for mental health, alcoholism, and drug abuse programs need increased funding if they are to fulfill their purpose. There is a need for special start-up grants for additional community mental health centers to meet the original goal of 2,000. This time around there should be clear-cut funding for rehabilitation and supportive functions.

As suggested in chapter 6, HHS could alter the medical model rules that restrict Medicaid reimbursement for community-based programs. In terms of cost to society, this would be an economy move.

In addition to providing grants to nonprofit groups wishing to set up housing with special services for the mentally disabled, HUD could endorse legislation making it illegal to use zoning to discriminate against the disabled.

Finally, NIMH and HHS should assume the task of clarifying the respective responsibilities for the mentally ill borne by each level of government.

States

Since Washington will surely resist efforts to federalize AFDC and GA, state officials, while continuing to press for federalization, should raise benefit levels for those programs. States with no GA should introduce that entitlement. All states would do well to follow the example of those that allow homeless people to use a shelter address when applying for aid. Funds for emergency and transitional housing can originate from state as well as national levels of government. Even more important are measures to offer financial assistance for several months to temporarily impoverished families unable to meet rent or utility payments, and assistance with mortgage payments to people in danger of eviction.

It is clearly in the domain of the states to take over the task of widening and improving mental health services (including drug-abuse and alcohol programs). In the past, state mental health agencies have had clear responsibility for organizing long-term care for the disabled. More recently, some of the responsibility has shifted to federal and local agencies, and even to shelters, with resulting confusion.

States need to take responsibility for planning a continuum of services, such as the range of graded treatment programs and housing alternatives proposed by Talbott. Guided by federal standards, states should monitor more closely the quality of treatment in their institutions and in private hospitals as well.

This kind of planning cannot be accomplished without a great deal of cooperation among all systems that affect the individual's mental health and well-being. State planning conferences should include reprsentatives from the housing sector, vocational rehabilitation agencies, the state employment service, and private business. Although their skills may be limited, many of the mentally ill are employable, particularly for the low-level jobs that have been multiplying. Even more important than its monetary value, work (including sheltered work) provides meaning and dignity to human lives.

All of this is pie in the sky unless states can create financial incentives to make it possible for local communities to develop a continuum of services. Ultimately, this will require more funding from the federal government to the states in the form of block grants.

Local Government

Cities and counties, of course, remain the front line in work with the homeless. Using federal and state funds as well as their own, local governments can set up public shelters, provide vouchers into hotels, and make food, equipment, and technical assistance available. The preferred pattern is to channel public funds to nonprofit groups for shelter and longer-term accommodations. Variations of this arrangement include setting up shelter trust funds for use by nonprofit agencies and selling city-owned houses, for $1 or so, to nonprofit groups, who turn them into dwellings for the homeless.

Municipal government can assume a positive regulatory function by modifying zoning laws to allow shelters, transitional residences, and group homes in neighborhoods throughout the city. Experiences in New York demonstrate that when authorities move judiciously in cooperation with churches, community boards, councils, neighborhood associations, and other grassroots community groups, they can deal with citizens' fears and successfully introduce small facilities for the homeless. Cities can also set standards for the various types of accommodations. However, as in the case of Cincinnati, there is always the danger that existing regulations will be used by politicians to close down a shelter.

Since it is important to work with every type of concerned group to assure a broad diversity of arrangements, cities, following Boston's example, could set up an emergency shelter commission to coordinate municipal efforts with those of state, federal, and private groups.

It is time that cities move away from the emergency shelter mind-set. New York offers the cardinal example of waste. The municipal government has been spending between $1,050 and $3,000 a month per room to house families in hotels, and nearly

$6,000 a month to place a family of four in one barrackslike shelter in the Bronx.[7] Yet it cost St. Francis Friends of the Poor only $9,000 per room to purchase and renovate a building that could provide permanent supervised housing to mentally disabled homeless people. Today a private room at St. Francis costs less than $450 (including meals and support services) per month. Homeless advocates propose that the city seize the hotels and turn them over to nonprofit groups, and that it set up a fund to help community groups renovate buildings for permanent and transitional housing, help community groups get funding from federal and state sources, and supply technical assistance to community developers.

These proposals deserve implementation in other parts of the nation. Cities could also contract with families that wish to let out spare rooms in their homes, a time-honored custom that can offer greater comfort and dignity to people who feel they have been squeezed through every crack of the system.

The most salient need, of course, is for permanent, affordable housing. Concerned Americans should push Washington to support low-cost housing, although it is probably unrealistic to expect significant federal initiatives in the near future. Until then, state and city governments need to share most of the responsibility. New York State and New York City are already working toward this goal.

States and counties can increase the basic grant and the shelter allowance components of public assistance stipends to enable recipients to find decent housing at rents that are fair to honest landlords.

Other suggestions in the realm of housing policy deserve recapitulation. Protection of low-income people from displacement requires action to change housing laws. Although it is late in the game (47 percent of the nation's SROs were demolished or converted between 1970 and 1982),[8] it is time to call a moratorium on conversions of SROs into condominiums. As long as the low-income housing crisis lasts, such conversion needs to be regulated, for example, through altering tax policies that encourage it. Resale controls and demolition controls require strengthening. Rent control measures (which usually allow annual increases in rent based on increased operating costs) need to be extended and in some cases expanded. In most cities antiarson laws are weak; they need reinforcement (and enforcement). Protection against eviction except for limited reasons such as nonpayment of rent, committing a felony, or the owner's clear desire for personal use and occupancy is essential; it has helped to stem homelessness in Washington and other cities. Another protective measure is a vacant unit tax, which creates a high level of property tax on vacant buildings or land, thus making it more profitable for owners to return units to the markets than to hold on to them in hopes of some future killing. Ultimately, one of the most effective measures would be an ordinance requiring that developers replace each unit removed from the low-to-moderate income stock with another such unit.

Even without federal back-up funding, cities can make a positive gesture to small landlords by setting up a technical and financial assistance program to help them maintain rental units, perhaps coupling it with special incentives to house low-income tenants. Cities can offer direct grants or loans to small groups for construction of innovative approaches to affordable housing, such as limited equity cooperatives and other forms of social ownership.

All these proposals imply reordering of a city's priorities—shifting from the emphasis on convention centers, office buildings, and luxury hotels, to housing for people. Is such a reordering possible? Current trends suggest that office and hotel room vacancies have risen to record levels. In the aftermath of a gold rush fueled by investors seeking high returns and tax breaks through real estate syndications and partnerships, some analysts have predicted a collision course with disaster in the future. In July of 1985, occupancy rates for hotels in Houston had fallen to 50.2 percent, and in New Orleans hotels were faring just slightly better at 56.5 percent.[9] With financial encouragement from federal, state, and city governments, some disillusioned developers might turn their attention to low- and moderate-income housing.

An extremely useful model for a range of housing programs that can meet the needs of both the homeless and other low-income persons has emerged from the work of the Philadelphia Committee for the Homeless. A nonprofit group with just six paid staff but hundreds of volunteers, the committee does outreach work, runs a day center, provides assistance to individuals and groups that want to help the homeless, and engages in advocacy and lobbying. As the committee's long-range planning group examined the situation, it became increasingly aware that the special housing programs set up by the county mental health–mental retardation office were filled with episodically homeless people, while the passive chronically mentally ill homeless, the original target group, remained in emergency facilities. It decided to undertake a comprehensive study of Philadelphia's homeless and how their needs were being met. That population was divided into four categories: unemployed adults, families, substance abusers, and the chronically mentally ill. The needed resources were classified under seven headings: initial contact, short-term shelter, case management, long-term placement, income, permanent housing, and further services. For each homeless category, the resources were analyzed in four ways (existing resources, their adequacy, resources needed, and roadblocks) to measure how well the needs for initial contact, short-term shelter, case management, and so forth were being met. The result, termed the Homeless to Housed Continuum, revealed, not surprisingly, that there is far more available at the left end of the continuum (outreach, short-term shelter, case management, etc.) than at the right end (interim and permanent housing). The Philadelphia committee has determined that the time has come for all those concerned with the homeless to focus their efforts on the root of the problem, the lack of affordable, permanent housing for *all* low-income persons. Armed with these charts, which illustrate the situation in a succinct and graphic way, the committee has begun an outreach campaign to enlist community support.[10]

Long-Term Proposals

Solutions to the crisis of homelessness must be truly preventive. They must address the problems not only of the very poor but also of the blue-collar and white-collar workers who have been skidding down the job ladder. In the long run we shall need new structures.

During the 1980s Americans have witnessed not only a widening of the gap between the rich and the poor but also growing attempts on the part of politicians to exploit the prejudices and class divisions in our society. The proposals set forth here have the potential, we believe, to bridge some of those divisions since they are based on the natural self-interest of individuals and on the mutual interests that unite us in community.

Social Welfare

We propose a social welfare system that incorporates many universal programs and services designed for the average citizen, not just for the dependents or cast-asides. By transcending classes, such programs do not breed resentment that *they* are receiving benefits that *we* do not. The stigma of receiving means-tested benefits creates debilitating despair and dependency. To break the stigma of poverty, good planning must integrate rather than isolate the poor.

Fees on a sliding scale could be charged for some services. Although this does not guarantee a single system—the rich could always buy their own services through the market—the great majority would use the same government-funded service, providing that it was of good quality. Since programs in which the middle class participates tend to enjoy a much higher degree of political support and funding (compare the support for AFDC and for Social Security, for example), they are also likely to be quality services.

In chapter 7 we advocated a comprehensive family policy, comprehensive personal social services, national health care, a multifaceted housing policy, a more equitable income policy, full employment, and a revised tax system. The keystone of sound family policy is adequate income, sufficient to help families stay together. A simple way to provide that is through universal children's allowances. They avoid stigma, are far less expensive to administer than means-tested programs, and would reach families that receive no AFDC grants now, either because of their own pride or because their income falls just above the maximum set by the state in which they happen to live. If the allowances are subject to taxation, as they are in many European countries, then a truly progressive tax system will cancel out most of the benefit to higher-income families that do not really need extra support. Family planning and maternity benefits would also be universal services, as would partially compensated leaves of absence for parents of young children who are ill. Child care and preschool education, too, should not be subject to means tests, but the enormous outlay of funds required to make it a free service would almost surely make it politically infeasible. More practical would be a plan basing fees on the household's income. With the availability of all these programs, the number of families needing AFDC would be greatly reduced.

National health care has received a bad press (and an onslaught of aspersion from the American Medical Association) in the United States. But it is instructive to note that contrary to popular belief, even the British like their much-criticized system very much. A 1978 poll, for example, revealed that 84 percent of the British were satisfied with it.[11]

National health care could be planned according to the insurance model, which contains some free market elements and is the prevalent form in most Western European countries. In Sweden, for example, county and municipal governments own general hospitals, specialists are salaried members of hospital staffs, general practitioners (who provide care only outside the hospital) are paid fees for service, and health insurance refunds most of the patient's costs. A patient pays a small fee (40–45 Swedish kronor, $4 to $5 in 1985) for a visit to a district medical office or hospital outpatient clinic, and the equivalent of $8 or $9 for a home visit. Swedes can also visit a private practitioner by paying a fee about 50 percent higher; the government compensates the doctor for the difference between the fee and an agreed-upon standard. Professional associations set guidelines for fee schedules, which tend to be much lower than in the United States. (The average yearly income for Swedish doctors is about $30,000 a year. In the United States the median net income was $94,580 in 1983.)[12] Drugs, dental treatment, x-rays, laboratory exams, and paramedical treatment are included among benefits. County council taxes, general state subsidies, state grants, and compensation from the national health insurance system cover over 95 percent of the cost; 4 percent comes from patients' fees.[13] The cost of administering such a system is far lower than the administrative overhead in the United States, which has some 1,800 health organizations. Although private practitioners exist in Sweden, it is mandatory that everyone be covered by government-sponsored plans. Hence the system is far more egalitarian than in the United States, where at least 35 million people have no coverage whatsoever and millions of others only grudging second-class care.

A national health service involves a unified system largely free of market elements and is the system adopted in Britain and Italy. In Britain this system allows everyone to sign up with the general practitioner of choice, pays doctors on a capitation basis, and owns and operates most hospitals. Care is paid for through general revenues with essentially no cost to the patient at the time of service. Many problems have arisen with National Health, particularly queuing up for long periods of time to get elective surgery. The basic reason for such problems is that Britain, besieged by fiscal woes, spends only $400 per capita (estimate for 1984) for health care, less than the United States, West Germany, France, and Japan. The United States tops the five countries with $1,500.[14] Increasing the outlay for care, rather than privatizing the system, would go far to doctor the ills in the British service.

If we, the citizens of a far wealthier country, decided to exchange our potpourri of public and private plans for a simplified national service, we could spend more than $400 per capita, yet far less than $1,500, and receive quality care. In the words of the Sidels, "While a national health service would certainly pose new problems, it would at least bypass the enormous costs of billing, payment, and auditing necessary for an insurance program and eliminate some of the temptations for overutilization, overbilling, and gross fraud inherent in reimbursements whether to the patient, or the provider."[15] It could also halt the trend in the United States toward a two-tiered system. Even a national health insurance plan as progressive as that proposed in the Kennedy–Corman plan tends to take funds initially from the poor and to provide guaranteed payments to health-care providers without adequately reforming the health care system. In contrast, a national health service supported by progressive taxation helps to redistribute wealth. The Sidels believe, and we concur, that it is politically realistic and not inconsistent to work for the most progressive of the national health insurance plans and at the same time advocate a national health service as the only rational long-term solution.

Mental health care, as pointed out earlier, is a natural component of a comprehensive health care program. Here, too, equity should become a paramount principle. Our present system tends to offer private psychiatrists and private sanitariums to those who can afford them, and overburdened mental health workers and state hospitals (sometimes) to those who cannot. Although good state institutions exist, many are warehouses. For the most desolate of the poor, the homeless, the final warehouse may be the shelter.

Housing

For the homeless, housing is the crucial issue. When the housing supply was more adequate, a far higher proportion of people who were mentally ill, unemployed, or on public assistance had some kind of roof over their heads, however thin and leaky it might be.

Short-term goals for providing more low-income housing have already been outlined in chapter 5 and earlier in this chapter. Fundamentally, there is little difference between short-term and long-term objectives, except that the latter would be more comprehensive, geared to middle-income as well as low-income people, and based on planning for decades to come. The goal should be to involve not only all levels of government but the private sector as well in planning that would benefit the society at large. (For example, lending institutions could be required to devote a certain proportion of their reserves to low-income housing.)

Programs should include a variety of subsidies, with the ultimate goal of ensuring that every American has the opportunity to obtain sturdy, affordable housing. A massive program to build more units would indeed be expensive. On the other hand, it would provide hundreds of thousands more jobs in the construction, lumber, cement, appliance, and other industries. To this end, the federal government should select one agency to coordinate plans for housing, employment, and economic development. Nothing less is required than a national commitment to honoring the right to decent housing.

Restructuring and Redefining Work

Although full employment is often deemed a utopian ideal, Harrington, Ginsburg, Hawkins, and Levison, among others, have proposed practical strategies to achieve that goal.[16]

Rep. John Conyers of Michigan has outlined a locally based national plan for full employment. Goals would be set up for every town, city, county, and region. Broad citizen participation would assure that the needs of each area be assessed. Priority would be given to employment in certain fields, such as rural and urban transportation, renewable energy, housing rehabilitation and construction, agriculture, natural resources, a high-speed national train system, and rehabilitating the decayed infrastructure. Basic social services, education, cultural activities, and reindustrialization would also get high priority. The federal government would retain a vital role. For example, it would finance projects, give special assistance to areas where unemployment is deeply entrenched and carry out plans of a regional and national scope.

The plan calls for special efforts for groups with more than their share of employment problems, such as victims of discrimination, the physically and mentally handicapped, ex-prisoners, alcoholics, and drug abusers. (These are also the people most vulnerable to homelessness.) The proposal includes plans for conversion from military to civilian production to avoid joblessness among workers now dependent on military contracts. To finance employment, Conyers proposes several measures, including more social control over workers pension funds, a major tax reform that would make corporations and wealthy individuals pay their share, and redirecting some military expenditures to useful civilian purposes.[17]

In stating the case for full employment, Harrington reminds us that employed people are taxpayers; effective job programs would eventually pay for themselves, reducing the federal deficit by $25 billion to $30 billion for every percentage point of employment gained. Employed people are also consumers, people who will buy the products of the new technology that is now being promoted. Full employment would help not only large numbers of new poor but nonpoor workers as well since the existence of a huge pool of idle workers makes people with jobs fearful and drives wages down. As long as there are frightened, impoverished people who will do any dirty job for a minimum or subminimum wage, dirty jobs will persist, sweatshops will thrive, and American businesses will feel little incentive to modernize. Full employment would help reduce crime and violence, benefit minorities, and give young people more reason for practicing the idealism that has been lost as they compete in a tight labor market. A full employment economy would set in motion what Harrington calls a virtuous cycle that would improve the lot of everyone in the labor force, yet it would not be incompatible with private enterprise.[18]

Full employment can become a reality only if government guarantees a job and becomes the employer of last resort, a prospect that clashes with traditional American suspicion of big government. However, it is not only the federal government that would be involved but also city, county, and state governments, together with private and nonprofit employers. The great need is for coordinated planning. Ideally, this should be predicated on active partnership between business, labor, and government. The experience of Sweden demonstrates that the relationship need not be an adversarial one.

Harrington proposes that no one who works *full-time* should be poor. He suggests setting up programs, including child care, that would make it possible for mothers to enter the labor market and would guarantee that their earnings will raise, not reduce, their income.[19]

We would go further. We would suggest that under the best of circumstances, it will be a herculean task to bring unemployment rates down to 3 or 4 percent. The goal may well remain merely utopian unless there is some redefinition of work and also some modification of our inflated expectations of what constitutes the good life.

As Celeste Mac Leod points out, we have still not reconciled the moral imperative "if you don't work, you don't eat," with the reality that there are not enough jobs to go around, at least under present structures. Politicians still capitalize on promises to rid taxpayers of supporting freeloaders on permanent free vacations.[20] Shelter providers, clergy, social workers, and others (the authors included) who have worked with the poor know that it is not true that most people on public assistance do not wish to work. Almost all human beings enjoy extended vacations but few enjoy permanent ones. The need for work goes far beyond the need for money; it is an activity that gives purpose to our lives.

The poor are not fundamentally different from the rest of us. True, many have become so demoralized from years of joblessness that they do not know what it is like to live with a sense of purpose, have developed fears of the unfamiliar demands involved in a job, and have lost confidence in themselves. Many need a little help to help themselves. In *The Underclass*, a detailed description of a program sponsored by the Manpower Demonstration Research Corporation (MDRC), Ken Auletta concludes that this effort was a success. What is significant here is that MDRC's various projects have been targeted at those often written off as hopeless: long-term welfare recipients, ex-convicts, ex-addicts, delinquent youths.[21]

Need everyone have a *full-time* job in order to be considered productive? Should the concept of full-employment not include a greater variety of job arrangements? Mac Leod proposes job sharing, shorter hours, and longer vacations.[22] West Germany, Sweden, and many other countries are already working in this direction. It would be important to make plans that assure that as far as possible these be arrangements of choice, and that they carry at least proportional fringe benefits. Many of the homeless wasting away in the streets or in shelters would benefit from part-time work. There are millions of other Americans among both the poor and middle class who would welcome such opportunities.

Mac Leod also proposes more adult education to help people develop new interests if they opt for early retirement, and programs to give teenagers useful and satisfying experiences while keeping them off the regular job market a year or so longer.[23] All these alternatives are productive, and most could fall under the rubric of work, broadly defined. So, too, could many of the activities carried on in rehabilitation programs for the physically and mentally disabled. At present there is a tendency to call some of it, rather patronizingly, sheltered work, to offer scant renumeration, and to limit it to tasks that present little challenge.

Does work need to be equated with a job? In past centuries this was not the case. Could we not expand the definition of work to include the labor that women, including *poor* women, put into a home? A study of the impact of AFDC mandatory work registration policy on AFDC clients revealed that only 5 percent reported positive effects; 28 percent reported negative individual effects (the strain of having to look for work in addition to performing other duties, lowered self-esteem as a result of failure to obtain employment, disappointment with the failure to get training or a better job); and 24 percent reported negative family consequences (expensive and inadequate child care, behavior problems of unsupervised children, and concern about children left at home to care for themselves).[24]

Theresa Funiciello, co-director of Social Agenda and once a welfare mother herself, oberves that

> If the "strongest" workers in the labor force (i.e., white men) continue losing relatively better-paying jobs (i.e., steel production, automobile manufacturing, etc.) and continue their downward mobility into lower-paid work, it isn't too difficult to guess which workers will get pushed out altogether. Welfare mothers can expect to face even stiffer competition for the jobs nobody else wants. Viewed in this context, pushing mothers (by dint of popular mores reinforced with social or welfare sanctions) to choose a poverty wage job at Chock Full o' Nuts over receiving AFDC and raising their own children can have questionable value.[25]

Voluntary efforts of poor women to enter the paid labor force should be supported by a whole range of services, especially income suplements and child care, says Funiciello. However, if we can also expand our definition of work beyond that for which one is paid a wage, we might be able to realize a new spectrum of programs.[26]

Perhaps it all comes down to a basic question: how real is our concern for America's families? The alarming growth of homeless families in cities, suburbs, and even small towns is merely a symptom of social and economic problems that are worsening. Such problems cannot be solved by AFDC, or indeed the rest of the public assistance system. What is needed is a clear family policy that integrates the employment, housing, social welfare, education, and health systems in the United States.

A Note on Inequality

In the past we could rely on constant economic growth to mask inequality and to cure poverty. That is to say, as long as the bottom strata of society could feel that their standard of living was rising, however slowly, their attention was diverted from perceiving that living standards of the upper strata were rising proportionately higher—that the gap between the haves and have nots was widening. Many liberals have bought this optimistic fixation with growth.

A concept more relevant to the present and the future might be balanced development. Here the focus is on the economy getting better, not just bigger. This means more efficient planning of human and economic resources and better distribution of goods and services.

Relying on ever-expanding economic growth involves ever-expanding exploitation of natural resources. They are limited. Americans, still having possession of vast natural wealth in this country and still able, because of relative affluence, to consume a grossly inequitable portion of the world's raw materials (estimates run as high as one-third) have been more insulated from that reality than others. Some time in the not-too-distant future, we shall have to come to terms with it. This will surely mean lowering expectations of what the good life is all about, trimming the American dream of an ever-rising standard of living. If average Americans are to simplify their life styles, however, they have a right to expect those in the upper income brackets to pare down *their* expectations and to recognize that finite resources should be shared more equally. In other words, we shall have to face the uncomfortable necessity of redistributing income and wealth.

Basically, there are three ways to make life chances more equitable; creating more and better jobs, with a higher minimum wage; providing more comprehensive social benefits; and making more adequate income transfers available through the tax system. In recent years the United States has not been pursuing any of these approaches.

Although it is important to make structural improvements in welfare programs for the poor, in the long term net redistribution of income will have more positive impact on their lives. The simplest, though politically difficult, way to move toward equity is through tax reforms. It is beyond the scope of this book to outline a blueprint for changes in the tax structure. Nevertheless, we can make a few observations.

The emergence of President Reagan's tax reform proposals demonstrates that it has become increasingly clear to both conservatives and liberals that there is an urgent need for reform. Joe and Rogers point out that before 1981 Congress tried to exempt families living below the poverty level from paying federal income taxes (although they were still subject to payroll taxes). By 1984, however, a low-income working family of four became liable for tax when its annual income reached $8,783 even though the poverty level was $10,613.[27] According to one source, the current so-called progressive tax system actually means that in 1985 the poorest tenth were paying an average tax rate of 29 percent, while the wealthiest tenth were paying 25 percent.[28]

There are several ways to ease the tax burden on low-income persons. Schorr argues that a general Refundable Tax Credit would be far more helpful to low-

and moderate-income people and much less costly to the government than doubling the personal exemption as Reagan proposed. It would replace not only the personal exemption but also the existing Earned Income Tax Credit (a refundable tax credit for families with children earning less than $11,000 a year) and special exemptions for age and blindness. The size of the credit would diminish as income rises. Under current law, Schorr says, 60 percent of the people who file a return would find a Refundable Tax Credit to their advantage.[29]

Joe and Rogers propose a strategy to assist low-income working families, which can be only briefly sketched here. The strategy includes expanding the Earned Income Tax Credit to supplement the wages of *all* low-income working families and extending it to all low-income persons; making the existing child-care tax credit refundable and thus available to families who do not earn enough to pay taxes; and raising the tax threshold so that the poor and near-poor are no longer liable for taxes. (They also suggest providing Medicaid to uninsured low-income working families, whether or not they receive AFDC.)

There are many advantages to the plan. For example, it would make working families better off than those who are not employed, thus supporting the work ethic. More poor people who need aid would receive it. There would be no financial incentive for mothers and fathers to separate. They would receive assistance without the stigma of "being on welfare." The move would shift some of the responsibility from the overburdened welfare system to the tax system. AFDC would become a program to ameliorate poverty, whereas the tax system would be used to *prevent* it. Income supplementation via the tax system would promote uniform assistance throughout the country. Finally, these proposals could be administered much more efficiently than AFDC is at present.[30]

The changes discussed here would lower the standard of material living for some people. However, these changes could heighten the general *quality* of living by making the United States a more secure and pleasant place in which to live.

Americans, we believe, are not innately more materialistic than their counterparts in other countries. Many Americans do become materialistic and competitive because of the insecurities built into the system of survival. Some devote their working lives to achieving high status. Fundamentally, however, what most people are searching for is security. Millions of Americans struggle and sacrifice most of their lives in order to feel protected in their old age. Social Security by itself is almost never enough to permit living in comfort, nor does Medicare pay more than 44 percent of health care expenses. The possibility of depleting life savings for extended medical and nursing home expenses hangs like an ominous cloud over their lives. Ironically, many of these oldsters, spent from the struggle, do not live long enough to enjoy the fruits of their quest for security.

Most of them leave money to their children, who have not worked to earn it. That legacy is taxed at a very low level (in 1985 the federal government taxed no inheritance under $600,000) compared to many other countries. Hence their life savings do not even contribute to a fairer distribution of income through the tax system.

By contrast, seniors in many European countries enjoy adequate retirement pensions, health benefits, and a wide range of services that provide certainty that they can live in dignity. During their preretirement years they had to work hard but with less pressure than Americans, who are haunted by fears of dropping into privation or dependency. In their last years they can afford to live with less money in the bank than their American counterparts because they can look into the future without foreboding. If we worked out a system of real social supports, based as far as possible on universal programs transcending classes, might we perhaps discover that our lives need not be focused on a constant striving for "more"?

Concluding Reflections

Some readers may feel that the framework outlined here runs counter to the American emphasis on individual responsibility. On the contrary, as we have shown, some of the most successful efforts to alleviate or prevent homelessness have been carried out by individuals as well as religious and other voluntary groups. America has a rich tradition of volunteer service, a tradition that is indispensable to the achievement of true community. The range of possible services is virtually unlimited. Efforts need not be confined to traditional gestures such as offering to help in soup kitchens and shelters. Individuals and groups can take measures to prevent homelessness by assisting families threatened by eviction till their lives are stabilized, sponsor shared-living projects, open boarding houses, join neighborhood associations to fight zoning that excludes the homeless or mentally ill, rehabilitate apartments, work with seed money from government to purchase and run group residences for the handicapped homeless, sponsor cooperative housing for low-income people, or form advocacy groups to press for better housing, mental health services, and social programs.

Most of these efforts imply not so much doing for low-income people as working beside them and pressing power structures to take both ameliorative and preventive action. Perhaps volunteer work should be redefined to include advocacy. Indeed, that seems to be happening among many groups concerned with the homeless.

Would putting such proposals into action require large outlays of funds? Certainly. Any investment in human life costs money. It should be borne in mind, however, that expending resources on a growing social sector (instead of mergers, for example) creates jobs. Moreover, although we complain about the cost of social welfare, in point of fact we lag far behind almost every other industrialized nation in the proportion of GNP devoted to social programs.

To the Reagan administration, almost every government program bears a dollar sign except defense. In 1983, every twelve seconds the federal government was spending $72,000 more on instruments of war than on AFDC, SSI, Medicaid, food stamps, earned income tax credit, work incentive programs, and the Job Corps *com-*

bined.[31] By 1986 the United States was spending more than $283 billion a year on military defense against foreign enemies. (Yet 45 percent of Americans are afraid to go out at night within one mile of their homes.[32])

When military spending devours a huge portion of the budget, social programs are cut. Melman observes that the cost of one 155 mm (conventional) high explosive shell ($439) would provide 460 meals for the homeless in Grand Central Terminal. The sum spent on one (F-16 jet fighter) antenna pulley tool, one antenna clamp alignment puller height gauge, and one antenna hexagon wrench, is $42,287, equal to the estimated cost of renovating an average five-room medium-income Manhattan West Side apartment.[33] Basing his estimate on Labor Department figures, William Winpisinger declares that defense industries are so capital-intensive that it takes $1 billion to create 45,800 jobs, whereas $1 billion spent in the civilian sector creates from 58,000 jobs in mass transportation construction to 98,000 jobs in public service employment.[34]

Massive defense spending is also a leading cause of the federal deficit. In the struggle to meet it, the federal government has borrowed funds by issuing high interest bonds, which foreign investors have been eager to buy. The result has been a strong dollar, but a loss of export markets to other countries that can offer more competitive prices. This trend has been so alarming that even the U.S. government has joined other nations in efforts to bring down the dollar.

Melman has amassed a body of research demonstrating that huge defense outlays are one cause of inflation. They deflect spending from goods and services that people can use (houses, food, clothing, public transportation, medical care, and the like) to hardware that no one can eat or wear and in the end either fails to be used or is employed to destroy consumer goods (and, incidentally, people).

One result is a growing mass of human beings who have nowhere else to go but the streets. According to Melman,

> A castoff nation is created when its working people—all grades—are progressively discarded by decision-makers determined to make money outside production, outside the country, and by military work that contributes no life-serving product. Being a castoff means being unneeded, unwanted, and that contributes to hopelessness and loss of pride and self-esteem. When that is made into a permanent condition, then social disintegration is set in motion: the castoff population becomes a concentration area for mental depression and illness, alcoholism and other drug addiction, family disintegration and abandonment.[35]

In other words, social costs should be added to the costs of defense.

Ironically, military authorities such as Admiral Gene La Rocque and General Gerard Smith have stated that no arms system can really defend us against annihilation in a nuclear war. It can even invite attack.

The programs proposed here *are* affordable if we change our priorities. The first step would be to make significant cuts in defense outlays. Not cuts in projected increases, but major progressive cuts in the current level of spending.

This would also be a visible sign to the Soviets that our leaders are serious when they talk of ending the arms race.

Inevitably, many of the ideas will encounter resistance, for they seem to fly in the face of a trend toward reduction in the scope of government. But how real is that trend?

Americans are traditionally suspicious of big government. There is some basis for this mistrust. In a big country it is harder to visualize where taxes go. Big government bureaucracy can breed waste and graft, but so can the bureaucracy of big business, especially at the conglomerate level. So can local bureaucracy, with its cronyism. Many federal government programs—Social Security, for example—have proved to be lacking in corruption and efficient at all levels down to the local areas. The reality is that some functions in our society can be administered or coordinated effectively only by the federal government. Yet the mystique persists that federal programs mean interference and therefore are wasteful and bad. Hence when a national leader declares that he has brought back less government, Americans tend to believe him.

The facts are that since the advent of the Reagan administration federal interference has grown. The Administration has broken strikes, set quotas on foreign imports, denied citizen access to an ever-widening array of classified information, and placed impediments on travel in Cuba and Nicaragua. Federal spending as a share of the GNP is now higher than when Mr. Reagan took office. The eight-year military budget plan he envisions would result in a taxpayer burden of $2,089 billion dollars from 1981 to 1988. All this hardly adds up to taking government off our backs.

Underlying much of the resistance to change is a gnawing fear that a growing welfare state would not only sap individual initiative but also foster alienation and pose a threat to both productivity and to individual freedom.

The ideology makers in America tend to identify democratic liberties with a free market economy. Average Americans accept the linkage, perhaps because small businesses do operate in a fairly competitive fashion. This is hardly the case with the many big corporations (especially defense industries) that frame the market with administered prices and frequently enjoy handsome government subsidies and tax breaks. That is not the main point, however. Wilensky notes that nothing in the history of the twenty-two countries whose social welfare systems he studied suggests that the welfare state might be a threat to democracy. In fact, civil liberties have not been threatened as much in Holland and Sweden, for example, as in the United States, whose spending on social programs ranks far behind that of other industrialized nations.[36]

We would add that there is nothing inherently demagogic in choosing to spend money on the welfare state. On the contrary, expending resources on the warfare state creates consequences that are far more dangerous to individual liberties.

There *is* some justification for misgivings about the welfare state. It is arguable that in some countries, certain perquisites (such as some kinds of disability benefits in Holland) have in the past been excessive. Certainly it is true that social expenditures are consuming an increased share of the GNP in almost all industrialized countries. At some point, a lopsided social sector could well become a threat to productivity because there would be little left over for reinvestment. Many welfare states are struggling with the need for balance as they plan for the future.

A crisis of productivity does not seem to have been reached yet, however. Indeed, by one index of productivity—output per hour—six countries with more developed social sectors than ours performed better than we did in 1983, a year that witnessed an economic upturn in the United States. This is hardly a sign that welfare states sap initiative.[37]

It is also true that more government bureaucracy can lead to alienation. This is already happening in America, despite the greater emphasis on market structures. In our own exploration of homelessness, we have talked with local welfare department employees who knew little or nothing about programs in the same department and did not even care. We have met budget directors of public agencies who did not know the ultimate sources of their funding. In a big country, especially, fragmentation leads to ignorance and often to apathy. In America we need to find new ways to balance central and local control.

Finally, it seems true that many Europeans are experiencing a certain disenchantment with social democracy—as ideology. Middle-class and upper-class Europeans constantly complain about taxes and tend to blame their troubles on the welfare state. Paradoxically, however, they have not been willing to give up most of its benefits. So many advances have been accomplished that these are now accepted as part of the status quo. Conservative governments may wish to retrench, but they incorporate social democratic principles into their programs—without, of course, referring to them as such. As ideology, the social democratic welfare state seems to be waning. As a fact of political life, it is very much alive.

Why the decline in its appeal? Some social critics complain that in Scandinavian countries it has produced a good life for nearly everyone, but a great life for too few. There is too much complacency, too little *angst*. Well, perhaps. But we suggest that most averge Americans would be willing to risk a little complacency for the sake of a good life for nearly all.

There is alienation and malaise, to be sure. They can be found in most industrialized countries today. We submit that the roots are complex and cannot be traced to one cause, much less the relative security built into the welfare state. The roots range from joblessness to the nuclear cloud that hangs over all lives.

Deep down, there is also the nagging awareness that life is no longer getting better and better. In the heady days of postwar prosperity, Europeans saw their standard of living steadily rise. Today the average European enjoys more comfort and more security than she or he did a few decades ago. Still, there is an undercurrent of uneasiness. It is not just that the momentum of material progress has slowed, in itself a situation that can generate a sense of confusion about one's direction in life. There is also a sense that the world is different today. Western Europe and the United States are no longer the omnipotent powers they once were. The players in the game are changing; the new entrants insist on being heard. Somehow, the world feels out of joint.

That malaise has been felt among Americans, too. Many sense that the inequalities in this country are only a reflection of the much greater disparities between the haves and the have-nots around the globe.

Any planning for redistribution of wealth and power should take these grosser inequities into account. There are no easy answers to these problems, but they are part of the challenge. If jobs have disappeared in the United States, if unemployment and homelessness have grown as a consequence, it is at least partly because the poor in other parts of the world are also seeking fair shares. To defend the American way of life by refusing to share resources or to enter international agreements aimed at fairer distribution of opportunities among members of the international community can only result in greater hunger, homelessness, and hostility in the rest of the world.

The malaise in America helps explain the fact that President Reagan has wrought changes in the role of government that are more radical than any wrought by previous administrations since the 1930s. A few years before his election, Reagan was considered to be too far to the right to make it to the White House, but by 1980 large numbers of Americans had become convinced that the old ways were not working. They were ready to try a bold new approach.

There is a growing sense that the new approach has not worked, either. It has brought greater affluence to the wealthy and release from fear of inflation to the middle classes, while the poor have slipped backwards. But most of those who belong to the middle classes, and even some of the affluent, do not feel more secure. There is something wobbly about the foundations of this rediscovered prosperity. Fewer and fewer Americans share in its fruits, our ability to compete in world markets continues to decline, the national debt has reached record levels, the number of farm foreclosures continues to increase, unemployment remains high, and the cost of basics such as housing and health care keeps rising. The growth in the GNP is fueled by the growth of deadly weapons to defend us and our way of life. Yet we do not feel more safe.

Across this land one can sense a groping for change: Where it will take us is hard to predict. It could lead to a benevolent dictatorship or to a patchwork of quasi-experimental programs that could muddle us through. However, it also could lead to a truly new approach that promoted a more equitable distribution of resources at home and abroad and matched the realities of the world in which we are living.

There are many signs of change that could lead us in the last direction: the growth of voter registration drives, tenants' rights groups, grassroots organizations, and coalitions of the young and the old; the new willingness in the women's movement to link forces with other Americans struggling to enter the mainstream; the once-conservative Catholic hierarchy's insistence that fulfilling human needs and increasing the participation of all citizens in the society should be the first goals in the investment of wealth, talent, and human energy.

In the nineteenth century, reformers had to fight against the prevailing ideas that free schools were only for pauper children. Prior to 1935, government-funded old-age pensions and unemployment insurance were largely regarded as inventions of socialism. Today they are regarded as rights. Increasing numbers of Americans are coming to see adequate health care as a right to which all are entitled. Navarro observes that a detailed study of major opinion polls from 1976 to 1983 shows continuous and undiminished majority support for an expansion rather than a reduction of health and social expenditures and for a tax-based comprehensive and universal health program.[38] As the Sidels suggest, the fact that medicine is widely regarded as a necessity rather than a luxury may make it an arena in which fundamental change in our society can begin.[39]

Shall we come to recognize food, clothing, housing, health care, and opportunity for work as fundamental rights? To develop such a change in American thinking—to say nothing of translating rights into policies—will require a concerted effort. But it is not too soon to begin.

It will take some clarification of American values, some recognition of the ambivalence in our attitudes. We support free universal education but not job training and retraining programs for all who may need them. We tacitly approve subsidies for the affluent, but begrudge benefits for the poor. We laud the family as the most sacred of institutions, yet fail to provide child allowances, day care, paid maternity leaves, decent housing, and other supports that could strengthen the ability of real families to remain together and to produce new generations of healthy Americans. We demand that welfare recipients take jobs, although we know that as our economy is presently structured, there are not enough jobs to go around. We tend to regard those who fail to make it as less worthy human beings, although millions of us fear losing our own jobs to computers, robots, or ill-paid workers in other countries. Today, we still tend to believe that our society has a moral obligation to *give* these necessities through the gift relationship but no moral imperative to see them as entitlements.

We value independence as the most American of virtues, although deep down we recognize that complete independence is an irrational abstraction in today's world. Indeed, who embodies that ideal of independence more than the homeless men and women who refuse to leave their heating grates for the safety and comfort of a shelter? When President Reagan made his famous *bon mot* that they were on the grates out of choice, he probably did not intend to imply that they should take their places beside the Lone Ranger in the Pageant of American Heroes. Instead, the implication was that they were not quite normal like the rest of us, not rational beings who knew enough to come in to receive the gift of warmth, and certainly not creatures who wished to work. There was, of course, no intimation that to some grate people their refusal made sense. No insight that shelters could be dangerous places, or that many chronic dwellers of the street have had painful experiences with shelter personnel, police, welfare workers, hospital staff, and other representatives of order and control. There was no perception that human beings hardly grow up preferring to be hungry and cold, that something happened on their journey through life to make them unwilling to do anything as instinctive as to come in from the cold.

What have they learned on that journey? Each has had his or her own distorting experiences, of course, but all have learned, among other things, that it is "wrong," unpleasant, and dehumanizing to accept help. Perhaps it is because they have internalized the virtue of rugged individualism so well that they have set up such homesteads on the streets.

Yet they are seen as unsuccessful people if they do come in for help and as "crazy" if they don't. Those who roam from city to city tend to be diagnosed as "drifters," not as human beings who keep moving on because they have not found work, or a home, or people who care. Once again the fault is located in the victim himself.

It is interesting that, although much of the recent literature on the homeless mentally ill castigates society for not offering better treatment or supportive services, very few writers discuss society's role in preventing pathology. Indeed, few point up the relationship between poverty and mental illness. Yet as Marc Fried emphasized years ago,

> The evidence is unambiguous and powerful that the lowest social classes have the highest rates of severe psychiatric disorder in our society. Regardless of the measures employed for estimating severe psychiatric disorder and social class, regardless of the region or date of study, and regardless of the method of study, the great majority of results all point clearly and strongly to the fact that the lowest social class has by far the greatest incidence of psychosis.[40]

Mental illness (like mental retardation and physical disability) is in large part the end product of poor nutrition, health care, education, and environmental protection, as well as the stresses arising from unemployment, discrimination, inadequate recreation, and crowded housing. Complex problems, these. It is easier to send the mentally ill back to asylum—for their own good, of course—and make downtown streets more pleasant for strolling and shopping again. The rest of us will enjoy a true safety net.

So we return to the same questions: Do we want to contain homelessness or prevent it? Do we want to bring the vulnerable people into the mainstream or keep them in their place?

The crisis of homelessness could actually be an opportunity, a new chance to take a long hard look at the inequities that produce homelessness and to create structures that will make America a more harmonious place in which to live. Instead of seeing homelessness in terms of shelters and souplines, we can take up the challenge of long-range planning for policies and programs that will make home a reality for all Americans.

The framework is there. For years workable plans for national health care, full employment, tax reform, affordable housing, and income maintenance have been introduced as congressional legislation. The human resources abound. In every corner of the nation there are committed service providers and advocates for the homeless. Today they are beginning to make common cause with low-income housing advocates, tenants groups, welfare rights associations, minority rights organizations, mental health advocates, children's rights groups, concerned clergy, and other groups pushing for fairer shares of wealth and power. What they need is clear support from the public.

The economic resources exist. They require choices, however. Choices between redistributing wealth and power upward and redistributing them downward. Choices between planning for programs that enhance life, and planning for a "defense" that brings us closer to death and universal destitution. Nuclear devastation would be the ultimate homelessness.

We do not need a policy on homelessness so much as a policy on poverty. We do not need a policy for the poor so much as policies that will protect us all.

The homeless are our other selves. They are the reflection of our own insecurity. They tell us that in the late twentieth century the American dream—the belief that anyone who tried hard enough in the competitive struggle could prosper—has become an illusion.

They are the face of our loneliness. They remind us of how estranged we have become from one another. In the large cities even neighbors can be strangers, and the human being who asks for help is someone to be feared.

The homeless recall something that seems to be missing from our lives: community. They challenge us to reach out, to forge those communal bonds, to imagine ourselves in their place. Deep down we sense that but for good fortune, we, too, could be those strangers huddled in the darkness of the cold street.

Notes

Preface

1. Physician Task Force on Hunger in America, *Hunger in America: The Growing Epidemic* (Boston: Harvard University School of Public Health 1985), 4.
2. Ibid., p. 5.
3. Ibid.
4. *Bread Crumbs*, Newsletter of Bread for the City, (January–February 1985):4.

Chapter 1. The Homeless: Types and Stereotypes

1. K. Hopper, "Whose Lives are These Anyway?" *Safety Network* (monthly newsletter of the National Coalition for the Homeless) (July 1984):1.
2. Phone conversation with Tom Styron, National Coalition for the Homeless, with authors, 21 January 1986.
3. Office of Policy Development and Research, *A Report to the Secretary on the Homeless and Emergency Shelters* (Washington, D.C.: U.S. Department of Housing and Urban Development, 1984), 19.
4. K. Hopper and J. Hamberg, *The Making of America's Homeless: From Skid Row to New Poor—1945–1984* (New York: Community Service Society, 1984), 74. Also available in *Critical Perspectives in Housing*, ed. R. Bratt, C. Hartman, A. Meyerson (Philadelphia: Temple University Press, 1986).
5. Hopper, "Whose Lives are These Anyway?" 4.
6. Ibid.
7. "Hearings Reexamine HUD Report; Previous Suspicions Confirmed," *Safety Network* (January 1986) 1.
8. E. Baxter and K. Hopper, *Private Lives/Public Spaces* (New York: Community Service Society, 1981), 8–9.
9. K. Hopper, E. Baxter, S. Cox, and L. Klein, *One Year Later: The Homeless Poor in New York City*, 1982. (New York: Community Service Society, 1982), 45.
10. T. Main, "New York City's 'Lure' to the Homeless," *Wall Street Journal*, 12 September 1983.
11. Baxter and Hopper, *Private Lives/Public Spaces*, 8.
12. Ibid., 76–77.
13. D. Roth, J. Bean, N. Lust, and T. Saveanu, *Homelessness in Ohio: A Study of People in Need* (Columbus: Ohio Department of Mental Health, 1985), 5.

14. Telephone Conversation with Tom Styron, National Coalition for the Homeless with authors, 21 January 1986.

15. U.S. Conference of Mayors, *The Growth of Hunger, Homelessness and Poverty in America's Cities in 1985* (Washington, D.C.: U.S. Conference of Mayors, 1986), 1.

16. C. Krauthammer, "For the Homeless: Asylum," *Washington Post*, 4 January 1985. © The *Washington Post*. Reprinted with permission.

17. E. Bassuk, L. Rubin, and A. Lauriat, "Is Homelessness a Mental Health Problem?" *American Journal of Psychiatry* 141 (12):1546–1550 (1984).

18. E. Bassuk, telephone conversation with authors, 1 April 1985.

19. Andy Raubeson, head of SRO Housing Corporation of Los Angeles, telephone conversation with authors, 5 February 1986.

20. Roth et al., *Homelessness in Ohio*, 134, 140–141.

21. *Washington Post*, 20 April 1985.

22. J.A. Talbott, former president of American Psychiatric Association, letters to authors, 28 February 1985 and 20 February 1986.

23. Office of Policy Development and Research, *A Report to the Secretary on the Homeless*, 24.

24. Krauthammer, "For the Homeless: Asylum."

25. Ibid.

26. M. Heckler, "Shelter," KCTS-TV, Seattle, May 1984.

27. Office of Policy Development and Research, *A Report to the Secretary on the Homeless*, 23.

28. Ibid., 26.

29. Ibid., 27.

30. Ibid., 29.

31. Ibid., 28–29.

32. Ibid., 27.

33. Ibid., 30.

34. Ibid., 19.

35. Ibid., 31.

36. U.S. Conference of Mayors, *Homelessness in America's Cities: Ten Case Studies* (Washington, D.C.: U.S. Conference of Mayors June 1984), 5; U.S. Conference of Mayors, *Growth of Hunger and Homelessness*, 2.

37. U.S. Conference of Mayors, *Homelessness in America's Cities*, 5.

38. E. Bassuk, telephone conversation with the authors, 1 April 1985.

39. Hopper and Hamberg, *The Making of America's Homeless*, 11.

40. Ibid., 28.

41. Ibid., 12.

42. Ibid., 13.

43. Ibid., 13.

44. Ibid., 4.

45. Ibid., 4–13.

46. H.M. Bahr, *Skid Row: An Introduction to Disaffiliation* (New York: Oxford University Press, 1973), 61.

47. *New York Times*, 9 April 1980.

48. *New York Times*, 20 April 1979.

49. *New York Daily News*, 9 July 1977.

50. R. Hayes, "The Mayor and the Homeless Poor," *City Limits* (August–September, 1985), 9.

Chapter 2. On the Street, On the Road

1. Personal letter from Todd Waters to the authors dated 2 December 1983. Reprinted with permission.
2. S. Crystal, "Homeless Men and Women: The Gender Gap," *Urban and Social Change Review* 17 (2):5–6 (1984). Reprinted with permission.
3. U.S. Conference of Mayors, *The Growth of Hunger, Homelessness, and Poverty in America's Cities in 1985* (Washington, D.C.: U.S. Conference of Mayors, 1986), 2.
4. J. Krauskopf, *New York City Plan for Homeless Adults* (New York: Human Resources Administration, 1984), 54–55.
5. H. Saver, executive director of Chicago Coalition for the Homeless, letter to authors, 21 March 1985.
6. See S. Crystal, *New Arrivals: First Time Shelter Clients* (New York: Human Resources Administration, 1982); House Subcommittee on Housing and Community Development of the Committee on Banking, Finance and Urban Affairs, *Homelessness in America—11*, 98th Cong., 2d sess., 1984, Serial No. 98–64.
7. *Safety Network* (October 1985):1
8. Office of Policy Development and Research, *A Report to the Secretary on the Homeless and Emergency Shelters* (Washington, D.C.: Department of Housing and Urban Development, 1984), 9.
9. Center on Budget and Policy Priorities, *End Results: The Impact of Federal Policies Since 1980 on Low-Income Americans* (Washington, D.C.: Interfaith Action for Economic Justice, 1984), 9.

Chapter 3. Homeless in Washington

1. *A Children's Defense Budget: An Analysis of the President's FY1985 Budget* (Washington, D.C.: Children's Defense Fund, 1984), 5.
2. D. Groner, telephone conversation with authors, 27 December 1985.
3. D. Coyle, Special assistant to the superintendent of Saint Elizabeths Hospital, letter to authors, 26 October 1983.
4. H. Thomas, public information officer of Saint Elizabeths Hospital, letter to authors, 17 April 1985.
5. Mental Health Law Project, *Summary of Activities 1982–83* (Washington, D.C.: Mental Health Law Project, n.d.), 12.
6. C. St. Clair and D. Doherty, "Deinstitutionalization: The Mental Health System and Homeless Women," *On the Street* (September–October 1982):4–5.
7. H. Thomas, letter to authors, 17 April 1985.
8. "Director's Corner," *The Advocate* (September 1982):2.
9. Ibid.
10. B. Simon, Metropolitan Washington Planning and Housing Association, telephone conversation with authors, 5 February 1986.
11. Various pamphlets of D.C. Law Students in Court; Rick Carter, telephone conversation with authors, 3 February 1986.
12. M.E. Hombs and M. Snyder, *Homeless in America* (Washington, D.C.: Community for Creative Non-Violence, 1982), 92.
13. Ibid., 93.
14. Ibid.

15. Ibid.
16. Ibid.
17. Ibid.
18. Ibid., 93–94.
19. Ibid., 97.
20. Ibid.
21. Max Schlueter, "Cage Count," *Jericho* 35:12 (Spring 1984).

Chapter 4. Down and Out in Cincinnati

1. C. Birdsall, City Planning Department, letter to authors, 12 June 1984.
2. S. Koff, "Power: Who Has It and How to Get It," *Cincinnati* (August 1983):44.
3. M. Goozner, *Housing Cincinnati's Poor* (Cincinnati: Stephen Wilder Foundation, 1983), 14.
4. D. Moran, City Planning Department, telephone conversation with authors, 6 January 1986.
5. B. Schwartz, Cincinnati Department of Human Services, telephone conversation with authors, 6 January 1986.
6. Hamilton County Bailiff's Office, letter to authors, 6 May 1985.
7. Hamilton County Sheriff's Office, letter to authors, 27 April 1985.
8. *World Almanac 1986* (New York: Newspaper Enterprise Association, 1985), 267.
9. C.S. Holman, Longview State Hospital (now Lewis Center), letter to authors, 3 January 1984.
10. Admissions Office, Lewis Center, telephone conversation with authors, 5 February 1986.
11. C. S. Holman, letter to authors, 3 January 1984.
12. Business Office, telephone conversation with authors, 5 February 1986.
13. D. Rohner, Hamilton County Community Mental Health Board, letter to authors, 22 April 1985.
14. Goozner, *Housing Cincinnati's Poor*, 1.
15. Ibid., 19.
16. Ibid., 9.
17. Ibid.
18. Ibid., 39.
19. D. Moran, telephone conversation with authors, 5 February 1986.
20. Goozner, *Housing Cincinnati's Poor*, 32.
21. Ibid., 30.
22. Ibid., 34.
23. C. Birdsall, "Housing Issue Related to Homeless Persons," report presented to Cincinnati City Planning Commission, 1984, 2.
24. *Voices* (June–July 1980).
25. Goozner, *Housing Cincinnati's Poor*, 53–57.

Chapter 5. Displacement and the Housing Crisis

1. *New York Times*, 3 February 1983.
2. H. Schechter, "Closing the Gap Between Need and Provision," *Society* 21 (3):40–47 (March/April 1984).

3. C. Hartman, D. Keating, R. Le Gates, *Displacement: How to Fight It* (Berkeley, Calif.: National Housing Law Project, 1982), 3.

4. K. Hopper and J. Hamberg, *The Making of America's Homeless: From Skid Row to New Poor, 1945–1984* (New York: Community Service Society, 1984), 54.

5. *New York Times,* 18 February 1985.

6. J. Newfield, "The Dirty Dozen: New York's Worst Landlords," *Village Voice,* 9 April 1985.

7. A. Downs, *Rental Housing in the 1980s* (Washington, D.C.: Brookings, 1983), 71.

8. C. Dolbeare, "The Low Income Housing Crisis," in *America's Housing Crisis: What Is to Be Done?* ed. C. Hartman (Boston: Routledge and Kegan Paul, 1983), 52.

9. Newfield, "Dirty Dozen."

10. Dolbeare, "Low Income Housing Crisis," 34–35.

11. U.S. Bureau of the Census, *Statistical Abstract of the United States 1985,* 105th ed. (Washington, D.C.: U.S. Department of Commerce, 1984), 736.

12. Dolbeare, "Low Income Housing Crisis," 57.

13. Hartman et al., *Displacement,* 3; C. Hartman, "Introduction," in *America's Housing Crisis: What Is to Be Done?* ed. C. Hartman (Boston: Routledge and Kegan Paul, 1983), 17–25.

14. Hartman et al., *Displacement,* 4.

15. Ibid., 12.

16. Ibid.

17. P. Hawley, *Housing in the Public Domain: The Only Solution* (New York: Metropolitan Council on Housing, 1978), 80.

18. R. Sanjek, "Playing Without a Full Deck," *Gray Panther Network* (January–February 1982):16.

19. R. Sanjek, *Federal Housing Programs and Their Impact on Homelessness* (New York: National Coaliton for the Homeless, 1982), 4.

20. Memo to members, National Low Income Housing Coalition, July 1984, 4.

21. Sanjek, *Federal Housing Programs,* 4.

22. Hartman, "Introduction," 12.

23. Sisters of Mercy of the Union, *Five Loaves and Two Fishes* (Silver Spring, Md.: Mercy Center, 1981), 20–22.

24. Dolbeare, "Low Income Housing Crisis," 55–56.

25. Memo to members, National Low Income Housing Coalition, 23 May 1985.

26. *Congressional Record,* 26 April 1984, S4976.

27. Hartman, "Introduction," 1–2.

28. Dolbeare, "Low Income Housing Crisis," 31.

29. Hartman et al., *Displacement,* 62.

30. Ibid., 62.

31. Ibid., 40.

32. Ibid., 40–41.

33. R. Carter, "Arson and Arson Investigation in the United States," *Fire Journal* 74:40–47 (July 1980).

34. J. Brady, "Arson, Urban Economy, and Organized Crime: The Case of Boston," *Social Problems* 31 (1):3 (October 1983).

35. Hartman et al., *Displacement,* 42.

36. Brady, "Arson, Urban Economy and Organized Crime," 1.

37. Hartman et al., *Displacement,* 42.

38. Ibid.

39. Brady, "Arson, Urban Economy and Organized Crime," 1–23.

40. J. Newfield and P. Du Brul, *The Abuse of Power: The Permanent Government and the Fall of New York* (New York: Viking, 1977), 5–6.

41. Hartman et al., *Displacement*, 43.

42. P. Dreier, "The Housing Crisis: Dreams and Nightmares," *Nation* (21–28 August 1982):142.

43. *The Wall Street Journal*, 16 April 1985.

44. D. Lauber, "Condominium Conversions: A Reform in Need of Reform," in *Land Reform: American Style*, eds. C. Geisler and F. Popper, (Totowa, N.J.: Rowman and Allenheld, 1984), 275. Reprinted with permission.

45. Ibid., 280.

46. B. Cicin-Sain, "The Costs and Benefits of Neighborhood Revitalization," in *Urban Revitalization*, ed. D. Rosenthal (Beverly Hills, Calif.: Sage, 1980), 55–68.

47. Ibid.

48. Ibid.

49. Ibid.

50. M. Gottlieb, "Space Invaders: Land Grab on the Lower East Side," *Village Voice*, 14 December 1982. Reprinted with permission.

51. Ibid.

52. Ibid.

53. P. Marcuse, "Measuring Gentrification's Impact," *City Limits* (May 1984):27.

54. Hopper and Hamberg, *Making of America's Homeless*, 34.

55. Hartman et al., *Displacement*, 150.

56. Ibid., 114–115.

57. Ibid., 119.

58. Ibid., 132–136.

59. Ibid., 170–175.

60. Ibid., 190–203.

61. "New Jersey Elections: Tenant Vote Makes the Difference," *Shelterforce* (July 1985):3.

62. S. Muwakkil, "Spreading Crisis Threatens Housing," *In These Times* (1–7 May 1985):5.

63. Ibid.

64. Hartman, "Introduction," 12.

65. E. Achtenberg and P. Marcuse, "Towards the Decommodification of Housing," in *America's Housing Crisis: What Is to Be Done?* ed. C. Hartman (Boston: Routledge and Kegan Paul, 1983), 202–231.

66. Hartman, et al., *Displacement*, 185–187.

67. John Davis, "The Community Land Trust," *CALC Report*, October 1983, 1.

68. Muwakkil, "Spreading Crisis Threatens Housing," 15.

69. Hawley, *Housing in the Public Domain*, 82–87.

70. Achtenberg and Marcuse, "Towards the Decommodification of Housing," 221–226.

71. Ibid.

72. Dreier, "Housing Crisis," 141–144.

73. M. Goozner, *Housing Cincinnati's Poor* (Cincinnati, Ohio: Stephen H. Wilder Foundation, 1982), 32.

74. *Congressional Record*, 26 April 1984, S4975.

75. C. Dolbeare, "New Tax Policy: The Good and the Bad," *City Limits* (January 1985).

76. "The Economic Situation of Swedish Households," Swedish Institute, Stockholm, November 1984, Fact Sheet 23.

77. A. J. Heidenheimer, H. Heclo, and C.T. Adams, *Comparative Public Policy: The Politics of Public Choice in Europe and America* (New York: St. Martin's, 1983), 99.

Chapter 6. Back Wards, Back Alleys: The Deinstitutionalized and the Never Institutionalized

1. J.A. Talbott, "The Chronic Mentally Ill," in *The Chronic Mentally Ill: Treatment, Programs, Systems,* ed. J.A. Talbott (New York: Human Sciences Press, 1982), 372.

2. D. Roth, J. Bean, N. Lust, and T. Saveanu, *Homelessness in Ohio: A Study of People in Need* (Columbus, Ohio: Ohio Department of Mental Health, 1985), 44.

3. Talbott, "The Chronic Mentally Ill," 372.

4. K. Hopper and J. Hamberg, *The Making of America's Homeless: From Skid Row to New Poor 1945–1984* (New York: Community Service Society, 1984), 33.

5. H.H. Goldman, N. Adams, and C.A. Taube, "Deinstitutionalization: The Data Demythologized," *Hospital and Community Psychiatry* 34:132 (2 February 1983).

6. M. Gittelman, "Developments in Foreign Psychiatry: An Introduction," *Hospital and Community Psychiatry* 34:158 (2 February 1983).

7. B. Morris, "Recent Developments in the Care, Treatment, and Rehabilitation of Chronic Mentally Ill in Britain," *Hospital and Community Psychiatry* 34:159 (2 February 1983).

8. Research and Liaison Unit, *Soldiers of Misfortune: Homeless Veterans in New York City* (New York: Office of Comptroller, City of New York, 1982), 6.

9. A. Scull, *Decarceration* (Englewood Cliffs, N.J.: Prentice-Hall, 1977), 152.

10. *Newsweek* (2 January 1984):27.

11. *Report on Federal Efforts to Respond to the Shelter and Basic Needs of Chronically Mentally Ill Individuals* (Washington, D.C.: Department of Health and Human Services and Department of Housing and Urban Development, 1983), 34.

12. M. Brewster Smith and Nicholas Hobbs, "The Community and the Community Mental Health Center," *The American Psychologist* 21:503 (6 June 1966). Reprinted with permission.

13. Mental Health Law Project, "Summary of Activities 1982–1983," 12.

14. J.A. Talbott, *The Death of the Asylum* (New York: Grune and Stratton, 1978), 36.

15. C. Lorber, "The Village's Worst SRO," *The Villager* (12 March 1979):12.

16. Talbott, *Death of the Asylum,* 69.

17. "Mental Health Is Not a Jobs Program," *New York Times,* 1 December 1983.

18. C. Bellamy, letter to *New York Times,* 22 October 1982.

19. *Newsweek* (2 January 1984):25.

20. H.R. Lamb, "Deinstitutionalization and the Homeless Mentally Ill," *The Homeless Mentally Ill: A Task Force Report of the American Psychiatric Association,* ed. H.R. Lamb (Washington, D.C.: American Psychiatric Association, 1984), 67–68.

21. P. Allen, "A Consumer's View of California's Mental Health Care System," *Psychiatric Quarterly* 48:10 (1974).

22. See S. Steindorf, *Community Support Systems: Local Demonstration and Replication Project* (Albany: New York State Office of Mental Health, 1982), 228–251.

23. N. Lehrman, letter to *New York Times,* 6 June 1981.

24. *Tenderloin Times* (April/May 1985):16.

25. *New York Times,* 12 August 1984.

26. M.M. Cuomo, *1933–1983—Never Again: A Report to the National Governor's Association Task Force on the Homeless* (Portland, Maine: National Governors' Conference, 1983), 47.

27. *Newsweek* (2 January 1984):27.

28. K. Collins and A. Erfle, "Social Security Benefits Reform Act of 1984: Legislative History and Summary Provisions," *Social Security Bulletin* 48:5–6 (4 April 1985).

29. Lamb, "Deinstitutionalization," 63–64.

30. K. Hopper, E. Baxter, and S. Cox, "Not Making It Crazy: The Young Homeless Patients in New York City," in *New Directions for Mental Health Services,* eds. B. Pepper and H. Ryglewicz (San Francisco: Jossey-Bass, 1982), 39.

31. *Journal of American Insurance* 48(4):18 (1984).

32. J.C. Turner and W.J. Ten Hoor, "The NIMH Community Support Program: Pilot Approach to a Needed Social Reform," *Schizophrenia Bulletin* 4(3):32 (1978).

33. *New York Times,* 8 October 1983.

34. Talbott, "Chronic Mentally Ill," 374.

35. See P. Solomon, J.M. Davis, B. Gordon, P. Fishbein, and A. Mason, *The Aftercare Mosaic: A Study of Patients in Transition—Discharged Psychiatric Patients in the Community* (Cleveland, Ohio: Federation for Community Planning, 1983), 1–32.

36. *UPDATE* (Cincinnati, Ohio: Hamilton County Community Health Board, 1985), 2.

37. E. Detzer, "Still Looking for the Rose Garden: The Effects of Deinstitutionalizing Mental Health Service," *Humanist* (November–December 1983):37.

38. Ibid.

39. Talbott, *Death of the Asylum,* 155.

40. Ibid.

41. L. Bachrach, *The Homeless Mentally Ill: An Analytic Review of the Literature* (Washington, D.C.: Alcohol and Drug Abuse and Mental Health Administration, Department of Health and Human Services, 1984), 44–55.

42. Report on Federal Efforts to Respond to the Shelter, 28–31.

43. W. Goldberg, letter to *New York Times,* 25 October 1983, © 1983 by the New York Times Company. Reprinted by permission of the author and publisher.

44. E. Baxter and K. Hopper, "Shelter and Housing Needs for the Homeless Mentally Ill," in *The Homeless Mentally Ill: A Task Force Report of the American Psychiatric Association,* ed. H.R. Lamb (Washington, D.C.: American Psychiatric Association, 1984), 118–119.

45. E. Baxter and K. Hopper, *Private Lives/Public Spaces* (New York: Community Service Society, 1981), 48.

46. C. Bellamy, "Giving a Hand to the Homeless," *New York Times,* 22 October 1982.

47. *Washington Post,* 24 April 1985.

48. Baxter and Hopper, "Shelter and Housing Needs," 115.

49. A.A. Arce, M. Tadlock, M.J. Vergare, and S. Shapiro, "A Psychiatric Profile of Street People Admitted to an Emergency Shelter," *Hospital and Community Psychiatry* 34:812–817 (9 September 1983).

50. "Health Care for the Homeless," *American Medical News* (12 April 1985):3

51. J. A. Talbott and H.R. Lamb, "Summary and Recommendations," in *The Homeless Mentally Ill: A Task Force Report of the American Psychiatric Association*, ed. H.R. Lamb (Washington, D.C.: American Psychiatric Association, 1984), 6.

52. J. Walsh, "Are City Shelters Open Asylums?" *In These Times* (23–29 January 1985):3.

53. *U.S. News and World Report* (15 October 1984):18.

54. *New York Times*, 4 June 1985.

55. "Workshops: Healthcare" *Senior Citizen News* 6(287):14 (July 1985).

56. V.W. Sidel and R. Sidel, *A Healthy State: An International Perspective on the Crisis in United States Medical Care*, rev. ed. (New York: Pantheon, 1983), 311.

57. J. Steinberg, "Failing Health," *Progressive* (December 1984):19–20.

58. A.J. Kahn and S.B. Kamerman, *Social Services in the United States: Policy and Programs* (Philadelphia: Temple University Press, 1976), 493.

59. Kahn and Kamerman, *Social Services in the United States*, 490–491. Reprinted with permission.

Chapter 7. Work, Welfare, and Well-Being

1. H. Rodgers, *The Cost of Human Neglect: America's Welfare Failure* (Armonk, N.Y.: M.E. Scharpe, 1982), viii.

2. H. Gans, "The Positive Functions of Poverty," *American Journal of Sociology* 78(2):275–289 (September 1972).

3. See M. Fried, "Social Differences in Mental Health," in *Poverty and Health: A Sociological Analysis*, eds. J. Kosa, A. Antonovsky, and I.K. Zola (Cambridge: Harvard University Press, 1969), 113–137.

4. Rodgers, *Cost of Human Neglect*, 52.

5. *New York Times*, 5 February 1985.

6. H. Ginsburg, letter to authors, 21 February 1985.

7. E.D. Huttman, *Introduction to Social Policy* (New York: McGraw-Hill, 1981), 179.

8. *New York Times*, 2 November 1985.

9. F.F. Piven and R. Cloward, *Regulating the Poor: The Functions of Public Welfare* (New York: Vintage, 1971), 147–180.

10. Social Security Administration, *Quarterly Public Assistance* (Washington, D.C.: Department of Health and Human Services, October–December 1982), table 22.

11. Social Security Administration, *Social Security Bulletin* (Washington, D.C.: Department of Health and Human Services, 1985), 72, 73.

12. Ibid., 72.

13. U.S. Bureau of Census, *Statistical Abstract of the United States 1984*, 104th ed. (Washington, D.C.: Department of Commerce, 1983), 396.

14. P. Cutright, "AFDC, Family Allowance, and Illegitimacy," *Family Planning Perspectives* 2:4–9 (4 October 1970).

15. M. Harrington, *The New American Poverty* (New York: Holt, Rinehart, and Winston, 1984), 224–225.

16. Office of Family Assistance, *Characteristics of State Plans for Aid to Families with Dependent Children* (Washington, D.C.: Social Security Administration, 1982), 335.

17. *World Almanac 1985* (New York: Newspaper Enterprise Association, 1984), 256.

18. Ibid.

19. *Characteristics of Households and Persons Receiving Selected Non-Cash Benefits: 1982* (Washington, D.C.: Consumer Income Series P-60, #143), Bureau of Census.

20. Huttman, *Introduction to Social Policy*, 181.

21. D. Pearce, "The Feminization of Poverty: Women, Work and Welfare," paper presented at the annual meeting of the Society for the Study of Social Problems, San Francisco, August 1978).

22. Rodgers, *Cost of Human Neglect*, 81.

23. *Newsweek* (10 September 1984):35.

24. Piven and Cloward, *Regulating the Poor*, 170–171.

25. Social Security Administration, *Social Security Bulletin* (Washington, D.C.: Department of Health and Human Services, 1981), 53.

26. S.B. Kamerman and A.J. Kahn, *Social Services in the United States: Policies and Programs* (Philadelphia: Temple University Press, 1976), 441.

27. Ibid., 494.

28. Center on Budget and Policy Priorities, *End Results: The Impact of Federal Policies Since 1980 on Low Income Americans* (Washington, D.C.: Interfaith Action for Economic Justice, 1984), 2.

29. *Characteristics of Households and Persons Receiving Selected Non-Cash Benefits*, Bureau of Census.

30. A. Stein, "Medicare's Broken Promise," *New York Times Magazine* (17 February 1982):82.

31. H. Ginsburg, letter to authors, 21 February 1985.

32. Rodgers, *Cost of Human Neglect*, viii.

33. H. Ginsburg, *Full Employment and Public Policy: The United States and Sweden* (Lexington, Mass.: Lexington Books, 1983), 53.

34. Center for National Policy Review, *Jobs Watch Alert* (Washington, D.C.: Catholic University School of Law, 25 June 1984), 2. Reprinted with permission.

35. Ibid., 4, emphasis added.

36. Ginsburg, *Full Employment and Public Policy*, 74.

37. Center on Budget and Policy Priorities, *End Results*, 19.

38. J. Bickerman, Center on Budget and Policy Priorities, telephone conversation with authors, 12 July 1985.

39. Ginsburg, *Full Employment and Public Policy*, 29–30.

40. J. Bickerman, telephone conversation with authors, 14 January 1986.

41. Center on Budget and Policy Priorities, *Unemployed and Unprotected* (Washington, D.C.: 1983), 4.

42. T. Joe, director of the Center for the Study of Social Policy, letter to authors, 8 July 1984.

43. *The "Flip-Side" of Black Families Headed by Women: The Economic Status of Men* (Center for the Study of Social Policy, 1984), 8.

44. T. Buss, *Estimating True Unemployment Rates For the Youngstown/Warren Area* (Youngstown, Ohio: Center for Urban Studies, Youngstown State University, 1984), 12.

45. See J. Bickerman and R. Greenstein, "High and Dry on the Poverty Plateau," *Christianity and Crisis* (28 October 1985):411.

46. *New York Times*, 2 April 1984.

47. Center on Budget and Policy Priorities, *End Results*, 11.

48. *New York Times*, 4 April 1984.

49. Center on Budget and Policy Priorities, *End Results*, 10.

50. *New York Times*, 9 October 1984.

51. *New York Times*, 24 October 1984.

52. *New York Times*, 25 October 1984.

53. *New York Times*, 13 December 1983.

54. J. Ridgway, "The Administration's Attack on the Homeless: Building a Fire Under Reagan," *Village Voice*, 14 February 1984.

55. Bureau of the Census, *Statistical Abstract of the United States 1985*, 105th ed. (Washington, D.C.: U.S. Department of Commerce, 1984), 452.

56. Ibid., 455.

57. *A Children's Defense Budget: An Analysis of the President's FY1985 Budget* (Washington, D.C.: Children's Defense Fund, 1984), 15–17.

58. *New York Times*, 27 November 1985.

59. *New York Times*, 29 August 1985.

60. Center on Budget and Policy Priorities, *End Results*, 14.

61. Ibid., 16.

62. "The 'Flip-Side' of Black Families Headed by Women," 8–9.

63. *A Children's Defense Budget*, 262.

64. "Work Shops: Health Care," *Senior Citizens News* 6(293):14 (July 1985).

65. *New York Times*, 15 January 1986.

66. J. Bickerman, telephone conversation with authors, 14 January 1986.

67. *New York Times*, 19 October 1985.

68. *A Children's Defense Budget: An Analysis of the President's FY1985 Budget*, 34.

69. Ibid., 35.

70. *New York Times*, 31 March 1984.

71. Harrington, *New American Poverty*, 46–62.

72. Bickerman and Greenstein, "High and Dry on the Poverty Plateau," 411–412.

73. S. Willhelm, *Black in a White America* (Cambridge, Mass.: Schenkman, 1983), 233. Reprinted with permission.

74. Bickerman and Greenstein, "High and Dry on the Poverty Plateau," 412.

75. *Economist* (23 February 1984):49.

76. *New York Times*, 27 November 1982.

77. House Committee on Ways and Means, *The Green Book* (Washington, D.C.: Government Printing Office, 1985), 322.

78. Ministry of Finance, *The Swedish Budget 1984–85* (Stockholm, 1984).

79. *News of Norway*, 7 November 1984.

80. *Wall Street Journal*, 13 August 1984.

81. A.J. Kahn and S. Kamerman, *Not for the Poor Alone* (New York: Harper and Row, 1977), 152.

82. Rodgers, *Cost of Human Neglect*, 105.

83. C. Leman, "Patterns of Policy Development: Social Security in the United States and Canada," *Public Policy* (Spring 1977):261–291.

84. Confederazione Italiana Sindacati Lavoratori, *Guida Pratica 1978* (Roma: Edizioni Lavoro, 1978), 30.

85. Kahn and Kamerman, *Not for the Poor Alone*, 172.

86. See *Swedish Employment Policy Annual Report 1983–84* (Solna: The National Labour Market Board, 1985.)

87. S. Kamerman, "Child Care and Family Benefits: Policies of Six Industrialized Countries," *Monthly Labor Review* 103 (11 November 1980), 23.

88. A. Schorr, "Women and Children Last," *Journal of the Institute for Socioeconomic Studies* (Summer 1984):9.

89. "Old Age Care" (Stockholm: Swedish Institute, 1983).

90. Rodgers, *Cost of Human Neglect,* 120–121.

91. *Newsletter from Sweden,* (Stockholm: The Swedish International Press Bureau), various issues 1980–1984.

92. H. Ginsburg, letter to authors, 21 February 1985.

93. "The Swedish Economy" (Stockholm: Swedish Institute, January 1985).

94. R.L. Sivard, *World Military and Social Expenditures 1985* (Washington, D.C.: World Priorities, 1985), 39.

95. *A Children's Defense Budget,* 84.

96. D. Wood, Health Care Financing Corporation, Washington, telephone conversation with the authors, 10 January 1986.

97. J. Quist, Ministry of the Interior, Copenhagen, letter to authors, 20 September 1984.

98. C.S. Prigmore and C. Atherton, *Social Welfare Policy* (Lexington, Mass.: D.C. Heath, 1979), 81.

99. Rodgers, *Cost of Human Neglect,* 199–202.

100. A. Schorr, "Against a Negative Income Tax," *The Public Interest* (October 1966), No.119.

101. Ginsburg, *Full Employment and Public Policy,* 215.

102. Ibid., 225.

Chapter 8. Work with the Homeless: Emerging Trends

1. *New York Times,* 10 October 1984.

2. A. Presley, "Interviews with 786 Homeless People on the Streets of Denver" (Denver: The Citizen's Coalition for Shelter, 1983).

3. K. Hopper and S. Cox, "Litigation in Advocacy for the Homeless," in *Housing the Homeless,* ed. J. Erickson and Charles Wilhelm (New Brunswick, N.J.: Center for Urban Policy Research, 1986), 314.

4. The 1984 Republican platform for at least one state, Colorado, did acknowledge the problem. Largely because of the persistent efforts of advocate Ann Presley, Colorado Republicans resolved to reaffirm a commitment to programs providing affordable housing and solutions for the poor and the homeless.

5. Subcommittee on Housing and Community Development, *Homelessness in America II* (Washington, D.C.: Committee on Banking, Finance, and Urban Affairs, 1984), 342–345.

6. "Report on the Resolutions Committee, Founding Convention of the Philadelphia/Delaware Valley Union of the Homeless," 6 April 1985.

Chapter 9. Prevention versus Containment: Conflicting Ideologies

1. M. Harrington, *The Other America* (New York: Macmillan, 1962).

2. Physician Task Force on Hunger in America, *Hunger in America: The Growing Epidemic* (Boston: Harvard University School of Public Health, 1985), 137.

3. Compare figures from January 1980 (1.334 million) from *World Almanac 1981,* 177, with those for June 1985 (2.317 million) from *World Almanac 1986,* 108.

4. M. Harrington, *The New American Poverty,* (New York: Holt, Rinehart and Winston, 1984), 21–23.

5. See C. Murray, *Losing Ground: American Social Policy 1950–1980* (New York: Basic Books, 1984).

6. R. Greenstein, "Losing Faith in Losing Ground," *New Republic* (25 March 1985).

7. M. Harrington, "Crunched Numbers," *New Republic* (28 January 1985), 7–10; Harrington, *New American Poverty,* 141, 144.

8. See G.J. Duncan, *Years of Poverty, Years of Plenty* (Ann Arbor: The Institute for Social Research, University of Michigan, 1984).

9. See H. Bahr, *Skid Row: An Introduction to Disaffiliation* (New York: Oxford University Press, 1973).

10. K. Hopper and J. Hamberg, *The Making of America's Homeless: 1945–1984* (New York: Community Service Society, 1984), 67.

11. Ibid., 68.

12. S. Schanberg, "Reagan's Homeless," *New York Times,* 3 April 1984.

13. National Coalition for the Homeless, "Report on the Federal Inter-Agency Task Force on the Homeless," October 1984.

14. See Task Force on Food and Shelter for the Homeless, *The Homeless: Background Analysis, Options: A Briefing Paper,* prepared by the Health and Human Services Working Group (Washington, D.C.: Department of Health and Human Services, n.d.).

15. "Catholic Social Teaching and the U.S. Economy" (first draft) *National Catholic Reporter* (23 November 1984):22 (paragraph 208).

16. U.S. Conference of Mayors, *Homelessness in America: Ten Case Studies* (Washington, D.C.: U.S. Conference of Mayors, 1984), 18.

17. L.M. Salomon, "The Results Are Coming In," *Foundation News* (July–August 1984):16.

18. Ibid., 17–19.

19. Ibid., 20–21.

20. Ibid., 22.

21. *Health Care USA 1984: National Citizens Board of Inquiry into Health in America* (Washington, D.C.: National Council on Aging, 1984).

22. *Encyclopedia Britannica,* 14th ed. (1958), v. 5, 248–253.

23. G. Will, "Washington's Little Miracles," *Newsweek* 5 (December 1983):134.

24. J.E. Cox, "Objectives of the UN International Year of Shelter for the Homeless (IYSH)—1987," *Ekistics* 307:284 (July/August 1984).

25. M. Gittelman, "Developments in Foreign Psychiatry: An Introduction," *Hospital and Community Psychiatry* 43:158 (2 February 1983).

26. L. Öjesjö, director Rattspsykiatriska Stationen, Linköping, Sweden, letter to the authors, 15 June 1985.

27. "Decay of Britain's Private Housing," *New Statesman* (31 December 1982):6; "The Decay of Britain's Housing," *New Statesman* (18–25 December 1981):6–7.

28. *London Times,* 4 January 1985.

29. See P. Friedland, "Homelessness in England: Impressions from a Brief Visit, 1983" (monograph available from the National Coalition for the Homeless).

30. A. Schorr, "Reacting to Cutbacks in Britain and America," *Christian Science Monitor,* 20 July 1982, 22.

31. Central Bureau of Statistics of Norway letter to authors, 10 January 1983.

32. Department of Health and Social Security, London, England, letter to authors, 25 February 1983. Used with permission.

33. Danmarks Statistik, Copenhagen, letter to authors, 3 February 1983.

34. *Safety Network* (October 1985); *Safety Network* (December 1985).

35. Harrington, *New American Poverty,* 93.

36. R. Titmuss, *Commitment to Welfare* (London: Allen and Unwin, 1969):133.

Chapter 10. Prospects and Proposals

1. "Preamble to Statement of Principles," National Coalition for the Homeless, 10 February 1984.

2. Ibid.

3. V.W. Sidel and R. Sidel, *A Healthy State: An International Perspective on the Crisis in United States Medical Care* (New York: Pantheon, 1983), xxvii–xxviii.

4. U.S. Conference of Mayors, *Homelessness in America's Cities: Ten Case Studies* (Washington, D.C.: U.S. Conference of Mayors, 1984), 24.

5. *New York Times,* 15 January 1986.

6. See J.C. Turner and W.J. Ten Hoor, "The NIMH Community Support Program: Pilot Approach to a Needed Social Reform," *Schizophrenia Bulletin* 4(3):319–348 (1978).

7. C. Bellamy, "Homeless Should Be Rehoused," *New York Times,* 18 May 1984.

8. K. Hopper and J. Hamberg, *The Making of America's Homeless 1945–1984* (New York: Community Service Society, 1984), 34.

9. *New York Times,* 13 July 1985.

10. For more information, contact Philadelphia Committee for the Homeless, 802 N. Broad St., Philadelphia, PA 19130

11. H.M. Leichter, *A Comparative Approach to Policy Analysis* (London: Cambridge University Press, 1979), 157.

12. "Are You Still Losing Out to Inflation?" *Medical Economics* (17 September 1984):180.

13. Swedish Institute, Fact Sheet 76, June 1983.

14. N. Macrae, "Health Care International," *Economist* (28 April 1984):18.

15. Sidel and Sidel, *Healthy State,* 339.

16. See M. Harrington, *The New American Poverty* (New York: Holt, Rinehart and Winston, 1984); H. Ginsburg, *Full Employment and Public Policy: The United States and Sweden* (Lexington, Mass.: Lexington Books, 1983); A. Hawkins, co-sponsor, "Equal Opportunity and Full Employment Act of 1976"; A. Levison, *The Full Employment Alternative* (New York: Coward, McCann, Geoghegan, 1980).

17. See Ginsburg, *Full Employment and Public Policy.*

18. See Harrington, *New American Poverty,* 232–255.

19. Ibid., 250.

20. C. Mac Leod, *Horatio Alger, Farewell* (New York: Seaview, 1980), 273.

21. See K. Auletta, *The Underclass* (New York: Vintage, 1983).

22. Mac Leod, *Horatio Alger, Farewell,* 274.

23. Ibid.

24. P. Spakes, "Mandatory Work Registration for Welfare Parents: A Family Impact Analysis," *Journal of Marriage and the Family* 44:685–699 (3 August 1982).

25. T. Funiciello, "Welfare Mothers Earn Their Way: Countering Myths of Dependency," *Christianity and Crisis,* 44 (20):472 (10 December 1984). Reprinted with permission.

26. Ibid.

27. T. Joe and C. Rogers, *By the Few, for the Few: The Reagan Welfare Legacy* (Lexington, Mass.: Lexington Books, 1985), 135–148.

28. "America Becomes Less Equal," *New Republic* (18 February 1985):7.

29. A. Schorr, "No-Loser's Tax Reform," *New York Times,* 6 September 1985.

30. See Joe and Rogers, *By the Few, for the Few,* 135–148.

31. C.A. Perales, "Myths About Poverty," *New York Times,* 26 October 1983.

32. R.L. Sivard, *World Military and Social Expenditures 1983* (Washington, D.C.: World Priorities, 1983), 5.

33. S. Melman, "The Butter That's Traded for Guns," *New York Times,* 22 April 1985.

34. W. Winpisinger, "What's Happening to Our Country?" *New York Times,* 4 March 1979.

35. S. Melman, *Profits Without Production* (New York: Knopf, 1983), 246.

36. H.L. Wilensky, *The Welfare State and Equality* (Berkeley, Calif.: University of California, 1975), 115.

37. Bureau of Census, *Statistical Abstract of the United States 1985,* 105th edition (Washington, D.C.: U.S. Department of Commerce, 1984), 853.

38. V. Navarro, "Where is the Popular Mandate?" *The New England Journal of Medicine* 307:1516–1518 (9 December 1982).

39. V. Sidel and R. Sidel, *A Healthy State: An International Perspective on the Crisis in U.S. Medical Care* (New York: Pantheon, 1982), 340.

40. M. Fried, "Social Differences in Mental Health," in *Poverty and Health: A Sociological Analysis,* ed. by John Kosa (Cambridge, Mass.: Harvard University Press, 1969), 113. Reprinted by permission.

Index

About the Authors

Marjorie Hope and **James Young** teach sociology at Wilmington College, a Quaker-affiliated institution in Ohio.

Separately or together, they have published over one hundred articles (mostly on social problems) in general and scholarly magazines. Their three books include *The South African Churches in a Revolutionary Situation* (1981). They also contributed "The Politics of Displacement: Sinking into Homelessness" to *Housing the Homeless*, edited by J. Erikson and C. Willhelm (New Brunswick: Center For Urban Policy Research, 1986).

In addition, they have contributed articles on homelessness issues to newspapers across the country, and to the *Urban and Social Change Review, Christian Century, Safety Network, Friends Journal, In These Times, Commonweal,* and *The Nation.*

Professor Hope has a master's degree in sociology from Columbia University as well as a master's degree in social work from New York University. Professor Young has a master's degree from Montclair State College in sociology and completed his pre-doctoral work in sociology at SUNY-Binghamton.

They have traveled extensively in over seventy-five countries on five continents, speak and read several languages, and often write about the people and social problems of the countries in which they have lived or traveled.